£5.00
IF

THE COMPLETE FLY-FISHER

THE COMPLETE FLY-FISHER

Edited by

C. F. WALKER

Former Editor of
"The Country Sportsman", "The Field Annual"
and the "Journal of the Fly-Fishers' Club"

BARRIE & JENKINS
COMMUNICA-EUROPA

© *Herbert Jenkins Ltd., 1963*
Reprinted 1964
Second Edition 1969
Reprinted 1972, 1976 by
Barrie & Jenkins Ltd
24 Highbury Crescent
London N5 1RX

ISBN 0 257 65718 5

Printed and bound in Great Britain by
REDWOOD BURN LIMITED
Trowbridge & Esher

EDITOR'S PREFACE

ALTHOUGH the sport of fly-fishing has probably produced a richer store of literature, both in quality and quantity, than any other outdoor recreation, the great majority of these books have been devoted to some particular aspect of the subject. This is especially true of recent years, when in every kind of sport the tendency to specialize has become more and more pronounced. In view of the rapidly increasing popularity of fly-fishing, therefore, the publishers of the present volume felt that an up-to-date book, covering all its various branches and describing the most modern as well as the traditional techniques, would meet the requirements of the ever-growing army of anglers who are catholic in their tastes and feel the need of some form of guidance at the outset of their fishing careers.

It is, of course, a truism to say that no sport or game can be wholly learned from a book, and to this the sport of fly-fishing is no exception. A knowledgeable and understanding friend by the waterside is worth more than all the words ever written on the subject, while practical experience and observation also have their parts to play in the making of the complete fly-fisher. But not every novice is fortunate enough to acquire a mentor with the requisite qualifications, and experience can only be gained with the passage of years. A book can at all events go some way towards filling the gap, provided that it is written by someone with both an intimate knowledge of the sport and an appreciation of the beginner's difficulties. As in cricket, however, there are very few all-rounders who have reached the top flight in every department, wherefore the publishers decided to employ a team of well-known experts, each of whom has made a special study of his allotted subject. Most of them, indeed, already have one or more books to their credit, while several have had practical experience of teaching the young idea on the lake or river. And here I should like to pay my tribute to all our collaborators, whose willing co-operation and readiness to adapt their writing to our requirements have made the Editor's task a relatively easy and pleasant one. I am deeply sensible of the privilege of being chosen as the captain of such a team.

While it is to be hoped that the combined efforts of our contributors will help the novice—and perhaps also some with a little previous experience—to understand and overcome the many problems which confront the angler, there is another aspect of the matter which has not been overlooked. Modern developments in the fixed-spool reel have made it so easy for the beginner to fish a

bait well enough to achieve a considerable measure of success, that
many have not looked beyond the threadline as a means of providing
sport. They thereby deprive themselves both of the chance of fishing
those waters where "fly only" is the rule and of a great deal of the
pleasure which might be theirs. But, worse still, it is generally
agreed by those who have the welfare of our inland fisheries at heart
that the wholesale flogging of our salmon and trout waters with
assorted ironmongery—especially in the hands of the inexpert—will
eventually ruin their sporting amenities, as it has already done in
many places on the Continent. If, therefore, the present volume
can be the means of introducing some of these misguided people to
the more beautiful and delicate art of fishing with the artificial fly,
which does no harm at all, it will not only open their eyes to fresh
horizons, but may also contribute in some small measure to the
preservation of our rivers and lakes for the benefit of future generations of anglers.

C. F. WALKER
Editor.

Dallington,
Sussex

CONTENTS

		PAGE
EDITOR'S PREFACE		5

CHAPTER

I. SALMON
by "Jock Scott"   17
Author of "Salmon and Trout Fishing Up To Date" and many other books on salmon and trout fishing

II. SEA-TROUT
by F. W. Holiday   54
Author of "River-Fishing for Sea Trout". Angling correspondent of the "Western Mail"

III. BROWN TROUT IN RAIN-FED RIVERS
by E. Horsfall Turner   82
Editor of "The Anglers' Annual"

IV. BROWN TROUT IN CHALK STREAMS
by Major Oliver Kite   113
Author of "Nymph Fishing in Practice"

V. BROWN TROUT IN LAKES
by Colonel H. A. Oatts   146
Author of "Loch Trout"

VI. RAINBOW TROUT
by Lt. Colonel W. T. Sargeaunt   170
Author of "Rainbow Trout" and "Reservoir and Gravel Pit Trout"

VII. GRAYLING
by Captain H. G. C. Claypoole   180
Author af "Grayling" ond other books on Angling

VIII. CASTING A FLY
by E. Horsfall Turner   193
Joint author, with Captain T. L. Edwards, of "The Angler's Cast"

IX. FLY DRESSING
by Peter Deane   219
Professional fly-dresser

X. THE ENTOMOLOGY OF LAKES AND RIVERS
by Commander C. F. Walker, R.N.   248
Author of "Lake Flies and Their Imitation" and six other books on fly-fishing, entomology and fly-tying

XI. RIVER MANAGEMENT
by F. T. K. Pentelow   281
Joint Author of Lonsdale Library volume on fishery management

INDEX   296

LIST OF PLATES

1. Two spring salmon from the Tweed. *Facing page* 32
2. A scale from a male springer. 33
3. The Spey near Aberlour. 48
4. The Awe, Errocht pool. 48
5. The Wye near Symonds Yat. 49
6. A 2½ lb. sea-trout from the Teifi. 64
7. Mr. F. W. Holiday fishing the Teifi. 65
8. The Annan at Dormont. 80
9. Loch Maree, Ross and Cromarty. 81
10 & 11. Mr. E. Horsfall Turner fishing the Yorkshire Derwent 96
12. The Eden at Kirkoswald. 97
13. The Severn at Glynhafren. 112
14. The Usk above Abergavenny. 113
15. The Avon, Gunville hatch pool. 128
16. The Wylye at South Newton. 128
17. The Test at Timsbury. 129
18. The Kennet: Crookham Manor water. 144
19. The Driffield Beck. 145
20. Loch Awe from the top of Kilchurn Castle.
21. Lough Currane, Waterville. *Between pages 152 and 153*
22. Lake Vyrnwy, Montgomeryshire.
23 & 24. Spring Lake, near Romsey, Hampshire.
25. Rainbow and brown trout. *Facing page* 176
26. The Derbyshire Wye at Ashford Bridge. 177
27. The Derbyshire Wye in Ashford Dale. 177
28. A 1½ lb. grayling from the Avon. 192
29. The River Dove in Dovedale. 193
30. The single-handed overhead cast.
31. The double-handed overhead cast. *Between pages 200 and 201*
32. The roll cast.
33. The Spey cast.

34. Typical forms of the insect food of trout.   *Facing page* 272

35. Some specific insects on which trout feed.   273

36. A chalk stream before being cleared of weed and vegetation. 288

37. The same stream after being cleared.   288

38. Clearing a trout stream of coarse fish.   289

COLOUR PLATES

  I.   Salmon flies.   224

 II.   Sea-trout flies.   225

III.   Flies for rain-fed rivers, lakes and grayling.   240

 IV.   Chalk-stream flies.   241

LIST OF DIAGRAMS IN TEXT

Page

1. Fishing a typical salmon pool with the sunk fly. 29
2. Fishing a salmon pool with a strong current in high water. 30
3. Extending the fishing arc by "mending" the line. 31
4. "Mending" the line. 32
5. Tailing a salmon (1). Gripping the fish. 35
6. Tailing a salmon (2). Lifting the fish. 36
7. Tailing a salmon (3). The correct grip to use. 36
8. Showing how the line is drowned when a hooked fish crosses the stream. 37
9. The popular and Wood greased-line methods of fishing a pool with a single stream. 40
10. The popular greased-line method of fishing a pool with two streams. 41
11. The Wood greased-line method of fishing a pool with two streams. 42
12. Hooking a fish with the rod-point raised. 43
13. The effect of hooking a fish with the rod-point raised. 44
14. An imaginary stretch of river showing typical salmon lies. 45
15. Greased-lined fishing by the controlled-drag method. 47
16. An imaginary salmon loch described in the text. 52
17. Diagram showing the time spent in the sea by different classes of sea-trout. 55
18. Approximate weights of whitling and first-winter fish on return from the sea. 56
19. Diagram illustrating the leverage exerted by rods of different lengths. 57
20. Table showing types and sizes of flies for different times and seasons. 60
21. Making use of background vegetation to screen the angler's movements. 63
22. Drifting a fly down a current. 65
23. Drifting a fly down a current near the angler's own bank. 66
24. The Drift-and-Draw method of fishing. 67
25. Skimming the Sedge. 71
26. Suitable points at which fish may be netted. 73
27. Correct and incorrect positions of the rod in relation to the sun. 76
28. Dapping: showing the different points at which a fish may take the fly. 78

Page

29. The theoretical cone of trout vision.   92
30. The visual picture seen by a trout.   94
31. The field of vision of a trout.   95
32. Turbulence area where fish almost invariably lie.   102
33. Typical lies of chalk-stream trout (1) Above and below a
    road bridge.   133
34. Typical lies of chalk-stream trout (2). Above and in a
    hatch pool.   134
35. Correct methods of casting a dry fly and a nymph.   142
36. Where to look for lake trout.   149
37. Bank fishing (lake).   165
38. Boat fishing (lake).   168
39. Rainbow and brown trout "windows".   176
40. Heads of grayling and trout compared.   181
41. The dorsal fin of a grayling.   182
42. The distinctive pattern of a grayling's scales.   182
43. The grayling's "window" and the way a grayling rises.   187
44. The effects of a section of line and a plug of the same
    weight.   195
45. The turn-over of the fly line.   196
46. Rod actions.   197
47. The relation of the cast to the reel line.   206
48. Faults in the single-handed cast.   210
49. The action of the off-rod hand in the single-handed cast.   211
50. The action of the off-rod hand in the distance cast.   212
51. Faults in the double-handed cast.   212
52. Two types of fly-tying vices.   221
53. The "catch" in use.   222
54. Winding the silk.   225
55 & 56. The whip finish (1) and (2).   226
57. The whip finish (3).   227
58. Red Hackle. Whisks tied in.   228
59. Red Hackle. Peacock herl wound on.   229
60. Red Hackle. Hackle tied in.   229
61. Red Hackle. Winding the hackle.   230
62. Red Hackle. The finished fly.   230
63. Hackle Blue Dun. Whisks, wire and quill tied in.   232
64. Hackle Blue Dun. The body completed.   232
65 & 66. Doubling a hackle (1) and (2).   233
67. Hackle Blue Dun. The finished fly.   234
68. Section of feather prepared for nymph wing cases.   235
69. Nymph. Seal's fur ready for spinning on silk.   236
70. Nymph. Seal's fur wound to form thorax.   236
71. Nymph. Strips of web tied down to form wing cases.   236
72. Nymph. The finished fly.   236

Page

73. Hackle Mayfly. Whisks, tinsel, ribbing silk and raffia
    tied in.   238
74. Hackle Mayfly. The body completed.   238
75. Hackle Mayfly. Partridge hackle tied in.   239
76. Hackle Mayfly. The finished fly.   239
77. Grouse and Silver. Body completed and hackle wound.   241
78. Grouse and Silver. The wing tied in.   242
79. Grouse and Silver. The finished fly.   242
80. Hairy Mary. The tag formed.   243
81. Hairy Mary. Wing hairs incorrectly secured.   245
82. Hairy Mary. Wing properly tied in.   245
83. Hairy Mary. The finished fly.   246
84. Irish Blue. First section of wing tied in.   247
85. Irish Blue. The finished fly.   247
86. Types of day-fly nymphs.   252
87. Day-flies: wing and tail combinations.   253
88. Mayfly body markings.   254
89. Fore wings of Baëtidae.   259
90. Hind wings of Pale Watery and Little Sky Blue.   262
91. Fore wings of Pond and Lake Olives.   264
92. Fore wings of True and False March Browns.   267
93. Repairs to a broken bank.   282
94. Clearing a stream of mud.   289
95. Restricting a channel to increase the current.   290

THE COMPLETE FLY-FISHER

CHAPTER 1

SALMON

by

"Jock Scott"

INTRODUCTION

THE majority of salmon fishers probably begin their fly-fishing careers as trout anglers, and it is to these people that I wish to stress some of the differences between the two arts. The novice who has never fished at all will probably take to salmon fly-fishing like the proverbial duck to water, but the trout fly man will find himself faced with the necessity of changing his methods, and very drastically at that.

So many men take up salmon fishing late in life, and it is difficult to change the habits of many years. No two kinds of fly-fishing could well be more different. The trout is hatched, lives and dies in fresh water, and to catch him the fly-fisher must offer something resembling his natural food. The trout takes it because he is hungry, and sees what appears to be an item of food. The salmon, however, does not feel hungry; he has no need to hunt for food. That is the first and major difference between the two fish. The second is that a trout will discover the fly to be an imitation and reject it in the twinkling of an eye. Not so the salmon; he is probably not thinking of food at all, and just takes the fly from curiosity or playfulness. That being so, he usually holds it in his mouth for some little time before letting go, and I have seen fish chew at the fly for several seconds before blowing it out. It therefore follows that quick striking is taboo where salmon are concerned, and that the trout fisher, if he is to succeed, must discipline himself. That is one of the hardest things to do.

Again, a double-handed rod is used instead of a single-handed one, and the line is cast across and downstream, instead of upstream as is often the case in trout fishing. Further, the study of entomology, so essential to the trout angler, is quite unnecessary to the salmon fisher.

The two forms of fishing are therefore poles apart, as are the fish themselves. The brown trout is a stay-at-home respectable citizen, and the salmon a wanderer through the ocean, whose goings and comings are quite unknown to man. The first is a fish whose life can be seen, diagrammed and studied; the second is a mystery, except for the time it spends in fresh water, and has therefore to be fished for in a different way, which to some of us is as mysterious as the fish!

B

THE NATURAL HISTORY OF THE SALMON

The salmon's requirements. The salmon is one of the few fish which can live in both fresh and salt water, and by means of a wonderful mechanism he can adapt himself to the change in a very short time. Hatched out in fresh water, he lives most of his adult life in the sea, returning to fresh water to spawn. Nature has provided for the life-cycle of the salmon in a most extraordinary way. To realize quite how wonderful is Nature's scheme, let us consider a typical salmon river, and one could not wish for a better example than the famous Spey.

This river rises in the high mountains, actually in a small mountain loch, and then falls through the wide, beautiful strath which leads almost due north to the sea. In its upper reaches the Spey passes through peaty land, and so can be very brown in colour at times. Lower down, it runs through well-cultivated farm land, interspersed with woods, mostly of conifers. The river bottom is rocky or gravelly, thereby providing the ideal quarters for salmon. The current is very fast; one of the heaviest in Britain. In its upper reaches there are, both in the Spey itself and its tributaries, excellent gravel beds for spawning.

Now these spawning-beds must fulfil certain basic conditions, namely, (1) shallow water. (2) A bottom of coarse gravel with a depth of from eighteen inches to two feet. (Unless the gravel is coarse, oxygen would be excluded and the eggs would die. Eggs laid in sand or mud would perish from lack of oxygen.) (3) The water must not be liable to heavy flooding, or the eggs would be washed away. Assuming that, as is the case on the Spey, the spawning-beds are good, we need sufficient food for the tiny fish. This, also, the Spey has, and it supports thousands of immature salmon. But what, you may ask, happens to the food supply when hundreds of salmon, averaging perhaps fourteen pounds each, swim upstream from the sea? They could easily consume all the natural food, leaving the youngsters to starve. But Nature has arranged for this; the adult salmon does not feed to any extent in fresh water; he lives on the accumulated fat acquired during his well-fed life at sea. He takes an occasional fly, perhaps, as a matter of sport, but he does not indulge in large meals.

Spawning. The time is autumn, and the male and female salmon have paired and are on the redds, or spawning-beds. The female fans out a trough in the gravel and deposits some eggs therein. The male, who has been mounting guard over his lady, moves over the trough and fertilizes the eggs, which the female then covers with gravel. The male has a very exhausting time; he has to fight off other males who may happen to be unattached, and chase away sea-trout, who are extremely fond of salmon eggs. This process continues, with pauses, until the female has voided all her eggs. If it

happens that one partner has eggs or milt remaining after the other
has completed the performance, he or she usually finds another
partner. The result is that the fish are very exhausted after spawning, and many casualties occur, the males generally suffering most.
Much, however, depends on the weather conditions. Should a big
spate occur just after spawning-time, many fish will die. They will
be too weak to control themselves in the heavy water, and will either
drown or strike their heads against the rocks. This, of course,
happens after the fish have left the spawning-beds and are back in
the main river. When spawning has been completed, the fish
gradually work downstream to the sea. The spent fish are known as
kelts, and are easily recognizable by their excessive thinness. Some
authorities state that salmon lose fifty per cent of their weight
during their stay in fresh water; they certainly are wretchedly thin
after the spawning period.

The kelt is of interest to the early spring angler, inasmuch as he
(or she) is frequently hooked while descending to the sea. Some
kelts recover quickly, and these well-mended kelts are occasionally
difficult to identify. The novice is always afraid of killing a kelt.
The best test is to lay a fresh-run fish and a kelt side by side, after
which there should be fewer doubts.

For some reason not fully known, the males usually hang about
the redds after the females have left and sought shelter in quiet
pools where they may recover a little. This may be one reason for
the excessive casualty rate among males as compared to females, but
there seems little doubt that the act of spawning is far more exhausting to the former. As the fish work downstream, they gradually
assume a more silvery colour—in angling terms they begin to
"mend"—and eventually they reach salt water.

From egg to smolt. To return to the eggs lying amidst the gravel;
the normal period before they become "eyed" is about three to four
weeks. The eyes show as two tiny black dots, and these are the eyes
of the embryo. The total hatching period is about ninety to one
hundred days, the temperature of the water being one of the chief
governing factors.

The baby salmon, when it emerges tail first from the egg, is very
small, usually under an inch in length. Attached to its body is an
umbilical sac, which contains its food supply for some forty to fifty
days. At this stage it is known as an alevin, and after the sac has
been absorbed, as salmon fry. In order to provide protection from
innumerable enemies, the young fish take on a colour which blends
with their surroundings, and have dusky "finger-marks" on their
flanks known in some districts as parr marks. When about three
inches in length they are called parr, and lead the same life as little
brown trout, feeding on flies, larvae, and in fact anything edible.
They have insatiable appetites, and after their second summer in
the river have usually grown to some six inches in length.

Then comes migration. Parr migrate at different ages, some being two years old, others three or four, and in due course they become smolts and descend to the sea. Nature has arranged for the protection of these youngsters by giving them a fresh camouflage, consisting of a dark back, silvery sides, and light belly. The silver scales grow over the existing scales and are very easily rubbed off at first. The little smolts then depart into the wide ocean, not to be seen again for some time.

Where do Atlantic salmon go to while at sea? In our present state of knowledge no certain answer can be given. The governments of this country, Norway, Sweden, Canada and other nations have carried out a good deal of research and the scientists have enunciated various theories, but it must be admitted that, so far, no concrete proofs have been produced. Salmon smolts just disappear into the ocean, but wherever they go and whatever they feed upon, one thing is certain—they grow very fast. In many countries smolts have been marked with metal tags, and when captured some time later their growth-rate has been recorded. The little smolt of six inches in length may return to its home river as a grilse of two feet or so in length and weighing, say, four pounds; and this after only thirteen or fourteen months' sojourn in the sea. Many salmon, however, do not return until they have spent two, three or even four years at sea, when their weight may be anything from eight or nine up to twenty or thirty pounds.

The return to the river. Salmon, like carrier pigeons, have the homing instinct, and almost invariably return to the river in which they were hatched, as has been shown by the tagging of fish. They return for one purpose only—to reproduce their kind.

It is here necessary to digress for a moment to consider the various rivers and their nature. River X is known as a spring river, because the runs of ascending fish occur in early spring, and very often these runs will cease in early May. After that there will be no fishing worth mentioning, wherefore the season is a short one. River Y, while having an early run in March and April, also has smaller runs of summer fish and grilse, so that it fishes from March to September. River Z, however, is purely a summer and autumn river. The first runs do not take place until late May or early June, and then continue into the autumn months. But rivers can change their character, and late rivers can become earlier ones.

The spring rivers are the most popular and command the highest rents. The reason is that the fish which enter these rivers are then at the very peak of their condition, they fight magnificently, and command high prices as an article of food. They have the blue backs, silver sides and perfect shape which the angler dreams of, and their strength is tremendous. These are fish straight from the sea, full of good living and *joie de vivre*, and they provide the cream of the sport. After one of these fish has been landed, the angler may hear his gillie say, "Fresh fish, sir! See the lice on him." Pointing to the fish, he will indicate two or three small brown parasites clinging to it. These are salt-water creatures which cannot live long in fresh water, and their presence is proof positive that the salmon is not long up from the sea. Lice die and drop off after some thirty to forty hours in the river, but their presence delights the angler and is eagerly looked for. Everyone likes to say, "I got a fish with sea-lice today."

The late rivers produce fish which are already in their spawning dress, and with the ova or milt well developed. These fish are not, and cannot be, in such fine condition as the early runners, so if the angler wants the best he has to pay spring rents for it.

When our salmon feels the urge to return to his native river, whether as a grilse or a fish of size, he heads for the river mouth. Spring rivers breed early fish and autumn rivers late fish. Let us imagine that our fish is a springer, and that he arrives off the mouth of the river in March. He senses the fresh water coming into the sea, but compared with the sea it is very cold, and probably it is full of melted snow. This may put him off, and he may hang about the mouth for some little time until the temperature feels right to him. Perhaps a rush of spate water finally tempts him, and up he comes. While he is waiting, however, he is in constant danger from the nets of the commercial fishermen at the river mouth. Indeed, a salmon's life is full of perils, for besides the nets he has to evade seals in the sea and otters, anglers and possibly pollution in the river. But we will suppose that our fish escapes these perils and swims upstream. How far he runs will depend on many things, such as the level of the water and its temperature, but he eventually reaches a pool which pleases him and takes up a good position, perhaps behind a rock, where he can lie without exertion and enjoy life. How long he will remain there is uncertain; possibly a spate will cause him to move upstream again. Then, as the summer advances, his colour changes. First he becomes more bronze than silver, and finally he puts on his full spawning dress. If a male, he will grow a hook on the point of his lower jaw, and his colour will change to red and copper. The slang name for a male in this condition is "Soldier", on account of the colour of his coat. Females, on the other hand, become rather black. The hook on the jaw of the male does not seem to serve any useful purpose, unless it helps to attract the ladies. No literary female salmon has yet gone into print to enlighten us on the subject!

With autumn coming on, the fish move up on to the spawning-beds and pair off. Now is the time for the water bailiffs to be on the *qui vive*, for nothing is easier than to gaff spawning fish, and the bailiffs usually have a somewhat sleepless time. This completes the life-cycle of the salmon, who may or may not survive and spawn again. Females frequently spawn more than once.

Scale-reading. No brief résumé of this kind can take account of the endless variations in behaviour, so I must request the critics to refrain from quoting instances from their own experience. To do full justice to the subject one would need a whole book! One point, however, must not be omitted; I refer to scale-reading. It is possible to obtain quite an accurate history of the fish's life by examining a scale under a low-power microscope. The scales have rings on them rather like those in a tree-trunk, and the life of the fish begins at the centre of the scale and works outwards. As the fish increases in size and age so likewise do the scales, and even with the naked eye one can form a very fair estimate of the life history. Furthermore, the size of the scale indicates the size of the fish itself, since there is a definite ratio between the two. The study of scales, therefore, has taught us a very great deal about salmon, and the photograph of a scale facing page 33 shows the results which an expert can obtain by this means. From a number of these scales taken from a single river, it is possible to gain a very fair idea of the life history of the fish it contains.

Characteristics of rivers. A word may usefully be said here about the river itself. Apart from whether they produce early or late runs, salmon rivers fall into several types. First there is the small river, which the salmon can only ascend while it is in flood. Such rivers depend upon rain, in the absence of which they become woefully short of fish, and they are not usually in great demand on account of their unreliability. The big river is very different, for the fish can run at any time, although a spate naturally induces a big run and often cause fish already in the river to move higher upstream. It therefore follows that the big river usually carries a good stock of salmon, unless, of course, pollution raises its ugly head. Salmon are very sensitive to pollution, and whether it be from village sewage or factory effluents they quickly become affected. I know of two pools below the outfall of a village sewer which are utterly useless because the fish will not lie there, but pass straight through until they are above the outfall. This, of course, implies a village where no sewage disposal plant has been installed.

Another important point is the character of the floods, or spates, as they are called in Scotland. If they are very dirty and take a long time to clear, they can seriously hold up the fishing. The Wye is an example of this, and the late J. Arthur Hutton wrote to me in the nineteen-thirties complaining bitterly that the river was so thick it looked as though one could walk on it, due, of course, to the red soil of the lower Wye Valley.

In Scottish rivers peat is probably one of the worst troubles. Peat can persist after a spate, and it seems to put the fish off. Under certain light conditions the water can look coal black, and I have seldom done any good in a black water.

TACKLE

Rods. Tackle is a very individual matter and depends to a great extent on the angler's physique and temperament. For example, I am six feet tall and weigh fourteen and a half stone, so that I have a liking for a long rod. A smaller man might prefer something shorter, although it is not altogether a question of the length of rod, but of the effort required to bend it when making a cast, that tires the fisherman. So far as length is concerned, the popular rod is probably thirteen feet; at least that is the length I see most often on the rivers I fish. Besides the personal angle, the size of the river to be fished is an important factor. A short rod can be a great handicap on a big river where a long line has to be thrown. Conversely, a fifteen-footer is quite unnecessary on a small river. As an all-round rod a thirteen-footer is probably the best compromise.

So much for length; the next point is strength. The majority of makers give the "test curve" of their rods, which is calculated as the load which will bend the rod into approximately a quarter circle, with the tip of the rod pointing along a line at right angles to the butt. I like a salmon fly-rod to pull about 2¼lb. This strength enables one to throw a good long line, and to put a useful strain on a hooked fish. At this point I must state my belief that it does not pay to fish too fine for salmon. Tackle has to match from fly to rod, if it is to work nicely. It is, of course, possible to fish with ill-balanced gear, but it is more difficult and not nearly so efficient.

Suppose, then, that we have decided on a thirteen-footer with a test curve of 2¼ lb. The next point is the material from which it is to be made. There are four main materials in use—greenheart, split bamboo, glass fibre and steel. Of these, greenheart is the oldest, the heaviest, but possibly the sweetest-actioned. A spliced greenheart rod is a beautiful tool to handle, but a greenheart with metal ferrules is not, in my experience, very satisfactory. A spliced greenheart is the rod for switch or Spey casting, which imparts a twist to the rod. If it is spliced—i.e. joined by two flat surfaces laid together and bound with tape or a thong—all is well. If it has metal ferrules the male ferrule on the butt joint is apt to turn slightly in the female ferrule, so that the rings get out of line, which is a nuisance. I only know of one type of lock-joint which is effective in preventing turn, and that is the stud-lock. The spiral lock-joints hold in one direction only.

Split bamboo is lighter than greenheart, and can be made with spliced joints. It must, however, be well looked after and kept thoroughly varnished, otherwise wet may penetrate through the joints between the segments into the material itself, with the result that the rod is seriously weakened. For use on a rough river, in the frequently bad weather of a British spring, the split bamboo has to be thoroughly protected.

Next we come to glass fibre, made in the form of a hollow tube. This, to my mind, is the rod of the future. It is the lightest type of rod for its power that I have ever tried, extraordinarily tough, impervious to blows against tree branches, it puts out a really beautiful line, and can be very tough on a hooked fish. It has its faults, of course, but these will probably soon be eliminated as the makers develop their products. I have used one for some time in very heavy water and found it excellent. Of steel rods I have had little experience, but I am told that they, too, have made great strides in recent years.

Rod fittings should be strong, plain and serviceable. I strongly advise the novice to eschew all fancy fittings and to concentrate on the practical. For example, I have fished with reel fittings which have allowed the reel to fall off at unexpected moments—even when playing a fish. (As a friend of mine says, "Never no more!") Any form of reel band which tightens on to cork is a snare and a delusion. Cork compresses, and at some inopportune moment the band slips upwards and down falls the reel. Make sure, then, that the reel is held absolutely securely on any rod you buy. My own rod has a metal sleeve on the butt with a thread on to which the reel band screws down, with a locking ring behind it. This provides a hundred per cent security.

The tip and butt rings of the rod should be agate- or synthetic agate-lined to prevent them being cut into grooves by the line. The intermediate rings should be either of the snake or bridge type if you are using the ordinary double-taper or torpedo-head line. If, however, you use the continuous-taper line—by far the best type for salmon fishing—the rings should be of the old fall-down pattern of our grandfathers, if you can obtain them today. The reason for this will be explained later.

I have purposely left the question of rod action until last in order to emphasize its importance. In over fifty years of fishing I have tried every kind of rod action, and for all-round salmon fishing there is one which stands out on its own—the stiff top and relatively supple butt. The action must come right down to the hand, and under stress the curve should be parabolic. The top becomes a straight line in the direction of the pull, and the curve becomes less and less down to the hands. Hence the greatest strain is thrown on the part best able to bear it; the butt. These parabolic rods throw a beautiful line, either switching or overhead, and will play a fish admirably.

Choosing a rod is difficult, but the best test is to grasp the rod firmly and flip the point up and down. The action should be felt right down into the hands, and the tip should not dither but should come to rest at once at the end of the stroke. Do not allow yourself to be persuaded into buying a rod with a supple top; it will never give satisfaction. The salmon fishing world is full of theorists who advocate all sorts of actions; so to save money, time and temper I suggest you take the word of one who has tried the whole gamut.

Reels. Reels are nowadays of very good quality, provided that one pays a fair price. The chief point is the diameter. I like a large reel of 4¼ inches, which recovers line quickly. The modern reels are made of very light alloys, so that their weight is not excessive. The check should be adjustable to suit the conditions under which it is used, i.e. with strong or fine casts, large or small flies. I like my reel to hold 40 yards of dressed line and 100 yards of backing. There may be occasions when 140 yards of line are needed and when this happens you need them very badly, believe me.

Lines. Lines are the next item on my list, and here I am certain to get into trouble! Three years before I was born the ideal salmon line was invented and it has never since been surpassed, even in tournaments. This line was cast a distance of 65 yards in a tournament in 1895, without shooting any of it. That is good enough for me. You can fish all day without pulling in and shooting line, and cast as far as you like. This is the square-plait continuous-taper line, tapering evenly from one end to the other. With this line you can do anything you wish—cast overhead, switch, or "mend" your cast in greased-line fishing, and all with great ease. As the greatest weight is near the rod, this line is inclined to go slack between the rod rings between the back and forward casts, the cure for which is to use fall-down rings, when the performance is superb. I have used lines of this type for more years than I care to remember, and have killed all my fish on them.

The modern alternatives are the double-tapered line, which has to be pulled in and "shot", but with which mending can be executed, and the torpedo-head line, which cannot be used for greased-line fishing as it cannot be mended. It is therefore only suitable for sunk-fly work. The reader must please himself, but if he desires maximum efficiency the continuous-taper line is the one to use, especially for switch casting. My own outfit consists of a continuous-taper line with a spliced greenheart or glass fibre rod fitted with fall-down rings. Some writers advise a lighter rod for greased-line fishing than for fishing the sunk fly, though personally I use the same rod all through the season. A special rod is not really necessary for greased-line work.

Casts. I always use monofilament nylon casts, and more and more anglers appear to do so. They can be knotted when dry, but—and it is a most important but—the knots used must be of a suitable type, correctly tied and pulled really tight. Some anglers aver that nylon is unreliable, but that has not been my experience, and I think it is less visible in the water than natural gut. However, I never use nylon of less than 8 lb. breaking strain and in that size and upwards I have found it very reliable, if the proper knots are used and well tied.

Flies. Flies are legion, and the fashion is changing. In late spring and in summer, the traditional feather wings are giving way to hair wings, which are more lively in the water. Wet feathers are inclined to cling to the hook and to show no signs of life in a strong stream, but hair—be it deer or stoat—does play in the current and seems to attract fish when feather wings do not. Two flies which come to mind are Hairy Mary and Stoat's tail, both of which are very successful in low water. My space is limited, but I must devote a few lines to the characteristics of salmon flies in general. These can be divided into two types, the sunk fly and the greased-line fly. The former is intended to be fished deep, and so is of considerable size. In my young days, sunk flies were tied on enormous hooks, either single or double. Now these hooks required a good deal of force to bury them over the barbs, and a fair proportion of hooked fish were thereby lost. Nowadays the flies are often mounted on small treble hooks, and the percentage of losses has dropped considerably.

While some anglers religiously adhere to the conventional dressings, such as Jock Scott, Mar Lodge, Thunder-and-Lightning and so on, others break away from tradition and use flies which resemble the original patterns only in the general colour scheme, and more and more fishermen are trying out the tube form of fly and its variations. This type of fly is mounted on a nylon tube, through which the cast is threaded and knotted to the eye of a triangle, against which the tube is then pushed down. When a fish is hooked, the tube slides up the cast and so exerts no leverage against the hooks while it is being played. Traditional flies, both single- and double-hooked, are still much used in sizes from, say, No. 4 down to No 10. For late spring and summer use, however, flies tend to become more sparsely dressed; indeed, the late A. H. E. Wood killed fish on bare hooks with the shanks painted red or blue, just as an experiment. But I shall have more to say of flies when we begin to fish.

Accessories. We now come to accessories. Fly boxes are a matter of taste, but in order to avoid the loss of flies at the riverside each one should be held firmly in a clip. Waders must be a good fit, otherwise they become most uncomfortable. A recent innovation is the Latex wader. These have two advantages; they are easily repaired and they dry almost instantly. Gaffs can be either telescopic or lashed (not screwed) to a long wooden handle. The former is very convenient unless the angler is using a long rod, i.e. anything above 13 feet, when a long-handled gaff is preferable. Tailers are much used today, and although I do not myself use one I hear good accounts of them from those who do. A final word on wading brogues. In my experience the safest are those with hammered felt soles and leather heels studded with hobs. This combination gives a most excellent grip, and slips are rare indeed. I have had an occasional fall, but only when the stones have been covered with green slime, to which I know no answer.

FLY-FISHING: GENERAL

So to our fishing, and the method we choose depends on the temperatures of the air and water. Thus we use an entirely different technique in the early season from that employed in the late spring and summer months. First, however, two questions have to be considered: Why does a salmon take a fly? and What does he take it for, since he does not feed in fresh water but lives on the accumulated fat and energy derived from his good living while at sea? The authors of two fairly recent books, Lee Wulff from America and Richard Waddington from Scotland, have propounded interesting theories. Wulff thinks that salmon take a fly from an instinct acquired in their parr days, and that the return to fresh water revives this dormant instinct. He also thinks that the longer a fish has been in fresh water, the more a sober-coloured, and hence more natural, kind of fly is likely to be successful. Waddington has other views, and thinks that the salmon takes a fly purely from the hunting instinct, and that when he sees something resembling his natural prey he will take it just to keep his eye in, as it were. We do not, however, know what the salmon feed on in the sea, although we can make a good guess at the size of the creatures. It is a fact well known to anglers that in the early spring a fly of about two to three inches in length is the one to use. This argues that a fresh-run fish has been living on marine animals of that size and from force of habit will take a pull at something similar in fresh water. He does not feel hungry, but he is in the mood to have a grab at a passing fly.

Salmon are particular as regard the size of fly they will take, and fresh-run fish in early spring, apart from the odd one, like something big. But when the water temperature rises to 48° F. or above, the salmon's taste alters. He now prefers a small fly fished near the surface, probably one of only about three-quarters of an inch in length. Why this change? Wulff would probably say that the salmon's memory of natural flies in his parr days induces him to take a small surface fly. Waddington believes that the warmer water reminds the fish of the small creatures he lived on in the sea in places where the water is warm, e.g. the Gulf Stream. Personally, I can make no attempt to solve the riddle. All I know is that with the water temperature low the salmon behaves in one way, and that as the temperature rises he changes his feeding habits, if you can call it feeding.

Here, then, we have a fish that does not feed. He is not hungry, but from motives of sport, playfulness, irritation or what-have-you, he sometimes takes an artificial fly. Let us see if he will take ours.

FISHING THE SUNK FLY

Choice of fly. We are fishing in the early spring—say, March. There is plenty of water in the river, and there has been a good run of fresh fish. The water can be, and probably is, very cold, but for good fishing the air should be a little warmer than the water. This applies at any time of the year. We need a big fly, say, 2½ inches long. Flies can be bought with long-shanked double hooks, and these are better hookers than the conventional single type with a wide gape. The alternative is a fly mounted on a treble hook, like a minnow. These flies both hook and hold fish very well indeed.

As to pattern, much depends upon the light. If the day is a bright one, put up a bright fly; if a dark one, a dark fly; in not very bright or dark weather use a moderately dark fly. When I first began to fish for salmon, many years ago, my mentor picked out three flies for me, saying: "Use this Silver Doctor if it is bright, this Jock Scott if it is moderately light, and this Thunder-and-Lightning if it gets dark." That is still very sound advice. If, however, the water is stained with peat, use a fly with plenty of yellow or orange in its make-up, as these colours show up well in peaty water. In early spring I do not vary the size of the fly, only the colour. What we need is a heavy fly which will fish deep in the water: in anglers' jargon we have to "get down to them". So we put up a 2½ inch fly of the colour we think the most suitable.

Cast and Lines. It is quite unnecessary to use a long cast; 2 yards of strong nylon (or gut, if you prefer it) is ample, but check the knots very carefully. The reel line must be heavy enough to throw the big fly and solid enough to sink in the water. If you are using a continuous-taper line of square plait, which is solid and heavy, you will probably have to cut some yards off the point. Having done so, whip a small loop in the end of the line and another in the part you have cut off. The two can then be looped together again when you are using small flies in late spring or summer, and you have lost none of your taper. With the fine point cut off the continuous-taper line becomes a very powerful fly-throwing instrument and it sinks very well.

Tactics. The question of where to fish next arises. This is early spring, the fish are fresh-run, and the water is cold. Under these conditions the salmon will be lying in deep water and not, as a rule, in the heavy streams. In order to attract a fish it is necessary for the fly to swim right in front of his nose, and to do so as slowly as possible. Success in early spring depends on the angler obeying the following precepts: "Fish slowly and fish deep." Depth can and must be gained, and there are several ways of doing so. Use a heavy fly and line, and fish in such a way as to get the fly well down.

The typical salmon pool has a strong stream at the head and deep water in its main part. When the water is cold the fish will be lying in the deep but slacker water inside the main stream, and the fly has to be brought across this deeply and slowly. The angler should get as far upstream of the lie as his casting powers permit and then consider the situation. There are two methods of approach, but before these are discussed it would be as well to explain what is meant by a fly "fishing". Fig. 1 shows the sequence of events. During that part of the swing marked A, the fly is dragging across the river. During the part marked B the fly is fishing; that is to say, it is heading upstream and swinging on the end of a reasonably straight line. A fish in sector B would probably be hooked if he came

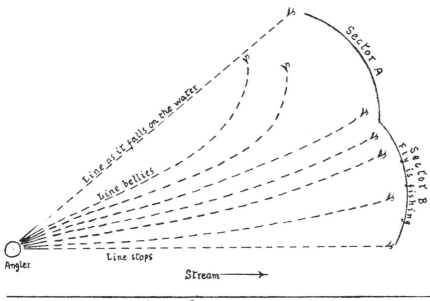

Fig. 1.

to the fly, and there is no reason why he should not take it. While the fly is in sector A, on the other hand, it is being pulled sideways at speed, and experience has shown that early spring fish will not chase a fast-moving fly. It is therefore obvious that, given a certain speed of stream, the line must be cast at an angle to suit it, or the fly will not fish properly.

The easiest and most straightforward method is to stand as far upstream of the fish as possible and to throw a long line. It is also necessary to wade well into the water, so as to narrow the angle. If the angler waded out towards the middle of the river he would be able to fish part of Sector A, while still fishing part of Sector B. But the farther across he wades, the less of Sector B can he fish, and if the water is heavy some fish will be lying in the slacker water near the bank (if it is deep enough). It is absolutely necessary to study the pool carefully and not to rush at the job. The angler should ask himself two questions: "Where will the fish be lying?" and "How will my line behave as it goes over them?" If he is trying the traditional long cast well down the stream, he will have to wade out as far as is necessary to prevent his line being dragged and to ensure that it comes slowly over the fish, The longer the line, the slower it will swing, exactly like a clock pendulum. But he will find that he can fish only one arc from any given stance, and he may well require to widen that arc.

Fig. 2 shows a pool with a number of fish lying in it, and the

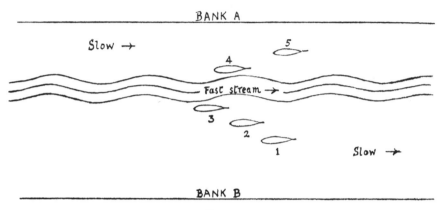

FIG. 2.

angler is fishing from bank B with no permission to fish from bank A. The water is high and the current strong, so that fish No. 4 and 5 are quite impossible to catch. (They could be caught in low water under greased-line conditions, but not in high water with a sunk fly). We are therefore left with the three fish on our side of the fast water. Consider the matter very carefully. If we wade in far enough to fish a fly properly over No. 3, the fly will have stopped before it reaches No. 1, and on the other hand, if we do not wade in so far, the fly will skid past No. 3 too fast to attract him. In other words, we must try to widen our fishing arc. We have to keep the speed of the fly down as it crosses No. 3 and to keep it moving past No. 1. The late A. H. E. Wood once showed me how he accomplished this feat, which is not quite so difficult as it sounds. Before describing it, however, I may say that Wood might even have killed Nos. 4 and 5, if the fast current was not too wide to cast across!

We are now tackling fish No. 3 in the Wood sunk-fly manner. In this way we are fishing the edge of the stream where No. 3 lies and coming round over Nos. 2 and 1. We have to accomplish two things; to sink the fly before it reaches No. 3 and to present it at the proper fishing angle, thereafter letting it come round over the other two fish. We do not wade in this case, as we want the fly to fish right round into the bank, so that it is still swinging when it reaches

No. 1. We therefore start above No. 3 and cast into the centre of the fast water, our cast being slightly *above* square across. The fly and line are washed downstream, sinking as they go down, while we carefully watch the small portion of line visible above the surface. If it is going downstream we follow it with the rod-tip. By the time the fly reaches the edge of the fast water it will be deep down and fishing as it should, when No. 3 may take it. If he does not, lead the fly round until it is under the bank, having crossed Nos. 2 and 1 *en route*. If, however, the slack water is *very* slack, swing the rod round until it is parallel with the bank and so move the fly across; or—and this is a deadly device—keep the rod-tip almost in the water and reel in slowly and jerkily. Fish in cold, slack water seem to like this method.

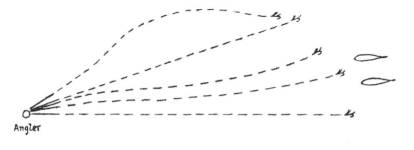

Angler

FIG. 3.

There is another way of extending one's fishing arc, also attributable to Mr. Wood, and this is known as "mending" the cast. If a greased, and therefore floating, line is used a mend may be made at any time, but when the line sinks the only chance is to make the mend the very instant it touches the water. The mend consists of lifting the line off the water and placing an upstream belly in it. By the time this belly has been converted into a downstream one, the line should be at a reasonable fishing angle. (Fig. 3.) Mending is not a very difficult trick to learn, but with an ungreased line it *must* be carried out before the water can grip the line. The *modus operandi* is to hold the rod horizontally with its butt against your waistcoat, and then to raise it, still in a horizontal plane, and gently swing it in a semicircle upstream. The whole movement is both slow and gentle, and as the swing is executed the arms are extended, so as to avoid a pull at the fly. One is, in effect, throwing the line forward as well as upstream (Fig. 4). Some anglers draw a yard, or perhaps two yards, of slack off the reel to prevent pulling on the fly.

We can now apply this to our three fish. By wading to a position inshore of No. 1, so that the fly will fish past him, and mending largely for No. 3, we should have extended our arc so as to cover all

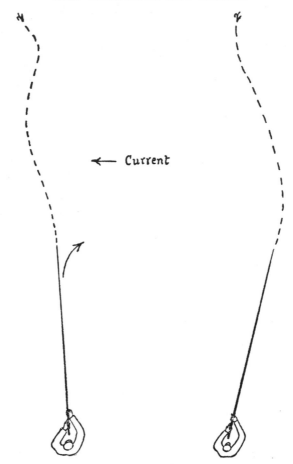

Fig. 4. *"Mending" the line.*

three fish. All this, of course, presupposes that the angler knows where the fish are lying, but unfortunately for the novice, salmon do not always lie in the same places. Their lies depend upon the temperature of the water and air, and also on the water level. In early spring, so long as the weather remains cold, the fish will be in deep, slow-flowing water. It is therefore useless to fish the streams under these conditions. As the water and air warm up, the fish gradually move into deep, streamy water, and later still into fast, shallow water, either at the head or tail of a pool.

Let us now imagine that we are fishing in later spring, which means that we are fishing deep, streamy water. We have to sink the fly, which is not always easy, since the current tends to lift the line. One way of sinking the line is to cast out the fly, then raise the rod to the vertical with almost a jerk, and finally drop the rod-point.

1. Two spring salmon from the Tweed at Sprouston: 10 lb. and 19 lb.

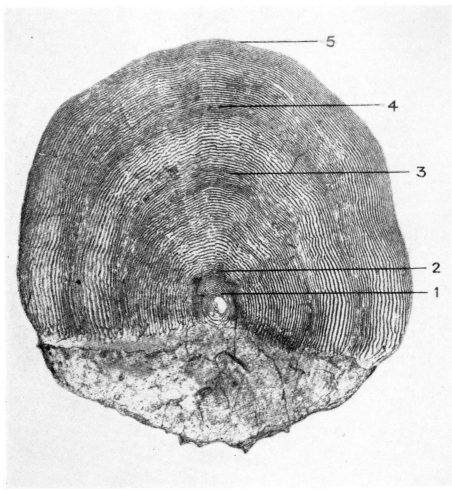

2. A scale from a male springer of 34 lb. The numbers indicate the years in the life of the salmon. Nos. 1 and 2 refer to its life in the river, Nos. 3, 4 and 5 to life in the sea.

This creates slack in the line and allows it and the fly to sink. The speed with which the line comes round can be increased by raising the rod or pulling in a little line, and decreased by lowering the rod and letting out line, or taking a step or two downstream.

Hooking a fish. Generally speaking, the fly should be fished very slowly; in fact as slowly as the stream and the skill of the angler allow. The early spring fish likes a slow fly, and the angler must watch his line—that is, the small portion visible above the water—to see how fast it is moving across the river. After a time the beginner will find a speed which brings results, and he should profit by that experience.

It is now time to consider what happens when a fish takes the fly. In early spring the angler will not see the rise, as the fly is fishing deep. The late Ernest Crosfield, a very famous salmon fisher, used to say: "If you see your rises in spring you are fishing too high, and if you don't see your rises in summer you are fishing too deep." The first indication of a fish's presence is a stoppage of the line in its swing across the water; a fish has taken hold. As the fish turns away with the fly in his mouth the angler will feel a heavy, solid, downward pull. That is the supreme moment in the salmon fisher's day, and no other fish can give you quite the same pull. Now many writers tell you to hold a foot of slack line in your hand, and as soon as the line stops to let this slack run out, so giving the fish time to turn before you tighten up on him. This presupposes that the fish holds on to the fly for a second or two. Where large spring flies are concerned he may or may not do so; with a tube-fly having a comparatively small treble he may do so but with a 4/0 to 6/0 single or double hook this is doubtful.

In practice, the angler has probably been casting for some time; he is becoming a little bored and his attention wanders. He does not notice the stoppage of the line, and the first thing he knows is a heavy pull. Up comes his rod, and the fish, we hope, is "on". Arthur Wood used to say; "He takes the fly into his mouth and spits it out fairly quickly directly he feels the big, hard hook, but if you have enough tension on the line to keep the fly moving you have a good chance of hooking him as he tries to let go."

Richard Waddington says: "Give him slack when the line stops, and he is your fish," or words to that effect. He, however, uses a fly with a small triangle, and fish probably hold on to it longer than they would to a big single or double hook. In any event, wait for the pull, whether you let go line or not; then up with the rod with a steady, firm pull, keeping the butt up and the button against your waistcoat.

Playing a fish. Now for it! As a rule the fish will not dash off immediately, but usually pauses for two or three seconds. In this valuable interval, glance at your line to see that it is all clear for running out. Then off he goes and the reel sings loudly. The very instant he stops,

C

try to wind in line, and keep on trying. Remember that you have a strong gut or nylon cast, so double your rod up into a deep curve and put on all the strain you dare. Never let up for a moment; if you do, the fish will soon be in charge of the proceedings and doing exactly what he likes. I once foul-hooked a fish in the back fin with a big fly and, his head being free, he could run as he wished. I landed him 300 yards away! Fresh-run spring fish are not easy to kill; they are in tip-top condition and have great stamina. I think that more fish are lost by the novice becoming impatient than by over-timid handling, although both faults are very common. Always keep abreast of your fish if you can; do not allow him to run out line and then remain in your present position. Walk after him, reeling up as you go.

Let us imagine a typical fight with, say, a fifteen-pounder. As soon as we have him hooked there are two vital matters which should be attended to at once. First, as I have said, make sure the line is clear, and second, wade ashore immediately. While we are getting ashore, the fish is probably running, so we let the reel buzz away to its heart's content until we are on the bank. Then we look and see where our fish is, and proceed to wind in until the rod has a good bend in it. Quite likely the fish makes another run, after which we again recover line. All the time we keep the rod nearly vertical, with the button against our waistcoat. Before long we shall have brought the fish to our side of the river, and then the awkward period begins. He will probably cruise about in a fairly small area, making only short runs, sometimes remaining still, but always unwilling to come any closer. He may only be a few yards away, but is still full of fight. Now here is the opportunity to exercise patience; we simply keep a steady strain on him and await results. A swirl on the surface shows that the strain is beginning to tell, and that he is coming up. We now find that his runs are getting shorter and much less vigorous. Then up comes his head, showing just above water. Another minute or so, and he is lying on his side. This is the time, above all others, to keep cool. We guide the fish in, pulling him downstream—never against the current—until he is within easy reach.

Landing a fish. Here I must emphasize the great rule which every novice must learn: never try to land a salmon until he is lying inert on his side. The expert may succeed in gaffing a fish which still has some fight in him, but not the beginner. We now have our fish right at our feet, completely played out. Let us assume that we are to gaff him. In an unhurried manner we lay the gaff over his back fin, point downwards, and give a short, sharp little pull. Then we lift the fish, walk up the bank, and hit him on the head with the "priest". If only the angler keeps cool, it is in most cases just as easy as that! A tailer is no more difficult to manipulate. Guide the loop over the fish's tail and give a little pull, when the noose will close with a snap, and all that remains is to lift out the fish.

If a beach is available the played-out salmon can easily be guided in until he is aground, when it is the simplest thing in the world to tail him by hand. Grasp him by the root of the tail, *the thumb pointing towards the tail*, and lift. The bones of the tail fin will prevent your hand from slipping, but you must make sure that your fish is out for the count first. (Figs. 5 to 7.)

Temperature. The thermometer is an important item of equipment, since it will tell us whether to fish sunk fly or greased line. Some novices appear to think that sunk fly should only be fished in the very early part of the season, but this is far from the case. I recently fished a sunk fly in June, because the air was very cold—a good deal colder than the water. In early spring there may well be some doubts as to whether the time is ripe for greased line. In this case I would try sunk fly, and only change over to greased line when other fishermen were doing well on it. The transitional period can be quite difficult at times.

Casting. Although there is a chapter on casting later in this book, I should like to add a word or two on the subject here. Unless you can Spey cast, or use the Highland form of switching (which I have never seen in the south), you will be unable to fish certain pools. I therefore strongly urge the beginner to learn one or both of these methods. He should realize that salmon fishing often requires a long cast, and that unless he is a good caster he will, on big rivers, fail to cover the fish properly. As a means of throwing a long line, the

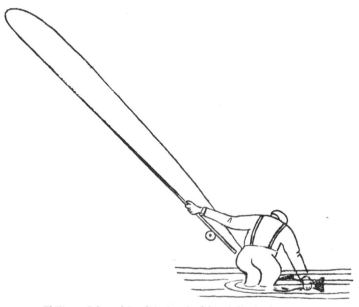

FIG. 5. *Tailing a Salmon* (1). *Gripping the fish as it lies in the water.*

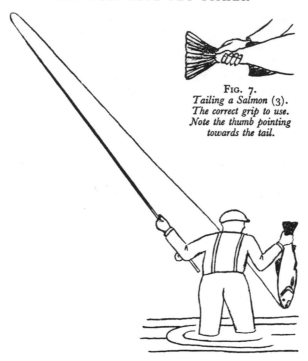

Fig. 7.
Tailing a Salmon (3).
The correct grip to use.
*Note the thumb pointing
towards the tail.*

Fig. 6. *Tailing a Salmon* (2). *Lifting the fish.*

switch cast, as practised in the Highlands, is the easiest, least fatigu-
ing and most effective. But the fisherman must not only be able to
throw a long, clean line; he must also be a good wader and know
where to place his fly. Given these qualifications, he is well on the
way to success.

GREASED-LINE FISHING

General remarks. Once the water temperature reaches 50° F., the
fish become interested in a small fly fished just below the surface,
provided that the temperature of the air is higher than that of the
water. In order to keep his fly near the surface, the greased-line
fisherman borrows a tip from the dry-fly practitioner and greases his
line to make it float. Some writers assert that only a light line will
float, but this is not correct, for if a good grease is used quite a heavy
salmon line will float excellently. There are various brands of
grease on the market, and the novice will soon find one that suits him.

The whole art of greased-line fishing can be summed up in a
sentence: "Fish a small fly, fish it slowly, and fish it high in the
water." I have written many thousands of words on the subject
during my thirty years as an angling author, but as my space here is

limited it is necessary to condense as much as possible. There are three main methods of fishing the greased line: the Wood manner, the controlled-drag method, and the popular modern style. The easiest, undoubtedly, is the last-named.

Equipment for greased-line fishing. First, however, a word on the equipment required. A fly-rod with a test curve of about 2¼ lb. will be quite suitable for this work. There is a tendency to use very light rods, but they are not really necessary. I frequently use a 14-foot rod, even in high summer, as the extra length is useful if a long cast has to be made, and it is a great help in other ways. The chief difference lies in the casts and flies used. Personally, I never use anything less than 8 lb. breaking strain, even in low water. Normally, I use nylon of 10 lb. b.s. and my reasons are these. Firstly, nylon of this size is extraordinarily tough, and less visible in the water than gut. Secondly, I have tried finer casts and have not risen any more fish, so I think that if a salmon means to take the fly he will not be put off by a reasonable thickness of cast, while 10 lb. nylon allows a small fly to be worked perfectly well. Thirdly, during the playing of a fish the cast may get scraped against a rock under water, and a very fine cast will not stand this. Fourthly, a fish often crosses the stream when hooked, towing a bag of drowned line behind him (Fig. 8). The pull on the line is then so heavy that a fine cast will break. Incidentally, the continuous-taper line has a considerable advantage in this respect, for the drowned line is the finer part, thereby lessening the strain on the cast. It must be remembered that the taper of a double-tapered line is quite short, so

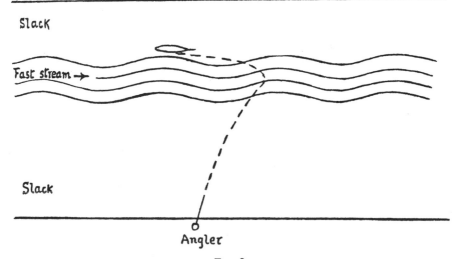

Slack

Fast stream →

Slack

Angler

FIG. 8.

that it is virtually a level line with plenty of weight in the drowned part and the finer end close to the fish. I should, however, add that in a small river in which there are no really heavy streams, this problem does not arise. As a final word on cast strength, the man who fishes too fine and so loses too many fish becomes very unpopular, because he is letting the side down; in other words, reducing the season's bag, and that, nowadays, is a deadly sin. Only when the water is dead low and the situation desperate is the fisherman driven to take risks of this kind.

Flies. Regarding flies, one can use either the conventional pattern or the tube-flies. The latter are gaining ground every season, and personally I think they are most efficient. They are tied on plastic tubes and consist only of a hackle made of a few strands of hair. The tube is bound with silk and/or tinsel to make a body, and that completes the fly. The small treble hooks on which they are mounted hook and hold very well indeed, and my own experience of these flies has been a happy one. They have the additional merit of being very light, and as the whole object in greased-line fishing is to keep the fly as near the surface is possible, this is a great advantage. It is also convenient to be able to vary the size of the fly without adding to its weight, and as a plastic tube is the lightest body foundation imaginable, a No. 6 tube-fly is hardly any heavier than a No. 10 orthodox pattern. These flies are extra suitable for very low and warm water.

The conventional fly has changed greatly in recent years. The dressing has become more sparse and hair has taken the place of feathers to a considerable extent. Hair is more lively in the water, and so creates the desired impression of a living creature trying to swim across the stream, while a very sparse dressing cuts down the bulk and there is consequently less for the current to get hold of and force the fly up to the surface. It often happens that, when the angler is fishing a smooth pool-tail, the fly skims along the top of the water, and a very sparsely dressed fly on a double hook is easier to keep down. If I were asked to give a selection of flies for greased-line fishing I think I should include the following patterns:

Hairy Mary: a hair-winged fly in other respects resembling a Blue Charm.
Logie: a very successful fly in clear water and bright light.
Silver Blue, with a hair wing.
Stoat-tail, with a black body and gold ribbing.

If the river was inclined to be peat-stained I should use a fly with a hair wing dyed yellow. As to sizes, I think the range should be from No. 5 down to No. 10, and the flies can be dressed either on long-shanked low-water single hooks, which Arthur Wood preferred, or on short-shanked doubles. In addition to the above I carry a series of tube-flies of varying colour schemes. The different types of salmon fly in use, both modern and traditional, are shown in colour on Plate I, facing page 224.

We now come to one of the most difficult problems of greased-line fishing, namely the selection of fly. Wood always maintained that colour was immaterial and that size was the vital factor. While I readily agree about size, I feel that colour is also of great importance. There are times when a green fly is very effective, and a Green Highlander has for long been one of my favourites. It is a good fly in a moderate light. I think the brightness or otherwise of the light, plus the colour of the water, determine the colour of the fly to use, of which the following are examples:

Clear water and bright light: Logie or hair-winged Silver Blue.

Clear water and moderate light: Hairy Mary or Green Highlander.

Peaty water and bright light: A fly with yellow hair wing and silver body.

Fairly clear water and dull light: Stoat-tail or any other dark fly.

The size depends on the height of the water and the pace of the stream, plus the temperature. A typical salmon pool has a strong stream at the head, a moderate stream in the middle, and a glide at the tail. To fish such a pool really well, three sizes of fly are needed. With regard to temperature, the rule is, the warmer the water the smaller the fly. A high temperature is usually combined with low water, and both call for a small fly. My own method of approach is as follows. I first take the water and air temperatures and then observe the height of the water. Let us say that the water temperature is 55°F. the air temperature 69°F. and the river at summer level. Conditions of this sort indicate the use of a smallish fly, so, for the faster water I should try a No. 6 or 7, for the middle of the pool a No. 8, and for the tail a No. 9. But—and this is important—it is very easy to fish too small in fast water, and I have seldom done well in such conditions with a very small fly: in summer a No. 6 has usually killed my fish in a fast run.

Richard Waddington, in *Fly Fishing for Salmon*, lays down a system of fly selection, but I have rather different ideas, based on Wood's method, which was practical and effective. Having sized up the general situation, he picked a fly which he thought was a trifle large and fished it until he saw a fish move to the fly. If the fish did not take he immediately tried smaller sizes until he found one to which the fish came without any hesitation. My own idea is to start with a No. 6—a very good size in late spring—and to vary from this basis.

The popular and Wood methods. Fishing with the greased line differs from sunk-fly fishing in that one has a very much greater control of the line, which is floating and easily visible. It can be either held back by mending upstream, pulled by mending downstream, or led across with the rod. The popular method, however, is rather like sunk-fly work. The angler fishes a straightish line, mending when necessary, and keeps his fly fishing through as big an arc as possible. Let us take as examples two pools which I have fished for many years. We will assume that it is early May, the water lowish and clear with a temperature of 51°F., and the air 67°F. The light being dull, we decide to use a Stoat-tail tube-fly on a 9 lb. b.s. nylon cast. Pool No. 1 (Fig. 9) is a simple one to fish. The water is slow on our side, gradually increasing in speed towards the far bank. Angler A, fishing in the popular style, has an easy time; his fly will come across by itself if the cast is made at the proper angle to the stream, and it is a fair bet that a fish will take his fly either just at the cheek of the stream or as it enters the slack water. In the latter case, the fish will probably have followed the fly for a few yards before taking.

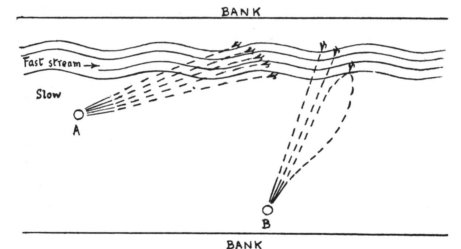

FIG. 9.

Angler B is fishing in the Wood style, his aim being to give the fish a sideways view of the fly, which Arthur Wood believed to be more effective than the almost end-on view presented by the popular method. He liked to let his fly drop down more or less sideways, and to achieve this he was obliged to carry out a good deal of mending. In this case angler B has to mend *downstream*, as the line in the slack water is lagging behind the fly. He therefore puts a downstream belly in his line, which is straightened out as the fly comes round. Notice that A has perforce to cast a longer line than B, who is almost abreast of the fish.

Pool No. 2 (Figs. 10 and 11) is more complicated, as there are two streams. Again our two anglers, A and B, are fishing in the popular and Wood styles respectively. A will probably wade out and fish the far stream first, making a mend as soon as his fly enters the

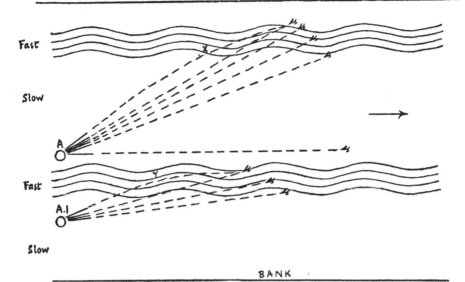

FIG. 10.

water. He may then wade to a position A1 and fish the near stream as shown in Fig. 10, or alternatively he could remain at A and fish the two streams by casting to the left and right. It could well be, however, that the near stream is too deep to wade, in which case the angler has to devise some means of covering both streams. He therefore wades in as far as he can and casts a long line to the point C (Fig. 11), making a big upstream mend at X. He will then be obliged to make a second mend at Y, or his line will be pulled down-stream to Z by the fast water, and the fly will be dragged away from the far stream where a fish is lying. But with the help of two or three mends he can make his fly come slowly over the fish, which, we hope, will take it.

Angler B's approach is a little different. He makes a cast to D (Fig. 11) and at once mends to V and keeps on mending until his fly has passed E. He then swings his rod downstream and allows the near current to pull his fly through the slack water from F to G, when he can fish the near stream. So long as the line is floating, the angler can see what he is doing, and if the fly is being dragged he can correct the fault by mending his line. The whole object is to bring the fly across slowly, which the angler can easily do by judi-cious wading, with a mend where needed, and by casting a long line.

Hooking a fish. Let us assume that we have now interested a fish, and up he comes to the little tube-fly. This is where the angler can easily spoil the whole affair. If he strikes as soon as he sees the boil,

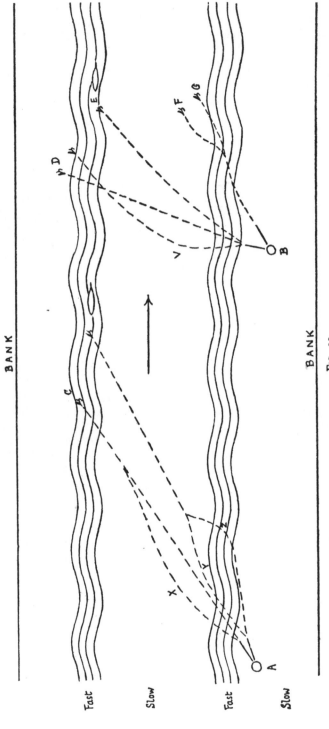

BANK

BANK

Fast

Slow

Fast

Slow

Fig. 11.

it is a hundred to one that he will miss the fish. If he is a trout fisherman he will have to resist his instincts, and this is very difficult. After some years of quick striking he has to throw these habits overboard and start *de novo*. To explain what he should do, we must retrace our steps a little. While the fly is fishing, there are two ways of preparing for the take, and there has been considerable argument over them. The first method, advocated by Waddington, is to keep the rod-point low, holding about two feet of slack line in the free hand. On feeling the slightest touch or strain on the line, this slack is let go. The angler should watch the end of his line like the proverbial hawk, and let go the slack the instant it stops in its swing.

The second method is to fish with a raised rod-point, which gives slack line in the air. This is the method advocated by G. P. R. Balfour-Kinnear and myself. I think that the slack given by a raised rod-point is sufficient for the purpose of hooking the fish. Note that the faster the current in which you are fishing, the higher should the rod-point be held. Arthur Wood used to hold his rod almost vertical when fishing a fast stream, and when he saw a fish come to his fly he dropped the rod-point to water-level. The whole object of giving slack line is to allow a belly of line to form alongside the fish and so pull the fly back into the corner of his mouth, where it usually obtains a secure hold. Figs. 12 and 13 explain the theory. The downstream belly in the line makes it difficult for the fish to get rid of the fly by opening his mouth. The chief snag lies in fishing a fast run when the surface is rough, and it is sometimes very difficult to see the line stop, especially with the sun at certain angles. If, however, the rod is kept well up, there will be some slack in the air, which will probably be enough to hook the fish in any case. If I can see the line stop, however, I just drop the rod-point and usually get the fish. Sometimes

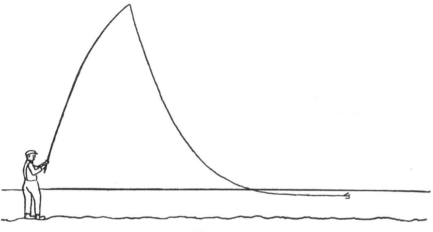

FIG. 12.

BANK

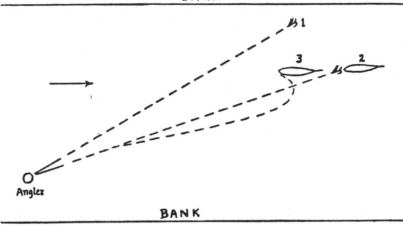

FIG. 13.

he will go quite a distance before the slack tightens. I once hooked a fish which went off with the fly, obviously back to his usual lie from which he had followed it, and just lay there until I lifted the rod and gave a pull.

Playing a fish. The playing of a fish on the greased line is similar to playing one on a sunk fly, but with one important difference. The gut or nylon cast is finer and the hook smaller, so that the strain put on a fish should be less severe. In greased-line weather, when the water is low and warm, salmon indulge in more jumping when hooked than they do earlier on. As the fish leaps, the rod-point should be lowered, to prevent him from falling on a tight line. While the finer tackle demands a lighter strain, too much timidity should be avoided. But the beginner will soon learn the art of handling a fish, which is not nearly as difficult as it sounds. Two main points require attention. First, if the fish runs through a fast stream, do not pull on him; the pull on the drowned line will usually bring him back in a short time. Second, never hold a fish hard on fine gear. Let him run, and the more he runs the sooner he will tire. Let me also repeat my previous advice: do not let a fish run too far away from you; use your legs and keep as close as you can—if possible, abreast of him.

Where salmon lie. The lies of salmon vary with the temperature and the water level. As the water heats up in spring, the fish move more and more into the streams, and when the river is low it is a safe bet to fish the fastest water on your beat. The fish lie in the streams because there is more oxygen available to them there. They will also be found in the tails of pools, where the water glides much faster than one would think before dropping down into the next run.

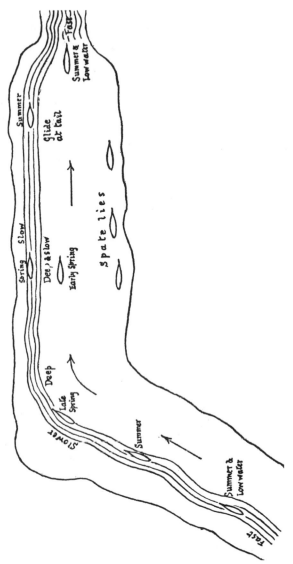

Fig. 14. *Sketch of an imaginary stretch of river showing typical salmon lies under various conditions.*

Frequently fish will be hooked on the very end of the glide—perhaps only just above the end of the pool. There is a pool on the Spey where, in summer, fish can be hooked a yard above the top of the fast run leading into the pool below.

Fig. 14 shows an imaginary pool and the likely positions of salmon at different times of the season. Of course, pools vary enormously, but the figure serves to emphasize the points previously mentioned. The principle is that the lower the water and the higher its temperature, the more will fish be found in the streamy shallows, while the higher and colder the water, the more they will be found in the quiet deeps.

The effect of spates. Summer spates can be very upsetting both to the fish and the fisherman. I do not mean a really heavy over-the-banks spate, but a small flood which causes a rise of a few inches. This kind of minor spate often causes the fish to run upstream, and so empties our pools. It is true that not all the fish run, but some of them will and they can be put off the fly completely. In the Scottish rivers a minor spate can bring down peat-stained water and will probably move the fish into the quieter parts of the pools. The angler should then increase his fly size to No. 4 or thereabouts, and if the water is peaty a yellow fly is the one to use. Nothing can be more annoying than a succession of minor spates. They thoroughly upset the fish, which begin to run up the river, and running fish are of very little use to the angler. He may catch the odd one which is taking a short rest, but the fish actually running do not take any interest in flies.

Real spates, bank-high or over, and with dirty water, frequently defeat the fly-fisher entirely. If the water becomes really thick, he may find the conditions impossible for a fly, and suited only to the worm-fishers. In such cases my fly rod is put on the rod-rack, but provided that the water is not *too* thick, a big sunk fly may work wonders. Fish the slack water near the bank, and fish it slowly as in the early spring. Get the fly down by the methods previously described, and when a fish takes, hold him really hard. Consider the situation; if the fish gets out into the very heavy main stream the combined weights of fish and current will be too much for any rod. You will be obliged to let him run, and the resulting pursuit may be a long one. I have seen a most experienced and determined fisherman pulled through three big pools by a fish with the weight of flood-water behind him.

The controlled drag method. Let us now imagine that the spate has subsided and that the river has gone to the other extreme, very low and with a temperature of, say, 55°F. Now is the time when the controlled-drag method comes into its own. There is a similarity between this and the upstream wet-fly technique of the trout fisherman; in each case the fly comes straight downstream to the fish. This, of course, is quite contrary to normal salmon-fishing practice, but it works. It is a curious fact that a fly dragging down the cheek of a stream can be quite remarkably deadly when the water is hot and low. If the fly is moving too quickly when fishing the far edge of the stream, as at A in Fig. 15, it can be slowed down by paying out line by hand. This will help to stop the cross-stream drag and to let the fly run down the water, as at B in the same figure. When

BANK

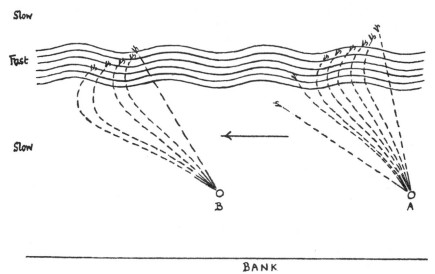

FIG. 15.

fishing in this way do not grease the final two yards of the line, as if that part sinks, together with the cast, it will help to prevent the fly from skimming when it is being dragged, leaving a V-shaped wake on the surface. If the fly does skid along the top, pay out some line, which should have the effect of putting it under.

When a fish takes, he is usually well hooked because the line is pulling from downstream and the fly is apt to hook him in the corner of the mouth—a very secure hold. This method was used by that very great Spey angler, the late Mr. Percy Laming. For many years he was the tenant of the famous Delfur beat, and his bags were quite exceptional. So far as I am concerned, any method which was good enough for Mr. Laming is good enough for me. It was about 1937 or 1938 when he first gave me a description of his low-water method.

Changing tactics. I have now described the three styles of greased-line fishing; the conventional method, the Wood method and the controlled-drag method. As I hope I have shown, there are times and places where each one of the three is likely to be the most suitable, and the complete greased-liner should be able to execute all the tricks. But the angler should always have a reason for every-thing he does; he should never try any tricks without thought. A change of method, a change of fly, a change of position—all should have a reason. For instance, if a fish is seen to come at the fly but refuses to take it, the fisherman should ask himself why. It could be due to several causes. The fly may be too large—a frequent cause of refusal—so try a smaller size. Again, the fly may have been coming too fast, in which case the reader will know what to do. In easy water the fly may have been swinging too slowly, to which the answer is to put on a drag.

Fish which have been in the pools for some time and are going bronze in colour are very difficult to catch; the fresh-run fish is always the easiest. The old stagers may sometimes be tempted by a smaller fly than the fresh fish will take, but it is a poor chance. "Potted" fish—i.e. those which have been up for a very long time—are usually almost uncatchable.

Practice. I would strongly advise the novice to take his rod and line to a river and practise fishing the fly in various ways. A river with no salmon in it will serve perfectly well. Cast in various directions and watch the line, which will be visible as it floats along. The effect of casting from various positions, and at different angles to the stream, can easily be seen, also the effects of drag, mending and raising or lowering the rod, or paying out line. The novice must learn the art of watermanship, and the quickest way to do so is with a floating line. When you see an effect, reason out the cause for yourself; it fixes things in your mind. Don't, whatever you do, become an automaton, slogging away mechanically. After a time you will look at a stream and know at once how it should be fished. Cultivate four main virtues: 1. The art of throwing a very long line—the longer, the better. 2. The ability to wade well, without getting into dangerous situations. 3. Watermanship. 4. The art of fly selection. And, most important of all, keep your mind on the job.

The effect of sun. If the sun is shining down the pool you are fishing, the floating line will probably scare the fish, as it is very visible and casts a shadow. The alternative, if the angler is using a continuous-taper line, is to sink it, which can be achieved by rubbing it down with a rag soaked in raw, refined (not boiled) linseed oil instead of greasing it. Fish a very small tube-fly like any other sunk fly. The line, being fine at the point, will fish shallow, and there will be no need to pull it in and subsequently shoot it. The oil makes for a smooth pick-up, and in fact makes the entire cast free and sweet. I have found nothing to touch these lines for salmon fly-fishing. They are the perfect instruments, on which you can play at any time you wish, either in early spring or mid-summer.

On patience. Before turning to the subject of lochs, I must warn the novice that salmon fishing requires the exercise of considerable patience. It has been my good fortune to fish some of the finest beats in this country, where from 800 to 1,000 fish are killed every season on the rod; and although one comes across some magnificent days, especially in April, when one grasses possibly eight or nine fish in the day, there are plenty of one-fish days and some blanks. On the less well-stocked rivers, particularly those up which the fish

E. W. Tattersall

3, 4. Two noted Scottish salmon rivers.
Above: The Spey near Aberlour.
Below: The Awe, Errocht pool.

A. V. Oglesby

5. A famous English/Welsh salmon river. The Wye near Symonds Yat.

can only run when they are in spate, since they are entirely dependent on rain, the angler will experience a good many blank days, or
even a blank week or two. Patience is therefore a very necessary
attribute.

The link with the sea. It may sound strange to the novice when I
say that the first point to consider in loch fishing for salmon is the
river which connects the loch with the sea. But the supply of
salmon depends entirely on the river, and the shorter it is the more
fish will get into the loch, unless it is so small that they cannot ascend
it except during a spate. The loch should also have good spawning
burns running into it. I know one small loch which provides good
sport after a spate, but which, in a dry season, is absolutely useless.
The most prolific lochs have short rivers up which the salmon can
ascend at any time. Loch Lomond and Loch Ness are good examples
of this. The novice, when contemplating a loch-fishing holiday,
should therefore study a map and concentrate first on those lochs
with a short connection to the sea. He should then find out, first the
annual bag, and second the times when the major part of the bag is
made. This will give him valuable information. Let us say that the
annual bag is 150 fish, of which 60 are killed during the period
from March to the end of April, and that the bag thereafter varies
tremendously. This is obviously an early spring loch and not much
good in the later months. Another may be mainly a summer loch,
producing bags which are very variable, no one month being consistently the best. This loch should be regarded with grave suspicion,
as it is probably entirely dependent on spates. Given a wet summer,
the fishing may be quite good, but in a dry season utterly hopeless.
If you see poor results in, say, May, June and July, followed by a
very good August, and you know that the summer was very dry
except in August, the case is proved.

Again, the fish may run into the loch earlier one year than the
next, for no apparent reason: the combinations are endless. When,
however, you see some such record as this year after year—May, 35
fish, June, 28 fish, July, 20 fish, August, 25 fish, September, 40 fish—
you know you are on to a good thing. Here you have a consistent
loch, to which the salmon have ready access all through the season,
so that fresh fish can and do arrive at reasonable intervals. If you
imagine that you are going to do well with the old stagers which
have been in the loch for a good few weeks, you will be disappointed.
Your hope of sport depends on meeting fish newly up from the sea,
and the normal times of the main runs must therefore be known.
If fish only run from March to April, it is obviously very little use to
visit the loch in July. Conversely, if the run is late, say from the end
of July to September, the loch is best left alone until then.

D

Boats. The next point to settle is the supply of boats. Make absolutely sure that a boat is available and that it is a seaworthy one. The boats on some lochs can only be described as death-traps, so do not take the boat for granted, but always examine it thoroughly before you embark. Take a tip from one who has had painful experiences in the past, and before pushing off make the oars fast to the boat by lanyards. In the excitement of playing a fish an oar can easily go overboard, and you are left with only one. If you can scull a boat with an oar over the stern you may recover the lost one, but not everyone has learned this trick. You may or may not be able to secure the services of a boatman, but if you require a man at the oars make quite sure that he is booked with the boat. Leave nothing to chance.

Tackle. Tackle for loch fishing need not be very heroic in character. A twelve-foot glass fibre rod will fill the bill. It is very light, and that is a blessing on a loch, where one must perforce cast more frequently than on a river. The rod should, however, have enough backbone to play a strong fish, and it is absolutely essential to use a reel which holds plenty of line, as loch salmon sometimes make very long runs indeed. I always use a 3-yard nylon monofil cast of 8 to 10 lb. breaking strain.

Flies. As to flies, I think that many patterns and sizes are unnecessary. Mr. Ian Wood, the Editor of *Trout and Salmon*, tells me that he uses only one pattern of fly on Loch Lomond, except on very rare occasions, the dressing being a black and white turkey wing with a gold body and either a brown or orange hackle. Mr. Wood is one of the most successful fishermen that Loch Lomond has ever known and I agree with him on this subject, but I will suggest two flies which are my own favourites. The first is a double-hooked fly with a yellow hair wing, silver body, and sparse claret hackle, and the second a Hairy Mary. Size is a question of temperature. In the early part of the season, while the water is cool, I use a No. 4, and as the water warms up I go to a No. 6 or 7, or maybe No. 8. Mr. Wood does not go beyond No. 6.

The lies of salmon. Where do the salmon lie? If you have a boatman, he should know where the favourite lies are situated, and you should have no trouble, but if left to your own devices the problem is more difficult. Lochs differ greatly in this respect, but I will make a few suggestions. First, look at the river which connects the loch with the sea. If it is obviously in spate, then fish will probably be running up it into the loch. Cast your eyes around for the first likely lie near the river mouth where a fish will rest for a while after his journey; shallow water from, say, 5 feet down to 2 feet in depth, with a sandy or shingle bottom. Now your chief hope is to contact a fresh fish, and if you do, or you get a rise from one, note the place in your mind by landmarks on the shore. You will then know where to encounter fresh-run fish.

If, however, the river is low, no runners are likely. Try the mouth of the main tributary burns up which the fish will later run to spawn, provided that the depth and bottom are suitable. Fig. 16 shows some likely lies in an imaginary loch, and the novice will see at a glance where his best chances lie. Ignore deep water; any fish showing there are travellers, not takers.

Tactics. Let us suppose that we are fishing at A in the figure. We have reed beds on either side, which may be awkward if we connect with a good fish. The golden rule here is to use one fly only, for if the fish runs through the reeds towing a dropper it is a hundred to one that the dropper will hook itself on to a reed, with a certain smash as the result. I have killed fish which ran through weed beds more than once when using one fly only, but in other places two flies are usual and to be preferred. It is not necessary to use a long line. Cast out your flies and work them towards you by raising the rod-tip until you are ready for a fresh cast. Always keep the fly moving, and in warm weather trip the dropper along the surface.

Hooking a fish. Watch your line very carefully. If a fish comes up to the fly and makes a good, heavy boil in the process, still watch the line. *When you see it moving away and not before,* tighten on the fish. If you strike at the boil, you will infallibly—or perhaps I had better say almost infallibly—lose him. The trouble is that the rise takes place under your very eyes, and this nearness gives the beginner an almighty shock! If it paralyses his arms, so much the better. Unfortunately, he usually strikes with a vigour capable of pulling the head off a twenty-pounder, the fish departs in alarm, and the one chance of the day has come and gone. That, I am afraid, is what happens far too often to the trout angler turned salmon fisher; he must learn restraint.

Playing a fish. When a fish is hooked he usually makes what a friend of mine calls "a dirty great dash" for deep water. At the conclusion of this athletic feat he sometimes turns sharp round and swims towards the boat, leaving a big bight of line drowned in the water. Wind in vigorously and get the line as taut as possible. Thereafter watch your fish very carefully, drop the rod-point if he leaps, and keep a steady strain on him.

Landing a fish. Landing a fish can be tricky, unless the angler goes ashore—the safest method of all. But if he is to lift the fish into the boat, he will need to be very careful. Just before the end, when the salmon is close to the boat, he sometimes dives underneath it. Here a 12-foot rod is useful, as its length may help to keep the fish away from the boat. Personally, I like, if I can, to play my fish out completely before I draw him in close. If he tries to dive underneath the boat a good boatman will pull away from his line of approach. When the fish is lying on his side, then, and only then, should the net or gaff be used.

Further tactics. Loch fishing is an art, and entirely different from

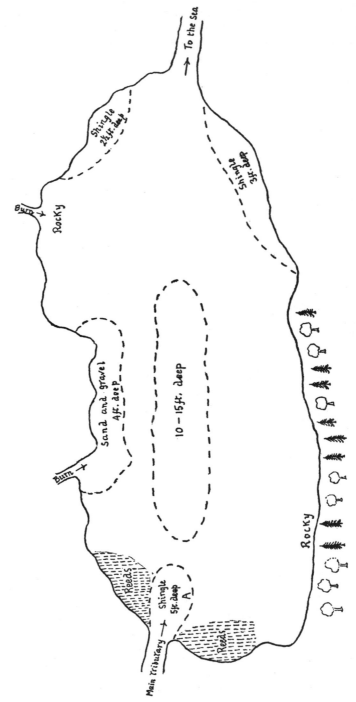

FIG. 16. *Sketch of the imaginary loch described in the accompanying text.*

river fishing. Each fisherman works his flies in the way which comes most natural to him, and that way will be found to suit particular patterns. That is one reason why angler A swears by a Silver Blue and angler B by a Thunder-and-Lightning, or what-not. I am a great believer in the fisherman using the fly which suits his style of fishing. Experiment is the answer.

The normal method of fly-fishing is to cast from a drifting boat, but a method of which I am very fond, and which requires the services of a boatman, is to row the boat very slowly up and across the wind, say at an angle of 45°. By this means the fly can be made to fish in an attractive manner, and it comes round in an arc behind the boat.

A point to remember is that the lies will vary with the height of the water, since in a high loch some of the lies will be too deep for comfort, and vice versa. In the same way, the beginner should remember that certain river pools are only fishable at certain heights of water. Pool A, for instance, will only hold fish in a big spate, while pool B is a low-water pool only, and so on. I once fished a beat where the results could be exactly forecast from the water level. In a spate and when the water was very low, you were on to a good thing, but if the river was at any intermediate height, you went golfing.

Wind-knots. I have purposely kept one hint until the end of this chapter. I refer to the knots which appear in the cast while one is fishing. These knots are made in the act of casting, especially in a strong wind. It therefore behoves the novice to inspect his cast very carefully at regular intervals. If a knot is left in the cast it will easily break under strain, for an overhand knot cuts the gut or nylon, and many a good fish has been lost from this cause. Intentional knots in the cast must therefore be of the non-cutting type.

Conclusion. Loch fishing, when you know your loch and its lies, can be just as exciting as river fishing, but even more patience is required. All forms of salmon fishing, however, can be wildly exciting, supremely boring, infernally exacting, or highly rewarding, and what more could anyone desire?

CHAPTER II

SEA-TROUT
by
F. W. HOLIDAY

NATURAL HISTORY

THE simplest questions are often the most profound. To the query: "What is a sea-trout?" there is at present no clear-cut answer. There are of course plenty of opinions. But these sometimes do not match with known facts or else they rest on observations which are suspect.

In a nutshell the sea-trout of angling parlance is a splendid fish of trout-like proportions and structure which spends roughly half its life in the sea and the other half in fresh water. Its flesh is pale pink and rich in natural oils. It is decorated with black spots some of which may take the form of crosses, almost of swastikas. Its nature is volatile and its habits are migratory.

Sea-trout hatch from eggs deposited by their parents in the upper waters of river-systems. The hatched sea-trout spends two or three years of life in these sheltered waters before dropping down to the sea. It is then known as a smolt. This journey to the sea usually takes place in May. The smolts gather in a deep tidal pool, as though for a final youthful get-together, before setting forth into the perils of the salt.

In the sea the wanderings of the smolts are not to be predicted. Some move up and down the estuary on the tides. Others cruise along the coast, feeding. After a few months a proportion of these fish return upriver—usually in late July or August, depending on water conditions. These young sea-trout are now known as whitling, herling or school-peal. Although many are caught by rods the percentage must be small compared to the slaughter inflicted by natural hazards.

The fish most desired and angled for is the maiden or unspawned sea-trout. Roughly speaking maiden sea-trout fall into four groups. First, there are the whitling mentioned above. Then we have the fish which have spent one, two or three winters at sea respectively before returning. Fig. 17 makes the distinction clear.

These unspawned fish with years of sea-feeding behind them offer the very cream of sea-trout sport. Small-headed, with shoulders rounded and heavy, they are veritable power-houses of living energy. In many rivers the two- and three-winter fish run early. May and early June are the usual times of migration. The numbers of potential two- and three-winter fish have been vastly reduced by natural selection in the sea; the lucky ones return to fresh water in small shoals, in twos and threes; perhaps only as stray individuals.

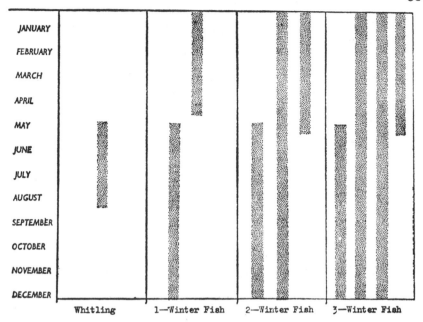

FIG. 17. *Diagram showing the time spent in the sea by different classes of sea-trout.*

The weight and condition of sea-trout varies a good deal in different parts of Britain. Fish grow in proportion to the amount of suitable food they can obtain. Although the sea may seem pretty uniform to our eyes it is clearly not so to the sea-trout. Irish sea-trout, for example, are known to be rather small in size. This could be because Irish rivers empty, so to speak, into the depths of the Atlantic. Possibly the sea-trout thrives best on life-forms most abundant in the shallow seas off the Welsh coast and the Scottish isles.

A good practical way of discovering the worth of a sea-trout river and the quality of sea-feeding available to the migratory stock is to discover the weight of an average whitling. If the fish went to sea in May and returned, let us say, in early August, it has benefited by some twelve to fourteen weeks of marine fare. If the typical whitling weighs about 12 oz. then the sea-feeding can be counted as good.

The table shown in Fig. 18 indicates how the average size of the whitling is related to the weights of first-winter fish. The second- and third-winter fish must vary in like manner since they are subject to the same conditions and food supply. The table is a practical pointer rather than a scientific statement.

The ruthless natural selection of sea-life means that the sea-trout runs upriver as a healthy, vital fish. It carries with it sea-lice, which it sheds. Once in freshwater various parasites try to worry it or it

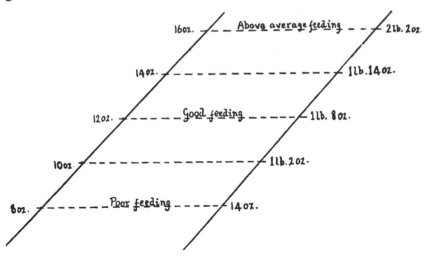

FIG. 18. Left: *Approximate weights of whitling on return to the river after fourteen weeks of sea feeding.* Right: *Approximate weights of first-winter fish on return after feeding in the sea.*

may fall a prey to a major disease such as furunculosis. But on the whole it is an adaptable fish and, unlike the salmon, often lives to spawn many times. Such, then, in brief is our quarry—perhaps the loveliest, strongest and most gallant fish in British waters.

TACKLE

Successful and pleasurable fly-fishing demands suitable tackle. Suitable tackle means that which is both efficient and pleasant to fish with. It is by no means synonymous with expensive tackle and even less so with new goods. Sound second-hand rods and reels are often advertised by reputable dealers at their end-of-season sales. I have a fancy for the well-chosen vintage outfit.

Rods. A sea-trout rod should be between 9 and 10 feet long and weigh, roughly, 6½ oz. Short rods are very much the vogue and it is quite true that they will cast as far, if not farther, than longer rods. But "matchstick" rods are not my choice. A rod is really a sort of special lever. Thus the shorter it is, the less leverage you obtain. Short rods seem to defeat the prime objective. They are of course light; but surely we have not reached the stage where a 6 or 7 oz. rod will strain the physique of the fisherman! (Fig. 19.)

The extra purchase of the longer rod is useful. One of the pleasures of fly-fishing is to be able to pick a line of about 15 yards off the water and cast it again without having to shorten it by hand-coiling. Short rods make this simple feat difficult.

A sea-trout rod should never be too stiff in its action because fresh sea-trout are notoriously soft-mouthed and unsympathetic

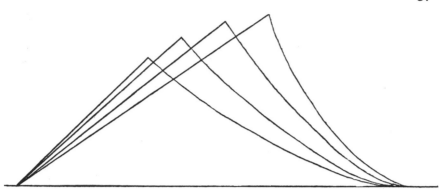

FIG. 19. *An exaggerated diagram illustrating how the leverage on the line decreases as the rod becomes progressively shorter.*

pressure will lose the angler many fish. When playing a fish a rod of moderate length makes it easier to follow its movements with the rod-tip and to get it on a short line.

I like split-cane rods. Glass is adequate and greenheart now almost extinct except for the veterans. Steel I mistrust after seeing a steel rod snap like a carrot in an angler's fist after no great abuse. The incident may have been exceptional.

The traditional school of anglers, even today, use rods of 11 and 12 feet for sea-trout. Where the fish run big and the angler expects to hook numbers of salmon it certainly gives him confidence if he is using a big rod, heavy line and stout nylon. However, on many rivers a sea-trout of 7 lb. is a good fish and salmon are not too profuse; on such rivers a lighter outfit gives much more pleasure.

Reels. Choosing a reel is a routine transaction. It should be well-designed and the drum wide enough to carry 30 yards of fly-line plus 100 yards of strong terylene backing. The number, shape and size of the handles are optional. A 3-inch reel is adequate for a 9-foot rod; a 3½-inch reel goes well with rods up to 10 feet.

Casting experts tell us that rods would cast better if they did not have reels fastened to their butts. This is another way of saying: "The lighter the reel, the better." I never feel any inclination to use a lightweight reel but prefer the more robust types. If a reel is to have a useful life it must be able to sustain knocks and even the occasional dropping. Be wary of reels which have steel spindles running in nylon bushes: these have a bad habit of sticking.

Lines. Despite its limitations and comparatively short life I still prefer a dressed-silk fly-line of the traditional type. This is not because modern advances have gone unnoticed but because change for the sake of change is foolish.

Double-tapered silk fly-line can be confidently expected to fulfil its function excellently within its limits. It must be admitted that these lines do wear rather quickly, especially when used on rods having steel rings. After a good deal of use they tend to waterlog and, finally, to rot. A firm who manufacture such lines assure me that, like most fishing tackle, a silk fly-line is a compromise. The angler demands a pliant line. Although harder dressings could be supplied it would be at the sacrifice of this pliancy.

The self-floating line has its many supporters and for fishing during high summer when fish rise readily into the surface film these are good lines to use. Lines of terylene and nylon are available, too, and some expert anglers will use no other.

There have been numerous modifications of the standard fly-line within recent years of which the forward taper and the casting-head type of line are chief. The merits of these are dealt with elsewhere. Young anglers with limited pocket-money should note that level silk fly-lines are available. Provided that they are of a size to suit the rod they are quite suitable for sea-trout wet-fly fishing and are a lot cheaper than double-tapered lines.

Silk lines, for most of the season, need to be greased, the exception being if one is fishing late at night when the fish are "down". There is a long-standing belief that they must be meticulously dried after use and that they will fall to pieces if not so treated. I think silicone-grease has banished this bogey.

In America there has been an admirable move to label fly-lines according to their weight. This step is an attempt to cut across the confusion posed by lines labelled variously by letters, numbers or such hopeful adjectives as "trout", etc. It took a second world war to standardize American and European bolt-threads: let us hope fly-line sizes succumb more easily.

Plaited terylene of 10–14 lb. b.s. makes the perfect backing-line. Rot-proof, square-sectioned and of small diameter, it quite displaces silk, flax and other materials which become unreliable through damp.

Casts. Most fly-fishermen have now faced up to the fact that silk-worm gut—the traditional material for fly-casts—is both inconvenient and expensive. Its place has been taken by the ubiquitous nylon monofil. Ample quantities of first-quality gut casts—which have a limited life—have become a luxury that few can afford.

As a material for fly-casts nylon is by no means ideal. The slightest contact with grease makes it float—and when wet-fly fishing there can be no more maddening trait in a cast. Moreover, it tends to kink and coil and the structure of its molecule-chains make it highly elastic. Its virtues are cheapness, durability and resistance to all forms of rotting.

Casts can be bought ready prepared for tying to the line. Anglers who do a lot of fishing usually prefer to have a 100-yard spool in their bag from which they can make up casts as required. For general sea-trout work 5 lb. b.s. nylon is a useful size. In clear water and fine weather it often pays to go down to 3 lb. nylon but with sea-trout such fineness carries risks.

Colour is a matter of conviction. I like casts of a dull sepia hue. Glitter is dealt with by giving the nylon a one-way stroking with what the trade knows as "crocus paper". Regarding length; the cast, normally, should be as long as the rod. In high winds the length can be cut to half.

Flies. Sea-trout wet flies may be usefully divided into two groups comprising (i) simulations of natural flies and (ii) traditional fancy patterns. In fact there is some overlapping between these classes since some fancy flies were undoubtedly designed to suggest sedges, moths and beetles. In general it can be assumed that a fancy fly, no matter how garish its appearance, which has a long history of successful killing behind it must, in some manner, suggest or resemble a creature on which sea-trout feed.

To list the hundreds of patterns of sea-trout flies would be point-less. It would be more fruitful to discover, if possible, what numbers of proven favourites have in common. A typical Irish fly, for example, is a ragged-looking thing bristling with straggly fur and unkempt of wing. Its hue is sombre, even dingy. Yet there is no doubting the efficiency of many Irish flies. Precision in fly-dressing seems to please the human element rather than the fish.

A great many fancy sea-trout flies are taken by the fish as sedges. Time and again I have known such flies draw a complete blank until there was a hatch of sedges when they instantly became attractive to the fish. Fancy patterns, in general, ought to bear at least some resemblance to the sedges encountered during a summer evening. In their various ways I think most successful patterns do this.

The newcomer is urged to buy a small selection of traditional patterns from a fly-dresser of repute. He should stick to these for most of his fishing until he has built up enough experience to make experiment worth while.

Three sizes of fancy flies are useful. Some anglers use less; others more. Flies of size 3* are often good for the late afternoon. No. 5 flies are good for the early part of the night, while sizes 7 and 8 are used from midnight onwards. Ordinary trout flies can be used during low water by day or the No. 5 fancy fly if the water is coloured. The table in Fig. 20 gives an indication of when to use which size and type of fly.

This table of course is only a guide. It is based on the assumption that the weather is fine and the cloud-base high. On a dark evening or if the water is coloured after rain it may be useful to increase the fly in use by one size.

Trout flies which simulate small insects should be chosen as if brown trout were the quarry. Sea-trout feed on such insects as the

---

* The sizes quoted throughout this chapter are according to the new scale.

MONTH	MAY	JUNE	JULY	AUGUST	SEPTEMBER
MIDDAY (HIGH WATER)	Fancy flies 5	Fancy flies 5	Fancy flies 5	Fancy flies 5	Fancy flies 5
MIDDAY (LOW WATER)	Brown-trout flies 1 to 3	Brown-trout flies 1 to 3	Brown-trout flies 1 to 3	Brown-trout flies 1 to 3	Brown-trout flies 1 to 3
8.0 to 10.30 p.m.	Brown-trout flies 1 to 3	Brown-trout flies 1 to 3	Brown-trout flies 1 to 3	Fancy flies 5	Fancy flies 5
10.30 p.m. to MIDNIGHT	Fancy flies 5	Fancy flies 5	Fancy flies 5	Fancy flies 7	Fancy flies 7
MIDNIGHT ONWARDS		Fancy flies 7 to 8	Fancy flies 7 to 8	Fancy flies 7 to 8	

FIG. 20. *Table showing the types and sizes of flies to use at different times and seasons. (Times are British summer time and hook sizes refer to the new scale.)*

Pale Wateries and Blue-winged Olives, which hatch during the summer months, with equal gusto. They feed equally readily on the nymphs of these and other flies.

The sea-trout fisher who wishes to stock a fly-box ought to include a few flies in each of the following classes if he is to be equal to any likely situation:

(i) A small selection of size 3 and 1 brown trout flies to imitate small summer naturals. Olive Dun, Hare's Ear and Gold, Red spinner and Half-stone are suggested.

(ii) A selection of fancy flies, size 5. These could usefully include Gold Mallard, Peter Ross, Invicta and Haslam.

(iii) A few flies of sizes 7 and 8. Mallard-and-Claret, Magpie Scad and Black Doctor are good.

(iv) A small number of dry flies running from sizes 3 to 5. A Coch-y-bonddu makes a good floating pattern. I dress them to the traditional recipe but insert two tiny chips of cork under the peacock herl and this makes for very positive floating. Even better, if you can get it, is a bit of expanded polystrene as used in modern life-jackets.

(v) A few two- and three-hook lures. A two-hook black lure dressed with a gantron tag makes a splendid top dropper for night work.

(vi) One or two patterns of tube-fly are worth having. They are especially useful when sea-trout are not being hooked properly on single hooks. The trebles for these flies should be kept sharp, in a cork-lined tin. I like patterns dressed with hair.

FLY-FISHING : GENERAL

Fly-fishing is not only the most sporting way of catching sea-trout; it is also the most effective way. Sportsmanship in the final analysis, it is true, depends on the person holding the rod. It could be fairly argued that to kill a very large basket with the fly demonstrates not sportsmanship but greediness. "Sporting", defined, simply means that a method gives sport. True; but the discerning angler wants rather more than that. More than anything else he wants the mental "kick" of seeing his quarry succumb to the Grand Illusion— for it to have fancied, for an instant, that the tasteless, inedible fragment of feather and silk was something good to eat.

This Grand Illusion is the heart and soul of fly-fishing. Bait-fishing permits of no such illusion: the bait is real and edible even though couched on a hook. And spinning seems to rely essentially on the fish's instant reaction to a moving object rather than to any belief in its edibility. Fly-fishing may be likened to bull-fighting in that the quarry is deluded by a scrap of material which is not what it seems. Both sports depend on bluff backed by skill. And both are tragic in that an animal's instincts are manipulated to encompass its own downfall. Like the bullfighter with his bull, the fly-fisher should know something of the psychology of his fish.

Fly-fishing depends for its success on the angler placing his fly at the right place, at the right time and in the right manner. These basic requirements are not always easily arranged. Atmospheric and other influences often introduce complications which are beyond the power of the angler to resolve.

RIVERS AND WEATHER

Sea-trout rivers vary between such wide limits that there can be no standardized approach unless we imagine some mythical "average" river. In parts of Ireland and along the Scottish west coast you encounter streams which hold their colour—that of good port— for weeks at a time. In parts of Wales and the west country the rivers quickly fine down to a sparkling clarity. Many Irish and Scottish rivers are treeless, the surrounding countryside being bog or machair. At the other end of the scale we encounter rivers winding through dense woodlands. Rivers vary in size (mean volume); the geology of the land-surface varies from muds and peats to bed-rock. Moreover, variation in the fall per mile means you may be dealing with anything between sluggish water and a fast torrent. Clearly, the sea-trout angler must be versatile.

When a sea-trout enters a river it seeks cover. Overhanging trees and undercut banks are the more obvious forms of shelter, but the fish may have to be content with rather less. Beds of weed, rocky pots and deep ravines, as well as debris such as the roots of trees half-buried in the river-bed, all help to provide a more or less safe harbourage. Above anything else the sea-trout dreads the otter. Latterly, it has encountered a new foe—the wild mink. Minks have already established themselves in parts of Wales and it is known that they can subdue sea-trout of up to 2 lb.

In Wales and rivers of the south-west sea-trout can be expected upriver on the first spate in May. In some Irish and Scottish rivers they run a little later. If May be a dry month the fish will work upstream nonetheless, although in smaller numbers.

These early sea-trout are often second- and third-winter fish. Late May and early June offers the angler the best chance of connecting with a heavy trout in all it sea-going finery. Big fish may be caught later in the season, true, but these often exhibit the undesirable features associated with the onset of spawning.

The fly-fisherman prays for good sea-trout weather. He wants days that are warm and seasonable without being arid. Moderate drought tempered with occasional thunder-storms can be first class. Probably the worst fly condition is prolonged flooding. Fishing seems to be best when the barometer is stable, and this in turn is associated with settled summery conditions.

It has been said that sea-trout are hard to catch by day. It depends largely on the river. A steep river, with plenty of rocky runs, possibly with a loch at its head, and fresh fish coming up on every tide, presents few special problems. Slower rivers, where the water is clear, are a different proposition. Many pools will be unfishable by day except perhaps by the very expert. The best pools on such rivers will be widely recognized as night pools.

WET-FLY FISHING

Time of day. Fishing by day in low water is not a job for the lazy angler. The man who saunters to the river after a 10 o'clock breakfast will catch no more than he deserves—which will probably be nothing. The heron—a professional worth watching—chooses and works his pools before the sun gets on them. It is a tip worth remembering.

Dawn in summer is early, but it is the best part of the day. Fish will be on the move for a last mouthful before retiring to their daytime lies. The light from the still unrisen sun is flat and oblique. In this shady half-light of the dawn hour the fly—mobile hackle and tinsel giving out attractive gleams—takes unto itself the magical illusion of life. A cruising sea trout turns in a short half-circle and swallows the colourful little animal. The grey shadow, which is the angler against the background of trees, lifts his rod-tip and takes up the strain. . . .

Dawn fishing is invariably deceptive as regards the strength of the light. If you start operations well before sun-up, conditions often favour the use of No. 5 fancy flies. On an overcast day it may be productive to persist with these until the sun has risen. But on a fine day (or a misty one where the mist presages heat) the quality of the light alters rapidly. So much so that the water is "killed": the angler and his tackle stand revealed in all their nakedness. Small trout flies may catch the odd fish before the fisherman is forced to cry quits.

Fish can sometimes be taken, even by day, in the rough tumbly water connecting the pools. Dark, overhung pools may also yield a fish or two, but the angler's chances increase in direct proportion to the size and colour of the water.

Camouflage. Camouflage of the person is worth serious attention. It can be placed under the three heads of: (i) Angling clothing, (ii) Direct use of cover, and (iii) Indirect use of cover. The sea-trouter who wants more than the occasional success is recommended to study the practical art of self-concealment.

Angling clothing ought to merge with its surroundings. A tweed jacket or a waterproof fishing-coat is as good as anything. The angler should not expose too much white skin—a point which has as much to do with preventing attacks by midges as it has with camouflage. A neck-muffler is useful.

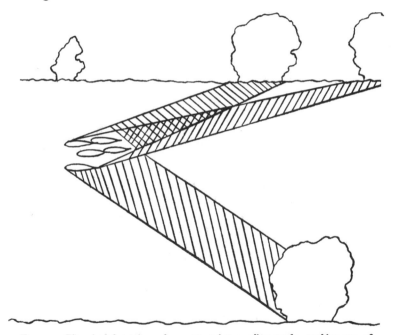

FIG. 21. *The shaded portions show appropriate wading tracks, making use of background vegetation to screen the angler's movements from the fish.*

Vegetation can sometimes be used as a direct screen. Most coarse-fishermen know how to use reeds and waterside bushes to their advantage. Greenery should always be placed between the angler and the fish where this is possible.

Indirect cover, or the use of background, is badly overlooked by many anglers. The worst error is to present a flagrant silhouette against the sky; this is quite enough to ruin many pools. Although this is well-known only a minority of fishermen seem to have learned the trick of using high banks, shadows and the like as a mask for their activities. By wading and using background cover sea-trout can be approached to within a short distance, which makes them easier to hook. Fig. 21 illustrates my point.

A typical incident in support of this happened during the present season. I was fishing the tail of a big pool at dusk. A shoal of fresh sea-trout had just run into the pool. By avoiding the open water and fishing in a direct line with background trees it was possible to place a fly over the fish on a short line without alarming them. Six fish were hooked and netted before the shoal moved on. A casual approach would certainly have sent them scattering much earlier.

Wading is essential on some rivers; unnecessary or even impossible on others. Wading enables the angler to station himself in the most favourable position for fishing. It also helps with camouflage by lowering his height relative to the water. If one is fishing a narrow, deep river the best approach is to kneel in the approved chalk-stream style. At all times try to fish as near to the surface of the water as is reasonably possible. This is important because sea-trout have acute water-to-air vision.

Casting. Casting is discussed elsewhere in this work. As regards sea-trout fishing it is only needful to remark that long casting, on the whole, is seldom necessary. By "long" is meant casts of over 20 yards. Some of my best fish—late at night, admittedly—have been hooked when the fly was a few yards from the rod-tip. Lengthy casting may of course be the only reasonable way of fishing a big river. Yet it should be noted that big rivers, by and large, are usually salmon rivers and tackle for these fish is generally in use. The sea-trout angler pure and simple often finds his best sport in the smaller rivers and, on occasion, even small streams.

A word here on the number of flies to use. With trout flies there is little to beat the usual three-fly cast. With fancy sea-trout flies of No. 5 and similar sizes I like a fly on point and a single dropper high on the cast. After dark a single fly on point is often enough, especially when the fish are lying low in the water.

Effect of currents. It is important to understand how river currents affect fly-lines—and their attached casts and flies. Currents are mysterious things: almost a law unto themselves. They flow fast and slow. For no visible reason they turn aside and move in some unexpected direction. In places, some travel in the direction of the river's source! These gentle, aimless, erratic movements of water are a study in themselves. The angler needs their co-operation and, unless he gets it, he will fish badly.

The fly-line is at the mercy of the currents. Given a chance they will drag the fly through the water at a speed quite ridiculous for such a small-seeming creature. Alternatively, they will leave it sagging lifeless—sinking inertly to the bottom under the weight of

F. W. Holiday

6. A 2½-lb. sea-trout from the Teifi.

7. Mr. F. W. Holiday fishing the Teifi for sea-trout.

its steel. No fly-fisher can know too much about currents. Almost his entire fishing effort depends on them.

The easiest of currents to use is probably the type shown in Fig. 22. A uniform current C flows parallel to and a little distant from the bank opposite the angler. A—A marks the fall of the line after the cast from the rod's position R2. The successive stage of the line's drift are marked by the numerals. The final rod position R1 shows how the rod should be shifted in sympathy with the line's drift. This helps to prevent fly-drag and gives the angler better control over a taking fish.

When the current flows strongest beside the bank occupied by the angler the line drift pattern differs. There is a tendency for the fly to fish too quickly due to the body of the line being subjected to a greater pressure of water. This can be off-set by fishing a longer line and by casting downstream so that the current strikes the line obliquely. (Fig. 23.)

Presentation and working of fly. There are so many schools of thought

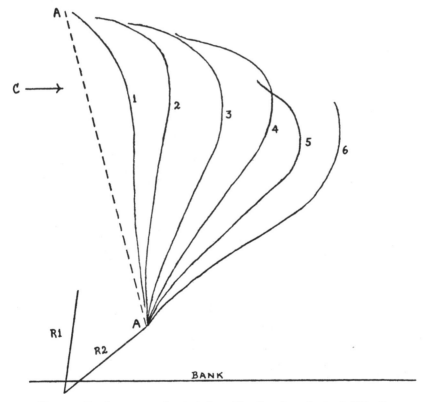

FIG. 22. *See the accompanying text for explanation. In order to simplify the diagrams all the line positions in figs. 22–24 are shown as springing from R2.*

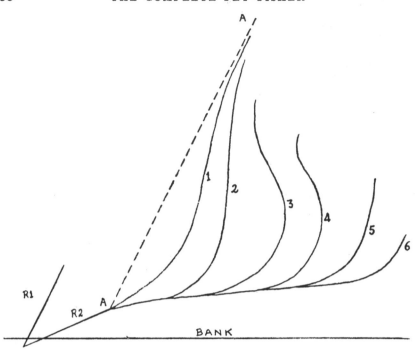

FIG. 23. *See the accompanying text for explanation.*

on the subject of placing and working the fly that it is obvious there
can be no one right way. Weather conditions, time of day, type
of fly in use and other factors are all relevant. Many anglers have
a characteristic way of fishing which they vary hardly at all. This
sort of approach catches fish; but it is not to be compared with the
adaptable methods of the angler who varies his technique to suit
circumstances. The former is easy and makes fishing a relaxed,
non-demanding pastime. The latter elevates it to the level of
artistic expression.

Small trout flies and nymphs should be allowed to drift with
little or no movement imparted by the angler. Such small organisms
move slowly and fish find rapid movement in small creatures a
matter for suspicion. Fancy flies of size 5 and upwards can be
given a measure of "life" or movement by the fisherman according
to the way the fish are feeding. This is found by simple trial-and-
error experiment.

Some anglers work the fly by jigging the points of their rods.
This can be successful if the fish are keen and fresh-run. Normally,
I find that a smooth even drawing of line is more effective. A
killing method, which could be called the "drift and draw" technique, is shown in Fig. 24. As soon as the fly touches the water it is
drawn towards the angler rather quickly for about a foot. Thereafter

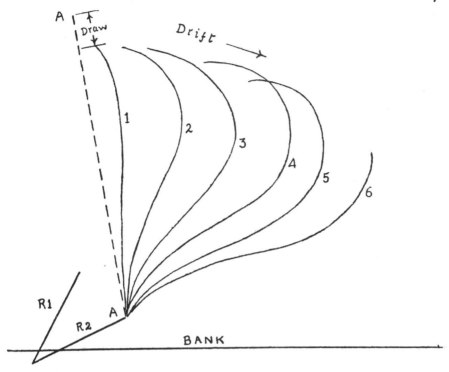

FIG. 24. *Drift-and-Draw. A-A shows the initial fall of the line, and the numbers indicate successive positions in the drift.*

it is allowed to drift round on the current. This simple method works well when sedges are hatching and no doubt the fish think the fly is a sedge trying to fly but not quite succeeding. It will take fish during daytime if the fly is cast beneath bushes out of the direct sunshine.

My own method when fishing a typical piece of water with No. 5 flies is to use drift-and-draw and vary the speed of the draw experimentally until I move a fish. Failing this, I try a few drifts with a slight amount of draw at varying intervals. The amount of draw is increased until it is quite rapid, more especially if the water is dark or high. If nothing results I try a few drifts with a longer line and work the fly not at all. Should this also fail I either give the pool a rest while I change fly-size or move on to fresh water.

A word might be said here about the angler's stance when fishing. Comfort and convenience are the first considerations. The rod should be held naturally at about 30 degrees to the water. The little "buffer" of slack line which thus hangs from the rod-tip is of the greatest value in hooking fish. It is obvious that unless the sea-trout takes the fly into its mouth it can't possibly be hooked. Sea-trout take a fly in two distinct ways—either by seizing it or by sucking it in. In the latter case the slack line method of fishing aids greatly by not obstructing the fish in its intentions. Moreover, the method gives a high proportion of fish safely and cleanly hooked in the "scissors".

There are places and occasions when it is useful to mend the line by throwing a loop or bag of line upstream with the rod-point. This again helps to put the angler out of direct contact with his fly—a fundamental point—as well as neutralizing the effects of a fast current on the line. Mending should be used when necessary; never through habit. No matter how neat the mend it is bound to cause some disturbance. The same, too, might be said about repeated false-casting, needless wading and other bad fishing habits.

Sea-trout take the fly in many ways—sometimes boldly, some-times with stealth. Sometimes they take near the surface; at other times in mid-water or even near the bottom. This behaviour is determined partly by weather (especially temperature) and partly by the fare on which they are feeding. Sedges, characteristically and delightfully, often elicit the surface rise which is so satisfying and thrilling. One may get half-a-dozen different rise-types in the same evening. From upper-water takes after hatching sedge the fish may switch to mid-water feeding on ascending nymphs. This may again be followed by an interest in minnows and stone-loach right down on the river-bed. The angler should be ready to exploit each type of feeding as soon as he knows it is occuring.

DRY-FLY FISHING

Many fly-fishermen prefer dry-fly to wet-fly fishing. This raises the question of the relative values of the two methods when applied to sea-trout. I speak here in terms of practical results rather than aesthetic appeal. Admittedly this is a bald approach because the number of fish in the basket is by no means directly related to the pleasure derived in catching them. There are plenty of anglers who would rather catch one sea-trout on dry fly than half-a-dozen on wet. No one can possibly quarrel with this attitude always provided that no attempt is made to make others conform likewise. Such lofty standards, however, are a personal matter, and for a discussion to be fruitful we are bound to consider results in terms of fish.

Sea-trout are sometimes very easy to catch with a dry fly just as they are with a wet. Fresh-run, they often rise keenly and will occasionally take almost anything put over them. This suicidal mood is of short duration. Once they have settled down they are less easy to tempt. Fish lying below trees, particularly during the heat of a summer day, can sometimes be roused by a big dry fly dropped over their heads. If the water runs slowly it is attractive if the fly is drawn an inch or two. A Palmer of ¾ inch diameter is hardly too big for such work.

Dry-fly fishing has a special value in cases where sea-trout are feeding cautiously on ascending and hatching nymphs in conditions of brilliant sunlight. A well placed dry fly will often produce a rise and a take when wet fly is quite hopeless. Bright light, especially if oblique, makes the finest wet-fly cast seem painfully coarse. On the other hand, a floating fly often finds acceptance under these conditions. The explanation, perhaps, is that the water surface in summer often carries a film of dust and scum and to a certain degree these help to camouflage the cast floating on them.

Although the dry fly makes an interesting change I never use it on those days or evenings when there is a culinary need to make a basket. Switching from dry to wet—as one must when the night draws on—means changing casts and ridding the line of grease, unless you have been using a self-floater. The advantage gained—strictly in terms of fish—by juggling with the two methods is nil. I find it more productive and a good deal less bother to stick to wet.

The angler who has an abiding love of the dry fly, however, should not let himself be put off by these remarks. Sea-trout *can* be taken on the dry fly—perhaps more often than the wet-fly angler imagines. If some of us fished a dry fly consistently perhaps we should be pleasurably surprised.

NIGHT FISHING

To many fishermen the sport of sea-trouting is synonymous with night fishing. Certainly the best of the sport with sea-trout may be expected after nightfall, the chief reason for this being that darkness lends the fish boldness while at the same time it offers the angler invisibility. At night, too, most of the larger insect forms are active—especially sedges and moths.

Night fishing is best practised in a good holding-pool or in a deep, slow run. The area should be thoroughly explored during daylight with a view to noticing snags. Background vegetation may need to be trimmed and it is essential to find a spot where fish can be netted and grassed without fuss.

Here is an incident to show how important the last of these points can be. This season I was tempted to pause at a strange pool for a few casts while on the way home. It was about 11.30 of a July night and the sea-trout were swirling at sedges in the pool-tail. They accepted a suitable No. 5 fly without hesitation. The first fish was no problem to grass since it ran downstream and was netted out of shallow water. The second went upstream and I found myself having to lie in soft mud in order to extend the landing-net through reeds. The fish snapped the cast in the reeds. The third went downstream and was netted. The next three went up. One buried itself in the reeds and shook the fly free. The other two snapped the casts, whereupon I packed up. A daylight inspection showed a good place for landing fish only a few yards from the impossible place I had picked in the dark.

In general, night fishing starts when the afterglow has faded from the sky. Fish often start feeding earlier, however, and the angler who is well-versed in gloaming fishing may well have two brace in his bag before the pukka night angler has wetted a line.

These early-feeding sea-trout are not always easy to catch. In the rivers that I fish one finds them feeding avidly on one of the small, quick-hatching sedges—a good answer to which is a No. 5 Gold Mallard. In search of a more effective fly for this purpose I asked Thomas Clegg to send me some flies dressed specifically for this type of sea-trout activity. The result was a chubby, rather drab-looking pattern and although it caught more fish than the Gold Mallard it was by no means a signal success. The reason, I found, was simple. Since the sea-trout were feeding in pool-tails cross-lit by the dying sun, they were highly sensitive to anything in the nature of a coarse and shiny cast. The answer to this was to soak some fine nylon points in hot water stained with a sepia dye; thereafter much better sport was enjoyed.

When the summer dusk settles heavily over the river there is usually a burst of intensive activity from the sea-trout. This is caused by the main sedge hatch. Whether the expected hatch in fact does take place is governed mostly by temperature and humidity. On a warm, dampish evening the flies, in some rivers, will leave the water in thousands. Some will alight on the angler and crawl trustingly over his hands. Fish activity should then be at a maximum.

Tactics. In these conditions my tactics are based on two points: (i) The fly must be fished shallow, since the sea-trout are surface-feeding and (ii) It should be fished fairly fast in order that it may not go unnoticed amongst the thousands of real and edible sedges. Catching fish during a heavy hatch is often a case of mathematical probability. The use of a larger fly than the natural on the water is advocated, very often, for this reason.

I use a technique which could be called 'skimming the sedge". A point-fly is used and a single dropper high up the cast. Usually it is the dropper that takes the fish. As a dropper pattern I like a Blae-and-Silver or a Buzzard-and-Silver both of which I dress fairly large to No. 5 hooks. (Fig. 25.)

The flies are cast to cover rising fish. The rod-point is raised steadily and evenly while simultaneously the angler recovers line with his left hand, drawing down from the butt-ring. The rod is raised almost to the vertical until—with a backward sweep—the angler recasts. If the operation is performed smoothly and at the

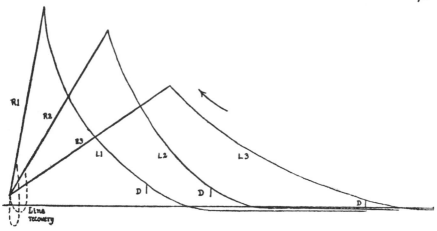

FIG. 25. *Skimming the Sedge. R3, R2 and R1 represent the successive rod positions during the retrieve and L3, L2, L1 the successive line positions. D is the dropper to which the artificial sedge is attached.*

correct speed—found by trial and error—the fish will rise and seize the dropper as it leaves the water.

With the onset of darkness these tactics fail and the fisherman must modify his approach. The sedges will have stopped hatching but there should be moths about. The sea-trout will now be cruising near the margins and under the bushes looking for water-borne moths. Some will drift to the pool-tail where the shallow water makes it easier to spot sizeable insects. The angler should cast to these places with a single size 5 or 7 fly and work it very slowly back. Pause frequently and expect fast takes.

Throughout nature creatures of different sizes and species exercise their right to feed by the aid of some system of priorities which seems little understood. There is a time when antelopes graze peacefully; there is a time when the lion prowls. And there is a short spell during the night—usually about three hours—when all nature seems to sleep.

Fish appear to be no exception to this universal rule. During a summer afternoon the tails of pools are full of feeding trout parr, minnows, stone-loaches and elvers. With the onset of dusk the small fry take cover while school sea-trout with a scattering of one-winter fish hold away. Towards midnight these, too, fade from the scene and the heavyweights take over. In keeping with their dignity these big sea-trout are deliberate takers. Occasionally one can be fooled into taking the skimming sedge but usually one expects to find them feeding in deepish water.

To obtain depth some anglers use a larger—and therefore heavier —fly. Others nick a scrap of ham-fat on the fly or affix a couple of maggots.* Others again switch to an outfit with a heavy ungreased line—almost like spring salmon tackle. Normally, my own method is to degrease line-point and cast thoroughly by rubbing in a little wet clay and to fish a fly of size 7.

Good night-vision is a valuable aid to the sea-trouter and it is easily spoiled by the too-liberal use of electric torches. Torches should be used sparingly for this reason; also to avoid disturbing the fish. A tip I find useful is to wear ordinary dark glasses during the early part of the night. Later, when these are removed, the angler will find he can see almost as well as in daylight.

A useful sort of torch takes the form of a square battery-case with a swivelled head containing the bulb. Fastened to one's middle by a belt there is little to beat it for night-fishing since the light is at the correct height for changing a fly and the angler's hands are left free.

PLAYING AND NETTING

"The smaller the fly the lighter the pressure" is a good working-rule for sea-trout fishing. Small hooks, obviously, can only take a small "bite". And since fresh sea-trout are tender about the lips it is not difficult to tear the hook from its hold. At the same time it is desirable, for practical as well as humane reasons, to net or beach the fish as quickly as possible. Beaching should be first choice—if there is a choice.

The easiest fish to deal with are those that head upriver at speed. The rod is held with the handle vertical and the angler lets the fish go. These fish soon spend themselves, when they can be reeled back and despatched. The awkward customers are the ones that flop about, jump, jig to-and-fro and end up by wrapping the cast round their pectoral fins.

The correct moment to net a sea-trout is when it turns on its side, spent. However I find that earlier netting than this often saves possible disaster, as when a fish may be drifting towards a fast glide. In that event it is certainly prudent to wade across its path and extend the net whether the fish is spent or not. Moreover, fish can be taken by surprise. I remember a 6-pounder that was netted from the surface a moment after it had taken the fly. It didn't know it had been caught! In the net it showed its disapproval by a violent display of acrobatics.

When netting a fish of size it is imperative to keep on eye on the river-currents. Never try to pull a fish against the current; in an emergency a fish can be *held* against the current. If it is impossible to get below a fish then it can be held in the current till it is half drowned—by keeping its head high—until such time as help arrives, Fig. 26 shows some netting situations. The usual netting stance is for the angler to hold the rod behind him at arm's length in order to

* But this can hardly be called true fly-fishing. Ed.

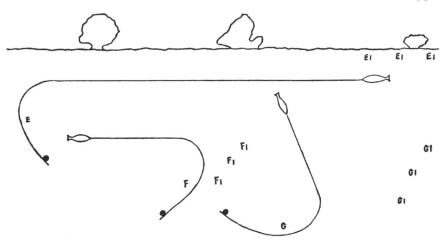

FIG. 26. *E1, F1 and G1 represent suitable points at which fish hooked at E, F and G respectively may be netted.*

save strain on the top-joint. Neat netting calls for much skill in judging the amount of line between rod-tip and fish.

LAKE FISHING

Lies of Sea-trout. I once spent several months on an Irish lough and during this period discovered that chuck-and-chance-it fishing is a waste of time. The newcomer must have local advice—even if it means going to a professional. An acre of water is a lot when it comes to guessing where fish are lying. A hundred or a thousand acres of water turns the game into the proverbial search for the haystack needle.

Luckily this penny dropped fairly early with me and the expert help of a professional fisherman helped to turn helpless guessing into confident knowing. In that great and (to my eyes) featureless lough it was uncanny to see the boatman rowing unerringly to a certain area which seemed identical with thousands of similar areas. He was, of course, using landmarks to give him the bearings of mid-lake shallows frequented by fish. A stranger might have rowed around the lough for years without stumbling on these spots.

Lake fishing would be much easier than it is if maps were available listing soundings taken over the lake bottom, together with notes about the ground-formation. Such maps are to be had for some of the largest lakes, especially where these are navigable. The Hydro-graphic Survey Office is helpful in these matters. The underwater features of the smaller lakes are usually a mystery except to the locals. The stranger fishing on his own needs a lot of luck if he is to find the paths taken by incoming sea-trout and the spots they favour as lies.

Sea-trout in lakes seem to like gravelly and rocky locations. They like to lie beside points and promontories—a predilection shared with their kin the lake-trout proper. Rocky bays, especially if they have sandy floors, are always worth prospecting. Shoals, whether of rock or gravel, should be fished carefully. Sea-trout love to lie in sheltered water where the deeps meet the shallows.

Earlier, I mentioned maps. A rough-and-ready fishing-map isn't too difficult to make provided you are not too ambitious. Given the use of a boat, a coil of string knotted at yard intervals and a weight, it is quite possible to map out a limited area. It takes two anglers to do the job—one busy on soundings, the other checking landmarks and preparing the chart. Such a chart will not only suggest where you should fish but also the size of fly to use.

Sea-trout still waters of course vary in character but hardly to the same extent as do sea-trout rivers. This is because sea-trout lakes are mainly confined to the west coasts of Ireland and Scotland—areas which have much in common geographically speaking. Most sea-trout lakes are glacial in origin and lie in that peaty no-man's-land which constitutes so much of the western seaboard. To hold sea-trout a lake must, of course, have direct access to the sea, whether by river or tidal channel. This access sometimes depends on spates or spring tides for its operation and unfavourable conditions in this respect simply mean that fresh fish can't run into the lake.

Most anglers agree that the ideal moment to put a fly over a sea-trout is the moment it pauses after its run up into fresh water. This is true of both rivers and lakes. In rivers where the fish follow a defined channel and enter recognized pools it is, of course, easier to find them than when they have entered the featureless expanse of a lake. The paths they follow in lakes are invisible on the surface. Lying-places, used by countless generations of sea-trout, are concealed from the view. Yet found they must be if more than an occasional success is desired.

Perhaps this over-simplifies the basic problem of lake fishing: that of finding fresh, taking fish. Because sea-trout, when they enter fresh water, seem to have a surplus of the energy that has driven them on their migratory run. This they often dissipate by a sort of nervous cruising round the confines of the area where they have chosen to lie. In rivers this will be a pool but in a lake it may be an area of many acres. And while shallow-water fishing is the accepted tactics in lakes it must be observed that good sea-trout are sometimes caught over the deeps—when they are, so to speak, on the prowl after running in fresh from the sea.

The serious lake fisher has numerous guides at his disposal and he should consult these with care. He will, of course, have a current tide-table and know the hour of high-water on the coast feeding fish into the lake. He will take due regard of the weather and its side-effects—especially in its relation to the level of the waterway up which the sea-trout must travel. His powers of general observation will be put to good use watching for "showing" fish.

The porpoise-like roll—almost as though the fish were attached to the outer rim of a wheel—of a salmon or a sea-trout bespeaks a fish on the run. Such fish are commonly regarded as non-takers, which I believe is true. Having reached fresh water these travellers slacken speed, as it were, and begin a prowl around the area's confines before settling into a lie. Non-takers can become takers in the time it takes to change a fly.

TACKLE FOR LAKE FISHING

Flies. I like a decent-sized fly for lake fishing, especially in peaty water. Flies of sizes 7 to 8 are not too big when the fish have to be attracted upwards through several feet of darkish water. Some loch anglers prefer the smaller salmon flies—no doubt after finding that the heavier irons sink better than do fine-wired sea-trout hooks.

Rods. Lake tackle really depends on how much lake fishing you hope to do. River tackle can be made to serve, although the advantages of a rod some $10\frac{1}{2}$-12 feet long are considerable. The longer rod certainly makes fly-manipulation a good deal easier, especially when sitting in a boat.

Casts. A nylon cast of 6 lb. b.s. makes a useful basis for experiments with terminal tackle. A cast of 8 or even 10 lb. would normally be used with the size 7 or 8 flies suggested and even this may be no more than adequate if the lake also contains salmon. Common sense must be the guide with the angler erring on the side of strength if in doubt. A fly on the point and a dropper fairly high on the cast is a typical arrangement.

TACTICS

The speed and manner of working the flies is again a matter for trial-and-error. Quick working for very fresh fish, slower working for those not so fresh, may be taken as the broadest of working rules. However, I am a firm believer in the virtues of casting up and along the ripple as opposed to casting athwart it. (Fig. 27.) This seems justified on the grounds that the cast in the former case is camouflaged by the refraction patterns formed by the waves. In the latter case the cast cuts cleanly across these natural shadows and must be correspondingly more conspicuous. Results bear out such a theory. Note the position of the sun in the diagrams.

Still-water fishing for sea-trout seems to be in a groove. Partly this is because most of it is managed by professionals who are satisfied with the old ways. A traditional fly on the cast, the time-honoured drift down the loch over the named grounds—this is still conducted as if it were some mystical rite. The angler who is so "different" as to

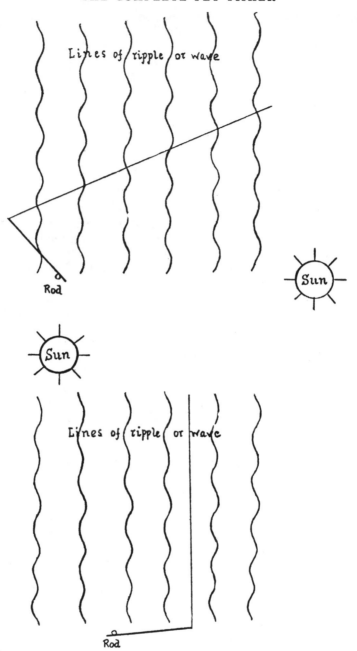

Fig. 27. Top: *Incorrect position of the rod and line in relation to the sun.* Bottom: *The correct position.*

don chest-waders to fish shallow bays and to use flies resembling natural insects is in danger of being regarded as an eccentric. Yet Mr. T. C. Kingsmill-Moore, amongst others, has enjoyed good catches of fish in the Irish loughs using trout-flies in conditions where the fish were clearly feeding on small naturals.

In a letter to the writer he says:

"Our Irish experience is this. Small flies tied in simulation of naturals are effective when the following conditions exist:

"(i) Sufficient small naturals, either of one species or of several species, to make the fish surface-observant and surface-minded.

"(ii) The water sufficiently calm as to allow the fish to spot the small naturals and artificials."

He adds: "In the open reaches big lure patterns are better because (a) There are few small naturals in exposed water. (b) In the rougher water small flies can't be seen by the fish. (c) It is not worthwhile for a big fish to rise from any great depth to secure a small fly."

The lake angler needs to think these and the other points over carefully when planning his campaign. The boatman's experience is invaluable for choosing a drift, but the angler should use his own judgement both in the selection of flies and in the method of fishing them. On the one occasion when I fished Lough Mask using large traditional flies (which caught nothing) it was interesting to find, on going ashore, that the rocks were covered with Lake Olives which had been hatching in sheltered water. Observation and adaptability are as useful on lakes as they are on the river. That the fish had been inshore feeding on Olives I had no doubt. This discovery came too late in the day to be of much use.

The angler who can "think like a fish" has a huge advantage over those who can't. This gift seems to be a mixture of intuition, experience and plain common sense. The lake fisher needs as much of it as he can develop.

DAPPING

On many of the Irish and Scottish lakes there is a traditional method of fishing known as "dapping", which is very effective for big sea-trout. In Ireland it is customary to use natural flies, either Mayflies or Daddy-long-legs, but as this is really a form of bait fishing it is outside the scope of the present book. In Scotland artificial flies are more popular, but no attempt is made to imitate the natural insects, and it could almost be said, "the bigger and hairier, the better". This approach, coupled with the automatic dapping technique (and the angler can become nearly mesmerised by his fly), has earned the method the label "dull" amongst some fly-fishers. But this, surely, depends on the sport being enjoyed.

A typical dapping outfit consist of a 14-ft. greenheart rod with a split-cane tip, a 4-inch reel loaded with as much line as it will carry, plus a 10-yard dapping line of floss-silk, ending in a yard of 12 lb. nylon. Dapping calls for a fresh breeze and a slow-drifting boat. Anglers commonly fish one in the bow and one in the stern, with the boatman amidships. An angler fishing alone should tie his oars to the rowlocks and straddle the midship thwart.

The breeze carries the floss-silk outwards to the critical angle, which is where the weight of line and fly exceeds the wind-pressure on the line. The dapping-angle is where the weight of the line and the wind-pressure are equal. By deft movements of the rod the angler can dance his fly over the surface. It should not be lowered or dragged through the water.

Many fish are lost through hasty striking, whereby the fly is pulled from their mouths. Fig. 28 shows that, although fish can rise from any direction, it is only when they rise with their backs to the boat that the angler runs little risk of this. In all other cases he runs this risk unless he pauses at the instant of the rise and allows the fish time to turn down. This is easier said than done—especially where there is a mighty swirl at the fly after perhaps hours of inactivity.

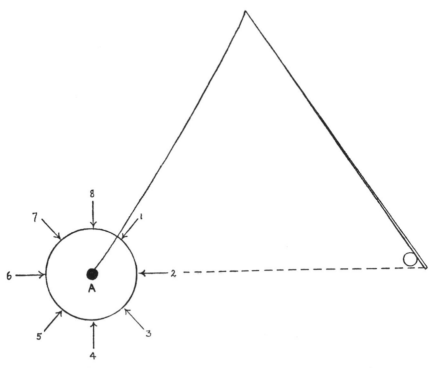

Fig. 28. *Dapping. A fish may take a fly from any point on the circle. Fish rising from positions 5, 6 or 7 should be given time to turn down before striking.*

TIDAL WATER FISHING

Fishing for sea-trout in tidal water is a distinct and valuable branch of the sport. Except in certain areas, where tidal fishing is studied and exploited, there is a disregard of tidal fishing which is not always easy to understand. Largely I think this is due to the change in outlook required of the angler in moving from the familiar greenery of the upper river down to the sands and mud of the estuary. There is, too, the fact that practical entomology—which most of us regard as one of the chief pleasures of fly-fishing—is of dubious worth once the water becomes brackish. River flies don't hatch in the sea!

Against these should be weighed the solid advantages: fish that are as fresh as they ever will be, pools full of water even during drought, and—not to be ignored these days—fishing which is, on many rivers, cheap or even free.

Voe fishing. Tidal water fishing may be divided into three categories. First, there is what the Scots call "voe fishing". This is fishing into the sea itself, especially along those beaches where there are beds of seaweed. The sea-trout move along the tangles feeding on copepods, slaters, shrimps and sand-eels. The best time to fish is on a rising neap tide in the months of July, August and September. Should the nearby rivers be badly effected by drought, so much the better; in this event shoals of sea-trout will be cruising and feeding along the shores, moving in and out with the tides, waiting for enough water to run. The angler should wade the shallow sandy bays and cast his fly down-beach over the tangles, working it back in jerks. Any No. 7 fly suggesting a shrimp is likely to serve. If this fails, a two-hook lure may be successful.

Estuary fishing. Secondly, we have estuary fishing. Some estuaries are almost unfishable due to glutinous mud. Others are a delight to fish—especially the ones composed of rock and sand. Quite often some of the muddy estuaries have small portions which make fishing possible for short distances. From the angling viewpoint the worst substance to encounter is clay.

Few experienced sea-trouters would care to risk their fly-fishing tackle in the salty waters of an estuary. Certainly I would never do so. If the angler is able to do a fair amount of estuary fishing it is well worth while obtaining a special outfit for this purpose. I use a tough 8 ft. hollow glass rod which will punch a line into the freshest breeze. A terylene line seems to survive the attacks of salt better than any other.

Flies need to be bright and of goodly size. No. 7 is not too big, although it often pays to drop to 5 during the low-water period, especially in sunshine. Lures kill well and their success may be due to their elver-like profile. Elvers and sand-eels are typical sea-trout fare. There is room for experiment with lures. Thomas

Clegg makes some of a special crimped nylon which is highly effective.

In estuary work the angler should study the area at low water. Note the position of the tidal channel, check the type of material forming the bottom and test the wading. It is prudent to know how to escape to dry land should the tide come in suddenly, as it will during the springs. In this connection do beware of tidal bores. I have seen three-foot bores come surging up quite small rivers and they are quite strong enough to throw an unwary fisherman on his back.

It is usual to fish the tidal channels during the low-water period. In this condition the fish are in known lies and the water is fairly clear of drifting weed and debris. Some anglers like to fish down with the last of the ebb and up with the first of the flood. This plan is ideal if the estuary is suitable and the shores firm. On the whole, slow, deep fishing seems to give the best results.

Although migratory fish often "show" when the tide is ebbing or flowing, it is uncommon to see them do so when the tidal channel registers low water—except perhaps when there is a heavy spate running to sea. As upriver, they seek cover partly for reason of the strong ultra-violet light which they seem to dislike. In estuaries cover takes the form of ledges, boulders and formations cut into the sand and gravel by tidal action. Rocky reefs covered in seaweed are a favourite haunt.

Brackish-water fishing. The third class of tidal-water fishing is what may be termed "brackish fishing". Strictly, it is river-fishing; yet it is in that part of the river which is under tidal influence. But in this case the tide is composed not of pure salt water but of fresh water slightly tainted with salt. The incoming tide pushes the river inland so that the tide is really the river flowing back on itself.

Sea-trout seem to perform their migratory run in two stages. Stage one sees them moving from the sea into brackish water. Stage two finds them moving into the fresh. This pause no doubt allows the fish time to adjust itself to osmotic changes in its system.

In brackish water it is usual to rely mainly on silver- and gold-bodied flies rather than representations of natural insects. Gold Butchers and Gold Mallards should be carried in a variety of sizes, Nos. 5 and 3 being the most useful. Light two- and three-hook lures catch well, especially when the water is murky with suspended mud. Lures dressed with light-coloured feathers are to be preferred. They look like silver sand-eels.

I normally use river-tackle for brackish water. The salt content is too small to do much damage. In any case, the best of the sport is enjoyed at or near low water when the stream is almost entirely fresh.

Most brackish reaches are rather exposed. The water is too fresh to sustain much seaweed and the tidal action is too pronounced to

L. S. Paterson

8. A Lowland sea-trout river: the Annan at Dormont.

9. A Highland loch holding big sea-trout. Loch Maree, Ross and Cromarty.

encourage tree growth. When the river is low the fish seek the deepest pools they can find. At dusk they come into shallower water to feed, and into the runs.

The beauty of brackish-water fishing is that the trout are always fresh-run. Taking periods vary through factors such as tides, weather, number of fish coming in from the sea and the success with which they are adjusting to their new environment. Sport is rarely mediocre. It is either completely off or very good indeed— assuming average ability in the angler.

F

CHAPTER III

BROWN TROUT IN RAIN-FED RIVERS
by
E. HORSFALL TURNER

TYPES OF RIVERS

BRITISH rain-fed river water can be divided into three types.

First, there is the fast upland water running in broken cascades, possibly interspersed with deep rock pools, over a bed with steep fall. In many ways this is the ideal water for the novice to fly-fishing, since he can often get near his fish without alarming them, and the broken water will make up for some deficiency in the ability to select the most effective flies. One or two treatises have been written recently on the suitability of the dry fly—indeed its preferability— on such water. I have fished a great deal on this type of water. There are occasions when the dry fly, in the sense that it is a fly that floats, can be used briefly to advantage as a tactical change with a difficult trout; but the fly used in such cases will bear little relation to the sparse life of these mountain streams, and will rather be a caricature of some land insect which finds its way by mistake, from time to time, on to the surface of the stream. The novice's catch on this type of water will not come near to that of the expert, but he will take a few fish which are obliging enough to hook themselves, which he is unlikely to do on the slower and more exacting waters of the lower valley, and will maintain his interest until his skill increases.

As these faster waters reach the foothills and the upper valley, their nature changes to the second type of fishing water. The river bed becomes wider or deeper to contain the volume of the mountain torrent at its slower pace. The broken water gives way, except when the river crosses sections of terrain with sharp fall, to shallow slightly-broken runs leading into deeper eddying tail-spins. These in turn lead into slow-moving unbroken pools. In the heavy water of spring, or during the run-off of a summer spate, the downstream wet fly, singly or in team, has its place on waters of this type, but, in my experience, the effectiveness of this method drops behind that of the upstream dry fly or the sunk fly cast upstream and drifted down, about the middle of May. It is on water of this type that the importance of relating the artificial to the natural insects begins to show itself to the full, though it is my conviction that the angler who ignores this relationship on the first type of water will reduce his chances of success.

Lastly we come to the third type of fishing water. The river which has splashed its lively course from the mountain and gained steadiness in the foothills and upper valley begins to receive the added volume of tributary feeders and widens into a deeper, more majestic flow in the broad plain to which the valley leads. On these leisurely waters, for all that one cannot watch and stalk the trout as in the clear chalk-stream waters, the technique of the dry fly need not be so very far removed from that of the chalk stream.

All rivers do not follow this three-phase plan of progress from the mountain cascade to the broad slow-moving waters of the alluvial plain. Fast heavily-broken water, again, may appear in many stretches of a river which has developed the general plan of the second or third of my types. It is for the angler to assess his water and the tactics demanded by its nature.

So far as the trout are concerned they are, on the whole, free rising and more catholic of taste in the fast upland waters. In the type of water found in the foothills and the upper valley, the hatches of fly are more frequent and more contained in period, which is reflected in the rather increased tendency amongst the trout to discriminate. In the slower waters of the river which flows gently through the plain, it is my experience that the discrimination of trout greatly exceeds that of trout in any other type of water, except that of the chalk stream.

Nature of river-beds. Before leaving the general description of rain-fed fly water, something should be said about the nature and effect of river-beds.

It goes without saying that the faster the water, the more it scours the river-bed; and in so doing reduces the weed growth of the bed, the home of insect life in a river. The slower the flow, the greater the accumulation of silt after spate and the greater the corresponding opportunity for the weed growth to take firm root. Since trout do not move appreciably about a river except when the mating urge grips them, the comparatively sparse feed of the headwaters permits less growth in the fish than the slower reaches of the middle and lower valleys.

River-beds also vary considerably in colour. This variation has its influence on the tactics of the angler. In some rivers, such as those in the mountainous areas of Montgomeryshire and Cardiganshire, the beds are worn from a pale grey granite. This gives the water, except when coloured by spates, a remarkable clarity. The angler has a clear view of his fish. In contrast, the beds of many Yorkshire rivers are worn from the dark rock strata with intermittent silting. These drab beds make it virtually impossible to see the trout unless the angle of light is precisely correct, which is of comparative infrequence during a day's fishing. On many occasions it is even possible to stalk trout on the less broken stretches of the clear mountain rivers, much as one stalks them on the chalk streams, but on rivers with darker beds such tactics are usually impossible. The angler can only look for the tell-tale dimple or rise-form of the feeding trout.

CHARACTERISTICS OF TROUT

Nevertheless, whatever their size and whatever their habits, the trout are the same fish in all types of water. So that before we consider the methods of fly-fishing these waters, it may be well to consider the characteristics of the fish we intend to catch.

The trout, unless tamed by usage to the comings and goings of the keepers of the stock pond, is a wild animal. Its actions are directed partly by instinct and partly by association of ideas. It can hear, smell and taste. Its life is a long endeavour to avoid the unfamiliar which is sinister to its senses (and therefore the potentially dangerous) and to obtain as much food as possible with the least possible expenditure of effort.

Our considerations can be confined to two main factors. The first is what the trout can see of the artificial fly. In this connection, we need not consider taste or smell, because the fly has neither; though we should not forget that an artificial fly moving at a different speed from that of the water surrounding it may well make a sound which is perceptible to the auditory system of the fish.

The second factor is the emotional influence aroused in the trout by detection of the fly. Detection may first take place by sight, as when a dry fly is drifted down into the field of vision of the fish, but it may also take place by hearing. On many occasions I have watched a trout turn towards a fly which has dropped at a considerable distance from it. The ultimate factor which impels the fish to take or reject an artificial fly, unless we accept Stoddart's obsession that the trout could smell it, is what it sees of the fly. We shall therefore make a start by considering the sensory and emotional elements in the trout, and then move to the fascinating, but largely speculative, question of what the trout can see of the bundles of fur and feather which it so frequently mistakes for the living things upon which it feeds.

Emotions of trout. The standard text book on animal mind remains G. R. J. Romanes' *Mental evolution in animals*, published in 1883. It requires something like literary trouser-waders to get through it, but a thorough study will pay the angler. Several other interesting but more elementary books have been written on the subject, such as those by Professor J. Arthur Thomson and Professor Lloyd Morgan. There is much of interest in these books, but it is to Romanes that we must turn for painstaking and thorough analysis.

There has been frequent reference to the "intelligence" of fish, trout in particular. Blakey credited the trout with a long catalogue of virtues including the fact that it "looked sagacious and intelligent", and kept up "a rigid system of order and discipline". Even Dr. Francis Ward, for whose photographic researches I have the utmost respect, makes the comment: "Many fish possess a certain degree of reasoning power, and there is often more truth in stories of fish intelligence than is generally supposed." What is the truth? It is that fish have no intelligence whatever as we understand the term. Innumerable tests have shown that they possess one of the lowest forms of animal mentality and that their mental faculties fall short of the power of reasoning. Unless reason is present, intelligence cannot exist.

Romanes analyses the limits of animal emotions with great care. He credits fish with capability to experience pleasure and pain, the faculty of memory, and the power to associate by similarity. Their emotions, in his opinion, are limited to fear, curiosity, jealousy, anger and a somewhat nebulous inclination to be playful.

The difference between reasoning and association by similarity is not difficult to translate into human terms. A townsman and a mountain crofter would see a pedestrian crossing in quite different ways. The townsman would be familiar with the design and would not notice it as such. He would merely regard it as a safe place to cross a busy highway. The crofter would notice and probably examine carefully a strange design in black and white on the road surface. At that, his understanding would end. If he continued to inhabit the area, he would notice the use made of the crossing by large numbers of people. Since he would have the human power of reasoning, he might work out the significance of the design after short observation of the way in which others reacted to it. But if he lacked this power, he would almost certainly learn the use of the crossing by associating it with the idea of large numbers of people crossing the highway at that point, and would ultimately join them in doing so. Nobody explains to the trout that a fly attached to a translucent tail, the point of the cast, has some sinister quality. If the trout has been pricked recently by a fly with this feature, its memory may alert the senses and it will leave such another alone—until it forgets. If it has had several such unpleasant experiences, the fact may be imprinted on its memory and it may become what we call "gut-shy". Gut-shyness, in my experience, is a transitory disease and never chronic! This process has nothing to do with reasoning and is merely the development of a habitual process of reaction which makes avoidance of flies with translucent tails into something like an acquired instinct. I say "something like" because instinct cannot be acquired, but only inherited.

Short-rising. The trout is extremely sensitive to the unfamiliar, as I have observed. The unfamiliar varies in nature. It may excite curiosity if it is not associated with the sinister, such as the sight of some small moving object which is reminiscent of the insect life of the river on which the trout is accustomed to feed; or, if a large shadow falls across the fish, its reaction is sense of the sinister and immediate arousing of the instinct of self-preservation. Curiosity is undoubtedly the reason for many "touches" of the fly instead of firm takes. These touches are frequently attributed to fish "coming short", in the sense that the fault lies in the mood of the fish, rather than in presentation or selection of fly. This is not a sound line of thought, even though it is a human failing to attribute our angling shortcomings to fortune rather than to ourselves! Let us consider this "short rise" in terms of our own behaviour.

One of our conventions is that we do not handle food which is put before us unless we intend to eat it. Let us suppose that this convention did not exist, and that we were confronted by a buffet containing a great variety of articles of food, some of which we knew and others we did not. Many of the unknown articles of food would cause us some mental association, by similarity, with others that we knew to be good to eat. What would our reaction be? Surely we should pick up the unfamiliar articles, smell them—and possibly lick them tentatively. That, precisely, is what the trout often does when it rises short. So that our first reaction to a short rise should be to ask ourselves a mental question : have we offered the trout something which it recognized only by association of ideas, rather than by conviction that it was edible—and preferably as edible as the familiar objects on which it had been feeding immediately before our offering came into its field of vision? Before moving further, it may be well to consider why a trout ever takes a fly into its mouth.

As I have said, the fish lives its life in a long endeavour to get as much food as possible with the least possible expenditure of effort. The primary reason why a trout takes a fly is that it fancies that the fly is something edible. If deception is complete, the take will be firm and fearless. The only exception to this is when the trout is already fed to repletion, but is carried away by the emotion of greed, and cannot allow further food to pass without going through the motions of taking it into possession. Deception, as I have suggested earlier, is not achieved by presenting a fly which to our eye looks the same as the natural insect. In his book, *Sunshine and the Dry Fly*, J. W. Dunne attempts to carry the theory and practice of exact imitation to about the ultimate. His creations, he contended, caused complete deception after they had been carefully examined by the trout. His arguments leave me without the slightest conviction. Sub-surface photographs show the limit of the picture of the fly which is there for the trout to see. The eye of the trout may see less than the lens of the camera, or it may see with reduced definition, but it cannot see what is not there. The spectrum line on the critical angle of the trout's visual field causes a remarkable distortion of the floating fly as it drifts into the direct visual field. This will be examined at a later stage. My only passing comment is that in the case of the floating fly, colour blend, shape and size all contribute their quota to deception in a quite different way from the contribution of the like features in the sunk fly. The trout should have quite a normal view of the sunk fly. In either case, for all that the hands of man have never come near to creating anything approaching a facsimile of the natural insect, the trout still take the artificial. Why should this be the case?

We know two ways of making a recognizable picture. The first is known as "sincere" and is an effort to reproduce a precise likeness to what appears to our eyes. Good colour photography is the ultimate, so far, in this kind of likeness. The second way is caricature. The effect of a good caricature is such that when we see it we cry instantly, almost with the enthusiasm of the ungrammatical monks of Rheims: "That's 'im!" Unless the trout were moved by a similar combination of senses and emotion, I do not believe they would ever take an artificial fly, except in such broken water that its characteristics were unrecognizable, or when they were in the mood to take anything which appeared to be alive and edible.

Our first reaction to a short rise, or a series of short rises, therefore, should be: "The fly is at fault . . . it is interesting *but not convincing.*" The trout are merely arresting the fly in its progress, and not attempting to eat it. The trout have no hands and use their mouths for this purpose, but the action of checking the fly for inspection is as different from the firm take as our action in picking up an article for inspection would be from a firm grab of that article. In one case, a light twitch would dislodge it from our hands, while in the other, our first instinct would be to hang on firmly. Moreover, in the case of the light pick-up, we should hold the article with the tips of our fingers (unless it were heavy), while in the second, our fingers would be round it in a firm grasp.

Before moving to other reasons for the short rise, something should be said of the speed of movement in the fly. The fish, as I have said, gets its food with the least possible effort. If it is hungry, it will move considerable distances with great energy; otherwise, it appears to balance off the amount of energy it must expend against the urge to get the passing food.

A fast-moving fly will often be ignored, whether natural insect or an artificial, if the balance is against the urge to secure food. This is particularly evident with the salmon, for all that the salmon urge is by no means certainly connected with some habitual urge to secure food, and the method of greased-line fishing devised by the late A. H. E. Wood was based on slowing up the movement of the fly. I have found on occasion that precisely the same slowing up of the sunk fly fished downstream with drag has taken fish, or rather has converted tentative takes to firm ones, when fishing for trout. The factor of fish-effort should never be left out of account. The marked difference between salmon takes and trout takes is that salmon often give the angler a second chance, whereas trout rarely do. A deduction that excessive speed is the reason for a short rise to the downstream fly for trout must usually be reflected in a slowing up of the fly movement for another trout, and not for the one which has come short. Another point about the speed of fly movement concerns the habit of the trout of getting into position to intercept the fly. This is a form of conservation of energy. For practical purposes it is my experience that the drifted fly, whether floating or sunk, is immeasurably more successful than a fly moving at speed. The reason is simply that its slow motion gives the trout plenty of time to take up the ideal position to intercept it.

Some emphasis has been laid on the importance of analysing the short rise. It is equally important with the floating or the sunk fly. A brief practical example of what induces me to emphasize the point happened on the top Yorkshire Derwent during the past summer. The stream is heavily treed at the point where I started fishing. Great numbers of the Hawthorn-fly (*Bibio marci*) were in evidence. This is a land fly, but considerable numbers drop on the stream and are readily taken by the trout. The fly has a characteristic of dropping its very long hind legs when flying or relaxed. The dressing I use is a body of black ostrich herl, with black cock hackle so manipulated during tying that a tuft of black fibres is concentrated into a short segment of the circle of the hackle. I had none of these dressings with me when I went up the river before lunch. The nearest thing I had was a fly to which I shall refer at some length later and call simply a beetle. The dressing of this is a cocoon of yellow wool overlaid with bronze peacock herl so that a little of the yellow wool shows at the rump, and three turns of short black hen hackle. The hook is No. 5 (new scale) down-eye. In terms of "general pattern", this beetle is not so far removed from the artificial Hawthorns I dress. I fished it upstream on a greased line and cast, an inch or two below the surface. Before lunch, I had a dozen touches of the fly but only hooked one fish. Its stomach content contained three Hawthorns. After returning to the car for lunch, I took some of the Hawthorn dressings left there and substituted one for the beetle. In a couple of hours, I had a dozen firm takes and not a single touch. This aroused my curiosity. Once again I mounted the beetle. In another half hour I had several touches and had convinced myself, beyond any shadow of doubt, that there was a completely different trout reaction to the two flies. In the case of the beetle, curiosity without fear was aroused; but in the case of the true attempt to imitate the natural Hawthorn, the fly carried conviction and the trout took firmly. Over the years I could quote many similar instances, although the facts were more complex and the evidence was suggestive rather than conclusive. For all that, I am sure the same principle applied. Short rises and touches of the fly were simply due to failure to convince the fish—which is not misfortune or fish mood, but merely the fault of the angler.

Let us now move on to short rises that are not due to failure to carry conviction with the fly. In these cases surmise takes a more prominent place than it does in mere failure in fly selection. The short rises I have described so far are due to failure to get further than arousing the curiosity of the trout, but Romanes allows several other emotions to fish. Fear, jealousy, anger and playfulness must be considered. Romanes does not mention greed in the sense that implies inability to let the chance of feeding go by even though the hunger is satisfied. How far fish hunger is ever satisfied, it is not easy to say. In waters with heavy feed, trout grow larger on average than in waters where the food supply is scarce, but this does not necessarily mean that if the small trout of the mountain stream were transferred to the better feeding grounds of the lower river, they would grow to the size of the natives of those lower reaches merely because they fed more heavily. There are times when trout appear to become gorged and disinclined to take firmly, or disinclined to take at all. Short rises may occasionally be due to this factor. That is as far as it is safe to go.

Fear undoubtedly accounts for many short rises by individual trout. As the trout approaches the fly it sees something unnatural about its movement, or sees that the fly is not what it appeared to be at a greater distance. This is evident when fishing across a current to chalk-stream trout whose movements can be watched. When the trout first sees the artificial fly it moves to intercept it without showing any trace of fear. The line and cast then begin to drag on the current and alter the drift of the fly. The interested trout immediately sheers away and drops to its lie. It has an uneasy quiver, and the slightest visible movement of the angler will send it scurrying to a more remote lie, or to a hiding place. On occasion, however, recognition of the unnatural or the unfamiliar comes so late that the fish makes what appears to be a snatching take before it sheers off. If the fish is not visible to the angler, as is so often the case in rain-fed rivers, this type of rise would usually be classed as "short".

Anger is not likely to play any part in short rises. It is almost impossible to attribute this emotion to a trout with any certainty, though I have seen a trout make a rushing onslaught which is reminiscent of angry movements in human beings. Usually this results in a firm take.

Jealousy, again, is unlikely to cause the short rise. If a trout fears interference with its take, or even inspection, of the fly, it usually makes a firm grab before it can be dispossessed. A year or two ago, a fly-fisherman on the Eden was using the beetle to which I have referred, with the drift method. The water was low and clear. He told me that on many occasions he was taken firmly when he drifted the fly past two or three trout lying close to each other, but that when he cast at a single trout, it rarely induced anything but inspection. I have noticed the same trout behaviour on many occasions, and have, indeed, used it to my own advantage when I wanted fish in the creel! Jealousy is a vice that can be turned back on the trout, rather than the cause of short rises.

We now come to the last two emotions: curiosity and playfulness.

The reaction of curiosity is difficult, if not impossible to distinguish from that caused by the urge to inspect potential food by feel, taste and smell. If any animal is without fear, it will always (unless overfed and lazy) investigate any unusual object, particularly if the unusual object has some association by similarity with food. Again, the boundary between curiosity and playfulness is not easy to define. What emotions urge a cat to chase a leaf that blows across the road? If we grant that the first emotion is recognition of a similarity between the fluttering leaf and the movements of a mouse or bird, we have further to go; because after the cat has caught the leaf and knows that it is inedible, it will continue to chase the leaf when it moves again. Halford observed that trout are frequently "quite silly" and will take any one of a number of patterns which bear no resemblance to their diet of the moment or to any natural insect known to frequent the water. Any experienced fly-fisherman will have noticed this occasional behaviour in trout. Is it not likely that the emotions which move the trout are much the same as those which move the cat in its chase of the leaf? Moreover, the passage of a fly through water may "sound" to the fish, much as the rustle of the leaf does to the cat.

The chase of the leaf by the cat probably starts with a mixture of curiosity and that overworked incentive, the predatory instinct. Once the cat has secured the leaf under its paw, inspected it and let it go again with the wind, any further chase must be induced, in the main, by playfulness. The difference between the cat and the trout chasing a fly, is that a touch of the fly is enough to alert the fish to danger, and the chase ceases sharply after that touch.

It has always struck me as important that the fly-fisherman should understand trout emotions and realize two points. First, the reactions of the trout to the sight of the fly do not result in any train of reasoned thought. Second, the reactions are predominantly influenced by the incessant urge to find food, and the instinct of self-preservation.

Vision of trout. We now turn to one of the most interesting of all fly-fishing questions: what does the fish see of the fly? The question can be answered quite easily for practical purposes: it must see something like our picture of the natural insect, and that something must be so near the appearance of our artificial creations that association of ideas causes the fish to take the artificial. All fly-fishing philosophy could be left at that for practical purposes. On the other hand, such a philosophy is pretty barren and has little appeal to the fly-fisherman as his experience increases. So that a careful examination of the facts, circumstantial evidence and possibilities of fish vision probably will not come amiss to the angler who has reached a stage (not all anglers do) at which the mere fact that his artificials catch fish, is not wholly satisfying.

We do not know what the fish sees. We know that in the game fish, which concern us here, the eye is covered by the skin. We know that water has a distorting quality, and—a point of some complexity with which I shall deal later—that the margin of fish vision is a spectrum which deflects various colours in light at different angles. Skues expressed the view that trout vision was "defective". It would have been a happier way of putting it to say that trout vision differed from ours. It is certainly not defective for the purposes of the trout. In the long range, the vision of the trout is remarkably acute in seeing our movements about the river. In the short range, it can show great discrimination at times in selecting some particular larva, such as that of the reed smut, from what would appear to us to be a host of similar small particles of food floating in the surface film. The possibility, if not the probability, is that the eye of the fish does not point focus; that is, the scene registers on the retina much as it registers, through the lens, on the negative of the camera. If we look at an object some yards away, we see it in sharp focus, but our vision also includes surrounding objects. These are not seen directly, but their presence is conveyed to the senses by our vision. The scientists have long suspected that the animal eye sees a panorama, rather than an object with an indefinite surround of other objects.

The circumstantial evidence, so far as the fish goes, tends to support this belief. The trout, for instance, will often rise to examine a fly at very close range, dropping back with the current to hold the fly at that range. Skues puts the angle from which the trout views the fly in this way at 45 degrees. It is much more likely, in my opinion, that the angle is slightly over 42 degrees, but that is a point related to the spectrum line of the under-surface viewpoint. At the moment we are concerned only with the fact that the trout comes close to the fly in order to examine it. This can mean one of two things: either that the eye of the trout has a very short focal length, or that its only means of making a careful examination is by "filling the field of vision" with the object under inspection. If the eye has a very short focal range, it is a reasonable assumption that objects tend to blur at a correspondingly short range. There is no doubt that the trout can see objects clearly, if not distinctly, at several feet of distance, so that very short focal range of sight is unlikely. The second alternative is therefore much more likely. First, the trout sees a panoramic picture of the scene, much as the image is registered on the negative of the camera; second, its view of an individual object in that picture is indistinct until it comes close enough to fill the visual field with that object. The importance of these conclusions will become apparent when we move on to deal with the characteristics of the effective fly and their relationship with the natural insect.

The next point for consideration is what there is in the way of a picture for the eye of the trout to see from its under-water viewpoint. The best evidence, as I have said earlier, is what the camera can see.

Many writers have described the "cone of vision" of a fish. Fig. 29 shows a cone with its apex on the eye of the fish, and an apex angle of 83 degrees. The base of the cone is an imaginary circle on the surface of the water. Objects in or above this circle are seen directly by the fish, while outside the circle, the under-surface of the water is a mirror, reflecting under-water objects which are sufficiently illuminated to register an image. So far as bank objects are concerned, they are "folded down", so to speak, around the margins of the base of the cone. This is due to the refraction of light rays by water. It is a neat scientific theory, but I am quite certain that it is an over-simplification of a much more complex problem. In any case the trout is uniocular and therefore has three cones of vision.

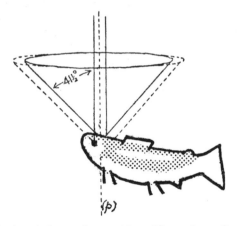

FIG. 29. *The theoretical cone of trout vision. The continuous lines indicate the binocular field and the pecked line the extensions due to the uniocular faculty and the spacing of the eyes.*

One is the straightforward cone in its binocular segment of vision. The others are marginal on this cone, where the one eye or the other has an extended field beyond that of binocular vision. Many times, when I am quite sure that neither my figure nor the rod could possibly have "folded down" into the vision of a fish lying in shallow water, I have watched the departing "V" of the disturbed fish. It must be remembered that the theory of the cone of vision, in its precise sense, is only tenable if the water surface remains at all times without movement. If it has ripple or even undulation, the angle of the base of the cone is sectionally variable. This means that the water surface may be "tipped" so to speak. In this case, instead of the cone wall being at an angle of 41½ degrees to the perpendicular through the eye of the fish, it may be at nearly double this angle for practical purposes. Whatever the upward visual field of the trout is, it is not a neat sort of horizontal port-hole. It is more likely to be an undulating spectrum line, roughly circular if the fish is lying deep enough. This spectrum line, the "rainbow line" as Skues called it, will be (if the surface is still) at an angle of $41\frac{1}{2}$ degrees to the perpendicular through the eye of the fish. Between the spectrum line and the perpendicular, all objects, whether floating or sunk, may be backgrounded by the sky. If so, their form will show clearly, but their colours will be dulled into half-tones. If the background is overhanging foliage, the object will be toned into that background, but its colours will be more evident. Moreover, if the light has penetrated to the fish, it will see its own image (and those of any sufficiently lighted surrounding objects) superimposed lightly, much as we see our own images superimposed on the objects in a shop window which is darker than the street outside.

On the other side of the spectrum line, the under-surface is a mirror. All that can be seen from beneath the water are objects in the water which are sufficiently illuminated to register an image in the mirror. If there is insufficient light, the mirror merely goes black and cannot, as at least one writer has suggested, become more transparent on dull days than on bright ones!

The appearance of a floating fly as it approaches a fish and crosses the spectrum line is distorted into a sort of "flare", which rises and falls during its progress. This flare is caused by the split of the colours of light by the prismatic border-line of the field of fish vision, and the fact that different colours travel down at varying angles through the water to the eye of the trout. Space does not permit of lengthy description of this feature of trout vision. It was covered generally in *The Field* of 7th April, 1960, with photographic illustration to show, so far as it can be shown in black and white, the singular effect of the colour break-down and blend.

The camera makes it quite clear that for practical purposes the angler should think of his dry fly in terms of a composition which, in size and colour, is likely to blend into the same flare as the natural insect. Shape is not of great importance as the fly drifts across the prismatic border of the trout's field of vision, but once it crosses this line, shape and size are likely to be of greater importance than colour.

So far as the sunk fly is concerned its appearance within the border is governed by the same factors as those which govern the appearance of the dry fly. Background, as I have observed, has an important bearing.

Outside the prismatic border, a singular phenomenon is evident with the sunk fly. The fish usually sees two flies. One is the fly itself in direct vision. The other is the unsteady reflection of the fly in the mirror beneath the surface film. The reflection will, of course, be reversed in shape, light and shade. The fly must also be in a position from which the incidence of its angle of reflection on the under-surface mirror does not fall within the prismatic border.

This double image has some importance, since a fly that may not be visible to the fish directly, or may be effectively camouflaged as its colours tone into a background, may be clearly visible as a reflection. When I first became aware of the existence of this second image I questioned whether many short rises might not be due to the trout confusing the image with the actual fly. Bearing the possibility in mind over the years, I am now sure that the trout make no such mistake. For all that the photographic recordings suggest the probability of a mistake, one must remember that they were taken in absolutely still water. The certainty is that on most occasions the trout see the reflection in a mirror that is not still, whereas the fly itself rides steadily at its own level.

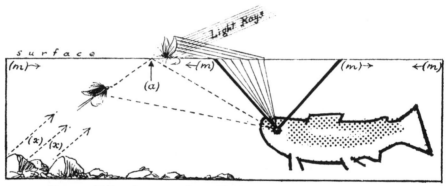

Fig. 30. *Various factors must be considered when attempting to assess the visual picture of the trout. The heavy black "V" denotes the limits of the theoretical "cone of vision". The under-surface between the points (m) is a mirror to the eye of the fish. It can see the sunk fly at point (a) in the under-surface mirror. This reflection will be backgrounded by the reflections of the stones to the left of the diagram if they are sufficiently lighted to register a reflection. The floating fly is outside the cone of vision. In direct vision, the trout will see any hackle fibres or part of the fly which pierce the surface film. It will also see the light rays falling on the fly from above, and reflected from the fly to the surface inside the cone of vision. These are split into basic colours by the prismatic factor as they enter the water, and the differing angles of entry present the eye of the trout with a blended "flare" of colour which rises to its height as the fly drifts over the margin of the cone of direct vision.*

Finally, there is the optical mechanism of the trout to consider. Unlike humans and many animals, the eyes of the trout are set on either side of its head and each eye covers its own field of vision in a way that is termed uniocular. The trout eyes can also be moved independently of each other. If one imagines the total visual range of a trout as something like an incomplete circle (the field is in fact nearly a complete sphere but at this stage it will be easier to think of the circular range) there are two large segments, right and left, of uniocular vision. At a certain point the two eyes can both focus on an object if the trout so adjusts them. This is the segment of binocular vision. Since the eyes are set forward in the upper part of the head, there is an upper arc of binocular vision extending from the horizontal through the eyes of the fish to somewhere past the perpendicular through its eyes. On the downward side, the flanks interfere with the binocular lines of vision and the arc is somewhat shorter. It is a common impression that the trout has a completely blind sector behind it. This depends on the relative level of objects in the rear. The trout can also, if suspicious, give a fractional turn either way and bring an object in its rear into the field of vision.

A trout in its lie alters its angle to the current from time to time. If the trout shows restlessness of this type during the stalk, assuming it can be watched, the angler must "freeze" immediately and wait for his chance to move when the fish settles to a steady upstream position. For practical purposes it is much easier to approach a trout unobserved from behind, but the idea that the angler can take advantage of a defined blind zone in the visual sphere of the trout must be treated with great reserve.

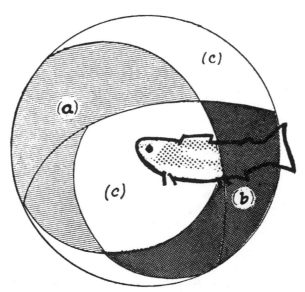

FIG. 31. *The Field Of Vision of a Trout.* (a) *represents the sector of binocular vision,* (b) *the blind sector, and* (c) *the sectors of uniocular vision.*

This brief commentary on the vision of the trout is enough for our purpose. It will give the reader a few pointers from which he can start his own researches during the ordinary course of fishing. There is no great certainty in the matter except that our flies bear some resemblance, in the eyes of the trout, to the natural insects of its diet; otherwise they would not be taken with the regularity they are—or indeed would not be taken at all. The discriminative ability of the trout is marked. On occasion the trout will take only one type of artificial to the exclusion of all others. At other times it will take artificials in a limited range. Sometimes it will take nearly anything in the fly-box. But the occasions of exclusive discrimination show its full capacity in terms of recognition, and this is always present except when water conditions make accurate assessment impossible for it and the urge to feed is predominant.

ARTIFICIAL FLIES

Let us now consider the potential and measure of deception which we can achieve with the artificial fly, and the extent to which imitation is practicable and effective.

There is a popular impression that Halford and his followers started the theory and practice of exact imitation of the natural insect during the closing years of the last century and the early years of the present. This is quite mistaken. It may well be that the ancient Macedonians, in the fourth century A.D., were arguing the merit and otherwise of exact imitation of their *Hippouras* fly! In this country we have an interesting and well-documented record of the violent difference between Professor John Rennie and the "routine" anglers (the "exact imitators" of those days) in the 1830's. By the time of Cholmondeley Pennell, in the 1860's, the "routine" anglers had become the "formalists"; and they waged equally violent war on Pennell's doctrine that three artificial flies for trout, and three for salmon, would catch as many fish as all the purported imitations of the natural. Halford has always struck me as a dull but quite realistic technician who based his fly-fishing on a belief that the flies he designed, from what he could see of the natural insects, did in fact deceive the trout into thinking that they were the insects upon which they had been feeding immediately before. There have been occasions when I have had no doubt that such was the case in my own fishing; and to that extent, I feel some sympathy for Halford and his philosophy. It was at least a thoughtful philosophy, and he showed his realism frequently by admitting that anything approaching exact imitation was usually unnecessary! It was the followers of Halford who built up a pompous and ridiculous edifice of "purism", with "exact imitation" as its corner-stone.

G. E. M. Skues then asked why an imitation of the immature stages of the fly, as a nymph, should not be as gentlemanly a way of catching trout as a copy of the floating insect. Skues firmly averred his belief that his nymph-type flies were taken by the trout as the natural insects, and went on to say that if he had believed otherwise, and indeed did not believe that his flies were taken by the trout for the diet of the moment, much of the joy would have departed from fly-fishing so far as he was concerned.

Against these beliefs, we face the fact that several competent fly-fishermen have fished the season through with only one fly, and have left themselves in some doubt as to whether, if they had known their

A. V. Oglesby

10, 11. Mr. E. Horsfall Turner fishing the Yorkshire Derwent near Scarborough.

E. Horsfall Turner

A. V. Oglesby

12. Ideal dry-fly water. The Eden at Kirkoswald.

entomology or rung the changes through a box-full of flies, they would have caught one more fish. I have tried this method myself at certain periods of my fishing life, and would not like to express a firm opinion on its comparative effectiveness. The only qualification is that presentation must be consistently good if the angler is to be fit to make any assessment at all.

Two very sound comments have been made on the subject of entomology and imitation. The first was that of Courtney Williams, who wrote: "I am always a little sorry for the 'one fly' man because he must lose some of the sport and a great deal of the interest and fun." The second comment was that of J. R. Harris, who wrote: "As one's fishing experiences increase, one's outlook changes, and, in so far as the catching of fish is concerned, the matter of importance is not so much how many fish are caught but rather how they are caught. When dry-fly fishing, one is apt to find that one loses interest in fish caught on 'a good pattern of general fly' and to get satisfaction only when it has been determined on what fly a trout is feeding and then to succeed in catching the fish on an imitation of that fly."

The only difference I have with these comments, both from remarkably good catchers of trout, is that Harris confines his comment to the dry fly. So far as the wet fly is concerned it is rarely safe, in my experience, to forget or ignore what is going on in the water before the angler. There are days when the fish will take anything; others, when a succession of short rises can be converted into firm takes by change of fly—either on a chance basis or after reasoning matters out with enough entomological knowledge to do so; others, when short rises are the order of the day and defy all attempts at conversion to firm takes; and lastly those days when the trout rise persistently to some natural insect but will have nothing to do with the artificial. The vast majority of days, so far as the fly-fisherman is concerned, are those on which the trout will take the right fly firmly, but will ignore the artificial which does not carry conviction.

Trout vision and the artificial fly. Let us pause at this stage in our reflections on the point and counterpoint of imitation, and consider the relationship between fish vision and our creations in fur and feather. Evidence suggests that a fish does not see objects in sharp detail as we do and that its ultimate best is at a couple of inches range when the object fills its field of vision. If the fish really has indistinct vision, what order of importance should be attached to colour, size and pattern in the fly?

The ability of fish to distinguish colours was in debate for many years. Scientific tests have shown, beyond doubt, that fish are sensitive to different colours, though it is not known exactly how they see the colours. Any experienced fly-fisherman will remember occasions when trout behaviour was such that it convinced him of their ability to discriminate between colours. It is probable that colour in the sunk fly has a definite bearing on its attraction value

G

if the fly is in the direct vision of the fish beneath the under-surface mirror; though if the fly is inside the 41½ degree angle, and the background is the sky, colour will have relatively little importance. Tones of colour, in my experience, matter little under any circumstances. One has to bear in mind that a scoop of the plankton net may bring up a dozen nymphs of the same species of fly, all having quite different colour tones—and even different colours to our eyes.

E. R. Hewitt held the opinion that the size of fly was more important than its colour or shape. So far as the dry fly is concerned, there is some reason in this belief because all adult flies of the same species, hatching in the same area at the same time, are very similar in size. Moreover the fly that drifts inside the prismatic border above the trout can be seen with enough precision to be distinguishable from the naturals it is supposed to represent if the size is wrong.

In the case of the sunk fly I have sometimes found that alteration in size has improved the number of firm takes, but I often question whether, in our efforts to relate the sunk fly to the natural insects, we do not make the error of using a smaller fly than we should. A widely-accepted principle of salmon fishing is that of starting in the heavily broken top water of the pool with a large fly and gradually reducing size as the water steadies into the dub below. In fishing fast broken water for trout, the fish must be offered something it can see in the turmoil. Fishing the dub below will not be very successful if the fly is dragged about unless the water is heavily rippled by wind —in which case the effect of the broken water is reproduced to some extent. The wet fly is a representation of a nymph, and nymphs vary considerably in size according to their ages. So that there can be little wrong with the principle of allowing predominant importance to using a fly large enough to attract the attention of the trout, and trusting that the trout will associate the artificial, by its colour, shape and movement, with nymphs of a different size.

So far as the dry fly is concerned, I find no reason to differ from Hewitt. The size should be related carefully to the size of the natural fly, bearing in mind that there is often a variation in natural fly size from time to time and from area to area, in the same species.

Shape of fly is a matter of considerable importance. The majority of shop-bought wet flies are still too heavily dressed, though there is, at last, a tendency to lighten these dressings. Light dressing has been a characteristic of north-country flies for generations, and were also a characteristic of the flies of that very great Welsh angler, the late Dai Lewis. A popular modern south-country fly is Frank Sawyer's pheasant-tail nymph, which has no hackle. I have tied up a few copies of this fly and have found it to be quite effective, but I must express a personal preference for two or three turns of short hen hackle on any wet pattern. They undoubtedly add mobility, and therefore life, to the fly when drifted, and when the fly is twitched or dragged they mill round the body in a manner reminiscent of action. Moreover, they tend to build up at the roots into a lump which bears some similarity to the humped wing-case of the nymph. If, as with many bought flies, the hackle is laid with a number of turns (often poor-quality cock is used) the fly loses mobility, and when it is in motion, the hackles fold down and completely hide the ribbing and materials of the body.

The body of the fly, whether fished wet or dry, makes a very important (if not the most important) contribution to the effectiveness of caricature. Caricature in human art is not a mere distortion of the facial characteristics of the subject. In 1928 the late Dean Inge, doubtless smarting under his representations by the caricaturists as a man of gloom, suggested that we should have a copyright in our features. The *Daily Express* cartoonist of the day, David Low, promptly drew most of the Cabinet without any faces. They were instantly recognizable from their stance, contours, and external idiosyncrasies. How much more important must be this attention to the external if the object is to be recognized by a creature with indistinct vision except at close range? The essence of good caricature is recognizable impression. The governing factor in the attraction of a fly may well be its shape—and its shape alone at times. Belief in this principle is apparent from the humpy wing-case dressing of modern nymphs, though I am not convinced that this feature adds much. A short soft hackle, as I have observed earlier, will turn over and give a similar appearance (and a livelier one) when the fly is in motion. When the fly is drifted or floating, the same appearance is preserved by the roots of the hackle.

A final point in considering the build of the fly is that of body roughness. There have been occasions when I found body material of quill, raffia, plastic or some other smooth body material to be effective when dubbed bodies were not, but those occasions have been rare. Some thirty years ago, we carried out some experiments on the Cardiganshire rivers with flies which had a better body resemblance to the natural insect than any I have known—to the human eye. We painted the hook shanks in various colours and wound them over with translucent Ja-gut, the fore-runner of monofil. These bodies, even to segmentation, had a remarkable similarity to the bodies of the nymphs. Even the opaque darkness down the centre had its relation to the alimentary canal of the insect. The trout, however, did not appear to see the flies in our way! We were soon back to our bodies of silk and dubbing, or herl. At that time, we did not attempt to deduce any reasons for the failure of the new method of dressing, which gave such promise at first sight. We were only concerned to catch fish in the most effective way. It was, however, a blow to any theories we had about exact imitation—so far as our eyes were the guide in such matters. In a subsequent discussion with Thomas Clegg about this point, he expressed the view that dubbed bodies retained a percentage of trapped air for some time during use. This trapped air is in minute bubbles distributed over the dubbing, which show as small, glittering pin-points of light. Clegg underlined the possibility by pointing out the undoubted effectiveness of tinsel bodies, such as those of the Butcher, and the Black & Silver, and the established effectiveness of wire or tinsel body ribbing, which is a nearly universal feature of wet-fly dressing. Wire and tinsel have a light-reflecting quality which the under-surface camera picks up much as it picks up the reflection in the bubbles of trapped air.

There is no certainty in these things, but the feature of trapped air and its relationship to fly design and materials should not be ignored. The Hare's ear, and the Pheasant tail, are two of our most effective wet flies under most conditions when considered as "general pattern" flies. Both have bodies which hold trapped air for a considerable time, when in use.

At this stage we have considered the type of rain-fed rivers, the nature of their fly waters, the emotions and vision of the brown trout, the effect of what the trout sees of the fly on its emotions, and the features of the artificial fly which are likely to influence trout reaction. It remains only to consider the features of the water which influence the positions of the trout, before we move to practical approach at the river-side.

THE LIES OF TROUT

The current of the river is the conveyor-belt of the food of the trout. It is round the current that its life revolves. This does not mean that the trout spends its life in the current: it would be a considerable tax on its energy to do so. But there is one important fact to remember. When a fluid substance, whether liquid or vapour, flows over a rough surface, such as the bed of a river, there develops what is known as an "area of turbulence" between the fluid and that surface. This is virtually a layer in which resting objects are completely protected from the force of the flowing liquid above. The existence of such layers near the river-bed explains why trout frequently lie in fast, broken water when it would appear that lies a few feet to one side or the other would call for far less expenditure of effort. The other reason is that if static objects lie in a current, there is an area of turbulence in front of and behind them. However fast a current may be, fish can usually find rocks near which they can rest with infinitesimal expenditure of energy.

The trout, from my observations, works in a limited area of activity. Its original choice of a lie is dictated, no doubt, by its sense of security. It finds a hide first. It then edges out within easy access of that hide as it becomes more familiar with its surroundings. But if it is disturbed, it moves straight back to the hide. This became very evident to us in less regenerate days when, as boys, we played the fascinating game of tickling trout, or "grouping" as we called it, on our Welsh mountain streams. As we began to know the pools, we could lay fair odds that if a trout was disturbed from a certain position, usually at the tail of the pool, it would go beneath a certain stone or overhang of bank. If we caught it there, the successor to its downstream lie would nearly always move to the same hide when disturbed.

Once the trout has settled its security arrangements, it is free to indulge in some measure of ranging for its food. This is regulated to a considerable extent by water conditions, but the conservation of energy is still apparent, and is only relegated to a secondary place when some particularly heavy feed comes down the main flow of the current. On these occasions the trout will move right into any current that is not too powerful, and lie high in the water—"on the fin", as the saying is. This, however, is not frequent. In the normal way the most certain position of the majority of trout is off the edge of the slackening tail-spin of the run. Backwaters are a favourite lie, or cruising ground, of the larger trout. The main current washes a great deal of food into eddies of this type. The larger trout, partly because they lack the strength of their younger days and partly because they have the weight to chase off intruders upon their feeding arrangements, find in these features of the water the ideal medium for heavy feeding and conservation of energy. The turbulence areas of mid-stream rocks are almost invariably fish lies.

These points, however, are only indications of the factors which lead the angler to develop "water sense". By that, I mean the faculty to glance at a stretch of water and recognize the likely lies of trout from force of habit. This faculty cannot be taught by books. It is most highly developed, in my experience, among anglers who started with the worm in their youthful days, but the faculty can be developed very highly without such apprenticeship. The general pattern does not vary much in any trout water.

A point of importance when considering the position of trout in the stream is the depth at which they are lying. If the majority are lying near the surface, it is a fair indication that they are prepared to take food—either nymphs struggling from their shucks in the surface film, or ascending nymphs, or, in my experience less frequently taken than the first type of food, the floating duns or spinners. Although I mistrust the full implications of the theoretical cone of trout vision, there is no doubt that the higher the trout are lying in the water, the easier they are to approach without detection. This has been attributed to the decrease in their visual range which corresponds with the size of the cone of vision. The easier approach may be partly due to this. But I suspect that the main reason is connected with the movements of other fish. The first reaction of a frightened fish is to turn downwards as it scurries to a hide. If all

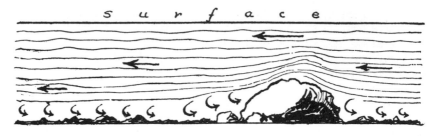

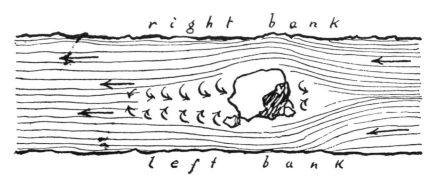

Fig. 32. *When a liquid, which includes vapours or air, flows over a rock, or a static rough surface, there is an area of turbulence at the contact point of the fluid and the static substance. The life of the fish requires the maximum conservation of energy. The fish can lie (and frequently do) in the turbulence areas with trifling expenditure of energy.*

fish are lying deep, the movement of a frightened fish which scurries past them at the same level is likely to alert them to danger. But if fish are lying high in the water (probably concentrating most of their attention on the surface feed as it comes down) it is probable that many disturbed fish pass beneath them without attracting their attention and alarming them.

METHODS OF FLY-FISHING

Now let us move to the river and consider our methods of catching trout with the artificial fly.

There are four fairly well-defined methods of fly-fishing.

First, there is the dry fly cast upstream, or upstream and across, and drifted down. Second, there is the fly which is thrown upstream on a greased line and cast, and allowed to drift down beneath the surface. Third, there is the single fly, or a team of flies, cast upstream and given some form of motion by manipulation of the rod and line. Fourth, there is the single fly, or a team of flies, cast across the downstream at an angle of about 45 degrees to the bank and brought round with the current until directly downstream of the angler.

WET-FLY FISHING

Downstream method. The fourth method is the one I propose to consider first. It is, as I have said earlier, the most simplified method with which a novice might be well advised to start. A brief excursion into my own development as a fly-fisherman will explain my reasons for making this suggestion.

My first trout of any size was caught in the Clwyedog, just above Llanidloes, shortly after the sinking of the Titanic—which was in 1912. It was a fish of about a pound and it erupted in a graceful arc over my head from a muddy swirling river in full spate. I promptly fell upon it, literally, to prevent any chance of its escape! My age was seven—and it was a "worm" job.

The criterion of an angler in those days, and in those mountain fastnesses, was the number of trout in the creel. There were salmon in the rivers at times, and a few chub. We learned to take limited interest in the salmon, later. The chub were scaly, inedible things that we regarded with contempt no matter how big they were. Trout were always "the" fish. It mattered little how one caught them. In a river clouded with spate, we fished with worm. As the river cleared, we changed to small Devons or natural minnows, spun. By the time we reached double-figure age, we knew something about flies. The rods and lines we used were the same for all purposes. The rods were about 10 feet long, and the level lines of braided pseudo-silk. The cast was a short length of gut (usually rotten because we could afford no better!) for worm and minnow, or about 6 feet of level gut, with two droppers and a point fly (if our pockets would stand the strain of three flies!) for what we called "fly-fishing". The top Severn and Clwyedog held a fine stock of fish in those days and they were lightly fished. By the time we were eleven or twelve, we thought nothing of a day which did not produce a score of sizeable fish in the sacking bag.

When I was about eleven my father did some minor kindness for a stationmaster at Pantydwr, eight miles up the old Cambrian line. In return, the stationmaster (his name was Pryce—no doubt "Pryce Pantydwr" to the locals in a country where surnames have always been in limited supply) who had heard of my interest in fishing, offered to take me for a day on the glittering little Marteg which flows past Pantydwr on its way to the meet with Wye. I remember five things about Mr. Pryce. He wore an old bowler hat with several fly-casts wound about the crown; he used an 8-feet greenheart fly-rod weighing about 4 oz and fished with a team of three wet flies—cast downstream and brought round; he was a very slow mover—though a jovial man; he caught a couple of score of trout before handing me the rod at tea-time, when he had to return to the station to see the second train of the day in and out; and he spoke in very disparaging terms of several who caught trout on worm and spinner.

Before I returned to the little station-house for a great feed of ham and eggs prepared by Mrs. Pryce at 7 o'clock, I had caught half a dozen trout with his tackle and had missed three times that number. Mr. Pryce then wrote a letter to my parents about the rod I had taken for his inspection (his comment when he saw it was: "Duw, bach! There's a thing for you . . . leave it by there!", and left in the parcels office it was) and a fortnight later I was presented with a replica of his tackle accompanied by strict Olympian injunctions that the items were "not playthings".

By the time I was thirteen, fly-fishing had a firm grip. There were occasional lapses to worm and spinner because fish in the creel was still the criterion. But they had already begun to give me less satisfaction than trout neatly caught with fly.

Fly-fishing was still merely a matter of ringing the changes on a few flies known to be effective in the locality: the March Brown, Blue dun, Coch-y-bonddu and Greenwell's Glory. But these flies, cast with the traditional downstream and across method, caught vast numbers of trout in those fast, sparkling waters. They did not catch so many for me as they did for the great Ben Blyth, the Llanidloes crack of whom it was said that he could spit on a stone, step backwards six paces and take a trout with a fly—from the spit! Nor did my flies take as many trout as they would have done for Ben's successor to the local title of "the Fish", Jack Owen. But they caught plenty and raised hopes that some day I too might add the honourable title of "the Fish" to my name!

Upstream v. downstream methods. It was in my middle 'teens that my faith in the traditional downstream-across was badly shaken. The manager of the local gas-works was a Yorkshireman named Hollings. After a poor day I came upon him fishing one of the slower pools, *upstream* with a floating fly. He had a dozen trout in his creel, all over the half-pound mark—while I had only a few smaller ones after a day's fishing.

The technique of Mr. Hollings was not mastered over-night, but before I was much older, I had experimented a good deal with the upstream cast and had found that if water conditions were right, it paid handsome dividends. It was varied with the upstream cast using the sunk fly, single or in a team. Usually the line was twitched down. Upstream casting was not easy with those light level lines and a cast of any distance was impossible, so that the traditional downstream method was the one generally preferred under normal conditions for the simple reason that it took more trout.

This last method has been dubbed "chuck-and chance-it" by many a protagonist of the dry fly. That is a point of view, but I can assure those who think in such terms that if they had tried their methods against Ben Blyth or Jack Owen, they would have realized that "chuck" was not a very good description of their accurate and gentle downstream presentation, nor "chance" the reason that these skilful local anglers caught tremendous numbers of trout when others were fortunate to take a brace.

There is a great art in this simple downstream game and the world of difference between the expert and the average angler, but it is still a game which is suited to the novice because it holds his interest from the start, and a few fish will hook themselves to his flies no matter how badly he handles his rod and line.

The dry fly had its place at times on the less broken stretches of these fast rivers, but on the really fast water, for all the dry-fly protagonism of such anglers as the American, G. M. L. La Branche, or the Rev. Edward Powell, and a few modern writers of lesser note, the experts fished downstream and across far more than otherwise.

Let us now take a step backwards to the third of my methods of fishing the fly: the upstream cast with a single fly, or a team of flies, with manipulation of the rod or line to give a semblance of life to the bundles of fur and feather.

In certain parts of these Isles a cross-country line can almost be drawn, on either side of which the downstream-across method or the upstream-down method is practised, the one to the exclusion of the other. The logic of the upstream-down is sound enough. The wet fly is a representation of the nymph, and no nymph has the power to defy the current as the downstream-across dragged fly does. The nymph may well drift and jerk *with* the current, as the upstream sunk fly is made to do by the manipulation of the angler. Moreover, the trout is usually facing or turning upstream when it takes a fly, so that if the angler is downstream the strike will jerk the fly back into the angle of its jaws, instead of dragging it away from the open jaws as must be the case if the angler is upstream of the fish.

Nevertheless, although I have watched experts in the upstream method on the Wye and Usk, and experts in the downstream method on Severn and Teifi, I would not lay money on either in like conditions. For my own part I regard the state of the water as the governing factor in choosing the method. If the trout are moving freely in a tea-coloured water running off after a spate, the upstream method on the less broken water is the more deadly in my experience. It is of little account whether a single fly or a team are used, though I prefer the single fly. If the water is very clear, no method will take more trout than the downstream-across method on heavily broken water—provided that the rod is in capable hands.

DRY-FLY FISHING

The next method for consideration is the floating fly. The only times when motion can be imparted to the floating fly with advantage are at dusk when sedges are about, or when the water is heavily clouded after a spate and odd trout are beginning to take an interest in surface feed under the banks. On such occasions the type of fly, so long as it is big enough and heavily dressed, matters little. Such an elementary way of catching trout may appeal to the novice. Most of us have resorted to it in earlier days. There is nothing "wrong" about it, and, as I have made clear from my comments on the downstream-across method, there is much to be said for methods which enable the novice to rise enough trout to maintain his interest.

Dry-fly fishing, however, is not merely a method of catching trout by offering something which nature prevents them from detecting as a fraud. In its ultimate best, it is a philosophy based on a continual attempt to deceive the trout in conditions which favour the fish rather than the angler. My own philosophy has never reached the heights of the "purist", who will not cast at a trout until he is convinced that he had diagnosed the insect it is taking at the moment, and he can put before it his own idea of the best imitation of that insect. That has always struck me as a narrow philosophy, its constriction no less than that of the man who fishes the season through with one fly only on the ground that it catches as many fish as a box-full. An old Yorkshire angler used to say that the trout would always take something—if one could only find it! That, in a way, is the epitome of my own philosophy. The search is the interesting part, and I am as convinced as J. R. Harris that knowledge of entomology, understanding of fly-dressing and ability in that art, and knowledge of the trout themselves, all play their part in that search.

It is not easy to describe a philosophy. Perhaps the most effective way of doing so is to take a practical example of a period of trout fishing. One that comes to mind happened during the 1960 season.

The summer was a busy one. I could only get to my water, some six miles away on a Yorkshire moorland stream, at about 8 o'clock on three successive evenings in mid-May. On each occasion I fished only about two-hundred yards of water before darkness. The river, in this stretch, is essentially of the second type of water described in the early part of the chapter. There are three runs, followed in each case by long shallow pools going down to about three feet in depth at the most.

On each of these three occasions the trout were taking reed smuts and very little else. On the third night there was tremendous activity. It showed how many trout the short piece of river (roughly ten miles of both banks are available to the angler on this stream if he wants to use them) contained. Most of my time was spent in experiments with various dressings of the smut. None achieved any success worth the name. I caught a brace of trout each night with the drifted beetle method in order to examine their stomach contents. Use of the marrow-scoop has its points, but I must confess a preference for examining the whole contents of the stomach if possible. The predominant feed was smut on all nights, though various other insects were in evidence. On the third night the stomach contents contained something like wads of smut remains.

The fish were there and the problem began to interest me, but on the fourth evening the rise was quite different. Blue-winged Olives were showing in tremendous numbers and the trout were taking the hatching nymph. The Orange Quill was ineffective beyond taking the odd fish. I noticed a few Pale Wateries about and questioned whether the trout might be taking these for preference. They were not, as examination of stomach contents showed later, but I put on a small impression of the Pale Watery, a simple tie with a raffia body and honey hackle on a No. oo hook. It was taken at once and consistently by several trout. I opened one for examination and found the stomach full of hatching nymphs of the Blue-winged Olive. The light failed slightly and the trout seemed to lose interest in the Pale Watery, but the rise went on. I tried the Orange Quill. It was now taken freely. The light deteriorated after half an hour and the trout seemed to lose interest in this fly also. I put on a Red spinner on a size larger hook, which renewed interest among the fish.

We had a spell of very fine weather during May and June of that year and I continued to fish that same stretch of river from about 7.30 p.m. onwards on nearly every evening for the next three weeks. The pattern of trout behaviour was much the same throughout, though rises varied considerably in intensity.

It was an interesting experiment and led me to a number of conclusions. Space does not permit a dissertation on these conclusions and, in any case, they are probably applicable to this river only under a certain set of conditions. I tried many other dressings during the period, of course. But the original plan, with its pattern selections, was the only one which seemed to carry consistent conviction with the trout. Then a spate upset things, and when the river ran down the trout returned to the smuts.

Only once during the period did I find another angler ahead of me. I watched him fish out the stretch with only one small fish to show. He told me later that he did not think it contained a very good stock of fish. I *knew* it contained several dozen!

The reason I recount this period of fishing (it is similar to many in my own fishing) is merely to raise a question in the mind of the reader. There is no doubt that by ranging over the water with some "good pattern of general fly", such as the Hare's ear, the John

Storey or my own beetle creation, I could have taken the limit of four brace of fish on most of those May and June evenings. But what would have been the interest value in such a performance compared with that of the intensive study of one short stretch of river, and the reactions of the trout to entomological conditions that prevailed during the period?

The reader must judge for himself. If he feels the trout in the creel will provide him with greater enjoyment, he should not trouble too much with entomology or the "difficult" trout. Rather, he should range widely and ring the changes on a very few flies known to be effective on the water he is fishing. He should also learn to cast well and read George La Branche on the subject of "hammering" a trout persistently with the dry fly until it takes. Better still, on most waters, he should experiment with my second method of fishing the fly, sunk and drifted down on a greased line and cast, which I shall conclude by describing and which is, in my opinion, the most consistently effective method of catching trout with the fly on rain-fed rivers.

Before leaving the subject of the dry fly, there are two practical points to which I should like to refer. The first is the position at which the fly should be presented to the trout. The second is the question of whether the cast should be floating or sunk.

Downstream method. The dry fly may be presented in four ways. The fourth is not one to which I resort frequently, but it has sometimes taken fish quite inexplicably when other methods have failed. It is a cast from upstream of the trout with plenty of slack thrown on the water to let the fly drift into the trout's visual field without drag. The reason for the occasional success of this method with a particular fish is possibly due to the incidence of light on the cast from other angles. At any rate, I merely mention it because it is sometimes worth remembering in the incessant search for the effective way to catch a trout.

Upstream methods. The other three ways of presenting are to lay the fly so far upstream of the trout that it floats from outside the field of direct vision, into that field; placing the fly on the nose of the trout; and placing the fly somewhere inside the visual field so far as the angler can judge the position.

The first method is the logical one, since the dry fly is a representation of either a dun that has just hatched and is floating down the surface as its wings dry sufficiently to enable it to take off for the bankside foliage, or of a spinner. I am assured by Test anglers that this method of upstream presentation has been "proved" over the years. Alas, I am not convinced. Its fault, in my opinion, is that it allows the fly to remain a bundle of fur and feather without suggestion of "life" or "activity". Theoretically, I suppose there is rarely any apparent life in the dun or spinner. But above all things to which trout react, I am sure that the semblance of "action" is the most influential. Another fault of the fly thrown well upstream is that it lets the trout have a considerable view of the cast.

One of our best northern chalk stream anglers, A. V. Oglesby, insists that the nearer the fly can be laid to the nose of the trout, the better. His record of trout caught with this method of presentation makes it impossible to disregard his contention. The reason he gives for selecting this method is that it gives the trout no time to examine the fly or become aware of unnatural behaviour in it.

My own method, which I have used for many years on both chalk streams and rain-fed rivers, is to present the dry fly as nearly as I can calculate to a point just within the visual field of the trout, so that the point of the cast is in the shortest perspective to the eye of the fish. This may entail placing the fly a little downstream of the fish at times, but much experiment has satisfied me that this position of presentation is no bar to success. Many a time I have watched a trout turn immediately to the fly and take it.

Floating v. sunk cast. The floating or sunk cast is another point of controversy in which logic is on the one side and practical experience, so far as I am concerned, is on the other. If the cast is floating, the capillary action of the surface skin causes a sort of ridge with the cast at its apex. In clear water, with bright sun overhead, the shadow of this ridge can be very marked on the river-bed. Eugene Connett describes the shadow as being "as big as a hose-pipe". The size of the shadow depends on water depth. I have seen a shadow as big as a drain-pipe! Both Connett and La Branche join many anglers in almost violent insistence that the cast must be sunk when fishing the dry fly. Once again, I do not agree. I have experimented with many types and colours of cast, and have now only one conviction. It is that the trout must always see the cast point. The best one can do is to show as little of the cast as possible by presenting it in the shortest possible perspective. If the cast moves at a different speed from the water which surrounds it, or "drags" as we say, trout usually show fear at once. But if the cast drifts at water speed, whether sunk or floating, they do not show fear except during transitory periods when they may be afflicted with gut-shyness. The shorter the perspective, the less the chance of drag being apparent. The merit of the floating cast is that both it and the fly can be picked up much more cleanly for the next presentation.

A FINAL WORD ON THE WET FLY

We now come, in conclusion, to the second of my four methods of fishing the fly: that of casting a single fly upstream and allowing it to drift down without any attempt to induce movement during the drift.

This method is, in my opinion, far the most deadly of all methods of fly-fishing on any water except that with a fast current.

There is nothing very new about it. I have found references to what appear to be a similar method in angling books dating back to the middle of the last century. We used it ourselves forty years ago on Welsh rivers when they were clearing after summer spate. The Coch-y-bonddu was usually the fly, and it is not very unlike the beetle, to which I have previously referred, but we merely regarded it as a variation in strategy and not a method on its own. It was not until the summer of 1940 that I began to develop interest in it as a technique.

Dibbing. During that year, the "Cold War" dragged on through a remarkably hot summer. A local doctor and I, tired of air-raid warnings of various colours and the general upheavals of a wartime state, took the first week of June off duty to stay on a neighbouring moorland stream. The Mayfly should have been up—but it was late. The trout smutted incessantly. After an indifferent morning and a rather heavy lunch we wandered down to some large elms and lay on our faces for an hour or more, watching the dozen of trout in the sunny pool below our high bank. One of these fish, a big fellow of just over the pound, cruised on a set beat right below us. Our worse natures got the better of us! We tried dibbing for him with various flies. He showed no fear—but no interest in our flies after dignified inspection. My companion tired of the exercise and returned to the hotel at which we were staying, but this big fellow seemed a challenge.

As I watched, with the fly poised a few inches above the surface against his return up the beat, a small land beetle dropped from the tree above, struck the water with a "plop" and began to sink slowly. The big fellow cruised up deliberately and took it without hesitation. This seemed to be a pointer. I trimmed the only suitable fly in my box, a big Norwegian-dressed variant, to something like the beetle in size and contour. Then I sucked it well. When the time came and I dropped it, the take was just as firm and unhesitating.

Dibbing is a game for lazy summer afternoons, and there is little water on the average stream where it can be practised—even if the angler has a mind to play such tricks on trout! It was clear that if the aim was to make capital out of the attraction value of this lure, some method of universal presentation must be devised. This was simple enough. It required merely a greased line and cast, thrown upstream. A check of the floating cast is the sign to strike. Various experiments led to a standardized dressing which I have given briefly in the earlier part of this chapter. Its main difference from the Black Pennell and similar dressings is that it has a yellow rump, and the cocoon of wool causes it to enter the water with a similar impact to that of a falling beetle, rather than the splashy impact of a sodden hackled fly. In subsequent years I caught a great many fish with this method, using the beetle dressing, on both chalk streams and rain-fed rivers as widely separated as Ireland, Scotland and Hampshire.

There are occasions when it is not wholly convincing, as was the case with the Hawthorn fly, but the occasions of complete failure are few, and the occasions of partial failure are far outnumbered by those on which it is completely successful. But the fact remains that this is *lure* fishing. It did not take me long, after experiments satisfied me that it could be taken little further in technique, to lose interest in such tactics. The only time I use the method now is when I want a trout to examine its stomach content, or when I want a brace for the table and they are not readily catchable in any other way.

The method, on the other hand, is not at fault if it is used to supplement other modes of presentation. It is much the same method as that described by Frank Sawyer in the book which he collaborated with Wilson Stephens to produce: *Nymphs and the Trout*. It will remain interesting to the fly-fisherman so long as he uses it as a means of presentation in his search for the ultimate in trout deception. It gives him, as Skues pointed out in his justification of the sunk imitation of the fly in its earlier stages of development, a wider basis from which to work than will be available to the man who confines his fishing to the floating of flies over trout which are evidently taking duns or spinners. The method becomes uninteresting when the angler merely throws a "good pattern of general *land-insect*" at the trout. In such circumstances he need only be a good caster, with knowledge of fish lies—and plenty of stock in the river.

That is, to me, the negation of the ultimate best in fly-fishing for trout, no matter what the type of water the angler is fishing.

CONCLUSION

It may be complained that there is too little of the firm definitive in these comments. One writer has gone so far as to say that unless they were definite, comments on angling were worthless. Such a contention is, in my opinion, wholly untenable. Little is certain in fly-fishing. The expression of a dogmatic view (to which many definitive writers tend for reasons of self-conviction) is no better than a lie if the fundamental facts are uncertain. Fly-fishing is stuffed with theories and dogmata founded on surmise.

I have tried to present the game as it appears to me after forty years or more of playing it on many waters, mostly those of rain-fed rivers. My endeavour has been to present a picture of progressive development of a philosophy which will extract the best from the game for the fly-fisherman; and in this respect I have tried to present the reader with stimulants to reflection, rather than assertions based on unstable foundations.

Whether the fly is floating or sunk, my own reactions to trout behaviour are now broken down to three questions: Why will the trout *not* take my fly? What fly *will* they take? *Why* will they take it? Only when a fly-fisherman is interested in the answers to these questions, will the full panorama of his fascinating game open out before him.

13. The Severn at Glynhafren: a fast stream suited to downstream fishing.

14. The Usk above Abergavenny : a broad, slow stretch where the dry fly may be used.

CHAPTER IV

BROWN TROUT IN CHALK STREAMS
by
OLIVER KITE

INTRODUCTION

Chalk-stream characteristics. Chalk streams are spring-fed rivers characterized by naturally filtered alkaline water of great clarity, conducive to the production of such nourishing protein trout food as fresh-water shrimps, crayfish and a variety of molluscs. These rivers are not so liable to sudden fluctuation in level as rain-fed rivers and are less subject to discoloration. They support a lush growth of water-weed for much of the year and this helps to keep up the water level during the summer months, when it also gives rise to various problems in fishery management. Weed affords good cover for the fish and many of the creatures on which they feed.

Maintenance of trout stocks. In some chalk streams, the Wylye being a good example, the natural regeneration of trout is adequate to maintain a sufficient stock of wild fish in the river to meet the requirements of carefully-controlled private fisheries. Elsewhere, for example on the expensive but hard-fished waters of the middle Test, periodic re-stocking is carried out with mature trout raised in adjoining hatcheries. Hatchery trout are, of course, easier to catch than wild fish when first turned into the river but they very quickly learn to be discreet, or die.

Importance of fly production. Regardless of the stock of trout it may hold, the sport afforded by a chalk-stream fishery depends on the presence of fly in sufficient quantity to attract feeding fish, for unless the trout are willing to take natural insects it would be difficult, if not impossible, to induce them to accept artificial flies. Although the amount of fly varies from season to season and river to river, indeed from place to place on the individual fisheries of a river, chalk streams in general provide suitable conditions for the breeding of many ephemeropteran species. It is on the nymphs, duns and spinners of these flies that the chalk-stream fly-fisher relies for his sport, augmented at times by sedge-flies which also breed freely in these waters, and by a few other important insects of other orders. The key to the successful management of a chalk-stream fishery is therefore the production of fly.

Limitations on fishing methods. Since it is possible to catch trout using imitations of these flies, either floating to represent them in the winged stages of their development, or beneath the surface to represent the later larval or nymph forms or the upwinged flies, and since two methods of fly-fishing have been devised which are selective

H

and allow the angler to fish for individual trout believed to be of take-able size, other forms of fishing, including spinning, bait-fishing, and wet-fly fishing, are normally strictly prohibited on the chalk streams.

The limitation of fishing to these highly specialized methods, the tolerably easy dry-fly fishing and the less easy nymph fishing, may or may not be right, but there can be no doubt that it commands the support of the overwhelming majority of chalk-stream anglers today.

The chalk country. Chalk streams are found in a number of English counties, especially in the south and, more especially, in Hampshire, Wiltshire, Berkshire and Dorset. Waters with many similar charac-teristics are found in several other counties. It would be wrong to assume that chalk streams resemble one another closely in character. Nothing could be further from the truth. They vary from the broad, swift-flowing Test to the impounded, canal-like reaches of the Itchen above Winchester, immortalized by the late G. E. M. Skues who fished the Abbot's Barton water from 1883 to 1938; from the crystal-clear, gravelly shallows of the Bourne at Hurstbourne Priors to the sedate and weedy Kennet at Ramsbury; from the tiny Ebble in the Chalke valley of Wiltshire to the many-faceted Upper Avon of Salisbury Plain.

The end and the means. Chalk-stream trout may, or may not, be more difficult to catch than trout elsewhere. Chalk-stream fly-fishers are, in any case, usually strictly limited in the number of trout they may keep each day and they are often less concerned with how many trout they catch than the manner in which they catch them. If it were otherwise, the chalk streams would quickly be denuded of their native trout stocks.

BASIC METHODS

Dry-fly fishing. In late Victorian times, a number of scholarly and inventive fly-fishers with enviable opportunities to fish the classic waters of the great chalk streams like the Test, the Kennet and the Itchen, evolved a pattern of chalk-stream fishing, the influence of which has persisted to this day. Francis Francis and G. S. Marryat set the stage for the more detailed work of F. M. Halford who, more than anyone else, formulated the cult of the dry fly, made feasible by H. S. Hall's invention of the eyed hook.

Halford's knowledge was profound and his writings were lucid and instructive, if somewhat dogmatic in his later works. He classified natural flies by types rather than by species, and for each type of upwinged fly he dressed separate artificial patterns for the male and female dun and spinner. He also suggested a number of patterns for artificial sedge-flies and other insects, to be fished floating on the surface. In this way, he laid down a dry-fly code which implied that artificial flies should always be imitations of natural flies in their *winged* stages and should always be fished floating on the surface.

Such fishing was and is known as dry-fly fishing, to distinguish it from fly-fishing in which one or more artificials are fished beneath the surface. Halford further defined dry-fly fishing as offering a trout the best possible imitation of the insect on which it is seen to be feeding, floating on the surface in the position which fly-fishers call "cocked". It is clearly implicit in this definition that before fishing can begin, a trout must first be seen to rise, the type of fly on which it is feeding must be identified correctly, and a suitably-matched artificial must be tied on the cast and presented to the trout floating on the water. And this is how some chalk-stream anglers practise dry-fly fishing to this day.

It is still customary to fish the rise rather than the water. On nearly all chalk streams there is a minimum size below which trout should not be taken, indeed, should not be fished for. By studying the rising fish, it is usually possible to determine whether it is of takeable size. With regard to matching the fly on the water, some chalk-stream anglers take this very seriously: others are content to rely on a few favourite well-tried patterns and hope to deceive the fish by delicate and accurate presentation of the fly. In these busy times, they find the Halford approach to dry-fly fishing unnecessarily complicated and sometimes their entomological knowledge is scanty. But they may still catch fish.

Halford was a great man and he invested dry-fly fishing with a scholarly and almost ritualistic charm which, for many, is a large part of its fascination. Yet it is almost certainly true that dry-fly fishing evolved on the chalk streams for the simple reason that it was an easy way of catching trout. It is probably the easiest of all fly-fishing methods, which is not the same as saying that chalk-stream trout are the easiest of all to catch. Some of them are indeed easy, and some are uncommonly difficult.

Some of Halford's followers, who have been referred to as dry-fly purists, held, and still hold, that the only rewarding, indeed the only legitimate way, to catch a chalk-stream trout is to fish for it with a floating imitation of the type of fly on which it is feeding. The snag is that the trout often elects to feed beneath the surface on flies which are still in the underwater stages of their development. Such trout may not be willing to rise to the surface at all, either to natural hatched fly or to artificial dry flies, especially when they are feeding on nymphs. The dry-fly purist accepts this with resignation, and may not cast a fly all day long. His fortitude commands our respect. The nymph fisherman, no purist, tries to catch these trout with artificial nymphs.

Nymph fishing. Nymph fishing owes its inception to G. E. M. Skues. His advocacy of a form of wet-fly fishing, specially adapted for use on the chalk streams, brought him into acrimonious conflict with Halford and his disciples. Skues discovered that a trout feeding below the surface which would not rise to an artificial floating fly would sometimes take the same fly if it became waterlogged and sank. This discovery led him to experiment with flies fished wet to individual trout seen to be feeding underwater. He published his early conclusions in 1910 in *Minor Tactics of the Chalk Stream.*

Skues's methods were every bit as selective as those of the most orthodox dry-fly fisherman but it is, perhaps, understandable that in an age at once more formal and conventional than our own, they were viewed with disfavour by many of his contemporaries. Some scorned his methods as ineffective; others feared they would be dangerously efficient; above all, his critics looked on them as unsporting. Some of them were guilty of an intolerance which threatened to bring discredit on the specialized but overtly simple art of chalk-stream fly-fishing, of which some trout fishers elsewhere cherish a distorted impression to this day.

Despite the hostility he aroused, Skues persisted with his experiments and began to dress imitations of the nymphs which he found in the stomachs of the fish he caught. He published a number of other books including *Nymph Fishing for Chalk Stream Trout* (1939) in which he recommended a series of dressings of nymphs based on direct imitation of individual species.

It was from Skues's early discoveries and experiments that the modern technique of upstream nymph fishing was evolved at Netheravon by Frank Sawyer, since 1926 head river keeper of the Officers' Fishing Association which controls six miles of the Upper Avon. This fascinating technique, which is discussed in some detail in the section on Nymph Fishing later in this chapter, is fully explained in Sawyer's second book, *Nymphs and the Trout* (1958). His first book, *Keeper of the Stream* (1952), had earlier drawn attention to its possibilities and had attracted to Netheravon outstanding fly-fishers of several nations to learn at first-hand the simple but effective methods which Sawyer had devised. Later, especially in France, manufacturers turned their attention to the production of suitable tackle expressly designed for modern nymph fishing.

It is important to understand the difference between wet-fly fishing, as practised elsewhere, and upstream nymph fishing as permitted and practised on the chalk streams. In wet-fly fishing, artificial flies are fished sunk in such a way as to represent various kinds of underwater trout food, including natural nymphs, but are not necessarily fished to a selected individual trout, as is the case in upstream nymph fishing. Wet flies, which may be fished singly or in teams of two or more, are dressed either as winged or nymphal patterns but generally include a certain amount of hackle to give them an appearance of life and thereby increase their effectiveness as lures. Artificial nymphs employed in the Netheravon style of nymph fishing are characterized by a complete absence of hackle of any kind. They are, in short, fished as nymphs, calculated to deceive, and not as lures, designed to attract.

In nymph fishing, as in dry-fly fishing, only one artificial is employed at a time. The term "upstream" should not be taken literally. Although fishing a nymph downstream and across, with a dragging action, is barred on the chalk streams, the artificial nymph is fished directly across the stream, or up and across, at least as often as it is fished directly upstream. The point to note is that it is always fished to an individual trout believed to be of takeable size and seen to be feeding *beneath* the surface.

Upstream nymph-fishing is therefore three-dimensional fly-fishing and, as such, presents a range of problems additional to those of the dry fly. It is more difficult to master and it calls for good eyesight and constant practice to bring the art to perfection. Once mastered, it is an indispensable asset to the chalk-stream fly-fisher, particularly during the long bright days of July and August.

On most chalk-stream fisheries today, nymph fishing and dry-fly fishing are regarded as complementary and both are tolerated on an equal footing. There are still one or two fisheries and a number of private waters, however, where nymph fishing is either not allowed at all or is confined to a limited period during the season. It is therefore as well to ascertain the rule applicable when visiting a strange water before attempting to employ an artificial nymph. When in doubt, stick to the dry fly rather than risk offering offence.

THE CHALK-STREAM SEASON

Duration. In general, the chalk-stream trout-fishing season lasts from May Day to Michaelmas but there are many exceptions at both extremities. Some Hampshire fisheries and parts of the Wylye open as early as mid-April but fishing does not start on the upper Test until May. Much depends on the usual spawning dates. The earlier the fish spawn, the sooner they can be expected to recover condition. In late-spawning rivers, the season may be extended to mid-October.

Most chalk-stream trout contrive to regain condition by mid-May and young fish make noticeable growth by the end of June. The trout of these rivers are generally at their best in July and early August. Appropriately, this is when they are usually hardest to catch!

Towards the end of the season, trout, and female trout especially, feed up hard preparatory to spawning. They then become rather vulnerable to the skilful fly-fisher and somewhat ripe and ill-conditioned. The great Skues consistently refused to fish for them after August for this reason, but his Itchen water, just above Winchester, was usually regarded as an early one and Skues used to begin fishing about a month earlier than we start on the middle Wylye.

Main phases. The chalk-stream trout season comprises three main phases: the first lasts from the beginning of the season until after the Mayfly hatch is over, in other words until early June; the second from early June until mid-August; and the third from mid-August until the end of the season.

The first phase. The first phase takes in the sweet of the year and, we optimistically believe, coincides with an abundance of natural fly. It is a biological fact that certain important species of upwinged flies, on the English chalk streams, produce their spring generation at this time. Consequently, when climatic conditions are suitable, their duns and spinners can be expected to appear on the wing in good numbers. Moreover, heavy falls of black fly may occur during this opening phase, if conditions are conducive, and these insects, Hawthorn-flies and Black Gnats, are beloved by trout above all others.

If fly does materialize, fish can be expected to rise freely, to suitable artificials as well as to natural winged insects, for they have not yet been hammered by fishermen into a state of extreme caution, as will be the case on popular fisheries later in the season.

In April, hatches of duns may be concentrated into a short period of an hour or so and may not begin until after noon. In May, the hatches tend to draw out and by the end of the month may last for much of the day.

It is only towards the end of May that a regular evening rise can be expected. Indeed, the earliest big evening rises may occur at Mayfly time when the spent spinner is on the water.

The dry fly is supreme during the first phase. Indeed, on some fisheries nymph fishing is not allowed before July 1st. In any case, it is not normally necessary to use it before June. My diary records that on the Upper Avon, where nymph fishing is permitted throughout the season, my first thirty-two trout of the 1961 season were all taken on the dry fly. Not until June 24th did I employ an artificial nymph to catch a trout from this water.

The second phase. The second phase, lasting from about mid-June to mid-August, is marked by a diminution in daytime small-fly hatches, coinciding with the end of the Mayfly period. The two are unrelated. Certain important chalk-stream species, some of the Olives and Iron Blues among them, produce two main generations; one in spring and one in the autumn. Accordingly, the duns of these species hatch in the greatest numbers early and late in the trout-fishing season. They give way during the second phase to daytime flies like the Pale Watery duns, the Small Spurwings and the slow-water Olives[1] and to flies which hatch well on some evenings at dusk, notably Blue-winged Olives and Pale Evening duns. At last light, sedge-flies may hatch in considerable numbers, prolonging the evening rise until darkness.

Spent spinners may be coming down in considerable numbers

[1] The Lake and Pond Olives of Harris, which are found in certain slow-flowing reaches on some chalk streams – Ed.

throughout the day, and on most evenings, bringing on an evening rise. On waters where the Blue-winged Olive is plentiful, there may be a fall of Sherry spinners on most evenings around sunset.

Trout may feed all day long on natural nymphs, especially over beds of water celery and in the runs at the tail of trimmed ranunculus beds. Indeed, nymph-fishing assumes great importance during this second phase, when it normally takes precedence, by day, over the dry fly. Between 24th June and 17th August, 1961, I took thirty-one trout on the nymph and only eleven on the dry fly, on the Upper Avon, and of those caught on the dry fly, all were taken in the evening: six on the Pale Evening dun and five on the Red spinner.

The third phase. The third phase, beginning about mid-August but somewhat retarded in a hot, dry summer, is characterized by increasing hatches of duns as the autumn generation of certain species begins to appear, by day-long hatches of Blue-winged Olives, by occasional falls of ants, by the appearance of numbers of Willow flies, by generous sprinklings of Black Gnats, especially on muggy days in August, and by the continuing hatches of sedge-flies at dusk on warm evenings. The month of September is traditionally one of the best for fly of the whole season and it witnesses the increasing employment of the dry fly by day to the exclusion of the artificial nymph. On the Upper Avon between 24th August and 30th September, 1961, I took twenty-seven trout, all by day, twenty on the dry fly and only seven on the nymph.

THE CONTENTS OF THE FLY-BOX

Introduction. Beware of those who pontificate on the subject of fly, those who say you should always use this or you never need that. "Always" and "Never" are terms of rather limited application to chalk-stream fishing. The contents of your fly-box can be as diverse or as uniform as you care to make them. If you want diversity, study the works of Halford, or Hills, or Carey, on the dry fly, and Skues on the nymph. If you want simplicity, you can have that, too, and still be successful, much of the time, especially if you know what you are doing, and why.

The nymph in relation to the dry fly. The chalk-stream fly-fisher generally likes to relate his artificial to what he thinks the trout is feeding on. Trout obtain a high proportion of the insect content of their diet beneath the surface of the water and if you examine their stomach contents, especially during the summer months, you often find that nymphs greatly outnumber hatched flies. It therefore stands to reason that a fly-fisher operating regularly and evenly throughout a chalk-stream season may end up by catching more trout on the artificial nymph than on the dry fly. I do so myself, in most years.

Your choice of artificial nymph patterns is unlimited, if you are tempted to try exact imitation. I use only one, Sawyer's Pheasant tail, dressed on hooks of sizes oo to 1, but mostly on No. o. Others may be necessary, somewhere, but not on the chalk streams which are our concern here. In 1961 this pattern yielded me good trout from the Avon, Bourne, Anton, Test, Itchen, Nadder, Wylye and Shal Bourne (a Kennet tributary), and no less than 551 of the 951 takeable fish I caught in 1957–61. Nymph fishing in the Netheravon style turns not on pattern but on the manner in which the artificial is fished. I believe, however, that chalk-stream fishermen should aim to master the dry fly completely before they concern themselves with learning nymph-fishing; I do not know anyone who fishes the nymph well who is not also a competent performer with the dry fly.

All-round dry-fly patterns. Certain dry-fly patterns, in competent hands, are capable of taking trout feeding on the surface on a variety of insects. An expert rod, using an artificial of this kind, can be counted on most days to catch more trout than a fly-fisher of moderate ability who commands a whole range of nicely dressed patterns. Successful all-round patterns include the Red Quill, which Halford recommended as the dry-fly man's sheet anchor on a strange river, the spent-winged Lunn's Particular, and the Pheasant-tail Red spinner, with white tails, a body and thorax of pheasant-tail herls, red tying silk, and a dark red hackle.

These three artificials are effective because they are reasonable imitations of female Olive spinners, and some of these natural insects, of which there are six fairly similar species, may be on the water every day of the fishing season. Trout expect to see them, spent, dead, and easy to capture, and are rarely averse from eating them. There is no other way of explaining my consistent success with the pheasant-tail Red spinner when trout are taking Blue-winged Olive duns.

My old friend, Colonel Peter Hammond, a distinguished fly-fisher who in these days operates mainly on the Abbot's Barton water on the Itchen, now contents himself with using a small Black Gnat and, sometimes, a Ginger Quill for variety. He still catches his share of trout: he is, of course, a master with the dry fly. There are decided advantages in this straightforward approach for skilled fly-fishers whose sight is no longer as keen as it was.

Some trout are more selective than others, even on the same river. On some chalk streams, they tend to be particularly finicky and easy to put down in the evenings, although on some evenings they can be relatively free-rising. Trout can also be momentarily rather choosey, just as a fly-fisher who enjoys Stilton cheese might not care to sample some when half-way through a bowl of strawberries and cream.

There are times, however, when trout settle to feed on one particular species of fly: Black Gnats, perhaps, on muggy August days, or Mayflies, or Pale Evening duns in the warm dusk of a summer evening when various other duns and spinners may be on the water. It is then that you feel the need for suitable related patterns to tempt them, although even when this happens, you can sometimes find the odd fish who is less pernickety than the rest. This knowledge may help to fill your basket, but the true chalk-stream fly-fisher does not readily acknowledge defeat by the selective feeder: a quarry worthy of his skill.

When you fail to induce a trout to rise to your fly, do not take it for granted that the pattern is at fault. Perhaps it is. But it could also be failure on your part to conceal from the trout that you are trying to catch it: by a faulty approach; by allowing the fish to see your line or cast, or their shadow on a bright, sunny day; by using the right pattern dressed on too big or too small a scale to look realistic; or by that most common cause of betrayal, drag.

Remember Hills's injunction to fly-fishers never to allow educated chalk-stream trout to see drag: you are lucky, in some ways, if you have access to chalk-stream fishing where trout are still naïve. You can get away with drag on some rivers to an astonishing degree, but if you think chalk-stream trout will put up with it, test your theory at Leckford, on fish lying under the far bank on one of the broad fast-flowing beats of this beautifully kept middle Test water, or on one of the tearing, racing fisheries of the upper Itchen or middle Wylye, or the Bourne just above its confluence with the Test, or the Avon below Figheldean Mill. There you may learn how drag affects chalk-stream trout, and how to overcome it. And thereafter you have a pretty good idea when your pattern is at fault, and when you are, yourself. But never be put off by the prospect of drag.

Although you may confine yourself, if you so wish, to the use of one or two patterns, and still catch trout, I believe that in so doing you may forfeit much of the pleasure, the fundamental charm of chalk-stream dry-fly fishing. Is there, then, a happy mean, some-where between the one or two patterns favoured by some, and the comprehensive but formidably complex assortment advocated by Halford and others? Of course there is.

The happy mean. In practice, not more than a dozen dry-fly patterns are needed during the course of a full chalk-stream season. The simplified table on page 145 may explain this more clearly. I believe it is more helpful to the beginner to teach him the practical use of a few sound patterns than to confuse him with a wide range, some of which have little practical value. Once he has mastered these, it is up to him to employ as many, or as few, as his fancy dictates. I respect any individual's estimate of the number of patterns he requires. I use only ten myself, those listed in the table less the spent Mayfly spinner, and I'll use that if I ever need it. In most cases I like to relate my artificial to what I reckon trout are feeding on.

The natural flies which the regular chalk-stream angler may encounter are briefly discussed below. I have grouped them, for convenience, in the orders to which they belong: Ephemeroptera, or upwinged flies: Trichoptera, or sedge-flies; Diptera, the order to which Hawthorn-flies and Black Gnats belong; and Other Insects to cover a few species outside these three orders. My aim is to show which are important to the fly-fisher and which I have found to be of less significance.

Upwinged flies (Ephemeroptera). I have recorded twenty-one different species of upwinged flies on the chalk streams in recent years. Six of these are uncommon. Some, indeed, have no English names. Two others, the Yellow May dun and the Turkey Brown, although becoming increasingly familiar to chalk-stream anglers, rarely feature in the diet of trout. Then there are two species of Iron Blue which may, for all practical purposes, be treated as one. This leaves us with twelve species, and only a fly-fisher who fishes most of the chalk streams and is on the water most weeks throughout the season is likely to see all of them.

Four are different species of Olive duns. The Olives—nymphs, duns and spinners—are the foundation of chalk-stream fly-fishing. The Iron Blue is their closest relative. Another is the Pale Watery dun. The Small Spurwing, the slow-water Olive and the Pale Evening dun also belong to the same family. All these flies have two tails. Finally there are three flies which have three tails: the Mayfly, the Blue-winged Olive and the *Caenis*,[1] or Broadwing as it is now called.

Some of these twelve species are of significance to the fly-fisher only at certain times of the year. Some, indeed, are usually on the water at certain times of the day or evening as well. Some are more likely to be found on one river than another. Some prefer fast water, others prefer slow. These notes on the natural flies are intended only as an introduction to a subject which can only be satisfactorily studied at the waterside.

The Olive duns. There are six species of Olive duns. Omitting the rare *Baëtis buceratus*, and *B. tenax*, inseparable from *B. vernus*, the common chalk-stream Olive, in the dun stage, we are left with four species which the chalk-stream angler is likely to encounter some time during the season. These are: the (common) Olive (*B. vernus*), the Large Olive (*B. rhodani*), the Dark Olive (*B. atrebatinus*), and the Small Olive (*B. scambus*).

Dark Olives, although widely distributed and locally abundant in the chalk country, are usually only seen in numbers in the autumn. They are therefore important to the grayling angler but of limited significance to the trout fisherman who, for practical purposes, can think of his Olive duns in terms of three sizes: large, medium and small. This explains the use of the widely recognized terms, Large Dark Olive, Medium Olive and Small Dark Olive, to describe them. In fact, the body coloration of these Olives is so variable, being

[1] A family name covering five species—Ed.

darker when the water is cold, that I neither use these terms nor teach them. You should, however, understand what they mean.

I use only one pattern of Olive dun, dressed on hooks of sizes 1, 0 and 00, to represent all the Olives. Others prefer to differentiate between them.

Large Olives may still be seen hatching in good numbers on chalk streams which open for fishing by mid-April. From about the end of this month Medium Olives, are increasingly in evidence and the Large Olive disappears temporarily, to return again towards the end of September at the tail of the season. May is usually a good month for hatches of Olives. September is another. Some Olives may be seen at any time during the season, for they hatch in every month of the year.

Small Olives, too, may be seen throughout the fishing season. The time of the peak hatches varies from river to river and season to season. Sometimes good hatches occur as early as April; Skues called the little fly the July dun, and I see quite a few at that time too; but Small Olives are generally most plentiful in September and October. The females are almost as large as Iron Blues and are sometimes mistaken for Pale Watery duns. The males are much smaller and also consistently much darker.

The Iron Blue dun. Darker still is the Iron Blue dun, a fly which no two writers seem able to describe in identical terms. This is understandable for it, too, varies slightly in size and, to some extent, coloration. Its comparatively small size and two tails, coupled with its distinctive blue-black wings and very dark purple-brown body, make it one of the easiest of all flies to recognize.

There are nearly always one or two days in the second half of May when Iron Blues come up in good numbers on both the Avon and the Wylye but it is a matter of chance whether one is out fishing on those days. They are usually wet, nearly always very windy, and not, in my experience, cold. Iron Blues have not been very important on the Wiltshire streams in recent years although there are signs that they are on the increase again.

In Hampshire, it is different. The Iron Blue hatches well on some Itchen fisheries and the Test also enjoys frequent, and at times, good hatches. The fly is much in evidence on the Leckford water, higher up at Longparish, and on the topmost beats of the Laverstoke estate during late May and much of June. Curiously enough, the Hampshire Bourne, which Plunket Greene linked for ever with the Iron Blue in his book, *Where the Bright Waters Meet*, seems to produce few hatches of this fly nowadays.

The somewhat smaller Iron Blues of September and October come up in rather less concentrated fashion than the flush broods of May and June but again you see the biggest hatches on wet, windy days. Once the weather turns cold, you have seen the last of the Iron Blue until the spring.

The Pale Watery dun. Although the natural insect, *Baëtis biocu-latus*, hatches freely on all the chalk streams I fish from about the end of May until early September, I have found little need for an artificial dry-fly pattern on most fisheries. This dun shares with the Spurwings and the slow-water Olives the characteristic of transpos-ing so rapidly from nymph to dun that trout simply do not waste their time and hard-earned calorific energy in pursuing the rapidly escaping duns.

Like so many matters appertaining to chalk-stream fishing, it is dangerous to generalize. Once in a while, I encounter an evening hatch of Pale Wateries and when this happens, the duns seem to sit a little longer on their shucks. Then, if fish come on to the duns to feed, you may be glad of a Pale Watery in your box.

There are also some chalk-stream fisheries where anglers do quite well with the artificial during a hatch of these small, pale duns. At Bossington, on the middle Test, a Pale Watery dressing, Fairey's Irresistible, accounts for many good trout. It was devised by the late Sir Richard Fairey, whose favourite pattern it was.

The trout of the Wiltshire chalk streams generally show little interest in Pale Watery duns and I have known day-long hatches of the fly at Itchen Stoke and Abbot's Barton to be ignored by Itchen trout. The nymph is another matter. I reckon to catch a great many trout every summer when they are taking Pale Watery nymphs.

The Spurwings. The Large Spurwing (*Centroptilum pennulatum*) is rarely seen in considerable numbers on any of the chalk streams and the average chalk-stream fly-fisher need not concern himself with this insect. The Small Spurwing (*C. luteolum*) is common on most of these rivers, where it may be seen hatching from February to Novem-ber, being most in evidence during the summer and early autumn.

Although the Small Spurwing is important in the scheme of day-time nymph fishing, it is of little consequence in the dun stage to the dry-fly fisherman because it spends little time on the water. I have therefore not found it necessary to carry a separate pattern of dry fly. In any case, if I did, my Pale Watery dressing would prob-ably serve the purpose well enough. The Spurwings were, for many years, regarded as Pale Wateries.

The slow-water Olives. Slow-water Olives (*Cloëon spp.*) occur locally on some chalk streams in the slow-flowing reaches, sun-warmed backwaters and, in one case, in the old gravel pits through which the head waters of a Test tributary flow. Although common in still waters in the chalk country, slow-water Olives are known to comparatively few chalk-stream anglers. As in the case of the Spur-wings, emergence from nymph to dun is rapid and the flies take wing so quickly that trout do not seem to bother much with them in the dun stage, even when they are hatching in fair numbers. Again, I have not found it necessary to carry an artificial dry-fly pattern. Trout take the nymph well at times.

The Pale Evening dun. Some chalk streams experience occasional heavy hatches of this crepuscular insect (*Procloëon pseudorufulum*), a fly I have yet to see on the Itchen. I usually see it on warm evenings from about the beginning of July to the end of August, especially from the impounded reaches above mills and hatches. The duns generally emerge at dusk and may continue to hatch after the light has failed. I have also seen a good hatch on a wet September evening. On such occasions, trout positively indulge in selective feeding and to take them, consistently, you need a suitably-dressed whitish artificial.

I have devised an effective pattern which, for the benefit of those who dress their own flies, is: hook, o; silk, white; hackle, cream cock; tails, cream cock; body and thorax, grey goose herls.

A heavy hatch of Pale Evening duns is one of the few occasions when I find it necessary to use a pattern other than the pheasant-tail Red Spinner in the evening. Given a simultaneous hatch of Blue-winged Olives and Pale Evening duns, trout, in my experience, usually elect to feed on the latter alone, and they obligingly take the hatched dun so that you don't have to contend with the difficult problems of nymphing in the failing light.

The Mayfly. The natural Mayfly again reached a low ebb in 1959 in its customary fluctuating cycle. I saw few good hatches that year, and not many more in 1960. More seemed to hatch in 1961, but the days when sport was good were few and far between on most chalk-stream fisheries. Parts of the Kennet fished well at times and there were some good hatches on one or two beats at Bossington and elsewhere on the middle Test. Slight improvements were noted on the Wiltshire rivers, especially the Nadder, but it may be a few years before we shall again enjoy the slightly barbarous excitements of an old-fashioned Mayfly season. When people tell you they dislike the Mayfly, watch their faces work when you reply that you won't offend them, in that case, by asking them to fish your water at Mayfly time!

Although in recent years I have not seen a fall of spent Mayfly spinners heavy enough to interest trout, you could be more fortunate and I would certainly advise fly-fishers visiting Mayfly water to carry spent patterns with them. I never go anywhere, at any time of the year, without a small fly-dressing kit in my car and if ever I should need spent Mayfly spinners or ants or anything else unexpectedly, it wouldn't take many minutes to turn them out.

The Blue-winged Olive. The Blue-winged Olive is one of the commonest of all chalk-stream flies, much commoner than is generally realized, for there is scarcely a day in the whole year when a few cannot be found hatching. The main emergence period occurs from about mid-June to the end of October. We may further generalize by saying that during that time, big hatches of this fly may be expected at about dusk in the evening from mid-summer to mid-August. Thereafter, good and prolonged daytime hatches are often recorded.

The attitude of trout to the Blue-winged Olive varies considerably and is not always consistent on one river, or even on one fishery. Sometimes a big dusk hatch brings on a good rise; sometimes trout ignore the fly almost completely or, to complicate matters, they take the nymph and disregard the dun.

It usually pays, when fishing the evening rise, to take advantage of the afterglow, if possible. You achieve this automatically by fishing upstream on most beats of the Kennet, Wylye, Nadder and Ebble and by opting for the east bank on the Test and Avon. The Itchen, above the Worthy villages, does not lend itself to this strategy.

Against the reflected afterglow, you can see the tall, backward-slanting wings of the Blue-winged Olive duns clearly silhouetted, and you know when trout are taking them. I catch such fish on all the chalk streams on the pheasant-tail Red spinner. This pattern is not an imitation of a Blue-winged Olive, but I do not allow this to distress me. The natural fly, which occurs in two distinct types, varies so much in size and coloration, within each type, that I question whether any other pattern, including the popular Orange Quill, could possibly serve me as well. Whether it would always be as effective in other hands is open to question. But many of my pupils now do very well with it on all the major chalk streams.

The Broadwings. Broadwings, as *Caenis* species are now called, sometimes hatch in great numbers early on summer mornings.[1] The only time I see them is if I am on the water long before break-fast-time. Fish seem fond of them but they are small flies, difficult to imitate, and the average chalk-stream angler need not concern himself with them unduly.

Spinners. So far we have considered only the dun, or subimago, stage of the important chalk-stream upwinged flies. To the dry-fly fisherman, however, the adult imagines, or spinners, are of con-siderable importance too. They lay their eggs in, on, or over the water, according to species, and thereafter perish and drift down, spent and lifeless, easy and acceptable prey to hungry trout. Male spinners, except for those of the Small Spurwing, only rarely occur on the water in appreciable numbers, but do not overlook the importance of spent female spinners in the scheme of dry-fly fishing.

It would complicate matters considerably, and clutter up the fly-box no end if it were necessary to carry separate patterns of each female spinner. It isn't. Reference has already been made to the advisability of including spent Mayfly patterns at Mayfly time. The early-rising specialist might find the need for *Caenis* spinners and a case could no doubt be made for carrying a suitable pattern represent-ing the apricot-coloured spinner of the slow-water Olive (*Cloëon dipterum*) in some localities. Apart from these exceptions, it is for-

---

[1] Some species of *Caenis*, however, emerge in the late evening—Ed.

tunate that the female spinners of other chalk-stream species share many common similarities and the pheasant-tail Red spinner, to mention only one effective pattern, is an adequate representation of them all, when dressed on hooks of appropriate size.

There is, however, no reason at all why those who like variety should not provide themselves with patterns representing the female Olive, or Red spinner, female Iron Blue, or Little Claret spinner, female Blue-winged Olive, or Sherry spinner, and so on, if they think they need them. I don't.

Sedge-flies (*Trichoptera*). These moth-like insects hatch from all the chalk-streams, but are more abundant on some than on others. The Grannom, a small spring sedge-fly, is locally important but much less common than in days gone by. The Kennet is traditionally a great sedge river and there are occasions, especially late on warm summer evenings, when trout may take natural sedge-flies on almost any chalk-stream fishery.

There are so many different species of sedge-flies that it is clearly impracticable even to begin to imitate them with separate artificials. Indeed, I content myself with one pattern, dressed in two sizes: hook No. 3 or No. 1; tying silk, brown; body, pheasant-tail herls; hackle, dark red, dressed palmer-fashion.

The smaller version may come in handy for daytime use in the summer, rather like Lunn's Caperer, the popular Test pattern, especially for luring trout in carrier streams. The larger version, named after me, was responsible for the capture of more large Avon trout (over 3 lb.) than any other evening pattern in 1961.

Diptera. Two insects of this order are of importance to the chalk-stream angler: the Hawthorn-fly (*Bibio marci*) and the Black Gnat, a convenient fisherman's name for several species related to but smaller than the Hawthorn-fly.

The Hawthorn-fly. This ungainly, leg-drooping insect is of great importance on some chalk-streams, more especially in Wiltshire, but appears to be of less significance on the Hampshire rivers. Its short season lasts from mid-April to early May. When you get a good Hawthorn-fly season, as we did in Wiltshire in 1959 and again in 1961, it may provide the best sport of the year. The prospects are usually good after a mild winter and spring, for the Hawthorn-fly is a land-bred insect, like the Black Gnat.

You do best when there is some sunshine first thing in the morning to bring these ugly insects out on the wing. Then you hope for wind to blow them on to the water. I look to the artificial Hawthorn-fly to give me my limit of three brace on the morning of May Day, which it does most years.

Skues once dismissed the Hawthorn-fly, in one of his minor works, as being of little account to the chalk-stream fly-fisher. He learned its worth eventually, but only when he came to live in Wiltshire, and in April 1943, almost at the end of his fishing career, we find him on the banks of the Nadder, mourning the untimely death of his old friend and fishing companion, Norman McCaskie, and deploring his absence from the water during a great rise of trout to the Hawthorn-fly.

The Black Gnat. Several closely related species of Black Gnat occur on the chalk streams, in appearance looking like smaller versions of the Hawthorn-fly. Black Gnats and Hawthorn-flies are sometimes on the water together during the opening days of the chalk-stream season. Trout seem very fond of all these black flies.

Black Gnats are most likely to be present on the water in numbers again in August, especially on close muggy days. Many fly-fishers will remember how abundant black dipterans were on the chalk streams of southern England in August 1953. In September, too, you may be glad of this pattern, for grayling as well as trout fishing.

Other Insects. A fall of ants is a possibility which has to be reckoned with, especially if you are fishing in the month of August. Some heavy falls did, in fact, occur on the Test at Bossington and elsewhere late in August, 1961. For some reason, trout seem to be fond of ants.

I carry no "Other Insect" patterns myself. Certain other insects are often plentiful along the banks of the chalk streams; Alder flies in late May and June, and Willow flies in September; but in my experience, they rarely seem to feature in the diet of chalk-stream trout.

Winged and hackled flies. All my dry flies are hackled patterns. I do not use winged flies, although it is always a joy to be shown the fly-box of a fly-dresser who commands the time and skill to dress winged patterns. As to which are more effective, individual fly-fishers must decide for themselves.

CLOTHES AND TACKLE

Dressing the part. Anglers visiting a chalk stream for the first time are usually struck by the exceptional clarity of the water which, except in the deeps above hatches or in reflected light, makes it possible to see trout clearly and to establish whether they are of takeable size. Equally, of course, the fish find it easy to see the fisherman, unless he takes care to hide himself from them. They may also hear him unless he treads very lightly as he moves along the riverbank. Wading is not allowed on many chalk-stream fisheries because it may disturb the water, interfering with sport downstream, or it may damage the banks, or it may cause the destruction of small living creatures on the bed of the river.

The main factors to be considered when deciding how to dress for chalk-stream fishing are:

(a) The paramount importance of hiding from the fish;

(b) the dirt and damp expected along the banks;

(c) the temperature and the weather generally; and

(d) the rules regarding wading.

O. W. Kite

15, 16. Major O. W. A. Kite fishing two Wiltshire chalk streams.
Above: The Avon, Gunville hatch pool.
Below: The Wylye at South Newton.

"The Field"

E. Horsfall Turner

17. The Test at Timsbury.

Avoid light-coloured clothes and shiny material. Be thorough about this. It is pointless to invest in an expensive willow-coloured fishing suit and then wear a white shirt with it. Khaki green, dark olive and such drab colours are the best for fishing clothes, shirts included. Expect to get wet and dirty while stalking your quarry, and dress accordingly. A cap may help to hide the face. Avoid tall hats, especially white straw hats. Rubber knee-boots are useful if the banks are marshy. Wear thigh waders if wading is allowed; these are also useful if the banks are very wet and you wish to keep your knees dry when kneeling.

The working tools. Carry no more than absolutely necessary to enable you to fish effectively and to deal with the trout you win by your skill. Some men fish the better for the comforting knowledge that they have come prepared for all emergencies. Good luck to them. But your requirements in fact, are few.

The rod and line. The length of the rod should be between 8 feet and 9 feet 6 inches, suited to the line you propose to use, rather than the other way about. The point is that if you only propose to use one rod for nymph fishing and dry-fly fishing, it is not a bit of good buying a rod so stiff that you need a No. 4 line to make it give of its best. You cannot master nymph-fishing technique with a No. 4 line. Buy a No. 2 line and then a suitable rod to handle it. Nymph fishing really demands a No. 1 line and an appropriate rod, but I manage very well without either, by using a No. 2 line for both nymph fishing and dry-fly work. I have handled some exquisite French tackle expressly designed for modern nymph fishing, for those who can afford it. For dry-fly work alone, of course, a stiff rod which takes a No. 4 line enables you to throw prodigious distances and once in a while you want to do just that. More often, you will find yourself casting 12–15 yards. Farther than 20 yards, hooking fish on the dry fly is not easy. Hooking them on the nymph is hardly "on" at all. The reel should balance the rod in the usual way and should carry enough backing to fill it.

Bear in mind that chalk streams are notoriously windy rivers, both the Test and the Wylye especially so, and that you will expect your rod to put a fly into the wind, once you have mastered the elements of casting. A soft rod can be an abomination on a rough day. Expensive split-cane rods are sometimes a delight to handle. This season, however, I have killed good trout on all the principal chalk streams using a glass rod. My only experience with a steel rod was unfortunate. It broke for no apparent reason except, perhaps, metal fatigue.

The cast. This may be of gut or nylon: nylon, if you want my advice. I recommend a cast of about nine feet, consisting of four or five links, of which the thickest should be at least three feet and the point at least three feet. The breaking strain of my point is 3·6 lb. (the equivalent of 3x gut) until after Mayfly, thereafter 2·9 lb. (4x).

I

Changing the fly and shortening the point to eliminate wind knots and frayed ends soon reduces the length of the point to less than a yard. Once it drops below 2 feet 6 inches, I have it off and tie on another, using the treble blood knot. When I am fishing, I always carry a roll of point-strength nylon in the right breast pocket of my shirt. Then if it is a hot day and I am tempted to leave my coat off, I do not find myself engaged in, literally, pointless activity half a mile upstream of my car.

If you do not tie your own casts, you need some spare ones with you: quite a few of them if you fish rivers badly overhung with trees. If you have no teeth, you might also be glad of a small pair of scissors.

Grease to make the line float. There are several proprietary brands. A floating line is absolutely indispensable to effective dry-fly and nymph fishing. The grease tin, too, has its place on my person when I am in fishing clothes.

A landing net. You need a big landing net for chalk-stream fishing. A satisfactory net is hard to find. Folding nets are for ever catching in barbed wire with which chalk-stream fisheries seem to abound, or you fall over them, or they won't open when you want them to, or they won't shut. An inexpensive net recently on the market may, in time, be developed to meet this very real requirement of the chalk-stream fly-fisher.

A bag to carry fish in. Chalk-stream trout are quite heavy enough to carry about in your bag. I see no point in cluttering it up with anything else.

Flies and nymphs, and something to carry them in. You don't need anything elaborate. The only fly-box I have ever possessed is an old tobacco tin, enamelled black without and white within, with a little grid made from pipe cleaners which provides horizontal bars on which the flies rest. There is also a magnetized needle for lifting them out and clearing eyes of hooks of bits of old nylon. I have always carried my nymphs in a little round pink box which, I think, once held face-cream: my wife gave it to me when it was empty.

Amadou and oil. I carry on me a bit of amadou, with which I dry my fly, and a little bottle of silicone floatant with which I anoint it to make it float better.

A ruler and a spring balance. Carry whichever is appropriate to keep you above the size limit of the water you intend to fish. If weight is the criterion the fish should, of course, be weighed in the landing net without being handled, in case they have to be returned to the water, the weight of the net then being subtracted.

A case could no doubt be made for burdening yourself with a great deal of paraphernalia over and above these few items. All I have set out to do is to indicate the items which I find necessary. The individual fly-fisher will add to this to suit his fancy. He is, I think, unlikely to be content with less.

THE DRY FLY IN THEORY AND PRACTICE

Basic theory. The basic theory of dry-fly fishing is simple: you arrive on your beat; put your tackle together and pull on the appropriate footwear; start at the downstream end, unless you have a particular reason for beginning elsewhere; watch for a trout feeding on the surface; when you find one, satisfy yourself that it is a takeable size, creditable as well as takeable; decide what it is eating—dun, spent spinner, sedge-fly, dipteran, ant or various; tie on the appropriate artificial, using a Turle knot (a two-circle Turle when using nylon), dressed on a hook of suitable size; oil the fly; approach the fish quietly and cautiously and not too closely, taking full advantage of available cover and background; present your fly so that it alights delicately on the water near the trout's head; and when the fish takes the fly, give it time to get its head down, then tighten smartly with a light movement of the wrist which is calculated not to break the point of your cast at the fly. Thereafter there is nothing unduly specialized about the procedure.

Preliminaries. Whenever you go to fish a chalk stream, do give yourself a fair chance. You may already have formed a poor opinion of chalk-stream trout on some underfished private water where the fish are naïve and easy to deceive, or on one of the great fisheries a day or two after stock fish have been turned in. Broaden your mind with a day on the Upper Avon around August Bank Holiday or, if you can get there, with a day engaging the big wild trout, shy as maidens, of the upper Test.

If you haven't fished for some time, loosen up with some preliminary casting practice *before* you go to the river. Nothing beats an open-air swimming pool for this, but a pond, a canal, a lawn, a park, a field, a parade ground, a big garage, a hangar, all will serve.

Try to arrive at your beat suitably dressed and equipped. You may be fortunate enough to receive helpful advice and suggestions from your host or his keeper as to where and when you are most likely to find worthwhile fish on the feed. Listen carefully to what they have to say. Unless you are visiting underfished private water, remember that you are faced with the problem of deceiving trout who owe their very survival to their caution, much of it inculcated by rods who have already failed. Accord the trout the respect they deserve, and resolve to teach them a lesson.

Making a start. Tackle up and tie on a fly appropriate to the season of the year. Hook the fly on to the second ring up from the cork handle. Run your fingers from the fly down the point of your leader to your reel and take the cast around it. Then reel up gently until all is taut. Make sure you have your bag, with a ruler or spring balance aboard; your net; spare nylon for renewing your point; amadou to dry your fly; silicone oil to oil it, and, of course, your fly-box. You will have greased your line before leaving home. If you leave this operation until you reach the waterside, you can never free your hands of the grease which gets on to the fine point of your cast and causes it to behave in a tiresome manner.

Choice of bank. If you can cast effectively back-handed or, better still, if you are left-handed, choose the left bank of the river (left, that is, when looking *downstream*) because fish under that bank are generally less educated than those under the right bank, which is the one normally favoured by right-handed rods. If you are out of practice, or if trees and other obstructions make the left bank difficult, settle for the easier right bank and accept the disadvantages of shyer trout.

Your choice may also be affected by wind. The worst wind to contend with is the one blowing from between a point directly downstream and directly across from you. I would rather have a cross wind at my back than in my face, and I prefer a light downstream wind to a light upstream wind. Strong winds are always tiresome, but they have to be faced, often, during the course of a chalk-stream season.

Locating a trout. Having made your choice—and you can always reverse the decision if you so wish—begin at the bottom of your beat and keep an eye on the water upstream for signs of a rising fish. Pay special attention to the water under the banks. Trout like to feed close to cover. Wherever there are likely hide-outs, near weed rafts, tree-stumps, cattle bridges, in the runs at the tail of trimmed ranunculus beds, in gravel pockets on beds of water-celery and star-wort, in the eddies of hatch-pools, under bridges, near groynes and hurdles, below carrier inflows, and near the abutments of disused hatches, there you may expect to find trout and to see them rise during a hatch of duns or when spent fly is coming down.

If you cannot spot a rise although a hatch is on, look at the duns themselves and follow their course with your eye, noting where the current tends to set towards the bank, stringing them beneath it. You may see one or more being sucked down by a fish making hardly any disturbance in the water. A good many trout also lie out in mid-stream during a hatch of duns, especially on the smaller, shallow chalk streams.

Fish in hatch-pools may be facing in any direction, according to the set of the currents. Trout sometimes come up out of these pools and lie just above the hatches, where they feed on spent spinners which have earlier laid their eggs by dipping in the sluggish im-pounded reaches above.

The main problem. When you have found a sizeable trout on the feed, do not imagine the main problem is to deceive it into mistaking your artificial fly for a natural. It is not. *The main problem on a hard-fished chalk stream is usually how to present a fly without the trout knowing, or quickly coming to know, that you are at the other end of the line.* This, I know, surprises many visiting anglers who are apt to ascribe their

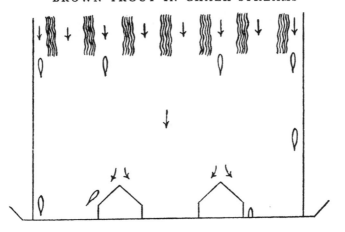

Road bridge

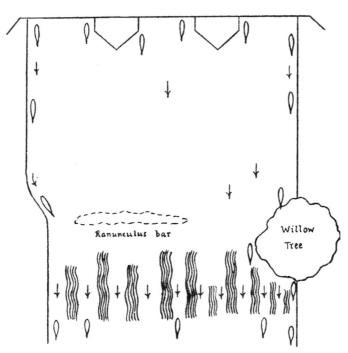

FIG. 33. *Typical lies of chalk-stream trout* (1) *Above and below a road bridge.*

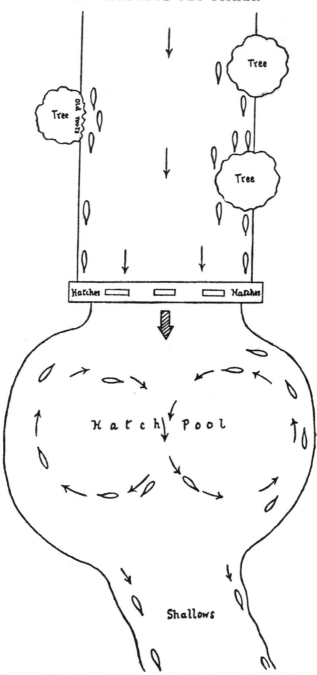

FIG. 34. *Typical lies of chalk-stream trout (2) Above and in a hatch pool.*

failure to catch fish to many other causes. They fail to realize that, in most cases, the game was up before they ever began to cast.

You may betray yourself in various ways. The most obvious is to let the trout see you by boldly walking along the bank instead of moving forward slowly and cautiously and getting down on your knees before you begin to cast. Occasionally you may be able to fish standing up, behind a screen of rushes, for example, or when you have a really good background of trees to conceal you if you are dressed appropriately, or late in the evening when you are fishing an artificial sedge-fly as the light is failing, or in the daytime if wading is allowed, which is not quite the same thing.

You may carry out a model approach but station yourself too close to the trout, so that the fish sees you or your rod the moment you begin to get out line. There are obvious gaps here and there among the bank-side herbage and it doesn't take long to appreciate that these are usually related to the lies of feeding trout. Stop short of these before you start to cast, and try to throw the extra yard or two. Trout get to know these gaps very well.

You may not be using a long enough cast, so that if you throw a shade too far, the thick line waves above the trout's head, in which case it will see it, whether the line touches the water or not. Or your cast may be all right but you may mistime your delivery and slam it down hard on the water and scare the fish in that way. Scared trout do not necessarily leave their lies; but you have the devil of a job to make them rise.

Reconnaissance. When you find a fish on the feed, don't be in too much of a hurry to put a fly over it. Watch it for a bit. Satisfy yourself that you know what manner of fly it is taking, to convince yourself that your own artificial is appropriate. If, when you left your starting point, you tied on a fly to anchor your line to your rod, do not hesitate to change it if your fish is clearly looking for something quite different. On some occasions, it may be.

Opening fire. When you do cast, aim to put the fly as close to the trout's head as your hands will allow. Above all, put it down lightly, and be inaccurate behind rather than in front of your fish. It helps if the first cast can be made to tell.

Aim always at an imaginary point three feet above (overhead) and slightly beyond the fish and shoot your line so that there is a bit of recoil, at the end of which the fly parachutes down like thistledown and alights on the water on the tips of its hackles, as susceptible to a breath of wind as a fragile dun. Never, ever let anyone persuade you this is difficult. With practice, it becomes automatic.

Provided a chalk-stream trout is unaware that it is being fished for, it will often turn aside a yard or go back a foot to take an artificial dry-fly presented in this way.

Take comfort in this knowledge as you prepare to engage. The late William Lunn said to a friend of mine, "It's better to change the fish than the fly." What he meant was that a fish, once alarmed, is no longer receptive to artificial offerings. Equally, a trout, carefully approached, may well accept a nicely presented, reasonable-looking artificial.

If the trout refuses your fly, it does so for one of two reasons. Either, despite all your care, something has happened to make it suspect that it is being fished for, or your artificial itself does not appeal to it as being good enough to eat. It is usually possible, by observation, to deduce which of these two reasons underlies the trout's refusal. If the fish has not been scared, it will continue feeding quietly and confidently and, if you are careful, you should know that such fish can generally be caught, however difficult they may seem, provided you have the patience to do nothing to give the game away.

You do better to change your fly frequently rather than accustom the trout to one particular pattern, and in cases like these, by no means uncommon on the chalk stream, you may be glad you do not restrict yourself to one or two patterns. You may change your fly many times before you eventually induce the fish to rise. I have caught a trout after forty or more casts, on an artificial which it had seen several times before and refused. If you watch some of these difficult trout, you notice that they allow many naturals to pass over them untaken. You can't hope to improve on the Creator's work, and you need patience to do as well.

It is always debatable whether you would not do better, in the long run, to pass on to less difficult quarry. If feeding fish are few and far between, you may have little choice. Then, of course, if you have found an exceptional fish for the water, one which is worth catching even if it means forfeiting a chance of several smaller trout, go ahead and persevere.

If you do rise the fish eventually, but miss it, you probably will not rise it again if you have pricked it severely, but if you mistime your strike and do not even scratch the fish, you may still succeed. On the Upper Avon in September 1961, I worked patiently on a good trout rising in shallow water below the lip of a hatch-pool. Eventually it took a Red spinner, and I missed it, being rather tired. I waited a few moments, rose the fish again and missed it once more. I gave it, and myself, a few minutes rest, cast, rose the fish again and this time hooked it firmly. It is a shameful thing to be beaten by a trout.

Some advice. If you are impatient and become fed up with trying to tempt a difficult fish, you may prefer to look for a less sophisticated trout elsewhere. You would certainly be well advised not to waste too much time over notorious Aunt Sallies; trout such as those who seem to be for ever feeding near popular car-parking sites and the junction points between beats. These fish are usually subjected to a hammering by most of the rods who frequent the water and they become educated to a superlative degree. At the other end of the scale, you may find good fish, especially in summer, in the carriers and side-streams, particularly lying out just below foot bridges. A small sedge-fly may be their undoing.

Smutting fish. Smutting fish, taking tiny insects on the surface, are not easy to catch. Sometimes all the trout seem to be engaged in this manner of feeding and it is not easy to tempt them with artificials, least of all with Black Gnats which are so much bigger, and basically unlike the tiny smuts. But I have found that such trout also intercept occasional Olive spinners as they come down spent in the surface film and I prefer to tackle smutting fish with a spinner than to try to imitate the smut itself, a very difficult thing to do.

Nymphing fish. If a fish is clearly nymphing, or feeding on something invisible to you beneath the surface, and will have nothing to do with your floater, do not bombard it with dry flies. Either try it with a nymph or pass on to more responsive quarry.

Handling a hooked trout. Trout vary tremendously in their reactions to being hooked. The struggle they put up is not always related to their weight, but when fish over 1½ lb. decide to run, there is not much you can safely do to stop them. Indeed I always feel happier about my chances of eventually landing a fish that does run hard than about recovering one which turns down into thick ranunculus the moment it feels the hook. The more acrobatics a fish indulges in and the faster it rushes about, the sooner it will tire.

Do nothing to alarm a trout once you have hooked it. Play it quietly and firmly but do not try to hold it hard, unless some fearful snag is close at hand. In principle, it pays to be firm rather than light. Far more fish are lost in weed than by the hook pulling out, though both account for a good many getting away during the course of a chalk-stream season. Remember that nothing takes the steam out of a trout like towing it downstream.

Sometimes a fish can be quietly coaxed over the net before it ever begins to fight seriously, but with large fish this can be a dangerous game, and if they are well hooked and the coast is clear, play them out before you try to net them. Very large trout, say over 4 lb. may decide to head for refuge some considerable distance away. You may then be obliged to go with them, at a respectful distance, especially if you have only a very fine point on your cast. You may end up by netting such a fish more than 100 yards from the spot where you hooked it.

Weed is the great snag on most chalk streams. Try to keep the fish's head up from the moment the hook takes hold. A fish fighting for its head has little thought for weed. If a fish tries to get into ranunculus, hold the rod low over the water and exert downstream pressure to comb it, as it were, through the weed tresses. When a fish goes to weed, your best ally in coaxing it out is the fish itself. Do not lose patience. Alternate between pressure and relaxation. Use your net to liven things up. Don't neglect hand-lining, and rapping the rod. And when, eventually, you do get your trout, congratulate yourself on earning it the hard way.

Fish to be returned to the water should not be handled, if possible. Kill a trout by striking it firmly on the head and weigh the fish at once, while it is fresh. Then wrap it in a generous piece of muslin, to keep it fresh, and put it in your bag. If the keeper comes along, he may be able to ease your load by taking the fish in for you. Trout do not improve in condition by being carried about in the hot sun all day. But do not leave fish cached about the river bank. Cats or rats nearly always find them. Don't kill more trout than you need for yourself or your friends and see that any you do kill are given to those who will appreciate and make good use of them.

NYMPH-FISHING TECHNIQUE

Natural nymphs. The nymphs of many species of upwinged flies occur in the English chalk streams, but the fly-fisher is concerned only with those which commonly feature in the diet of the trout and, more especially, with those on which trout regularly feed during the daytime in the summer months, when dry-fly fishing is least rewarding. There are relatively few of these.

They belong, for the most part, to the genus *Baëtis* (the Pale Watery, certain Olives, and perhaps a few belated Iron Blues), *Centroptilum* (the Spurwings, and especially the abundant Small Spurwing) and *Cloëon* (the slow-water Olives). All except the latter occur in fast-flowing reaches which are a feature of most chalk streams. Spurwings also occur in the sluggish waters above hatches, mills and other obstructions, together with slow-water Olives.

When the insect first hatches from the egg, and during the first instars, or stages, of its larval existence, its species may be impossible to determine. Up to the time when its wing-pads first appear, it is known as a larva. After the wing-pads appear, it is properly called a nymph. A nymph is designated young, half-grown or full-grown, according to the length of its wing-pads.

Nymphs of different generations of the same species vary considerably in size. Structural differences have already been explained. In addition, nymphs undergo colour changes, in whole or in part, at various stages in their development. These facts have naturally influenced the dressing of modern artificial nymphs.

Artificial nymphs. Pattern is of much less significance than size and careful construction to imitate the general appearance of natural nymphs in the water. The artificial nymph is dressed to sink quickly and is fished *under* the surface in such a way as to simulate the behaviour of the natural nymph it is intended to imitate.

This method, the Netheravon technique devised by Sawyer, differs from the style of nymph fishing first advocated by Skues. His numerous patterns were dressed as exact imitations of ripe, full-grown nymphs of various species about to transpose into duns, and were intended to be fished in or just beneath the surface film. Skues was primarily concerned with the full-grown nymph during the last few moments of its subaqueous existence. The Netheravon-style nymph-fisherman is concerned with the nymph throughout its existence as such, a period taking in several instars and amounting to days, or even weeks. A knowledge of the habits and behaviour of the natural nymph during its underwater lifetime is therefore essential for its practical application.

Patterns necessary. Few patterns are required. Sawyer himself advocates three, and there are obvious advantages to being able to ring the changes a bit, but for all that, I only use one of them, the Pheasant tail, dressed in sizes oo to 1. I take most of my fish on a size o hook. Pheasant-tail herls are wound on over a core of gossamer-fine nymph wire which gives the artificial its characteristic outlines and ensures its free-sinking capability which is so essential. These wire-bodied nymphs, an original and imaginative construction evolved by Sawyer, are the very foundation of modern nymph-fishing. Even after the pheasant-tail herls have worn away completely, I catch many trout on the almost bare hook, merely by fishing it in an appropriate manner.

When trout are feeding freely on or close to the surface, they often take natural duns and hatching nymphs impartially. Pale Watery, Spurwing and slow-water Olive nymphs, all of which transpose rapidly, are often taken a moment before emergence, especially on a fine, warm day when the transition from nymph to dun is very swift indeed. When trout feed in this way, they accept nymph-like patterns fished in the surface film, including patterns such as Skues devised for his impounded Abbot's Barton water where these species commonly hatch. This canal-like fishery has little in common with the fast, shallow, well-aerated reaches of many chalk streams, including the upper lengths of the Itchen itself where artificial nymphs of the kind Skues devised are whirled away downstream like confetti on the surface, and achieve but modest success.

A test of suitability. Natural nymphs live *under* water. That is where artificial nymphs should be fished. You can test the suitability of your own artificials at home, with the aid of a glass of clean water. Place your artificial gently on the surface skin of the water. It should sink to the bottom at once, without dithering. Unless it does, it is unsuitable, indeed useless for nymph fishing in the modern style.

Tackle. Nymph fishing calls for a fairly fine line, not thicker than No. 2. You can catch trout on the nymph on a No. 4 line—I catch a good few myself when demonstrating with other people's tackle—but you handicap yourself in speed of reaction to the take by doing so. The rod should be suited to the line.

Use a yard, at least, of fine nylon or gut on the point to allow the artificial to sink freely and rapidly after entering the water. Do not allow any oil or grease to come into contact with the point, or its sinking capability will be impaired. During fishing, keep the point well rubbed down with soft mud to give it a good entry into the water.

When to fish the nymph. Provided its use is permitted, the artificial nymph should be fished to any trout, believed to be of creditable size, which can be seen feeding consistently beneath the surface. A nymphing trout visible to the fly-fisher can be seen making little movements, lifting slightly in the water from time to time and half turning sideways to intercept food particles which may not themselves be visible. Such fish are on the fin, as fishermen say, and their tails are working busily to keep them balanced for interceptory movements.

Nymphing trout, in fact, are usually feeding on a variety of creatures borne down by the current but, more especially, on freshwater shrimps, migrating snails and the nymphs of upwinged flies at various stages in their development, as you discover when you catch them by the score and examine the contents of their stomachs.

Even if it is not possible to see the trout itself, in reflected light or other circumstances, it may be possible to estimate its size either from the nature of the swirls as it moves under water or from past experience of the trout which usually occupies its lie.

Windy days. On very rough days, when duns are hatching in numbers but fish are frustrated in their attempts to seize them on the wind-whipped surface, nymph fishing may be the only practicable way of making a basket. This sometimes happens in September during what should be good dry-fly fishing time. It was so in mid-September 1961. In these conditions, when it may be impossible to see the trout, it pays to grease the thicker links of the cast to make it lie more visibly in the rough water on the surface and so act as a float to give you some indication of the whereabouts of your artificial.

Tailing trout. It is during the daytime in July and August that nymph fishing is most necessary, but it may sometimes be helpful to use the nymph earlier in the season, especially if trout are seen "tailing"—feeding on the bed of the stream with their tails showing occasionally through the surface. Such trout are easy to catch with an artificial nymph, provided you offer it to them when their attention is momentarily withdrawn from the bottom. It was in these circumstances that I employed the nymph for the first time this season (1961), at Polhampton Mill on the upper Test on June 6th as the guest of Mr. J. C. Marsden. Although there was no hatch of fly on that hot, bright day, and the large trout were shy and difficult to approach, an almost bare oo hook yielded me six weighing over 14 lb.

Tailing trout, feeding on caddis, snails and so on, are usually vulnerable to the nymph fisherman with quick-sinking artificials. So, occasionally, are trout minnowing on the gravelly shallows when the little fish are spawning at mid-summer.

Evening nymph fishing. Sometimes the nymph is useful in the evening, especially early on before the presence of much spent fly brings on the evening rise proper. After the light begins to fail, however, the indications of a take are not easy to detect and nymph fishing then imposes a strain on the fly-fisher who may be seeking relaxation after an arduous day.

Basic technique. The basis of modern nymph-fishing technique is deception. The nymph fisherman relies for success on deceiving the trout with a representation, similar in outline, size and general appearance to the natural nymphs it is expecting to see, fished where it expects to see them, and behaving as it expects them to behave.

The first problem, then, is to deceive the trout into taking the artificial. The second is detecting when it has done so. The third is hooking it when this has been established. To be successful, the three must take place almost simultaneously.

Nymphs in fast water. The natural nymphs which a trout expects to encounter in fast water during the daytime in summer are primarily those of the Pale Watery and Small Olive, with some common Olives and Small Spurwings. All belong to the swimming group of nymphs and, indeed, are closely related.

Trout intercept these nymphs over beds of water-celery, in the gravel runs between clumps of starwort and close under the banks and, more especially, in the runs at the tail of ranunculus beds which have been barred during the main summer weed-cutting operations in June. Such nymphs are fairly helpless in the faster currents by which they are borne to the waiting trout. It follows that the artificial must also swim down freely, unimpeded by lateral drag which, in these circumstances, would appear unnatural and alarming to the fish.

Nymphs in slow water. The two most important species occurring in slow water in summer are the abundant Small Spurwings and the locally common slow-water Olives, mainly *C. dipterum*. These nymphs, especially the latter species, are fast swimmers which dart about among the weed fronds in which they live and from which they periodically emerge into open water, perhaps to frolic. Trout take them at all levels and the artificial should accordingly be fished at the depth at which the trout can be seen feeding. Unless favourable conditions of light and background enable you to see into deep water, trout feeding well below the surface may be quite invisible. This is the case on some reaches of the middle Test where opportunities for employing the artificial nymph may be limited.

Trout in slow water may take an artificial as it is sinking, like a natural nymph settling back into deep water, or, if the fish seems likely not to notice the artificial, movement may be imparted to it with the rod-tip to simulate the sideways dart or the upward glide of a natural nymph, and so induce the trout to take.

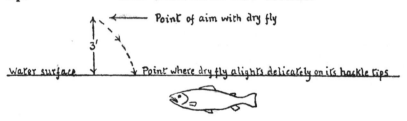

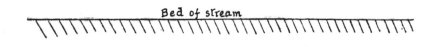

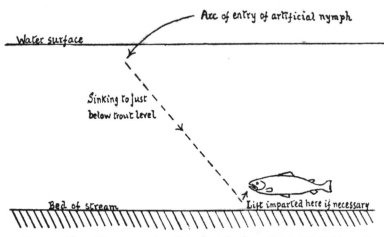

FIG. 35. Top: *The correct point of aim for a dry fly, so that it falls lightly on the surface.* Bottom: *A nymph should be pitched directly into the water, so that it sinks immediately.*

Nymph pitching. Casting a nymph is in some ways the opposite of casting a dry-fly. Whereas the latter should be aimed at an imaginary point above the water and from there drop lightly on to the surface on the tips of its hackle, the artificial nymph should be pitched, as it were, to arc over and into the water with the minimum of surface disturbance to interfere with vision—an otter's entry.

According to the speed of the water and the depth at which the trout is judged to be feeding, the nymph may have to be pitched into the stream anything from a few inches to 15 yards above the fish's lie. The aim is to present the nymph in front of the fish at its own level and correct for line, without treacherous lateral drag. Fish directly upstream to overcome the latter, whenever this is possible.

Timing the strike. Nymphing trout see the artificial with astonishing speed, especially during the summer months, the moment it penetrates the surface to their approximate level and they may shoot forward several feet to take it with savage eagerness. Stock fish seize a nymph with great deliberation and are easy to hook. Wild trout eject an artificial with a rapid movement of the jaws and you must be keyed up to strike the moment they take to have any chance of hooking them consistently.

The first requirement is to gather in the slack line as the artificial is drifting down to the fish, so that your strike, when you make it, is immediately effective. You must also be prepared for forward acceleration by the trout as already described. When the trout does shoot forward to take, you do well to strike at once, for if you wait to see what happens when it reaches your nymph you may be too late. Trout hardly ever hook themselves in nymph fishing, as is quite common in wet-fly fishing.

Although you may not be able to see your artificial in the water, you can follow its progress by watching the dipping-point of your floating cast—the place where the fine nylon or gut turns down into the water over and above the position of your drifting nymph.

When you judge that your artificial has reached the fish's head, you can and should expect the trout to take it, whether or not you see any sign of this. If your cast has been accurately gauged, the trout should take first time and it therefore pays to assume that it has and strike as a matter of course. Every season I catch a good many trout in the presence of other fly-fishers who see no sign of a take. Very often there is no sign, but usually there is some slight indication recognizable with experience.

A visible trout generally lifts slightly or turns aside a little as it intercepts the artificial. The more accurate the cast, the less it needs to do so. In favourable conditions, the take may be clearly seen as the trout's mouth whitens when it opens its jaws to seize the nymph. In reflected light, when the fish cannot be seen, the indication of the take must be obtained by watching the dipping-point of the cast.

This will check and draw under as the fish grips the nymph momentarily. The strike must follow at once to be effective.

Once a trout has ejected an artificial due to a delayed strike, it is not easy to persuade it to take it a second time until it has forgotten the incident. This may take anything from some minutes to a day or more. Always wait a little before trying again, preferably until the trout has restored its confidence by taking several natural nymphs.

Should a trout refuse an artificial nymph, after appearing to show interest in it, it may pay to put on an artificial dressed on a slightly smaller hook. Once again, give the fish a chance to take a few naturals before you offer it the smaller artificial.

Practice. Some fly-fishers use polarized glasses to help their underwater vision in bright conditions. There are times, however, when good eyesight is essential for effective nymph fishing. Even this, in itself, is not enough. The eyes must be trained to detect the take in reflected light, in rough conditions, and in poor visibility. Train them at grayling time, in the autumn, when these obliging, quick-taking fish readily accept an artificial nymph during the murk and gales of wet November and December days. After that, nymph fishing for trout in the clear water and bright weather of July and August may be found less difficult.

18. The Kennet: Crookham Manor water.

19. A Yorkshire chalk stream: the Driffield Beck.

NATURAL FLY	SCIENTIFIC NAME	RECOMMENDED ARTIFICIAL AND HOOK SIZE	REMARKS
		First Phase—April to Early June	
Large Olive dun	*Baëtis rhodani*	Olive Dun (1)	Good hatches possible well into April; body darker in cold conditions.
Small Olive dun	*B. scambus*	" " (oo)	Early hatches sometimes occur in April; " " " "
Olive dun	*B. vernus*	" " (o)	Peak hatches occur late April to late May.
Hawthorn-fly	*Bibio marci*	Hawthorn-fly (3)	Especially when wind follows sunshine in late April and early May.
Spring Black Gnat	Bibionid species	Black Gnat (o)	" " " " " " " " "
Iron Blue dun	*Baëtis niger/pumilus*	Iron Blue (o)	Sometimes hatches well in rough, showery conditions.
Red spinners	*Baëtis* species	Pheasant tail Red spinner (o)	A pattern for evening use as a matter of course.
Mayfly	*Ephemera* species	Mayfly (5)	Mid-May to early June on some rivers.
Spent Mayfly spinner	" "	Spent Mayfly spinner (5)	Evenings in late May and early June, if naturals are on the water.
		Second Phase—Mid-June to Mid-August	
Nymphs	*Baëtidae,* all species	Pheasant tail nymph (oo to 1)	Most days, during the daytime when trout are feeding under water.
Pale Watery dun	*B. bioculatus*	Pale Watery dun (oo)	For those occasions when trout take the natural duns.
Small Olive dun	*B. scambus*	Olive dun (oo)	
Red spinners	*Baëtis* species	Pheasant tail Red Spinner (o)	Most evenings and, sometimes, during the day if trout take spent fly.
Blue-winged Olive dun	*Ephemerella ignita*	" " " (oo)	Most evenings at dusk. Orange Quill is the accepted imitation.
Sherry spinner	" "	" " " (oo) (1)	Most evenings around sunset, if naturals fall on the water in numbers.
Pale Evening dun	*Procloëon pseudorufulum*	Pale Evening dun (oo) or (o)	Occasionally on warm evenings after sunset in slow water.
Sedge-flies	Order Trichoptera	Sedge fly (3)	When too dark to see the Red spinner on the water. For daytime use, especially in carriers; or use Lunn's Caperer.
Black Gnat	Bibionid species	Black Gnat (oo) (1)	Sometimes, on muggy days, especially in August.

Third Phase—Mid-August to the End of the Season

As for the Second Phase but add Olive dun (o) and Iron Blue (oo), especially on damp, showery days in September

Notes: (i) A fall of ants is always a possibility in August.

(ii) This table is only one possible effective combination favoured by one fly-fisherman and may be varied or augmented to suit both local conditions and personal inclinations.

(iii) For the benefit of those who dress their own flies, the dressing of the pheasant tail Red spinner is given on page 125 and of a Sedge-fly on Page 127.

K

CHAPTER V

BROWN TROUT IN LAKES
by
H. A. OATTS

INTRODUCTION

THROUGHOUT this chapter I propose to use the word "lake" according to its dictionary meaning of "a large body of water entirely surrounded by land". In the British Isles there is every form of lake between Watten and Blagdon and all vary both in name and character. Even the term "reservoir" covers a vast number of different types of water and the popular west-country reservoirs are not all the same.

I shall also call the trout "lake trout" rather than "still-water trout" for it always seems to me that the term "still water", although descriptive, conjures up visions of dull, uninteresting stuff, and I doubt whether Sir Walter Scott would have sold so many copies of *The Lady of The Lake* had the title been *The Still-Water Woman.*

It will only be possible to deal with factors which are common to most lakes and to point out the main differences which occur as between river and lake and between natural and artificial waters.

TACKLE FOR LAKE FISHING

Rods. The rod for general purpose lake fishing should cast, and fish, a short line well for boat fishing and a long line well for bank fishing. It should fish the wet fly well and the dry fly well enough where great accuracy is not required. These conflicting requirements are technically impossible, but, nevertheless, our leading British rod makers can produce a rod which, for practical purposes, is near enough to perfection. My own favourite is a 10-footer of medium action, made of split bamboo. It is in three pieces for convenience of carrying and weighs 7½ oz.

The rod must suit the physique of the angler, however, and a "best rod" by a good maker is a sound investment. The rod described above is for the general practitioner. For the specialist there is the rod with the long, slow "Scotch action" for drift fishing, the fast rod for accurate dry-fly work, and the powerful weapon for distance casting on reservoirs.

Reels. A reel has to be lifted every time a cast is made—and a lake fisherman does a lot of casting. It should not be too heavy, therefore, and a good modern reel would be 3½ inches in diameter, weighing about 5 oz. and with a capacity of 30 yards of line and 60 yards of backing. A check which can be regulated is desirable.

Lines. A double-taper line is the best for general use, the forward taper being favoured for reservoir fishing. As line materials vary in weight, the correct weight for a given rod should be ascertained from the rod maker.

Casts. Gut is the best material for sinking the fly and for fishing in an unfavourable wind, though nylon is quite satisfactory for all general purposes. The thickness of the cast depends upon the size of the fly, for all the angler's tackle must be properly balanced. Useful sizes are 2x gut and .008 nylon. The standard length of 3 yards is generally satisfactory, but it pays to lengthen or shorten the cast according to the conditions. It is logical to use a tapered cast with a tapered line.

Landing-nets. I use a pear-shaped net measuring 15½ inches by 13½ inches. This screws into a strong two-piece handle, each section being 3 feet long, with a "lock-fast" joint between them. One section does for bank fishing and both sections are joined to make a 6 foot handle for boat work.

FINDING THE FISH

The man who drifts upon a lake
In search of trout to slaughter
May weep like anything to see
Such quantities of water:
"Could this be only drained away,"
He says, "My quest would be much shorter."

This, I think, expresses the feelings of many people who go fishing on great areas of water without either a good gillie or knowledge of the ways of lake trout. It always seems to me that the first task of an angling writer should be to help the reader to find the fish and so I will endeavour to drain away some of the water.

It is a popular belief that the lake trout is an energetic, active fish which spends most of its time swimming about all over the place while hunting for something to eat. It is a belief which probably arises from the fact that lake trout cruise at times and can be seen while doing so. I will deal with cruising elsewhere and it will be sufficient to say here that it is not a normal habit of every day. Very far from it, for the lake trout is a lazy creature which takes no more exercise than it can help.

The trout of the river takes up its position in some favoured spot and stays there, or thereabouts, while the stream brings the rations with no bother. The lake trout is not so fortunate, for there is no stream to do the work. It therefore has to go to such parts of the water as may contain a good food supply under existing conditions, and, having found a good place it stays there until conditions change and it has to go somewhere else.

Now it so happens—fortunately for the fisherman—that the best food supply of any lake is only to be found in water of no great depth. Ten or twelve feet is generally the depth limit for good feeding and therefore great areas of water can be eliminated straight away. In the average Highland loch hardly more than twenty-five per cent of the whole area is actually worth bothering about, but the fishing area will generally increase in flatter country. If one fishes the same waters constantly throughout the season it is worth while to find out the depths with a lead, but for ordinary purposes most people can make a fair guess when they know that depth of water is worth thinking about.

The effect of wind. The direction of the wind can often be a help in leading the fisherman to the fish, for wind blows food items from the land on to the water and then carries all manner of things across the surface until they accumulate along the downwind shore. The trout in many hill waters depend quite largely upon the wind for food supply, for such places are seldom rich in feed. The shore from which the wind is blowing is worth trying and the shore to which the wind is blowing is often even better. If the wind is blowing from a good land area of trees, shrubs, heather and general vegetation, the effect upon the location of the trout is considerable, particularly when such a direction has been constant for a day or two.

A constant steady breeze is the lake fisherman's best friend, while the changing type is his worst enemy. During a changing wind the trout go to the bottom and stay there until the direction steadies, and the fisherman might just as well take time off in which to read this book for, in the words of Ecclesiastes "*The wind goeth toward the south, and turneth about unto the north; it whirleth about continually, and the wind returneth again according to his circuits.*"

The bed of the lake. It is generally possible to obtain a fair idea of what the bed of a lake is like from a study of the contours of the ground which surrounds it, for the character of the surroundings does not change abruptly just because there happens to be water. Rather does the character continue under water. So we find that a lake among steep, high, hills is likely to be a deep, steep-sided, water-filled hollow, whereas in the midst of flat country a lake is probably a shallow pan. Between these two extremes there is every variety and an extensive lake often provides all these varieties. A steep fall down to the lake means a continuation of fall under water, with consequent deep water right up to the edge. A more gentle decline produces a reef along the shore, and shore reefs are common features for they are also formed by the slow process of land erosion.

A promontory does not end at the water's edge but continues for some distance into the lake in the form of a reef, and if there is a corresponding promontory on the far side the reef may run right across the lake. Were it not for the water, this reef would be a ridge.

There is generally a reef of sorts round an island, and if there are two or more islands close together there may be a reef which joins them up for, on dry land these islands would be knolls or hillocks. There is usually a reef at the mouth of an inflow stream caused by the silt which is brought down, and a landslide also forms a good reef.

It is impossible to overstress the importance of reefs in lake fishing, for they are ideal feeding-places for trout. They are generally not too deep for a food supply, and they have deep water just off them for sanctuary. Trout do not remain on the reefs unless these are very extensive. Rather do they watch the reefs from the deep water and go on and off them when feeding.

Other features. There are other features which attract trout, and the more important of these are outflows and weed-beds. Outflows create a drag which carries with it the food supply from a wide area, and weed-beds form a natural larder. It is always worth while to fish the edges of a weed-bed with care, but it is only worth while to fish over the weeds if trout are seen to be moving near the surface. If fish cannot be seen they will probably be below the weeds where they cannot see the angler's flies. Weed-beds which are not too

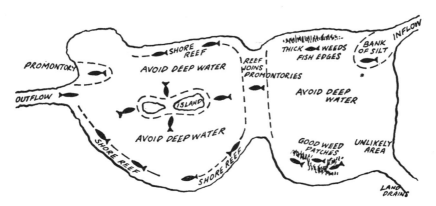

FIG. 36. *Where to look for lake trout.*

dense and which have gaps or "rides" are excellent holding place for trout.

Drains running into lakes are generally best avoided, for they are apt to carry sour bog-water, road washings, or some other form of minor pollution which affects the area around the mouth of the drain.

These, then, are some of the important factors which help the fisherman to find fish in natural waters. A single factor may not prove sufficient, but a combination of several is certain to provide results.

Artificial reservoirs. In general these are more difficult to cope with, for they are liable not to follow natural rules. Wind direction, water depth and weed-beds apply, but the important reefs are lacking, and the surroundings often give little indication as to the nature of the water. Under water there may be all manner of important things depending upon what existed before the land was flooded, and unless the water level is very low, there is nothing to indicate objects or features below water. I have encountered the same sort of thing in Highland lochs which have varied from a ruined causeway to a submerged fort, and such things are always great places for trout. There is no alternative to local knowledge in such cases and, fortunately, such knowledge is generally available. If flooding has taken place so long ago that the original state has been forgotten, the artificial has probably reverted to the natural to a considerable degree.

Under natural conditions the shore line is much favoured by trout, for many things fall into water from the land, minnows and small fry haunt the shore shallows, and caddis and snails are to be found among partially submerged stones. Heavy fishing can affect the habits of trout and where reservoirs are much fished from the bank the fish become bank-shy. They will be attracted towards the shore but will not come in too close, and they will be very wary of movement from the direction of the shore.

All this seems to add up to quite a lot, but there are many factors involved in the search for any form of game, even down to the case of that mouse in the room when, poker in hand, one is guided to the quarry by knowing where to look. Lake fishing is a very fascinating form of sport for the man who knows sufficient about it, for there is a great deal more to it than just the catching of fish.

MORE ABOUT THE TROUT

The brown trout of lake, loch, river, reservoir and pond are all, scientifically, exactly the same fish, but environment brings about such enormous changes that the scientific fact is often difficult to believe. No two waters produce exactly the same environment or exactly the same brown trout. It is not difficult to understand that an English reservoir should contain trout which differ from those of a Highland loch, but no two Highland lochs produce the same results either, even when they are close to one another.

The basic similarity between the trout of river and lake is that both are omnivorous and the chief difference is that one lives in running water and the other in water which is static. These are obvious platitudes, but they help towards understanding the ways of trout.

Food supply. The food of the lake trout exists in varying depths of water. The least important items are found at or near the surface and the food value increases until the bed of the lake is reached. The main and fundamental part of the diet is found on the bed of the lake, which is also the main source of supply for the rest of the water. All waters vary as to what they can produce, just as soil varies in this respect, and the main factor in trout growth and habit is the fundamental bottom feed. It is for this reason that in one lake there are small, free rising fish, for in that lake there is a lack of bottom feed and the trout are therefore dependent upon what they can get at, or near, the surface. In an adjacent water the fish may be large and dour, for the bottom feed is good and the trout less dependent upon surface feed. In some Irish loughs it has been found that eel fishing affects both growth and rising, for eels consume a lot of bottom feed, leaving less for the trout.

It follows that when trout are not at or near the surface the fly-fisherman must try to find the right depth, which varies according to existing conditions. The bed of the lake may be out of the question, depending upon depth, but there are generally such things as nymphs and shrimps at a depth which can be reached and the trout can be tempted to rise off the bottom even when they will not come right up to the surface.

Variation of fishing depth is really a matter of patience and slowly-fished wet flies will sink quite far enough if given time in which to do so. Many lake fishermen acquire the habit of fishing much too fast, which is a tiring and not very productive habit, perhaps the result of fishing from a fast drifting boat.

Movement of trout. The effect of water which has no flow is that trout cannot face upstream although they do, to some extent, face up-wind when surface feeding. A stream maintains the trout's breathing apparatus in good order more or less automatically, and if one examines the gills of a fish it is apparent that these are quite complicated pieces of mechanism which have to be kept in working order and assisted in their work. The lake trout is therefore encouraged to move about by nature, for a trout which is moving, however slowly, is breathing easily and freely, whereas when it is at rest the gills are operating with an effort akin to panting.

The lake trout generally has to move about sufficiently while feeding, but when the oxygen content of the water is low and the trout are full-fed the gills have still to be kept working and, as the trout is a lazy creature which will not take exercise for the sake of exercise, nature stimulates movement by providing plankton as an incentive. This, in my opinion, results in cruising, and the angler swears because there is no discernible direction or method in this form of exercise. The fish takes a fly here and there but takes no notice of other and better flies, including those of the exasperated fisherman. The latter cannot, of course, see the plankton for it is too minute. Probably the trout cannot see it either, but has other means of finding it.

In a lake there is none of that sub-surface turmoil which exists to a greater or lesser degree in all rivers and streams, and which helps the angler in many ways. It is therefore fortunate that the lake trout

never attains to quite the same degree of sophistication as does the
trout of a heavily-fished river. Even in the hardest-fished reservoir
there is a lot of water in which the trout are undisturbed, and there
is never the same degree of close contact with the world outside the
water as there is in the case of a river.

An important point is the rise of the lake trout and the method by
which it seizes its food. The river trout is generally accustomed to
some degree of rapid action when food items are passing with the
current. The trout of a mountain stream has to be out in a flash
from behind a stone or the food will be whirled away, and even the
large, fat aristocrats of the chalk stream have to move quite fast in
many parts of the river. The trout of the lake seldom has to hurry,
for the various creatures upon which it feeds do not move at any
great speed and are not assisted by any stream to do so. Even when
a lake trout is chasing a minnow it does not have to move fast for,
although the small fish may appear to do so, this is an illusion
caused by its diminutive size. As a consequence the lake trout is
used to feeding in its own time and will not bother to go beagling
after objects which are not obeying the local rules. It can, of course,
put up a pretty turn of speed, but it has to be thoroughly scared
before it does so.

It is very easy to fish too fast for lake trout.

THE LAKE FISHING SEASON

The life cycle of the trout is concerned with reproduction and the
continuity of the race. Nature pays little regard to the survival of
adult fish after spawning in late autumn or early winter and spawning
leaves the fish spent at a time of year when food supply is almost
non-existent and the water too cold for feeding. Fortunately the
trout is a hardy creature which manages to survive until the spring
food supply arrives.

It follows that the trout are hungry and feed voraciously in the
early spring, and the opening of the fishing season is timed in order
to allow sufficient feeding to take place prior to the opening date.
This opening date cannot allow for local conditions, which determine the food supply of any water, and the quality of the trout
varies in different parts of the country.

The effects of temperature. When the season opens the trout will still
be hungry, whatever the water, and they are likely to remain hungry
throughout most of April. This hunger does not mean that they will
be too easily caught, for the surface of the water will be cold and
night frosts may keep it so. The air, too, may be cold and may even
be colder than the surface of the water. This means that there will be
little in the way of surface feed and the trout will be discinclined to
rise into surface water which may be colder than that which is
deeper down. If the air happens to be warm there may be a surface

20. A Scottish loch. Loch Awe from the top of Kilchurn Castle.

C. V. Hancock

21. An Irish lough. Lough Currane, Waterville, showing both bank and boat fishing in progress.

22. A Welsh reservoir. Lake Vyrnwy, Montgomeryshire.

C. V. Hancock

Alex Behrendt

23, 24. A South Country lake. Two views of the Spring lake, which forms part of the Two Lakes fishery near Romsey, Hampshire.

Alex Behrendt

rise about midday, but the general tendency will be to stay down.

Gradually, as the surface warms, the trout will be more willing to come up and during May and June they are both free-rising and anxious to feed. These are the best fishing months and the trout are in peak condition and full of fight. They are neither ravenous nor over-fed and the fishing is neither too easy nor too difficult.

Summer fishing. During July fly-fishing gradually deteriorates for, as hatches of duns tend to decrease, trout find their food at, or near, the bed of the lake. By the time August comes this tendency has increased and the fishing is therefore generally at its worst. Even so, it is certain that they will feed at some time during the day and a lot depends upon local conditions and the general weather pattern of the summer. There is a lot to be said for a bad summer from the fishing point of view, particularly when the water never gets a chance of warming up too much.

The end of the season. During September the fishing of every lake undergoes a change, for spawning-time is again in sight and the trout gradually tend to leave their normal feeding-places and to congregate in the vicinity of spawning areas or feeder streams up which they will later run in order to spawn. Large trout, which are difficult to locate at other times, are now more in evidence and can often be caught. A great change takes place in feeding habits and there will be active feeding in order to put on condition and to develop the spawn.

The condition factor at this time gradually becomes spawning condition rather than condition suitable for the table and the fish may be soft and slimy. To those who do not know trout well condition is not so obvious, but a trout which is not in good firm condition is rather a horrible fish. A further consideration is that back-end trout fishing can amount to killing off good breeding stock. It can also be a good time to cull out stock.

All these things are worth considering in relation to any given water and it is up to local fishery management to control fishing as local conditions indicate. There are no fixed dates and rule of thumb in nature.

WET-FLY FISHING

I hope that I have sufficiently introduced the reader to the fish, and will now get on to the important matter of catching them. The most effective means of fly-fishing for lake trout is with the wet fly, and in Scotland this fly is something of a tradition among loch fishers, many of whom seldom or never use any other method. It is also the method most in use on artificial waters, such as reservoirs, where there is a "fly only" rule, although in certain high-class waters in southern England the dry fly is more favoured.

The artificial fly. The type of lake or loch fly which has been in effective use for generations is a very curious creation, for in the dry state it resembles nothing in nature and is even tied as a winged insect, which seems very odd for something which is intended to be fished submerged. There are hundreds of different patterns tied in this style, and when American and other patterns are added, the numbers become thousands, and all of them catch trout. The reason for this is that when the fly is wet and fished the appearance changes to something quite different, and the result gives an impression of some form of aquatic creature.

No two fishermen ever agree as to exactly what any single pattern represents and most patterns can be made to convey an impression of more than one form of aquatic life according to the method by which they are fished. A good example of this is the March Brown, which has been said to be capable of representing everything and anything, except a March Brown.

Years ago a very expert Canadian fisherman visited the lochs around my home in the West Highlands and, hearing that he was doing remarkably well, I sought him out and discovered that his fly-box contained nothing but North American patterns. I asked whether he had tried local patterns and he replied that he never changed, for he knew what his own flies looked like.

A secret of successful wet-fly fishing is, surely, for the individual fisherman to decide, by trial, error and experience, which patterns represent which main groups of aquatic life according to his own style of fishing. By "main groups" I mean nymphs, pupae, beetles, small fish, and surface creatures such as insects, spiders and caterpillars. Having decided this matter it is up to the fisherman to fish his selections in a reasonably natural manner.

Many people, who have not given much thought to this subject, put up a selection of different patterns and hope for the best. The result is, probably, that one of the team of flies will be fishing in a natural manner, and taking fish, while the rest are doing no good. How often does it happen that every fish comes to the tail-fly or perhaps the bob-fly, while the others are ignored, and flies which are not fishing in a reasonably natural manner may cause alarm which is often manifest by what is known as "short rising" or "coming short". So would we "come short" if offered a sardine served up as a mutton chop.

I have said that it is for the individual to make up his mind with regard to this problem, since no two anglers work their flies in exactly the same manner. If two men of equal skill are set to fish the same identical cast of flies one will almost certainly do far better than the other, for the flies have been more suited to his style of fishing. I can therefore only describe my own approach, which may serve as a general guide.

Nymphs and Chironomid pupae. I would hazard a guess that about half of the total of all trout caught on the wet fly have been deluded into thinking that they were taking something in this class, and that about the same proportion of wet-fly patterns are capable of giving an impression of nymphs or pupae. There are many species, but they all behave in much the same way which is not difficult to understand.

Both types progress from the bed of the lake to the surface in a series of rises and falls. They swim upwards, stop, sink back a bit, swim upwards again and sink again, gradually making the grade. When they arrive near the surface they swim slowly along under water before coming to the surface.

Fishing the artificial. This whole action can quite easily be produced with a fly rod: cast the flies and allow them to sink, then slowly raise the rod-point about a foot and slowly lower it again. Repeat this and gradually bring the flies to within about a foot of the surface and then slowly retrieve them at about the same depth under the surface.

Cast-sink-raise-lower-raise-retrieve: it is no more difficult than that. It is "sink-and-draw" followed by a normal retrieve. The "sink-and-draw" part brings the fish up, and the retrieve catches them. If the fish are already close to the surface, the ordinary cast and retrieve catches them, as every wet-fly fisherman knows, but even then the complete action is better for it conveys a natural impression.

Where trout are shy, as they often are in hard-fished reservoirs, it is a good idea to fish in this manner with a single fly on a tapered cast, for this allows for more delicate fishing and the fine taper of the cast allows the fly to sink quickly. A single fly well fished is better than a team more clumsily handled and droppers are always liable to cling to the cast and to create some degree of wash at the knot.

A further development is the fishing of a single weighted fly on a greased line and tapered cast which is also partly greased. The idea is that the fly should sink rapidly for a foot or so and it is then worked slowly along at about the same depth in order to represent the nymph searching for something to hold on to. This is another method which is worth trying on well-fished reservoirs but, of course, it can only be really effective when trout are high in the water.

Fly Patterns. Useful patterns which I use are: Invicta, Greenwell, Golden Olive, Blae and Black, Woodcock and Hare's Ear, Teal and Green, Grouse and Green, but a lot depends upon the part of the country in which one is fishing. I am not quite so independent of local patterns as was my Canadian friend and am generally ready to give anything a trial. Flies which are fished as nymphs should not be heavily dressed and I often strip bought flies down a bit. A little stripping is also worth trying when fish are coming short. There are also a number of special nymph tyings which appear to be more accurate imitations of the natural and these may be worth trying, provided that the actual species of nymph upon which trout are feeding is known.

Water-boatmen swim steadily towards the surface at a rather acute angle and at a speed which is faster than nymphs. This suits the simple action of casting out and retrieving which is generally practised, particularly by beginners, and probably accounts for the popularity of the Zulu as a lake fly. Another good artificial of this type is the Coch-y-bonddu, and I am inclined to think that Hardy's Favourite, which is an excellent lake fly, comes into the same category. It certainly always seems to do well when fished in simple fashion.

Small fish may be at any depth and progress rather jerkily on more or less the same level. The rod-point is kept low and the retrieve done by 'hand twisting'', which produces the jerky movement. Take the line in the thumb and forefinger of the spare hand, palm towards you. The fingers and thumb are pointing upwards and pivoting from the wrist, which is stationary. Draw the line back with the thumb and forefinger to the full extent of the pivot from the wrist. Bring the remaining three fingers down on to the line and twist downwards while releasing the thumb and forefinger. This will bring the thumb and forefinger into position to take hold again. Follow these movements with a rod in the hand and the method becomes apparent. It is a very useful method which can be carried out at varying speeds, and it is worth while to acquire the habit of it.

Useful patterns to represent small fish are Alexandra, Teal and Black, Teal and Silver, Butcher.

Surface insects (*Duns, spinners, sedges and land-bred species*). These are found at or near the surface and are represented by the top-dropper or bob-fly, which should be made to work on the surface when fishing out the cast. The fishing of the bob-fly is important, for it can be most productive. It takes a fairly long rod and short line to make the bob dance along the surface as it should do, but it is generally possible to give it a short innings just before the flies are lifted for a fresh cast. A slight pause is always a good thing before lifting, for it is extraordinary how often a fish will take as the flies are leaving the water.

Useful patterns for bob-flies are Woodcock and Yellow, Black Pennell, and most of the patterns which I have given as nymphs when these are tied in the style known as "parachute" with the wings sticking out sideways. A good large, dry, hackle fly also makes a good bob when the flies can be fished on a short line, as do the Red, or Soldier, Palmer, the Black Spider, and the March Brown Spider.

The above are all standard patterns available anywhere. Better imitations can be obtained under most headings, but it must be remembered that the closer the tying is to nature the more natural must be the manner in which it must be fished. The fisherman can get away with something which conveys a general impression, but it is not so easy to get away with an imitation of nature.

One sometimes makes curious discoveries, particularly in the case of nymphs, and I recently found trout taking both the Invicta and the Greenwell as nymphs of the Mayfly.

In addition to patterns which I have mentioned there are some which are "patent safeties", which come in handy when one does not know what else to do about it. These are Teal and Red, Peter Ross, Claret and Mallard, March Brown and the popular Worm-fly—but the best "patent safety" is the old warrior which has taken many fish. It may have lost most of its identity, but it has acquired charm. This is one of the curiosities of fishing, for I have often tried to produce the same effect by stripping down a fly but it does not work and, apparently, the stripping has to be done by the trout.

Change of method. I have described some of the basic ways of fishing the wet fly, but there is much more which can be done by varying pace, depth, and the working of the fly which any fisherman can try for himself according to his individual touch. It is always necessary to consider the conditions when fiddling with flies, for the existing ripple or wave is also working the flies. Thus it may be a good thing to work the flies quite actively in a light ripple but to do so in a good wave might result in an action which is too accentuated.

The effect of light. In bright weather the water is full of silver, while on dark days it contains nothing but lead. In between these extremes there is both silver and gold in varying proportions. I have not suddenly become romantic, but am thinking about the effect of light upon the myriads of tiny air bubbles which water contains. Normally we do not see these air bubbles and their effect, for we are looking from the wrong angle, but they are very prominent through the window of an observation tank.

There is a very excellent observation window at the Pitlochry salmon ladder in Perthshire which is well worth studying under varying conditions of light, particularly when there are smolts in the tank. Smolts are not unlike trout in habit and, on a bright day, they are to be seen to be attracted by everything which carries a silver bubble. When the gold effect is present they are still attracted but rather less so. When there is little light the smolts inspect solid things such as bits of stick or leaves.

There is silver or gold tinsel in the tying of many flies and such patterns must surely appear out of place and unnatural on a dull day, when there is neither silver nor gold in the water and everything has a dull look. It is possible that the unusual may attract, and sometimes this does happen, particularly when the trout are themselves dour and dull, but as a general rule it is safer to present that which looks natural. If this is agreed it becomes a reasonable preliminary to look at the sky, decide that it is not sufficiently bright for silver, and tie on a Teal and Red instead of a Peter Ross. At the same time it would be a good idea to exchange the Silver Butcher for one with a gold body and there are, of course, many variations of this theme.

This is the sort of thing which an experienced fisherman does without, perhaps, being able to give on-the-spot reasons. Sometimes there are reasons and sometimes there is just a feeling, or sense of the natural, which has been acquired during the course of much fishing. Sometimes, of course, even the experienced expert does not get the right answer, for there is still much to learn about fish, and fishing would lack interest were this otherwise. Part of the charm of fishing is that one is always experimenting and learning.

Fly sizes. All fly-fishermen agree that the size of fly is important and most will change when there is good reason to believe that the size which is being fished is at fault. Short-rising fish make a change of size necessary and when small fish rise and larger fish do not it is often an indication that the size of fly is wrong. Some years ago I published my own guide to fly sizes and, as I have heard of nothing better, I offer it again here:

1. When the light is bright use large flies. The reason for this is that fish do not see well in a bright light. Give them something which they can see and hope that they will not see too much.

2. When the water is deep and the fish are not showing use large flies, for lake trout will not bother to rise out of deep water unless there is an incentive which looks to be worth the effort.

3. When the light is dull use small flies. Trout see well in a poor light and will see a small fly. They will also see a large fly, but they will see it too well, and decide that there is something wrong about it.

4. When the water is shallow use small flies. Trout see near objects very well and should therefore not be shown too much.

5. In doubtful conditions of light and water start small and change up if necessary. It is always safer to start small, and there is no truth in the big fly for big fish idea. Big fish are less easily fooled than small fish.

It is impossible to be definite about actual fly sizes for these vary so greatly in different parts of the country and what would be large in one locality would be small in another. Loch Leven sizes, for example, are smaller than those in use on Highland lochs. Two sizes in each pattern with a difference of two sizes in between them are enough to carry, and good tackle-makers know the sizes for different localities.

The tendency nowadays is towards small flies and these can be fished on a finer cast than large flies. It is largely the size of fly which determines the thickness of the cast, for cast and flies have to be balanced. Small flies do not fish properly on a thick cast nor do large flies fish on a fine cast. Large flies sink better and faster than do small flies.

Practical application. The fisherman, armed with rod, tackle and all this information, arrives at the water. He may see fish moving, but the chances are that he will see nothing but water. There may be nothing to indicate what is happening below the surface, and he has to fish in order to find out what the trout are doing. That is part of the interest in lake fishing. Weather conditions may give some guidance, for in warm weather the nymphs might be tried first. Under colder conditions one might start by trying the water-boatman or small fish techniques. Whatever is done should be done on some form of reasoning and not just "chuck-and-chance-it", which is a poor way of fishing.

Start shallow and go down deeper. Give each method a fair trial until the best one is found, then stick to it until it becomes apparent that the trout are doing something else. Method is more important than fly pattern.

The lake fisherman is assisted by ripple and wave, which help to conceal both man and his efforts from the trout, and that is why good baskets are often made when there is a considerable "sea" running. But wave, or not, it is very necessary for the flies to land lightly upon the water without the slightest splash or disturbance of any kind. Should there be an accidental splash it is better to retrieve the flies normally and cast again than to pick them immediately off the water as one is tempted to do. The trick of light casting is to aim slightly above the water and to shoot some line through the rod rings.

It is every bit as important for the flies to be lifted quietly off the water for another cast to be made and there is a fatal trick of lifting the flies with a flick which affects us all at times. This flick will scare fish away as quickly as anything does and the best cure for it is to take a short rest.

There is no hurry or bustle about the sport of fishing. Modern man is forced to rush about in order to survive, but this is not a case of survival and the fisherman must attune himself to the unhurried ways of the trout. Flogging away at the water is both unproductive and tiring and the flies will only catch fish when they are in the water. The less they are whisked through the air the better, for they are dried during the process and will not sink properly.

Hooking a trout. It remains to say a few words about the hooking of lake trout which many people, with reason, find so difficult. I can not do better than to quote what I wrote, in *Loch Trout*:

"Whatever the method of fishing there is only one occasion upon which to strike a fish and that is before putting it into the basket. It should then be given a smart 'dod on the heid' with a blunt instrument. A hook is not a blunt instrument. It is not designed for striking.

A hook, whether it be a fish hook or a meat hook, is drawn into whatever substance is required to be hooked.

Draw in a hook—draw in a gaff—fishing never demands jerks."

DRY-FLY FISHING

There are some forms of loch and lake which compel me to fish the dry fly, for it seems almost like sacrilege to do anything else. It may be some lochan among the hills which has this effect, or perhaps a small sheet of water, among rhododendrons, which was once a gravel pit. It is not so much a question of size as of character, and in such places I will go to an immense amount of trouble in order to present a dry fly to a rising trout. When the effort is successful I am very pleased about it and the fact that I could probably have taken the fish out easier, and quicker, with a wet fly is neither here nor there. On suitable water the dry fly is a most fascinating method of fishing. It has also got to be interesting in order to be worth while.

The dry fly can be fished with some measure of success on every loch, lake or reservoir, and I have known men who never fished in any other way if they could possibly help it. There does not, however, seem to me to be much fun in sailing a dry fly about in the manner known as "fishing the water" when there is no obvious rise to anything in particular, and when the trout are below the surface. The trout, too, in very many lakes are not in the least selective where surface insects are concerned, for lakes seldom produce any great abundance and variety of insect life. Trout are as selective in their feeding as they can afford to be and on many Highland lochs they will take almost any pattern of dry fly, irrespective of what may be on the water. They like something which looks large and juicy and will break off in order to take it.

Lakes vary in this as in all other respects, and there are waters where the trout are almost as selective of pattern and critical of presentation as those of the chalk stream.

When to fish dry. Although the great majority of British lakes are more suitable for wet fly than for dry, every lake presents opportunities for the dry fly on occasion, and these opportunities are worth taking for they often produce the best fish of the day. The fish which is seen to be rising steadily in some favoured spot is generally a good fish, and not the sort of character to be easily fooled. A team of wet flies thrown at him may put him down, whereas he may accept a floater even when it may not be a representation of the particular insect upon which he is feeding. Again, there are often beds of reeds and trout are to be found among reeds. It is difficult to fish wet flies among reeds, but a single dry fly can be dropped almost anywhere. Finally there is the flat calm which descends upon the water at some time during many fishing days, and there is often a good rise during a flat calm. A single wet fly will take trout provided that it is fished slowly and very carefully, but I have often done better with the dry fly under such conditions.

For these reasons I like to have a spare rod in a boat, set up ready for an immediate change to dry fly, and when shore fishing I always carry a spare reel with greased line in my bag. In a boat it is a clumsy business changing reels and tackle and one is tempted to miss a good opportunity in order to save trouble. It is a different matter when on one's feet and able to move freely.

Practical application. The waters of a lake are generally clear and, as I have already mentioned, they are free from sub-surface disturbance. It is therefore essential to drop the floating fly very carefully and gently at the end of a fine cast, free from curls and twists which a stream often corrects. Use should be made of any wind there is in order to drift the fly over the fish and the cast should therefore be made slightly upwind of the rise. The use of oil in order to help the fly to float is best avoided, for a skin of oil is liable to hang on the water around the fly, and I have noticed that lake trout will not take a fly when there is a suggestion of oil.[1]

It is not difficult to cast a dry fly to a lake trout, but what is difficult is the picking of the fly off the water when it is not taken the first time. If the fly is towed away from the spot where it is floating it leaves a wake behind it, and if it is lifted straight off the water there will be a commotion of some sort, and in neither case will it be worth casting again to the same fish. That is why dry-fly fishing in a flat calm is difficult, for it is a case of only one shot at a fish and it is useless to fire a second barrel. When the fly is fished on the ripple there is a breeze to take it well clear of the fish and it should not be lifted until it is really well clear.

Drag. A curious but understandable difference exists as between river and lake over the matter of drag which, as everyone knows, the river trout are very sensitive about. Flies on a river are borne along by the current and the trout itself is in the same current. It is little wonder that the fish knows exactly how the fly should behave. On a lake a fly is either borne along by its own flutterings or by the wind, and as the trout is not itself in the wind the movements of the fly are unpredictable. Within reason, therefore, the dry-fly fisherman on a lake is not much bothered about drag and may even, with advantage, apply a little gentle drag. A few twitches given to a floating fly will often bring a fish up. The fly must never be moved against the wind, for that would be a form of drag which any trout would object to.

Hooking a trout. Hooking a fish on the dry fly is more difficult on a lake than a river, for the fish may come to the fly from any angle and a strike at a rise is just as likely to remove the fly from the mouth of the trout as otherwise. The only method which I have found to work reasonably consistently is to watch the line and raise the rod when the line moves forward. This movement of the line surely indicates that the fly is in the mouth of the fish.

It is not easy to concentrate attention upon the line unless it is coloured white, which exerts much the same influence on the eye

---

[1] But the modern silicone floatants obviate this—Ed.

L

as a chalk line does on the eye of a hen. It is almost impossible not to see what a white line is doing, and white is a very good colour which is easily seen from above and not easily seen from below. The camouflage effect of white on water is shown by the white or light colour of the undersides of both fish and birds which swim. Such a line takes getting used to for at first it looks as if it would scare every trout into the next parish, and I well remember the reactions of the manager of a tackle shop, years ago, when I demanded a white line. I thought that he was going to dial 999, but the white line is now widely accepted by the tackle trade.

Fly patterns. I have never found any reason or value for special lake patterns and all the well-known river patterns are suitable except for the matter of size, for lake trout seem to be attracted by a somewhat larger size of fly than the trout of the river. A case of value for swallow perhaps, but lake sizes are always larger in all types of fly and the experience of generations of fishermen show this to be correct. When I am in doubt about what fly the fish are taking, and that happens often enough, I throw a Black Spider. That is not likely to be the fly that is being taken, but few lake trout seem inclined to refuse it.

SHORE V. BOAT FISHING

Fishing any form of lake from the bank or shore, wading or otherwise, is a matter of fishing the shore line or such shore reefs as may exist and, as has already been explained, the shore line is always a good place for trout. In some ways bank fishing is akin to river fishing, but it differs from river fishing in several important respects.

In the first place there is seldom much in the way of cover available and the fisherman must therefore depend upon background to conceal his movements, and if he can blend with his background he is not very easily seen. If he stands out in contrast to his background, or if he has no background other than the sky, he will be very obvious to the trout. Besides using background he must also fish a sufficiently long line to keep him outside what is called "the trout's window", but this does not mean any form of real distance casting, as the surface ripple or wave conceals a great deal from the trout.

The shore fisherman must move quietly and with great caution, for clumsy movement causes vibration under water where there is no natural underwater disturbance. Again, all fish are not facing the same way, or rather in the same direction, and there is no question of coming up behind them, for some, at least, are pretty certain to be facing the fisherman.

Boat fishing changes the whole basic situation. Fish are not frightened by a well-managed boat and the boat therefore affords the fisherman the cover he requires, so long as he does not leave his cover by standing up. In a boat he is moving smoothly and silently, unless vibration is created by clumsy movement within the boat.

Shore fishing is, perhaps, the more interesting form of lake fishing and gives a greater sense of personal achievement, for it depends upon personal knowledge and effort which is not shared with whoever is managing the boat. Lake fishing can be rather a poor form of sport when all the thinking and work is done by a professional gillie and the angler merely casts as directed. Shore fishing is also the best approach to lake fishing for it is the more natural approach. I will therefore consider it first.

SHORE FISHING

When shore fishing I fish a single fly on a tapered cast with a tapered line having the heavy part of the taper greased. This is a personal choice and I do not lay it down as "correct". Many wet-fly men do not feel confident without their team of flies, and confidence is of great importance in fishing. I have never, myself, found that the number of flies fished has made much difference to the result, and in my youth it was not unusual to put down a "hatch" of eight or even more. I fish a single fly in this case because I doubt whether a team can be fished well enough on a longish line to make up for the trouble they cause.

Choice of beat. A shore fisherman selects his beat with due regard to the wind, but wind is feckless and unreliable. In shore fishing, too, one has to cast in all directions at times, and also to cast in places where there is obstruction to the back cast. There are also such things as weeds to cause trouble with and without assistance from a hooked fish. Droppers and bobs get into trouble sooner or later and are liable to take one's attention away from the fish.

Wind is one factor which must be taken into consideration when making a final choice as to where to commence fishing, and another is background. A high bank may be easy to cast from but there may be no background other than the sky and the fisherman will be very obvious to the fish. It is generally better to fish from water-level, and better still to be in the water, even if only a yard or two from the shore. This means wading, and there are points about that which are worth attention.

Wading. Wading in a lake is safe enough if done with care, but it can be dangerous if done carelessly. If one takes a toss in a river the stream helps one to get out, but to fall into deep water in a lake, when wearing waders, may mean staying there. There is no reason for such a thing to happen for it is nearly always possible to see the bottom and a foot should never be put down without knowing where it is going. A wading staff is a good thing so long as it is not furnished with one of those horrible iron spikes with bank-hook attached. Such a thing grates against every stone and sends out a warning to every fish within range. A strong, plain stick without a ferrule is much better and should be attached to the person by a lanyard of some sort so that it can be dropped when not required. A long-handled landing-net can be used in much the same way, but it is rather a clumsy thing.

This grating against stones which alarms fish also applies to hob-nails on waders, and felt soles are better for lake fishing, where it is not a case of standing up against a heavy volume of water. Rubber soles are just asking for trouble.

There is always a temptation for the shore fisher to go straight at or into the water and having got out as far as possible to cast out as far as he possibly can. The man in the boat does just the opposite, for he tends to hug the shore and to cast into the bank. The shore line is a favourite resort of trout and even in hard-fished reservoirs where the fish may have become somewhat bank-shy it is unwise to think that they must be well out. There is always a chance, and more than a chance, that a good fish may be lying right in at the shore. Those large reservoir trout do come in close, and often stay in close, until driven out by fishing and movement on the bank. The larger the trout, the more it seems to be attracted to the shore, particularly in the evening, when I have often had good fish while wading well out and casting into the shore.

It follows that the fisherman should mount his rod well back from the water and then fish his way to the water and into it. Commence fishing well back from the bank, as a river fisherman often does, and fish out the water over twenty yards of bank up to about five yards from the shore. Move forward and do the same thing with the next five yards out, and so on until the desired starting point has been reached. A patient process, but no waste of time when it is remembered that a single fish which bolts in panic takes all the others with it. Quiet, slow progress into the water will cause fish to go into deeper water, but they will not be seriously frightened, and I have often caught trout which I have seen to move off in front of me.

Method of fishing. Having got into position, either on the shore or in the water, the fisherman moves slowly along casting methodically from the shore outwards. It is this slow, methodical, progress which gives him the advantage over the boats, for he covers most fish while the man on a drift only covers an occasional fish and drifts over many. Some, in fact, never get a chance to see the flies, particularly if the bed of the lake is broken up by boulders or rocks. Trout are often on the wrong side of a stone, but the shore fisherman shows them the fly from several angles.

When a reef is being fished the reef itself should be explored first, then the edge of the reef, and finally the deep water outside: a matter of perhaps half a dozen casts for each step forward. At the edge of a reef there are often shelves at varying depths and these

FIG. 37. *Bank Fishing. A typical inshore reef, with deep water beyond and a background of vegetation.*

are good lies for trout. It therefore pays to sink the fly well at the edge of a reef.

It is generally best to keep to the same length of line as far as possible, for altering the distance of the cast may result in "lining" a fish and that causes panic. A fish which is seen should be covered immediately and the risk taken of another fish being close in.

On a popular reservoir, where there are other rods fishing, it may not be possible to move far and perhaps moving along will not be possible at all. Having got into position the angler has to wait for trout to come to him, rather than go in search of the trout. This is not really so tedious as it sounds, for the large trout in such places seem to have a habit of patrolling, and one of these may arrive at any moment. In any case such a fish is worth waiting for, and I often wonder what Blagdon and Chew regulars would think of the wee trout of Highland lochs.

I have spoken of "lining" fish, which is a thing that the shore fisherman is very apt to do. Trout are seldom cast-shy but they are always reel-line-shy. It is therefore a good thing to use the longest cast which conditions permit in order to keep the reel-line as far as possible from the fly. In a favourable wind which is not too strong, I go as far as a twelve-foot cast, while in wilder conditions and a blustery wind seven or eight feet are enough to handle. This works out both ways, for when the long cast can be fished the surface ripple will be slight and the need for it apparent. Conditions which call for a short cast also produce a good surface wave which helps to conceal the reel-line.

I would finally stress the value of absence of hurry in shore fishing. There is nothing to be gained by flogging miles of shore line. Rather like the dog which rushes about as if the devil was after him and finds little, except by accident, while the close worker, who quarters his ground, fills the game bag.

When the day is spent in looking at waves and ripples, polaroid glasses are of great value.

BOAT FISHING

Boats vary as do lakes, and the lake fisher has to be prepared to cope with all sorts from the well-found craft of a well-managed fishery to the semi-derelict contraption which can only be made to float by the continual use of the rusty paint tin which has been provided as a baler. Having experienced everything in the shape of boats I always carry my own baler, and before I set forth I check whether the hole in the bottom of the boat, which generally exists for the purpose of letting water out, has been properly closed with a cork or other means. I also carry a length of strong cord with which to secure that which is insecure, and particularly the oars when the boat is fitted with rowlocks and not thole-pins. Oars slip out of rowlocks when the former are dropped, as they often have to be during a day's fishing. It is best to secure them in some way which does not make it possible to lift the rowlock out of its socket and drop it overboard.

The best way to regard a boat is as a means of closely approaching fish which could not be otherwise reached. This is an old-established principle of lake fishing based upon the fact that fish are not frightened by the boat itself but only by the occupants thereof. If full value is to be got out of boat fishing the fisherman should endeavour to make himself part of the boat by sitting quietly and not showing himself any more than can be helped. It is a matter of keeping to cover. If one man stands in the boat and fishes a long line while his companion is seated and fishing a short line, a little thought will show that he who is standing must be keeping the trout away from the other.[1]

Apart from this matter of standing it is not very good fishing manners for one man to fish a line which is much longer than that of his companion, for the reel line is a factor in keeping fish away from a boat. It is, of course permissible to lengthen line for some special purpose such as to cover a rising fish.

I continually stress the need for quiet movement in lake fishing and it is very necessary to avoid such noise as is made in contact with the boat. Such things as foot shuffling and knocking out a pipe cause a form of vibration which is conveyed over a wide area of water, and in order to prove this it is only necessary to try the old gillies' trick of stamping the feet in order to turn a hooked fish and stop it from running under the boat.

Fishing the drift. Boat fishing is largely a matter of drift fishing or "fishing the drift" as it is called, and the man at the oars is said to be "holding the drift". The boat is taken up wind, turned sideways to the wind, and allowed to drift with it.

[1] Standing up in a boat, especially in a strong wind, can also be dangerous—Ed.

When fishing the drift the conventional wet-fly cast of three flies is perfectly satisfactory. The team consists of the tail-fly, the middle-dropper, and the top-dropper, which is the bob-fly. The cast is generally three yards in length with the bob about 2 feet 6 inches from the butt of the cast and the middle-dropper half way between that and the tail-fly. The two best flies are the tail and the bob. The dropper generally does least good and the reason may be that fish which come to it see the main part of the cast. I also strongly suspect that a fish coming to the dropper sometimes fouls the cast, although I have never been able to see this happen.

The length of line which is fished on a drift depends upon the speed of the drift, and should only be just sufficient to allow the flies to sink before commencing the retrieve. Thus on a slow drift a very short line only is required, while a faster drift calls for a somewhat longer throw. In no case should more line than is necessary to sink the flies be thrown, for the less line there is out the less there will be for the fish to see. Another consideration is the fishing of the bob-fly on or about the surface which can only be done well on a short line. The length of the rod also has a bearing on this matter, for the longer the rod the better can the bob-fly be worked. That is why the older school of loch fishermen still favour long rods and I, myself, like a rod of not less than ten feet for boat fishing.

When fishing the drift it is important to remember that the man in the boat is moving towards the flies and he is moving down wind. If, therefore, the flies are fished too fast, and the retrieve is made too fast, the flies will be moving up wind. Sub-surface wet flies can be moved against the wind for they are below the water which the wind affects, but no form of surface fly, be it dry fly or bob, should move against the wind, for to do so would be unnatural. The combination of down-wind drift and up-wind retrieve really results in the flies remaining in much the same place, although it does not look like that.

Whichever method of retrieve is fished the flies should be brought right up to the boat before being lifted for another cast, and the lift should be slow for a trout often takes as the flies are being lifted.

Netting a trout. When a trout is hooked it should be guided round to the up-wind side of the boat. There are two reasons for this: the first is that the fish is less likely to run under the boat which is drifting away from it, and the second is that the water down-wind, and in front of the drift, is not disturbed.

The landing-net for boat use should have a long handle in order to enable the fish to be brought to the net without having to lean over the side of the boat. In the event of two fish being on at the same time the trick is to net the upper fish, seize it with the hand, and then net the lower.

Tactics. The tactics of boat fishing depend greatly upon the wind, but the wind must not be allowed to dictate the tactics. It often happens that a boat will drift along very nicely and without any attention, but much time may be spent in drifting over water where there are no fish. The drift must be held to the right line, for even a few feet of deviation can make all the difference, and it is better for one rod to fish where there are trout than for two to fish where there are none. When there is no third person to hold the drift this not unattractive duty makes a change from casting.

The wind must not be allowed to dictate the speed of the drift either, for a fast drift is of little value and leaves much water un-fished. The speed can be held by the oars and slowed by hanging something over the side of the boat. There is nothing much better for the purpose than a camper's canvas bucket made fast to one of

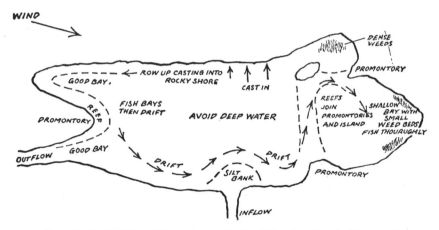

Fig. 38. *Boat Fishing. The angler's tactics should be adapted to the direction of the wind.*

the thwarts. An anchor is also useful, for the boat can then be anchored at favoured spots in order to fish such places thoroughly, but anchoring is not permitted on some lakes in the general interest.

Certain combinations of wind and sun can be very troublesome owing to shadow. Shadow is not very apparent on ripples and waves, but it is there nevertheless, and the trout see it even when the fisherman does not. The worst case is when the wind is blowing straight out of the sun, for the sun is then directly behind the rod, and it is hardly worth while fishing under such conditions: better wait until the angle changes. The same factor of shadow applies in shore fishing, but the shore fisherman is better able to control his shadow.

Fishing alone in a boat is a delightful form of sport and for this it is sometimes better to drift the boat stern first with a bucket attached to the bow. The fisherman can sit with an oar at each side of him and facing the way in which the boat is drifting. A touch at either oar will take him where he wants to go and he can hunt for trout.

When a drift is finished and the boat is being taken up wind it is common practice to trail flies behind the boat. Many trout are caught by this somewhat doubtful method, which requires no skill, and which provides little sport, for a trout so hooked is about half drowned by the time it is brought in. It is bad for both line and cast, which may become twisted or kinked. A better method is to cast a long line sideways and allow the flies to come round as far as the wash of the boat. This method can be great fun when rowing up a broken shore line, for the flies can be thrown into all sorts of hidey-holes and many a good trout is the result.

CHAPTER VI

RAINBOW TROUT
by
W. T. Sargeaunt

NATURAL HISTORY

The rainbow trout is a native of the Pacific shore of North America and has been found from the Bering Sea in the north to Lower California. Some rainbows have settled down as inhabitants of lakes, spawning in the carrier streams, others spend part of their lives in the sea coming into rivers to spawn, being then known as Steelheads.[1] Some spend their life in rivers, others travel from rivers to estuaries when they are known as coastal rainbows.

Mr. Leney of the Surrey Trout Farm, who has had, I suppose, more experience than anyone in the acclimatization of rainbows, tells me the first English stocks came from a hatchery on the McCloud River running into Lake Shasta. Those were the days when it was popular to give specific names freely, and fish out of the lake were known as *Salmo shasta* and those out of the river *S. stonei*. No one has ever been able to establish any constant and certain method of distinguishing these from each other or any other rainbows. They did, however, breed in the autumn, unlike most rainbow which breed in the spring. This has since been established to be due to water temperature, and introduced into the Derbyshire Wye they revert to spring spawning.

The demand eventually exceeded the supply, and eggs were used from early spawning seagoing coastal rainbows, so that one can now speak only of a *shasta* type. It was hoped that the *shasta*, being land-locked, would have lost its seagoing habits, but this does not appear to have been so and if put into rivers they tend to set off seawards, never coming back.

Recently a variety called *kamloops*, first described in 1892, from a lake of that name in British Columbia, have been used. These feed on a land-locked species of salmon called koakanee, which grows to only about half a pound, while *kamloops* have been recorded up to 40 lb. They spawn in the tributaries in the spring when the ice has left the lakes and the water temperature in the rivers reaches 40°F.

Maiden *kamloops* can easily be distinguished from the *shasta* type as the former are without the rainbow markings, having a steel-black head and silvery body. All rainbows can be distinguished from brown trout as the tail of the former is thickly spotted. That of the latter never carries more than a few spots, and that rarely.

Rainbows reach maturity and spawn in three or four years, and

[1] Cut-throat trout in seagoing stage are also known as Steelheads.

the size reached depends on the food available in those years. After they have once spawned they grow little more, and if the food supply is small few will survive the first spawning.[1]

Rainbow waters. With two exceptions,[2] rainbows flourish only in alkaline water. They do well in large reservoirs alongside brown trout. They are most successful in small artificial waters if stocked alone and the water is kept alkaline by introducing lime. In rivers they have only stayed in an occasional stream, chiefly in the Chilterns and in the lower reaches of the Derbyshire Wye. Where they succeed they squeeze out the brown trout.

The Derbyshire Wye is a tributary of the Derwent and I think they have settled in the Wye because only a few fish care to penetrate into the Derwent. Those that do so grow large. Similarly in the Chess, a tributary of the Colne, the rainbows have driven out the browns, but few penetrate into the Colne. The Thorney Weir Fishery in the Colne was stocked, but they never stayed.

It will be seen, therefore, than an angler will find rainbows alone in only one or two rivers, and in, I think, an increasing number of small gravel pits. In great reservoirs they will be fished for alongside brown trout. But one observes that some rods invariably catch a higher proportion of rainbows than others. Most writers either ignore the differences or remark on them without comment, but their feeding habits differ substantially from those of the brown trout.

The rainbow has four years to grow, and if it can't make the weight in those four years it probably perishes after the first spawning. One would therefore expect it to have a prodigious appetite, and so it has. That is why it is better to stock with rainbows alone in small waters, and why it has in places driven out the brown trout.

The advantages for the angler are that there are few times in the day where rainbows are not on the feed. Studies of what rainbows feed on have been made, particularly in New Zealand and Ireland. Unlike brown trout, they generally feed in shoals.

LARGE RESERVOIRS

The food of rainbows. In rivers, and to some extent in small reservoirs, it is usually possible to see what the fish are feeding on, but in large reservoirs it is very largely a question of knowledge gained by long experience. One rainbow fisherman I know, who fishes a large reservoir stocked with both species, keeps a map of all rainbows caught on which he records the month, fly, hook size, depth fished and wind direction. He has kept this map now for four years, and in his fishing diary he records the result of autopsies. He tells

[1] Authority, Charles M. Mottley, Aquatic Biologist, Division of Fishery Biology, USA. Sir Robert Saundby has stated that no rainbows in Britain live more than four years, but does not give the reason.

[2] Loch Shore in Eire and a stream near Haslemere in Surrey.

me he now knows where and how deep the rainbows will be feeding in accordance with the time of year and the direction of the wind, and what they will be feeding on. In some lakes they may specialize wholly on one species of food. The Inland Fisheries Trust in Eire report that on most of their waters the rainbows feed on midges and gnats, turning to duns, spinners and sedges when these are on the water. But in Lake Labe, says the report, "the big rainbows are feeding amongst the stones on crayfish, which suggests that big flies fished really deep are more likely to be successful than wet flies fished (as they usually are) only a foot or so below the surface".

Tactics. I have no very extensive knowledge of fishing for rainbows in large reservoirs in England, most of my fishing for them in this country having been in small reservoirs and the Chess and Derbyshire Wye. But such experience as I have has convinced me that catching rainbows is largely a question of keeping on fishing even when fish are not showing up, and of knowing the right depth to fish and the right size of fly.

The angler must, of course, be ready to take advantage of any surface feeding which takes place on midges and gnats, day-flies (including on some waters the Mayfly), sedges and demoiselle dragon-flies. But surface feeding will be more easy to observe on smaller waters and may be left to the next section. This does not mean that rainbows in great waters do not feed on such things. There are few days when there will not be a time—sometimes no more than a few minutes, sometimes for hours on end—when they are not feeding on midge pupae. And quite often a big, stiff-hackled floating fly fished at a venture will give results, just as it will on a small reservoir. But it is more usual on large deep waters to use large flies, fished deep.

Flies. Skues said something to the effect that he would never fish again if he did not believe that the trout took his flies for the natural insects they were feeding on at the time. But, of course, he thought Halford absurd for refusing, in his later years, to use the Gold-ribbed Hare's Ear. He believed that the trout took the Hare's Ear for the Medium Olive dun, possibly in the act of hatching. My theory is something like this: if you want to catch a fish feeding on, say water-boatmen, it is better to use a fly on which you have caught fish which were feeding on water-boatmen, rather than go away and try to make an exact copy.

I mention the water-boatman (*Corixa*) because I am inclined to think that rainbows take it more often than brown trout. It is an active creature and rainbows are perhaps more energetic. I have so often taken trout with *Corixae* in their stomachs on a large thinly-dressed Wickham's Fancy, that I think there is evidence that they look similar to the trout. It should be allowed to sink and then be recovered quickly, and is especially effective when an on-shore wind is stirring up the *Corixa* population.

I often wonder whether, as I have frequently heard argued, the Teal and Red is taken for a shrimp and whether Peter Ross owes its success to being an even better representation. Some lakes in which I am interested were stocked with shrimps for several years, but they never became really established and we gave it up. Peter Ross is not now in such demand. Of course, this is no evidence, but it is suggestive.

C. F. Walker's dressing of the water louse has a mixed grey and brown hare's ear body ribbed with silver tinsel and a grey-brown partridge hackle. This is not far from the silver-bodied March Brown, which I think rainbows take for *Asellus*.

I think anglers fishing Lake Labe might well try a pattern known as the Missionary. It is very similar in general effect to a New Zealand fly, Craig's Night Time, which was tied to represent the crayfish. The Missionary has been used with great effect in New Zealand as a substitute, although the actual patterns are quite different. The dressing is:

Body: White wool, pulled, and spun on.

Tail: A tuft of white cock's hackle.

Wings: Black turkey tail feather with strips of dark teal along the side, extending well beyond the hook.

Hackle: White cock's.

The old Black Palmer of our childhood keeps on reappearing under other names, such as Black and Peacock Spider and Peacock and Black. But it is a reasonable representation of the Alder larva and of the snail *Limnaea stagnalis*, whose shell is very fragile when partly grown. There is a variety found in the Cam, a rainbow river, called *fragilis*, whose shell is even thinner.

With these five flies:

Wickham } Missionary }	Sizes 7 or 8[1]
Peter Ross	4 and 5[1]
Silver-bodied March Brown	3 and 4[1]
Black Palmer	5, 6 and 7[1]

you are well equipped to deal with rainbows feeding on Lesser water-boatman, crayfish, shrimp, louse, Alder larva and water snail.

At some time during the day, if there are sufficient numbers in evidence, as there usually are, rainbows will be feeding on one or the other of these throughout the season, usually without a perceptible rise.

On principle I am against fishing with more than one fly, because no two species of natural food behave in the same way. I do, however, sometimes start with a team of three flies, a "reconnaissance in

[1] New Scale.

force" in the military phrase. If you are lucky this will tell you the pattern to use and the proper depth to fish it.

As a general rule I think rainbows like flies on the large side when feeding deep, and most of the sizes given are larger than the natural. The most important thing is, of course, movement.

Methods of fishing. Wickham. Let it sink and recover quickly.

Missionary. Recover very slowly, keeping near the bottom all the time.

Peter Ross. A fairly quick but jerky recovery.

March Brown. Slow sink and draw.

Palmer. Sink to bottom and draw for snail. Slowish steady recovery when representing Alder larva.

The stickleback is hardly a fly, but the pattern known as Reckless William is quite a good imitation. The dressing is:

Hook 8.

Tip Round gold 4 turns.

Body 1/3 flat silver followed by 4 turns flat gold and then by white floss.

Head Green cellulose.

Hackle Hot orange.

Wings The dyed olive feathers of a hen pheasant's tail tied in as cheeks with a strip of dark green swan flat over back of hook. Wings should extend beyond the bend of the hook.

Usually you will see the fish pursuing the shoals of sticklebacks, which often attract the more active rainbows. Keep out of sight and cast so that line and cast do not cross the vision of the fish before they see the fly, or else they will turn away in a body. Quite often the rainbows will take sticklebacks deep with little or no surface indications. Then fish as for the Wickham.

Fishing for rainbows in deep lakes and with sunk flies differs mainly from fishing for brown trout in such lakes in that experience in locating the shoals is of even greater importance. Flies may be larger and, on the whole, more gaudy. In Kenya they say that nine out of ten rainbows are taken on a Coachman. This must imitate some local insect. If, which Heaven forbid, I was limited to one fly, I should plump for the Wickham. I would ring the changes, large and thinly dressed for deep fishing, tied nymph or pupae-fashion on small hooks, tied dry and small to represent duns, large and dry to represent sedges. But fortunately there is no such restriction and we can now go on to consider the, to my mind, much more interesting fishing with floating flies and nymphs in small lakes and gravel pits of (say) up to twelve acres.

SMALL RESERVOIRS AND GRAVEL PITS

There used to be a prejudice about rainbows—one might almost label it snobbery. Thus, in the official guide to the Kenya Fishing, there is a preface by Sir Robert Mitchell, then the Governor, who finds it necessary to apologize for his preference for rainbows. In the upper Derbyshire Wye at Monsal, where only the occasional rainbow gets up, they are treated like vermin and knocked on the head at sight. Only in New Zealand have they come into their own, and that mainly so far in the North Island, particularly in Lake Taupo. But even in the South Island, the brown trout strong-hold, things are changing, and a cousin of mine recently over in England, whom I asked how the brown trout fishing was going, confessed, rather apologetically, that he had now gone over to rainbows.

Stocking. I would not suggest stocking any more rivers with rain-bows. The results are apt to be doubtful. But the ideal places are small gravel pits and reservoirs of some twenty acres or less. And I would always put them in alone. You must keep the water alka-line, but this can easily be done by the addition of an appropriate amount of lime. And stock two- and three-year-old fish of eleven inches upwards. These are substantially cheaper than brown trout of similar size. These trout will spawn and mostly die at four years. Little of the spawn will come to anything, so that you can control the number of fish and adjust the number of rods accordingly. This sounds very artificial fishing and, as Mr. Leney said to me, "rainbows can be very stupid at times", but, believe me, when they are in form, they will exercise all your skill. This is, of course, to attribute human thinking to the trout. But they soon get very wary of the sight of gut, and deeply suspicious of any fly which behaves in an unusual manner. Many times I have seen a rainbow circum-navigating the fly and, seeing the gut, turn away. A line in the air over his head is sufficient to turn him aside off his beat.

Playing a rainbow. But when you do hook him, after that magnifi-cent head-and-tail rise, how splendid is the battle! And you must be specially cautious when a rainbow appears to be dead beat and ready for the net. My New Zealand cousin was telling me he hooked a very big rainbow in a creek running into Lake Te Anu, and having subdued it after a fierce struggle, was looking for somewhere to bank it (they seldom use nets in New Zealand and gaffs are for-bidden). "The fish," he said, "turned a baleful eye on me for about two seconds. I could almost see him making a plan. Then suddenly he decided that the lake was the place for him. So far as I know he is still going with all my thirty yards of line and a hundred yards of backing!"

The brown trout, when it realizes it is being fished for, according to its degree of education, either retires into the weeds or goes on rising with extra caution, but the rainbow shoal will simply move away.

Manner of feeding. As to his manner of feeding, the rainbow lies low in the water, so that he has a much larger "window" than the brown. (See Fig. 39.) A couple of days before writing this I had an

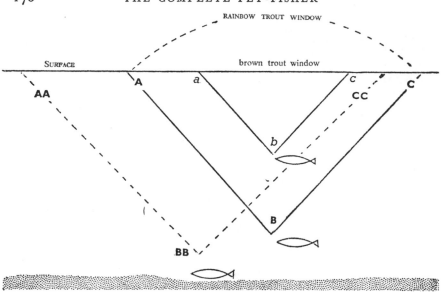

Fig. 39. *A brown trout lies near the surface when feeding and has only a-c for his "window". A rainbow trout lies near the bottom and has a much larger "window" (A-C). While a brown trout on the feed usually stays in one position, a rainbow will move about, e.g. from B to BB.*

interesting experience of the way rainbows feed. It was the rainbow part of the Derbyshire Wye, a bit called a dam, which is really a mill pool above the mill dam where the conditions approximate to those of a small lake. The water was gin-clear, some 6 feet deep over the weeds, and there was a shoal of rainbows all of a pound or so feeding. They were taking the nymph of a Pale Watery, mostly standing on their heads and taking the creature in the weeds. But every now and then a nymph would escape into mid-water, quickly followed up by the trout, who usually caught it before it reached the surface. Some, however, surfaced and were then taken.

Of the feeding in the weed there was no surface sign: the mid-water take gave what I think Mr. Skues calls a hump on the water. The head-and-tail rise was, of course, plainly visible, and sometimes a fish would leap clear of the water, I imagine after a fly on the wing. I took one fish on a leaded nymph, striking on chance when I saw the white of his mouth. But I do not like this sort of fishing, so I put on a oo Pale Watery, dry, with no success. Then I put on a largish Coachman, dry, and one or two fish came up from the bottom and rose half-heartedly at it. Just round a bend there was a more open stretch ruffled by the breeze, and watching carefully I saw a fair few head-and-tail rises. So I went there, cast my Coachman well ahead of a rise, and allowed it to drift down in the wind. It floated some 6 feet before being engulfed.

T. Vinney

25. A 5½-lb. rainbow (*above*) and a 4¾-lb. brown trout from the Two Lakes fishery, showing the difference between the species. (Note the spots on the tail of the rainbow.)

R. M. Robson

26, 27. The Derbyshire Wye, one of the very few English rivers where rainbow trout have become established. *Above :* At Ashford Bridge. *Below :* In Ashford Dale.

R. M. Robson

Now the point about this story is this. A brown trout might have been tailing or nymphing or taking duns, but it is very unlikely he would have been doing all three at the same time. The rainbows were. They had an eye cocked on the surface all the time.

Flies. In the lakes where I do most of my fishing we get a big Mayfly hatch and the fish feed on the nymph, pursuing it up to the surface and sometimes into the air after hatching. They can be caught with a deep-sunk leaded Mayfly nymph, or if there is a ripple a fish which has pursued a nymph up to the surface will take one's artificial floater, but not usually unless there is a little ripple.

The flies with which the rainbows will behave in this way are in general: Mayfly, Pond Olive, Lake Olive, Claret and Sepia duns, and sedges. Walker, in his book *Lake Flies and their Imitation*, gives suitable patterns. Tie them on the large side and load your nymphs with wire.

Another situation arises with spinners, spent demoiselle flies and insects blown from the land, particularly brown and black ants. It is to be observed that spinners may get blown on to the water at any time, the male as well as the female. Of course, in rivers the brown trout will stay put to take such food, and even in still water his movements are pretty sedate. But the rainbow shoal will cruise at considerable speed, sometimes with their backs out of water and mouths open, as they do when feeding on midge pupae, but more usually coming up from the depths, with a head-and-tail and away.

This they will do with spinners of the species previously mentioned, Blue demoiselle, Crane-fly, Ants, *Caenis* (Broadwing), and Reed Smuts.

The method of fishing is to drift a floating fly for as long as possible until it is taken or drags. You can avoid the drag for some time by letting out line. As to flies:

Spinners. I usually find a Pheasant-tail of appropriate size will suffice.

Blue demoiselle. Get from the chemist a length of nylon tubing size 3 (*not* polythene, which won't dye). Dye it with a royal blue and tie a detached body with a long black hackle behind a white. A turn of fluorescent white hackle helps. It is a bad hooker, but by far the most successful of all imitations I have tried for raising fish.

Crane-fly. *Body;* Rubber valve tubing. *Legs:* Fibres from tail of golden pheasant. *Hackle:* White dyed in Drummer brown dye.

Black Ant. I use a oo Coachman.

Brown Ant. Ditto, but body tyed with red pheasant-tail fibres.

Caenis. Walker's pattern of Broadwing spinners.

Reed Smut. *Body:* Black tying silk. *Hackle:* Black cock. *Wing:* Fluorescent white floss tied in flat and varnished, cut off above bend of hook.

In the summer months and usually at some time during the day or evening throughout the year, rainbows will feed on midge pupae. A

M

certain sign is the shoal swimming with backs out of water and mouths open. I confess I usually go away when this happens, but some anglers are very successful fishing Walker's midge pupa, size oo or even ooo, cast in amongst the shoal and recovered rapidly.

RIVERS

Some rivers are stocked with rainbows and you will catch them incidentally when fishing for brown trout, but the rainbows will usually navigate seawards and eventually disappear. Of course, the natural habit of rainbows is to migrate to the sea and return to their own rivers to spawn. But, so far as I can discover, no transplanted rainbows anywhere have produced a run of steelheads, except possibly in Lake Taupo in New Zealand.

There is pretty conclusive evidence from various parts of the world that rainbows will stop in the upper parts of rivers and breed where the lower reaches are too hot for them, as in Kenya, or where there is some element in the lower waters they don't like. In the Derbyshire Wye a few fish will face the Derwent, into which it runs, and grow big, though mostly they will not. They stay in the Wye and spawn. Similarly with the Chess, which runs into the Colne.

The immediate differences the angler who comes fresh to a rainbow river will observe are the distinctive head-and-tail rise, the habit of feeding in shoals and the way the shoals will move out of his way if he bungles or shows himself. It is almost always best to fish above an observed rise. The fish has probably moved up or another of the shoal will have done so.

Flies. As rainbows will be found in chalk and limestone streams, the usual chalk-stream dry flies will suffice. But I would never be without a Coachman or Wickham in various sizes. Rainbows seem to be particularly attracted to these flies. The best rainbow I caught out of the Derbyshire Wye, just short of 2 lb., was taken in a run along the wall of the gardens above Bakewell Bridge on a size o Wickham. I had been taking a number of smallish fish on an Olive, when I saw a head-and-tail rise from what looked a huge fish in the tail of a rapid. The head-and-tail rise always makes them look much bigger. He would have none of my Olive, but took the Wickham without hesitation, and made for the bridge, below which no doubt he lived. By good luck my 3x point held and I turned him. After two immense leaps he made for a bush upstream, I managed to turn him again and he was skilfully netted by another rod before he had recovered his balance. Or, I should have said she, for it was a hen fish.

The standard pattern nymphs, in my experience, are often very successful, while a No. 3 Wickham or Peter Ross, fished down and across in the pools, will be more likely than anything to bring up the big ones. On some waters, however, you will find your ticket endorsed "Dry fly only", and of course you must obey that. Quite recently I paid a visit to a hotel which controls a length of rainbow water where this rule obtains. The average size is not much more than about ten inches, but they told me that one or two rods were regarded with deep suspicion because they regularly brought in pounders and over. They were suspected of the dark crime of nymph fishing. The local paper was lying in the bar with an account of the conviction of a poacher for fishing the hotel water. He had eleven fish all over the pound and up to 2 lb., taken at night on an Otter! But for the dry-fly restriction the hotel guests might have had some of those fish.

I, personally, would always prefer to fish a dry fly because I find it much more amusing. But I do think that the larger rainbows get wise to "dry fly only".

I was fishing a deep backwater on that same river, but not on the hotel water, when there were several brown trout visible near the surface rising to Olives. Amongst them were a couple of rainbows coming up from the depths, taking a fly and going down, as the keeper said, "in a flash". I kept my fly waving in the air until one of them rose, when I at once covered him. He took the natural fly and my artificial almost in one gulp.

I think this experience clearly shows the difference in habits between the two fish.

CHAPTER VII

GRAYLING
by
H. G. C. CLAYPOOLE

ORIGINS OF GRAYLING

SURELY grayling represent the strangest enigma of the whole world of freshwater fish. That they are members of the *Salmonidae* family there can be no doubt whatever; the adipose fin is sufficient proof of that; yet grayling spawn between the months of March and May (at the same time as coarse fish) whereas trout spawn between October and February.

Generously distributed in the rivers of the Baltic countries, Russia, Central Europe and in some rivers of North America, where they thrive and multiply, they are found only to a lesser degree in the rivers of the British Isles.

Are they indigenous to our waters or, if not, how did they get here in the first place? Were they introduced to our rivers from the Continent of Europe by human agency? That is unlikely, for they are not easy to transport long distances even in these days.

A possible suggestion is that if, as is generally supposed, they were at one time marine dwellers they were also inhabitants of Arctic waters during the era before the coming of the Ice Age, when those waters were a great deal warmer than they are now. At that time the British Isles as we now know them were not islands at all but were merely a part of the great European Continent. Many of the rivers of our eastern seaboard were then merely tributaries of a great river which followed the course of what we now know as the Rhine. In those days this broad river debouched into the Atlantic between Iceland and Norway and, as the ice pressed southward, so the grayling retreated before it and entered the river mouth and, in course of time, into its tributaries.

When the great icefields melted new oceans came into being, and our islands assumed approximately their present form. Those rivers which were originally tributaries of the European River then became main rivers on their own account. Some of them were too fast and turbulent to allow grayling to survive in them—notably some of the Scottish rivers—but in many of the tributaries of what is now the Humber, grayling became acclimatized, and in such waters they multiplied rapidly.

Grayling were probably introduced to more southerly rivers such as the Hampshire Avon, the Kennet, Test, Itchen, etc., by human agency, perhaps during the monastic era and later. Certainly the monks were responsible for the transfer of other freshwater fish to their streams and stewponds for, in their day, freshwater fish formed a large part of their everyday diet.

ANATOMY OF THE GRAYLING

A grayling in prime condition could not possibly be confused with a fish of any other freshwater species. Its body has a graceful symmetry, slim and streamlined, tapering sharply towards the "wrist" near the tail.

The head is small and short, rather pointed at the mouth, the upper jaw projecting slightly beyond the lower. The mouth has been described as being soft, but this is a misleading description. Certainly it is *smaller* than that of a trout of a similar weight but the lips of a grayling are firm (even gristly on the larger fish) and there

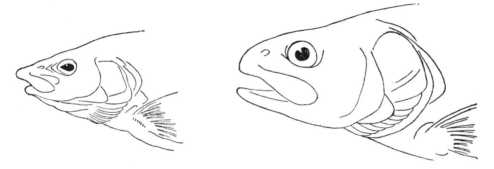

FIG. 40. *Head of a grayling (left) compared with that of a brown trout of the same weight.*

is no more reason why a hook should tear free from such a mouth, once it is driven home, than from the mouth of, say, a carp.

The eyes are large and particularly bright in aspect. The pupils are dark, pear-shaped and distinctly pointed at the forward edge.

The pectoral and ventral fins are somewhat delicate in texture but the anal fin is strongly formed, rather squarely shaped and convex on the outer edge.

The caudal fin is markedly forked and is reminiscent of that of coarse fish, but the adipose fin is as clearly defined as in other members of the *Salmonidae* family.

It is the immense dorsal fin, however, which is the most prominent feature of this singular fish. When opened to its full extent it is almost one third of the fish's total length and nearly two thirds of its depth. Angling authors have described it as being "wing-shaped" or "sail-like" but its outline varies to some degree in different fish and comparison is best left to the individual angler.

The scales are slightly flattened on the exposed edge and when seen

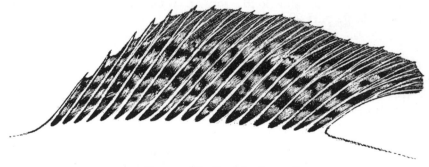

FIG. 41. *The dorsal fin of a grayling.*

on the fish's flanks they give the impression of a hexagonal pattern over-ruled with horizontal dotted lines.

Coloration. Except for the unusual dorsal fin the smaller grayling are not unlike dace in appearance, but are opalescent rather than silver in colouring. In their first year they have no distinctive spots and the dorsal fin is often almost transparent. At this stage they are known as "pinks". In the second year they begin to develop faint spots and are then known as "shotes". It is in their third year that they begin to reach maturity and the lilac, purple or reddish hues begin to intensify in them—colours which grow more pronounced as the fish develop and come into condition, but which vary according to the rivers in which the fish are found. It is particularly noticeable that the grayling of the southern counties are sometimes of more delicate colouring than those of the rivers of the Midlands and northern counties, but this is not always so. From my own experience the Lambourn and the Kennet have surrendered grayling of up to 3 lb. in weight whose backs and dorsal fins were dark blood-coloured, whereas two two-and-a-half pounders from a weir pool on the Hampshire Avon were almost purple on the backs, and nearly burgundy-coloured in the dorsal and caudal fins. These fish were taken in mid-winter and were in the very best of condition.

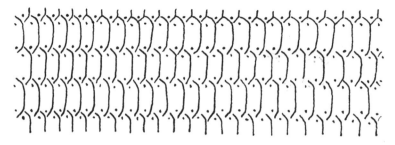

FIG. 42. *The distinctive pattern of a grayling's scales.*

HABITATS

River conditions. It is generally supposed that any trout water will suit grayling equally well, but this is not necessarily the case. Trout may live in an *ideal grayling water* in company with grayling if the natural food supply is sufficient to support them both, but it does not follow that grayling will find every *trout water* to their liking.

It is true that in stretches of many chalk streams both trout and grayling are sometimes found together in considerable numbers, but grayling demand streams that are clean and free of impurities as their habitat, and will soon disappear from waters which show any marked degree of pollution. Trout do not appear to be so strongly affected by adverse conditions and are sometimes to be found in stretches of rivers which have become so discoloured by sewage that one would suppose that fish could not survive in them.

It is therefore important when seeking grayling fishing to consider not only the river's many aspects, but also the stretches of the river which provide the right conditions for grayling if they are to live and thrive. Obviously every river undergoes many changes in its appearance, nature and degree of purity of its waters, between its source and its estuary, or junction with the main river in the case of a tributary.

At its source it may be pure and crystal clear, yet the nature of its bed, the turbulence of its current and its persistently low temperature, if its origin is in some rocky hillside, may not be conducive to the production of the natural underwater insect life, larvae and crustacea, which are the main diet of most freshwater fish. On the other hand it may well be that in other reaches where the river-bed is ideally gravelled, sanded or is even of clay, the river banks are so industrialized and the river itself so laden with industrial traffic that its discoloured and impurity-laden waters are unable to sustain either vegetation or natural insect life.

Food supply. One of the first necessities of almost any form of fish life is an abundance of natural food. In addition, as already explained, grayling require a clean and unpolluted current if they are to survive. In these circumstances the most likely stretches of a river to hold grayling are those where there are runs of clear streamy water over a gravel, sandy or even earthy bed where shallows alternate with channels and deeper pools and where underwater vegetation provides shelter not only for fish but cover for their natural food.

The bank vegetation of such pleasant spots would almost certainly harbour an additional food supply in the shape of grubs, beetles and winged insects. These may either fall or be carried by the wind on to the current, where they would be eagerly taken by questing fish.

Alkaline content and temperature. Both trout and grayling seem to prefer waters with a slightly alkaline content, no doubt due, to some extent, to the fact that their insect food supply also finds such conditions to its liking; limestone or chalk streams being the classic examples; but water temperature, too, plays a considerable part where grayling are concerned. They are particularly sensitive to drastic changes in temperature and, probably for this reason as much as any other, are more often found in lower mid-water rather than near the surface where changes in temperature can vary continually, or actually on the bottom in deeper water where the degree of warmth may be too high for their comfort. It is the middle course which best suits their temperament, and while they will take food from either the surface or the bottom impartially, it is often to the lower levels of mid-water that they will return when idly cruising.

Stocking experiments. From time to time rather half-hearted attempts have been made to introduce grayling into some rivers of our southern counties, which till now have been notable for other types of coarse fish. As far as I know, these attempts met with no success, but in February of this year a large number of grayling of all sizes were netted from the River Lambourn, and I was asked if I could find a home for them. At that time our own syndicate water on the Avon already carried a generous number of these fish and I was on the point of regretfully turning them down when I happened to mention them to the secretary of an angling club which held fishing rights on part of the Kentish Stour and Little Stour. He approached the River Board in question, who gave their permission for the introduction of the fish to their waters, and the transfer was duly carried out. It is too early yet to form any conclusions as to the success or otherwise of the venture, but it will be extremely interesting to see how they take to such a river as the Stour, this being the first serious attempt to bring grayling to that river, as far as I know.

A further consignment were also placed in the Upper Medway following the apparently successful transfer of a small number of grayling to that river in late 1960, but here again, it is too early to draw a definite conclusion as to whether or not the water has proved to be to their liking.

SPAWNING

Opinions vary as to whether or not the mature grayling prepare redds for the reception of their eggs, and indeed there is considerable doubt whether in fact they do. It would be unwise to be dogmatic on this point, but it may well be that, where spawning takes place on a sandy river-bed, a shallow depression is formed in the sand and the eggs are deposited therein; but where the bed is gravelled it is more common for the female fish to deposit her eggs among the gravel whilst swimming in close company with the male fish, which become extremely restless and excited at such a time and discharge their milt in a milky stream. Nature appears to have considered this somewhat haphazard treatment of the eggs and has endowed the female fish with an extraordinary fecundity to offset the loss of eggs from natural causes.

It is generally accepted that a female grayling produces approximately two and a half times as many eggs as a female brown trout of the same weight. In addition the eggs hatch comparatively quickly if the temperature of the water is favourable—between two and three weeks being a reasonable estimate of the period of incubation; whereas the incubation period of the eggs of brown trout is between two and three months under the same conditions. Thus the grayling eggs are not exposed to the depredation of other fish or of birds for as long a period as are those of their more aristocratic cousins. Nevertheless, a large proportion of them undoubtedly find their way into the stomachs of predators, but even after allowing for such loss a great number survive, eventually to hatch, and in waters favourable to them grayling will soon outnumber fish of other species if left to breed unhindered.

The eggs are orange or opalescent globes about one sixteenth of an inch across and, when hatched, grayling fry are tiny and almost invisible to the human eye; but in six months they can measure up to 5 inches in length. At twelve months they weigh about 2 oz. and in two years, with favourable conditions, they can weigh up to 6 oz. In their third year they are reaching maturity and will weigh about $\frac{3}{4}$ lb.

It is at about this age that they first spawn and for each succeeding year they add about 4 oz. to their weight until they reach between 4 and 5 lb., dependent on the food supply.

Weights. The largest grayling taken in British waters to date weighed 7 lb. 2 oz. and was caught in the River Melgum in July 1949. This must be reckoned to be an unusual weight for a grayling in this country, although somewhere or other in our rivers fish as large or even larger may still exist. Nevertheless, grayling of 4 lb. are to be reckoned as notable fish and those of 3 to $3\frac{1}{2}$ lb. above average.

Of the thousand or so grayling which I have taken from southern counties rivers in my angling life a good many ranged between 2 lb. and $2\frac{1}{2}$ lb. in weight and only three fish reached a weight of 3 lb. each.

Nevertheless, I have seen heavier grayling in private fisheries, although I have not been privileged to attempt to catch them. I know of one case, however, when an angler spinning with a small Vibro lure hooked a grayling which, when landed, proved to tip the scales at a shade over 4 lb. The fish was cleanly hooked in the front of its gristly upper lip and until actually landed was thought to be either a very lively chub or a fair-sized trout. The fish had certainly attacked the spinner, but this is the only case that I have ever known where a grayling has taken a spinning lure. Walton suggested that they could be taken on a minnow, but I cannot visualize any angler successfully angling for grayling by such a method.

Of the fish which I have taken from midland and northern waters, only a small proportion have weighed in the region of 1 lb. each, but I must hasten to add that I have not had the same opportunities to fish these most attractive rivers as I have their southern counterparts. Nevertheless, I believe northern anglers will agree that a Yorkshire grayling of 1 lb. is a good fish and that the average fish would be nearer ½ lb. On the other hand, such rivers as the Derwent, Severn and Swale often yield very large bags and I must confess that the Yorkshire rivers are more likely to yield the larger number of fish in a day's angling, given good conditions, than a grayling river of the south. However, the chances of larger fish would possibly be better in the south, as the following table of notable grayling taken from the rivers Avon, Wylye and Test suggests:

River Wylye	1885	4 lb. 8 oz.
River Test	1905	4 lb.
River Test	1873	3 lb. 12 oz.
River Test	1917	3 lb. 12 oz.
River Test	1832	3 lb. 11 oz.
River Avon	1960	4 lb. taken on a spinner and returned alive.

SHOALING HABITS

Unlike trout, grayling are gregarious by nature and are usually found in some numbers when found at all. On several occasions I have seen the surface of a particular pool so dimpled by feeding grayling that the effect was as if a light shower of rain was striking the water, but this is a matter with which I shall deal later. Do not be misled, however, into believing that because a shoal happens to be in one stretch of a river today they will necessarily be there tomorrow. As already explained, grayling are susceptible to changes in water temperature and fish that are in the shallows today could well be in deeper water tomorrow if the temperature drops.

Lies. The larger and perhaps more shrewd fish are likely to be found in deeper water where the temperature may not be so subject to sudden change. From such a point of vantage they command a view not only of flies on the surface but of larvae and crustacea on the river-bed and shrimp, etc., in midwater Thus they may take their choice of the varied food supply.

In southern waters, particularly, I have noticed this tendency of groups of larger grayling to lie in the lower layers of deeper water while the smaller fish, in larger numbers, throng in the upper layers. A period of bright sunshine can bring about a rapid change, however, and under such conditions I have known big grayling rise to the surface with their backs half out of the water and their dorsal fins lying flat; not feeding but merely enjoying the sudden sunshine.

SURFACE FOOD

Method of rising. Grayling are inquisitive yet exasperating creatures, but have the advantage of particularly keen eyesight: a gift which may have some association with the manner in which they will rise almost vertically from a position below midwater to take a floating fly before returning just as steeply to their former position. This fashion of rising to a floating insect is typical of grayling and would be expected to create a considerable disturbance on the water surface. Oddly enough the reverse is more often the rule and, apart from the fact that the insect has disappeared, the manner of its going is often betrayed only by the merest dimpling of the surface or the sudden flash of the fish as it is completing its elliptical

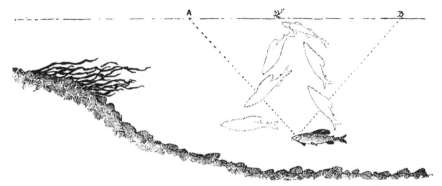

FIG. 43. *Diagram showing the grayling's "window" and the way in which a grayling rises to a fly on the surface.*

movement. It may sometimes miss its objective at the first attempt, but undeterred by such a preliminary failure it will often come at the insect again and again until it is finally successful.

This procedure, so different from that of feeding trout, will undoubtedly prove disconcerting to the confirmed trout angler, but when considered from the grayling's point of view may be more readily understood. A fly on the surface of a stream does not necessarily pursue a straight course, its passage being governed partly by its own movements and also by the vagaries of every air current. Now consider the fly to have been observed by a hungry grayling from a point some four or five feet below the surface. The fish must estimate where the fly *will be* by the time it has covered the intervening distance. Remember also that the upper lip of a grayling protrudes beyond the lower, so that the fish must turn partly on its side if it is to take the floating fly. It must now be apparent that the fish is at some disadvantage and must be governed by the maxim of "If at first you don't succeed . . ." In fact the whole operation is not so dissimilar from that of a predictor and an A.A. gun; the plane is the fly, the projectile is the fish and the predictor the fish's brain estimating the course, speed and angle of the target. Any "ack-ack" gunner will agree that it is seldom that a hit is achieved with the first round, even by the best of gun crews. Do I hear him reply with some relief, "at least the misses don't return just as steeply to their previous position"?

THE ARTIFICIAL FLY AND THE USE OF COVER

Flies. Angling with a floating fly is no modern innovation. Even two thousand years ago live insects were used by anglers as lures. In those days the fly was tied to a barbless hook and the angler did not have the advantage of the use of many yards of floating line.

From angling with a live insect it was comparatively a short step to its simulation by scraps of feather and fur and such artificials were used by the Macedonians in the third century.

Patterns of hooks and hook materials improved. Fly-tying became an art. In the fifteenth century artificial flies were more widely accepted as angling lures, and in the seventeenth century, when Charles Cotton wrote the second part of the fifth edition of the *Compleat Angler*, it was obvious that he was aware that a wide variety of artificial flies could be utilized in angling and also that the manner of their presentation was of paramount importance to the success of the venture, not only in the actual casting of the fly but also in the steps taken by the angler to merge himself with his background.

Taking cover. On this subject he wrote ". . . and if you are pretty well out of sight, either by kneeling or the interposition of a bank or bush, you may be sure and take him too if it be presently done; the fish will otherwise, peradventure, be removed to some other place." Anglers today are even more conscious that self-effacement on the river bank is an important contribution to successful angling. W. H. Canaway expressed the whole matter most succinctly in his book *A Creel of Willow* thus: "Wear sober clothes. Stand by a convenient piece of vegetation, concentrate as hard as you can and try and fade into it. When someone comes along and attempts to water you then you may count yourself ready to commence fishing."

DRY-FLY FISHING

Throughout the warm summer days trout anglers may have been pestered from time to time by immature grayling which have not only taken their artificials but in doing so have also put down their trout. During the early part of this period the larger grayling will have been recovering from their spawning activities and are concerned not so much with floating insects, which may or may not come down on the current, as with the generous supply of shrimps and larvae which are nearer to hand and call for less effort in their capture.

Now the delicate colours which were one of the distinguishing features of the mature fish during autumn and winter are faded and tarnished, the fish themselves lank and flaccid. As the autumn approaches again, and the trout season draws to a close, the position is reversed. The grayling recover and are at their peak of condition. The lack-lustre appearance has gone, their bodies now full and strong. Such fish may not have the gymnastic ability of a healthy trout of the same weight, but there is no doubt of their fighting qualities; and with the added assistance of their expanded dorsal fins they will present the angler with a variety of problems.

The very manner in which they may now take a floating insect will often result in them hooking themselves, and when this happens and the line tightens there will be some anxious moments. A lively grayling when hooked produces every trick in the book, at least one of which will be new to the trout angler. Although I have read of grayling which leapt clear of the water when hooked I have never actually experienced it myself, but that dorsal fin when expanded by a fish travelling across the current produces an effect similar to that of a dinghy when the boat is tacking across a breeze.

To the angler the sensation is as though he has hooked by the handle an open umbrella which is being tugged across the current by a second angler on the far bank who has hooked it in the edge of the cover.

Tactics. Obviously, then, when once feeding grayling have been located by the angler the cast should be made *upstream* for a variety of very good reasons:

1. The angler, being downstream from the fish, is less likely to have been observed.
2. If the fly is taken the hook is more likely to be driven well home instead of being snatched from the fish's mouth by a too hasty strike.
3. The dorsal fin will not be able to be used to its full advantage in the current so long as the angler stays downstream from the fish.
4. The angler is assisted by the current in bringing the fish to the net and the rest of the shoal suffers the minimum of disturbance as the action takes place behind them.

We know that grayling are not put down by having missed the fly at the first attempt, and will often come at it again at each successive cast. It must not be inferred from this, however, that the angler can allow coils of line to slap down on the water in haphazard fashion. The cast should be made with as much care as when casting for trout, for unnecessary disturbance of the surface will scare off grayling as surely as it will any other fish.

The object of the angler should be to endeavour to allow his fly to alight on the water surface, a few feet upstream from the fish as lightly as possible, with the line almost straight from the rod tip to the fly. A little line drag does not seem to have the same effect on grayling as it does on trout and more often than not the former will still attack the fly, whereas the latter may leave it severely alone.

Tackle. Rod, reel, line and cast may be the same as when trout fishing, but the outfit may be improved a little by using slightly finer material in the gut or nylon cast. 3X tapering to 4X or its equivalent in nylon over a length of 6 feet is a useful type of cast, although some anglers prefer the length to be up to 9 feet. It is a matter of individual choice.

Fly patterns. The average trout angler is usually something of an entomologist and will be accustomed to "matching the fly on the water" as nearly as possible. This is sound common sense and on many occasions produces the required result, but grayling are perverse creatures and will sometimes persistently ignore the angler's artificial even though it be a faithful representation of the natural. At such a time an artificial with a touch of silver in its make-up is often the answer, and if I were asked I would say that a Red Tag with a hint of silver tinsel at the base of the tag is the most useful fly for any grayling water. A Witch, a Tup's Indispensable, a Greenwell's Glory, a variety of Bumbles, Water-hen Bloa, Wickham's Fancy, Sherry spinner, Bradshaw's Fancy, and Poult Bloa should all have their place in the fly-box, tied on size o and size 1 hooks. King's Austrian Wasp, though little known in this country, is another useful pattern.

Grayling fly-patterns are almost as numerous as those for trout, but if the angler were to be allowed only six patterns I would suggest the following with the confident expectation that one of them would attract surface-feeding grayling on almost any grayling water: 1. Red Tag 2. Witch 3. Greenwell's Glory 4. Wickham's Fancy 5. Bradshaw's Fancy 6. Sherry Spinner.

WET-FLY FISHING

Tackle and flies. Very little change is needed in tackle if the fly is to be allowed to sink instead of to float, but certainly a longer cast length could be used to advantage. One of 9 feet in length should serve the purpose and the flies named in the preceding paragraph can be fished either wet or dry.

Variants that carry rather less hackle may be found to be more suitable when fishing a sunk fly and some anglers may prefer to use a dropper in addition to the tail-fly. If two flies are used the dropper should be tied to a 9-inch point and attached to the cast about 15 inches above the tail-fly.

Combinations of any two of the flies already named may be tried, but it may well be found an advantage to start the day with a Red Tag as the tail-fly and perhaps a Wickham or a Greenwell as the dropper; changing to one or the other of the remainder if the first two are found to be unrewarding.

Deliberately to fish the fly wet is not always the shrewdest approach with grayling, however, and I have often found it more rewarding to start by fishing the flies dry but after a few casts, when they become waterlogged, to allow them to sink gradually. A semblance of life can then be given to them either by alternately lifting and lowering the rod-tip a few inches at a time or by lightly jerking the line with the left hand.

Upstream or down? Many anglers when fishing a wet fly cast down and across, but this practice, too, may at times be varied by casting upstream and across. On many occasions anglers have complained to me that they have continually lost fish by fishing wet downstream and because the hook "tore free". I am not at all sure, however, that this is the real reason for them losing fish.

Downstream grayling are more often lost not because the hook tears free but because the fly is snatched from the fish's mouth in the angler's act of striking. The hook is far more likely to be driven home if the fish is hooked upstream, or even across the stream, and fewer fish will be lost in consequence.

Striking. One other point on this matter of striking is worthy of discussion. Why do so many anglers strike by bringing the rod upright? It is certainly not always the surest method of driving home the hook. Why not try striking an upstream or an across stream fish by drawing the rod *sideways* to a position when it is parallel with the water surface and would be pointing at a spot behind the fish if the rod were straight? Try it; I think you will lose fewer fish!

Nymphs. Of the numerous artificial nymphs available almost any one will attract grayling if it incorporates in its make-up a turn or two of silver or gold tinsel and is given a semblance of life when sunk by light twitches on the line.

The main points to bear in mind are, first to see that the lure sinks well and next to make sure that its movement back to the surface is under control and is by a series of short jerks rather than as a continuous movement.

CONCLUSION

Grayling are where you find them and, when once they are found, the angler should not be persuaded to try other stretches of the river merely because the fish do not appear to be feeding where they are first located. Experiment and perseverance are the secrets of success if the angler follows the primary principles of his art.

The inveterate dry-fly angler will not be persuaded to fish in any other fashion. Why should he be? The angler with the wet fly or even with the nymph *may* have more sport, but does it matter? There are many pleasant days during our English autumn and during the winter, too. Why put away your fly rods in September when you could continue to enjoy their use?

H. G. C. Claypoole

28. A 1½-lb. grayling from the Avon.

R. M. Robson

29. Noted for its grayling since Charles Cotton's day : The River Dove in Dovedale.

CHAPTER VIII

CASTING A FLY

by

E. HORSFALL TURNER

I HAVE heard the comment, frequently, that casting is the most difficult part of fly-fishing. This, in my opinion, is absolutely wrong. Casting is indeed the easiest part of fly-fishing for trout, because it is the only exercise with something like a known potential, and can be reduced to a drill. So far as the potential of the casts is concerned, we can make an accurate assessment, both in terms of accuracy and distance, from the performances of the top tournament casters: Tarrantino and Dieckman, of the United States; Schöpp and the elder Kolseth, of Norway, and Daubry, of France. In the stiff test of the Trout Fly Accuracy, under the intense strain of the World Championship platform, they have all scored the "possibles" of 100 points. Several tournament casters can exceed 50 yards consistently with what we regard as standard equipment for long fly-casting on lakes and reservoirs. The average competent fly-fisherman would be lucky to exceed 50 points in the trout fly accuracy test, and few anglers can cast over 30 yards with any tackle they care to use.

Nevertheless, these apparent shortcomings of the competent angler are not serious for the practical purposes of his fishing. He rarely requires the accuracy or distance of the good tournament caster. This fact has permitted great anglers like Dai Lewis or Pashley to use tackle and methods which left a great deal to be desired in terms of really good casting by tournament standards, and yet catch many more fish than their contemporaries. I do not imply that the precision and power of the tournament caster is without point, as some would like to believe. The motorist will get along happily with a family saloon in the middle cost; but given freedom of choice, would he select it against a car with double the acceleration and a much higher cruising speed? The point I make is merely relative to the comparative ease of casting, which can be raised to perfectly satisfactory angling standards at half its full potential.

In dealing with the topic so far, I have confined my comments to the fly cast for trout, both wet and dry. There are three other casts: the wet-fly cast with heavier tackle, for grilse or sea-trout; the long cast with wet flies on lakes; and the double-handed salmon cast. The first two types are covered in a large measure by the general comments on the ordinary trout-fly cast. I shall draw certain distinctions later, but the reader will be well advised to think of them, for the present, as one. The double-handed cast will be considered separately, for all that, as I shall point out, it is really no more than the single-handed cast with the lower hand taking the weight of a rod that is too heavy to be used with one hand.

Basic principles. The basic principle of the fly cast is that the line is a weight, and the rod is a spring. The rod is also in part a lever, but the point is confusing. For our purposes, we shall confine ourselves to the principles of the weight and the spring. If a spring is compressed, it will recover sharply to the inert if the pressure is released. If a weight is attached to the spring (whether the attachment causes the weight to be pushed or pulled) the action of the spring during recovery imparts velocity to the weight, provided that the weight is not so heavy as to be immovable when the compression on the spring is released. This velocity in the weight is a constant, but the movement of the weight is affected by a number of factors, the two most important being the force of gravity and air resistance. So that once the weight has been given velocity and is no longer under the influence of the rod-tip, it is these two forces, in the main, that bring it down to earth.

A weight may be in a great variety of shapes and sizes, according to design and the density of the material of which it is made. We need take only two instances for the sake of example: a metal ball or sphere, weighing $\frac{3}{4}$ oz., and a trout fly-line of about 41 feet in length made of a material which gives it precisely the same weight. The ultimate effect of both these weights on the flexing of a flexible rod will be precisely the same, but the effect of air resistance will be quite different when the weights are given velocity, owing to the difference in surface exposed to air resistance. The additional surface of the fly-line will subject it to greater air resistance; and for that reason, the greater the initial velocity of the line, the more slowly the effect of air resistance becomes apparent and the more the line holds to the course on which it has been projected. In terms of practical angling, this means that accuracy can more easily be achieved with a medium length of line outside the rod-tip, than with a short length or a long length, because, for reasons we shall next examine, the velocity of the line drops on either side of a certain *weight* of line outside the rod-tip.

In the case of the metal ball, we have a compact weight. Immediately the force of the rod-tip is exerted on this weight, every part of it is influenced—for practical purposes. In the case of a fly-line, however, the design is such that a part of the weight can be influenced but the influence will die out long before it has reached the *whole* weight. In these circumstances, the compressing factor of the weight of the line upon the flexible rod, the spring, will be quite different from that of the metal sphere, unless enough of the line is outside the rod-tip and is influenced simultaneously for all practical purposes. It is this fact that has provoked the common advice to halt the rod at the vertical in the back cast "to allow the line to straighten" behind the angler. I dislike this advice and do not give it when teaching a beginner, because it encourages a cast with a jerk in it; whereas the cast must, ultimately, be a smooth, integrated action from start to finish. This point will be dealt with at a later stage.

A simple experiment for the novice is to take his fly-rod, with both a weight and a length of line of the same weight. First, let him attach the weight to the rod as though it were the line; then lay the weight behind him on the ground, with the rod held ready to cast it forward. As he brings in the power by applying torque to the rod

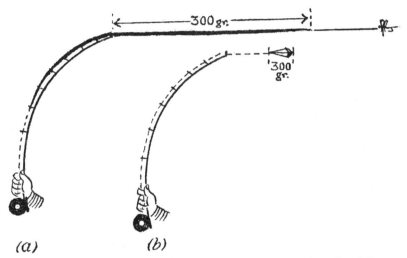

(a)   (b)

Fig. 44. *Diagram illustrating the similar effects of a 300-grain section of line outside the rod-tip and a plug of the same weight.*

grip, he will both see and feel the flex of the rod. If he substitutes the line for the weight, and lays it straight behind him on the ground, application of torque will have precisely the same effect; and in both cases the weight, whether a solid ball or a line, will be impelled forward. If he wishes to carry the experiment a stage further, let him double a little of the line back on itself. He will find that the effect of a little doubled-back line will make no appreciable difference, but as he continues the experiment with a greater length of doubled line, he will find that a stage is gradually reached when the line will not lift and the "feel" is that of casting no weight.

Aerial manipulation. This takes us to the next point, which is that the fly-fisherman cannot go on his business about the river laying the line down behind him every time he wishes to cast it forward. He must devise a method of aerial manipulation which enables him to bring *enough* of the line behind him, in such a position that the forward movement of the rod-tip will influence the whole, or virtually the whole, weight of the line at the same time. This must be an integrated double movement. In other words, he must throw the line back in such a way that its weight compresses the spring of the rod to the greatest possible extent; and at the moment it does this, it is in a form which subjects it substantially to a forward movement of the rod. It is the ability to co-ordinate the instant of maximum flex of the rod with the ideal state of the flying line, and to start the forward movement of the rod, which we call "timing".

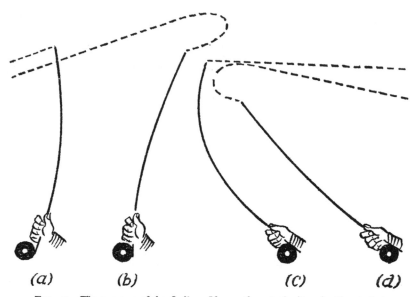

(a)   (b)   (C)   (d)

FIG. 45. *The turn-over of the fly-line. If correctly cast, the line should not drop below the level of the rod-tip, either in the back cast (a) and (b) or in the forward cast (c) and (d).*

It may have been noted at this stage that the complete movement of the fly cast is really two movements of a nearly identical nature; the first, a cast of the line backwards; and the second, a very similar cast forwards. This is precisely the case, and underlines most forcibly the comment that a good fore cast cannot be made unless it is preceded by a good back cast. Moreover, neither can be made unless the line lies, whether ahead or behind the angler, in such a position that a movement of the rod brings it under immediate and virtually complete influence. These principles apply, of course, to every type of cast with a fly-rod and line.

Rod action. Before leaving this elementary analysis of the mechanics, there is one important point to be considered: that of rod action in relation to the weight to be cast. The first thing to understand is rod action. The angler who knows his rods will pick one up and classify it immediately from feel, as slow, medium or fast. He may vary this to soft, medium or stiff, but he means the same thing. In Fig. 46 the curves of three types of rod are shown, when the curve is caused by a weight suspended from the tip. The polytechnicians have devised names for various so-called rod actions. "Parabolic" and "Progressive" are two that spring to mind. For the purpose of the polytechnicians, those terms may mean something. For practical purposes, they mean nothing. The term "test curve" has also been given its share of learned exposition, but unless it is applied to rods with known tapers and texture, it is equally meaningless. So long as the angler knows the difference between slow, medium and fast actions in fly-rods, it is enough. It is important that he should know

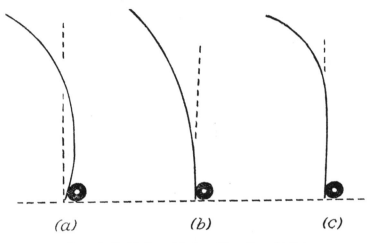

(a)   (b)   (c)

Fig. 46. *Rod Actions.* (a) *slow:* (b) *medium:* (c) *fast.*

these differences; otherwise, he cannot match a line to a rod, or understand why a line does not match a rod.

The reason why he should have this knowledge takes us back, briefly, to the case of the rod and its capacity for projecting a weight. Let us suppose the rod is attached to a composite weight, made in sections. The complete weight is so heavy that, when it is laid behind the caster, the rod refuses to move it when the attempt is made to do so. Sections of the weight are removed until the rod will move what remains. The first move is a sort of budge of the weight. When lightened further, the weight will swing slowly forward. Lightened further still, the weight will describe a slow parobola from behind the caster to in front of him. Ultimately the weight will be lightened to such an extent that it comes forward in a lively manner, full of velocity. That weight of line, precisely, is the best for the rod in use; making allowance, of course, for the different reactions between a solid ball of weight and an elongated weight which is subject to considerable air resistance. My example is primarily to illustrate the importance of rod action. Because it will be found that a rod with slow action, in which recovery to the inert when compression is released is not so rapid a process as with the fast rod, will generate velocity in a lighter weight which would not compress the fast rod, that is, the spring, for reasons of its lightness. This means, in terms of practical casting, that whereas a No. 3 line with a weight of, say, ¾ oz. would flex a medium to fast action rod ideally, and cause the utmost speed in rod recovery to the inert, it would over-flex a soft rod, and its weight would retard recovery of that rod to the inert. In common parlance, it would "overload" the soft rod. Conversely, a No. 1 line, which might be admirable for the soft rod, would "underload" the fast rod.

So that, when an angler tells you that he likes a 9-foot rod and a No. 2 line, without telling you the material of the line (since today line materials vary considerably in weight) or the action of the rod, he merely tells you that he has found *a* rod and *a* line which work well together.

TACKLE

Rods. The modern fly-fisherman faces a much more complex problem in tackle selection than did his counterpart of fifty years ago, although, as a compensating factor, he has a much wider range of choice. His choice of rods, fifty years ago, was limited to bamboo (or "split cane" as it is commonly called) and greenheart. By that time, these materials had superseded the long, composite weapon of the eighteenth century. Today, good greenheart has become difficult to obtain. Fly-rod materials are almost entirely confined to built bamboo, fibre (often called "hollow") glass, and steel. Space does not permit of a lengthy discussion about these materials. My comments are merely the outcome of trial, and discussion with some of the best rod makers and casters of the day.

Perfectly good fibre-glass and steel fly-rods are available for trout and salmon fishing of all types. Both materials, particularly glass, make for extremely durable rods. Steel rods are on the slow side, weight for weight, when compared with other materials. Fibre-glass rods are very light and extremely powerful, weight for weight. The majority of the fibre-glass rods on the British market have a fast action. The disadvantage of both materials is that they cannot be varied in the making to give the action required. Built bamboo, on the other hand, is constructed by feel, and is designed by the maker to have a particular action. The rod-making craftsman is trained to achieve this design in the rods he makes. This situation has led to a widespread opinion that bamboo still holds the day, for the reason that bamboo rods have a better "feel" to the angler. I must confess

that out of a considerable number of rods I have felt, only one glass
rod has impressed me as having a "feel" similar to that of bamboo.
The makers told me that it had taken them seven years of experiment to produce an article which satisfied them on this point, and
the rod is not yet on the market. In the hand, I have the impression
that steel sometimes gives a better feeling than glass, but this is a
personal preference limited to certain rods, and I would not compare
rods of either material with bamboo as a medium of "feel" to the
angler. On the other hand, it is every angler to his fancy—or to his
pocket—and I know many anglers who are finding what they want
in steel or glass.

So that, since we must settle for some definite type of rod in this
brief commentary, let us make it, for ordinary fly-fishing for trout,
a bamboo rod of 8 feet to 8½ feet in length, weighing 5 oz. or slightly
less. Its action must be decided only after we have determined the
line it is to carry. It will handle trout up to 2 lb. comfortably, and
fish up to 5 lb. at a pinch. If the rod is to handle a considerable
number of 5 lb. fish and up to 10 lb. fish occasionally, many anglers
prefer a longer rod of from 9 feet to 9½ feet, weighing about 7 oz.
Personally, for this type of fishing, I prefer a powerful rod of 9 feet
at the outside, weighing under 6 oz. The intermittent angler, however, may find that his wrist tires rather quickly with these heavier,
or more powerful, rods. His answer, or that of the lady, is a light
double-handed rod of about 11 feet. It will throw a good line; is
far less tiring; is useful for the specialized work of greased-line
fishing with small flies on low summer salmon rivers; and gives an
accurate enough cast for the type of fishing.

The salmon rod will depend on the type of fishing which the angler
contemplates. If his fishing is to be spring work on broad rivers,
particularly the Norwegian type of river, his rod must be powerful
enough to cast big flies in the 4/0 to 8/0 range. My own choice would
be a 14 foot bamboo rod, weighing about 26 oz. For lighter work,
common on most rivers of this country, the purpose would be served
by a rod of from 12½ feet to 13½ feet. It will cast smaller flies in the
No. 2 to 2/0 range in comfort, and, at a pinch, flies down to about
No. 6. The ideal rod for these smaller flies, from No. 4 to No. 10,
is the 11 foot double-handed rod I have already suggested as a
substitute for the powerful single-handed rod.

A safe compromise for the salmon angler who cannot afford a
range of rods, or who fishes for salmon so infrequently as to make a
range unwarranted, is a medium-action rod of 12½ feet. The precise
action, again, must be assessed when the type of line is known.

Before leaving the subject of rods, one point should be mentioned.
Built bamboo rods have often been decried as unsuitable, if not
unusable, for the roll cast with Spey action—a type of cast which
will be described later. This cast is executed in a manner which
twists the rod. Greenheart has been advocated widely as the only

suitable material for a rod which is to perform the Spey cast effectively without damage to the rod structure. Unless an angler has a
beat which calls for something near exclusive Spey casting, he can
disregard this advice with safety. The limited Spey casting which
the average angler will do in his normal rounds will not do the
slightest harm to a well-made built bamboo rod. The advantage
greenheart has for the roll cast is that it will only make up, except
at an outrageous weight, into a soft action rod. This soft action is
essential to good Spey casting, but it can be matched by the craftsman in the making of a bamboo rod. Against this possible advantage,
assuming one compares a medium to fast bamboo rod with a greenheart for the purpose, the weight and softness of greenheart makes
for poor overhead casting. One can, of course, carry two rods about
the river, but I have yet to meet the competent caster who does not
take advantage of the versatility of bamboo to carry one rod, and
make it do all that he requires on any normal beat.

Lines. Emphasis has already been laid on the vital factor of line
weight when considering the operation of rod and line. Indeed, I
have suggested in a textbook on casting that the angler should choose
his line first and then proceed to select a rod to match that line. This
is sound advice in that it is the line that will determine the quality
of an angler's cast in the conditions, and for the purpose, that
require the cast. A light line will descend on the water very gently,
but if the angler has to cast it into or across a wind of any strength,
he will have trouble in controlling it. This will be due partly to the
lightness of the line, and partly to the fact that, as such a line
demands a slow rod which it is capable of flexing properly, the rod
will not drive the line as would a fast rod. On the reverse account,
if the line is heavy and has a fast rod to drive it, wind has little effect
if the caster knows his job, but the line cannot, for reasons of its
weight, be made to fall as lightly.

The angler, then, starts with a number of questions which he must
answer for himself before he decides on his line. Is he likely to fish,
in the main, where windy conditions are fairly frequent? Will he
pick his conditions and confine his angling largely to days when
conditions are fairly tranquil? Or will he fish preponderantly on
wind-swept moorland, or upland, waters where the day without
wind is an exception? Or again—and this is much more likely to
be his question—will he find it possible to select a general-purpose
line which falls fairly gently, and yet has a moderate performance
in windy conditions? Fortunately, this last question can be answered satisfactorily. For myself, I keep three lines, with rods to
suit them, for differing conditions. But out of these three sets, the
medium one has always struck me as a nearly perfect all-purpose
match, and I use it far more often than its heavier and lighter
counterparts.

Let us now consider the lines available today. Until a com-

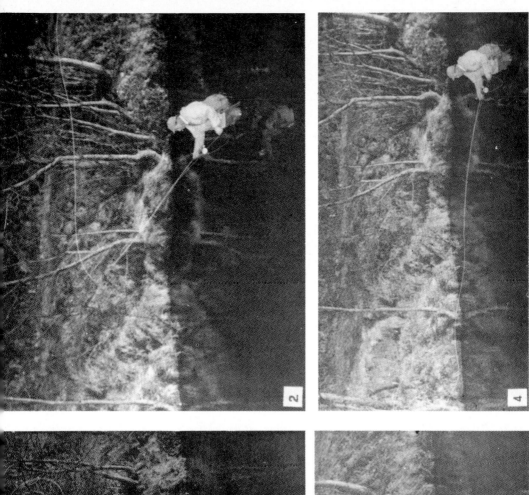

A. V. Oglesby

30. Four stages in the single-handed overhead cast.

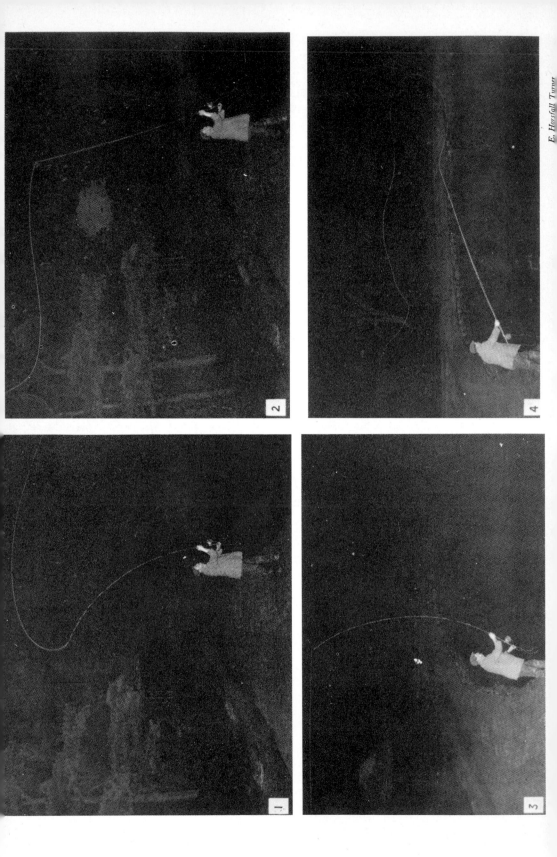

E. Horsfall Turner

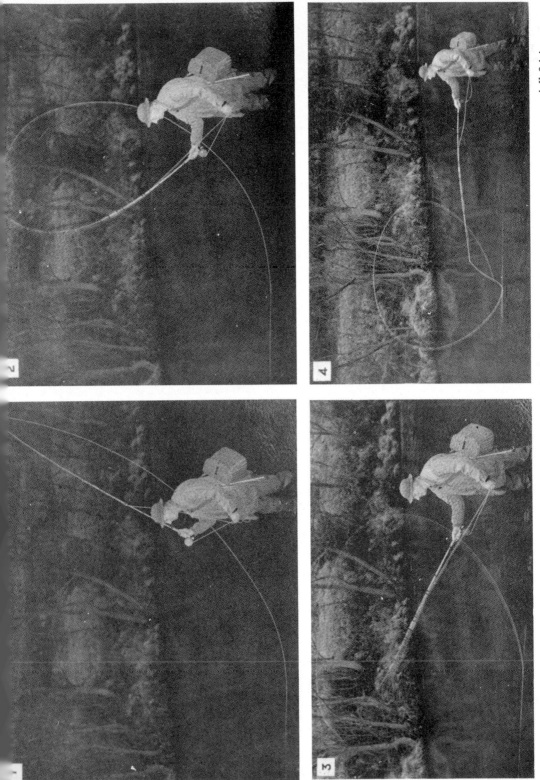

32. Four stages in the roll cast.

F. Horsfall Turner

paratively few years ago, fly-lines were made almost exclusively of braided silk. The consistency and diameter of these lines varied a little, according to tightness of braiding and oil saturation, but the gauging of them was a comparatively simple matter since they were all made of the same material. Tapered lines were well known in the early years of the last century, and Pennell devised something like our forward-taper design in the 1880's. Wire cores, even, were introduced to enable the lines to be driven into the wind. Today, however, lines are made of a number of materials: for instance, silk, nylon, terylene, and the synthetic-coated lines called Wet Cel and Air Cel. The gauging of these lines is extremely difficult. A number of attempts have been made, but I have yet to read one which gives the angler a really reliable guide as between material and material. In the first place, the materials differ in weight. The lightest is nylon, followed by silk and terylene, in that order. The Air Cel line is comparatively light, falling between nylon and silk, while the Wet Cel is considerably heavier than terylene. The gauging of silk lines became something near standard with the "Kingfisher" scale. A Scottish firm made a range of lines with this trade-mark, and numbered them according to belly diameter, in graduations of ·005 inch. The No. 1 line, for instance, had a belly diameter of ·035 inch, while the No. 5 line had a belly diameter of ·055 inch. The disadvantage of this gauging is that it tells the angler nothing about the weight of the line; nor does it tell him the tapers, from which he might make a fair estimate of the weight. The Americans then tried to remedy this by allocating a capital letter to each belly diameter, so that a double-taper HEH line has a belly of ·040 inch, and tapered ends to a diameter of ·025 inch. This was an advance in some respects, but unless all tapers were uniform, which they were not, the angler still had some guessing to do. An HEH line in nylon was completely different in weight, and behaviour, from an HEH line in terylene. Neither were of the same weight as a silk No. 2. The vendors of the Wet Cel and Air Cel added to the confusion by using letters, though they have now, in some cases, come to the more sensible course of publishing a graph with the letters, belly diameters *and weight*, included. This, again, is an advance, and a further advance is the inclusion of plans of the tapers in the latest graphs. No doubt the makers of nylon, terylene and silk lines will be forced to follow suit in self-defence!

I have dealt with this problem of line specification in some detail because, unless the angler knows the background of the confusing modern situation, he will be unable to assess the method I shall now suggest for simplifying his own problem. He will realize that any advice to use a rod of stated length, with a line of stated number, means nothing beyond a general indication of the type of equipment, roughly, which the adviser has in mind. If he chose a fast 9 foot rod and a nylon line with a specification of No. 2, or "E" belly, or ·040 inch belly diameter, he would have a poorly balanced outfit; whereas a terylene or Wet Cel line of the same specification would flex the rod well and provide a useful outfit. The problem is to find some yardstick by which to gauge lines of differing materials. Several attempts have been made by trying to relate silk numbered gradings to letter grades and belly diameter. None of these attempts have resulted in a scale which is accurate enough for comprehensive recognition. One or two of the larger rod-making firms, however, now produce a complete schedule showing the correct lines (in all materials) for rods of their own range. Fundamentally, this is what the angler wants for all types of rod, no matter by what firms they are made. As this is not procurable, those firms who do make some attempt to ensure that the angler gets the correct lines for their rods are entitled to reap the reward of their enterprise in helping him.

It should be borne in mind that there is a good deal of latitude in the factor of line weight as it compresses the spring of the rod. Otherwise, the ideal length (that means weight) of line outside the rod-tip could not be varied to make long or short casts with the same equipment. The aim of the angler is merely to find a line and rod which will work together to maintain an ideal length of line in the air, so that there is the widest margin of variation on both sides of the ideal to allow for longer and shorter casts.

These principles have the same application to salmon lines.

General application. Application of the principles I have outlined to the selection of good tackle is a comparatively simple matter. Let us start, once again, with what I have termed a yardstick: that is, a good general-purpose kit, which will handle well in moderate winds and allow a fairly light fall of the line. For normal fly-fishing, with preponderance of dry-fly work, a No. 3 silk line, with a medium to fast 8½-foot rod weighing 5 oz. or less, will perform well. For work in heavy winds, a fast rod of the same length and weight will carry a No. 4 silk line well. Personally, I use a No. 4 silk line in these conditions; or, in extreme conditions, a line of equivalent diameter (·050 inch) in terylene. During comparatively calm weather, if the angler requires a very light lay-down of the line, a slow-action rod of the same weight and length should give him all he wants with a No. 2 silk line. In dealing with this question of lay-down, I find much to support the view of the American angler, E. R. Hewitt, who places some insistence on the desirability of maintaining the line weight to keep the casting power, but lengthening the cast, or leader; and thereby achieving, for practical purposes, the light lay-down at a sufficient distance from the fish.

The grading of other line materials from silk, inside this specification, needs no further comment. I have alternated a No. 3 silk line with an HCH "Air Cel" line during the last two seasons, with very satisfactory performance, on the same rod.

While the foregoing equipment is primarily for dry-fly fishing, most anglers turn to wet fly from time to time, as occasion demands, during periods of dry-fly fishing. By wet fly, I mean sunk fly dragged across broken water. Upstream sunk-fly fishing and nymph fishing (a distinction I have never understood except that the former was practised widely in my boyhood days, while the latter has become fashionable in recent years on southern streams where it was formerly "dry fly" and dry fly alone) are forms of fly-fishing which require the same presentation as the dry fly. The dry-fly equipment, for the dragged fly over broken water, can be used, but obviously the tackle is not the best for the job. The line should be on the heavy side to encourage sinking, and the rod must be faster to match the weight of the line. This type of fly-fishing does not call for the same degree of accuracy or delicacy of presentation, so that the use of heavier tackle is not of account.

This brings us to the tackle usually preferred for wet-fly fishing. On ordinary trout streams, my own preference is for a fast rod of about 9 feet, weighing 5 oz. or less, and a terylene line of about "C" belly rating. I use one outfit consisting of a terylene "B" classification line, with a very powerful $8\frac{1}{2}$-foot rod, on occasions, but only in head winds of exceptional strength. These lines control well and, if rubbed over with detergent, sink quickly. For handling trout up to 2 lb. frequently, and occasional 4 lb. to 5 lb. fish, this tackle is ideal. When it comes to handling grilse or sea-trout from 5 lb. to 10 lb., the general run of anglers appear to prefer a 9 foot to $9\frac{1}{2}$ foot rod, weighing something nearer 7 oz. This type of rod, with fairly fast action, will cast any normal line up to terylene of ·055 inch belly diameter, or Wet Cel of something like that equivalent in weight. My preference still remains with a rod of under 6 oz., of 9 feet at the outside. Some very powerful rods of this type are on the market, and for all that I have moderately strong wrists, in regular practice, I have never understood the preference for weight in the hand, either in casting or during the play of the fish. In casting, of course, weight in the hand reduces velocity and is to be avoided for that reason.

Much the same applies to tackle for use on lakes and reservoirs as applies for the heavier tackle for sea-trout. If long casting is needed, the outfit must be moderately powerful, but by that I do not mean heavy. Fast 4 oz. rods have been made to carry lines of considerable weight, such as the terylene HBG grading, with a belly diameter of ·055 inch. A slightly heavier rod, in my opinion, is the ideal, since it will undergo considerable strain. Anything over 6 oz., however, is unnecessary. The action must be fast and the line matched to it. In the right hands, the caster will cast consistently over 35 yards, and if he uses the right technique he will not tire. If his technique is unsound, and he does tire, it is merely correcting one fault with another to use equipment which must inevitably slow the velocity of the cast.

For the double-handed salmon cast, with the heavy 14 foot rod, silk line with a belly diameter of ·065 inch to ·070 inch is required. This is rated about No. 6 in the "Kingfisher" range, or No. 10 in the Hardy range. The general-purpose rod of about 13 feet still requires a No. 6 line if it is other than slow in action. Fairly large flies can be cast with this combination, though when the size rises to from 6/0 to 8/0, the tackle is not heavy enough to obtain good performance. Personally, I dislike using anything above 2/0 with a lighter rod and line than the 26 oz. rod previously described. Finally, we come to the light double-handed rod of about 12 feet. Unless it has an exceptionally fast action, it carries a No. 5 line comfortably, and is the ideal combination for greased-line fishing with small flies.

The last point concerning lines is a differentiation between what are called "double-taper" and "forward-taper" designs. A double-taper line has a long belly, tapered down to ends of the same dimensions. It can be put on the reel from either end with the same result. The traditional length for trout lines is 30 yards, and for salmon lines, 40 yards. The forward-taper line has what is known as a "casting head" of about 36 feet. It is designed as a sort of elongated plug. The traditional backing line is of braided silk, something less than the point of the line in diameter. The principle is that, in the case of the double-taper, the distance of the cast is limited because the propelled head of the line cannot draw out stripped line of the belly weight that remains wound to the reel when the maximum controllable line is outside the rod-tip; whereas the lighter backing of the forward-taper line does not have the same retarding effect, and can be "shot", that is to say, pulled off the reel in advance and allowed to flow out under the pull of the forward-moving line during the fore cast. Although the forward-taper design has minor disadvantages against the double-taper, I used such a line for some time without experiencing any trouble. Latterly, however, I have bought double-taper lines, cut them in half at 45 feet, and backed each half with about 50 yards of 18 lb. test monofil. It is rare, during ordinary fishing, that the angler wants more than 35 feet of line outside the rod-tip, which, with a line of 45 feet means that a couple of coils of casting head are still round the drum of the reel; and whether the rest of the line on the reel is expensive braided silk or synthetic, or monofil, is of no account whatever. If the angler wants real distance, he can work the whole of the 45 feet outside the tip, with a couple of yards of monofil after it, and go into the distance cast of 35 yards or so—assuming, of course, that the rod is powerful enough. Moreover, the remaining half of the double-taper line can be properly stored until wanted, instead of suffering the deterioration inherent upon being wound to the reel beneath the line in use. Again, 45 feet is not a hard-and-fast point: the two lines may be varied, at the choice of the angler, to, say, 40 feet and 50 feet if he so wishes.

Reels. There is only one principle to be observed in picking a fly-reel. It should be the lightest possible to carry the amount of line that will be required. The maxim, "the reel should balance the rod", is meaningless. If a rod requires a reel to balance it, the design of the rod is faulty. The ideal is to cast without any reel on the rod. I am assuming, of course, that the reel is soundly made. For the last twelve months I have been using a fly-reel that cost under 30/-. It is a bit heavy, but I have no other complaint.

Leaders. This is an American term for the six to ten feet of gut or monofilament attached to the point of the reel line. We, by tradition, call this a "cast". Etymologically speaking, I prefer "cast", but its use can be very confusing if applied both ways in a technical treatise on casting. In a major work on casting the authors faced this problem and settled firmly for clarity, rather than etymological preferences. So that here, too, I propose to use the term "leader" for the point of the fly-line.

The angler has a choice of three materials for his leader: horsehair, gut and nylon monofilament. I have used horsehair, partly out of curiosity and partly because one or two anglers insisted that it laid the fly down more gently than any other material. I was not very convinced about the latter point, after trial, and the inherent disadvantages of horsehair make it quite plain why it was virtually ousted by gut when the latter became available.

When we turn to gut and monofil (to give it the familiar abbreviated name), we face a point of much controversy over recent years. Let us start with a comparison of the two materials.

	GUT			*MONOFIL*	
					Dry
Grade.	Diameter.	Breaking Strain.		Diameter.	Breaking Strain.
1X	·010 inch	3·5 lb.		·010 inch	6 lb.
2X	·009 inch	2·7 lb.		·009 inch	5 lb.
3X	·008 inch	2 lb.		·008 inch	4 lb.
4X	·007 inches	1·5 lb.		·007 inches.	3 lb.

On these figures, even if one makes the generous allowance of $33\frac{1}{3}$ per cent for the wet against the dry breaking strain of monofil, the balance of strength is well against gut. Monofil is also very cheap. Its alleged faults are two: the first, that it is difficult to knot securely; the second, that it does not turn over and extend, in the cast, as well as gut.

Monofil first became procurable about twenty years ago, when the medical profession obtained supplies for stitching. It was very springy and my first attempts with it were disappointing. The knots "gave" frequently. Modern monofil, however, is quite different in composition. I have used it for fly leaders for years, and do not remember a knot slipping. The knots I use are a four-turn blood for making up; a turle for dry fly (trout); a half-blood for wet fly (trout or sea-trout); and a tucked half-blood for salmon.

So far as turn-over is concerned, I have examined the tackle of many of the top casters in the World trout-fly accuracy event, and have yet to find a preference for gut. A perfect turn-over is vital in this event, and if gut gave a better turn-over than monofil it would be used universally.

We then come to latter-day expositions on the advantages of forward-taper leaders. So far as leaders of this design are concerned, several of us have given them exhaustive trial for tournament work. We have had various impressions and fancies, but they all broke down when we tried to distinguish a normal-taper leader from a forward-taper, blindfold! There was no difference in "feel", and after further experiments in turn-over we came to the conclusion that there was nothing in it between taper and forward-taper. Since these experiments, we have turned to leaders of about 8 feet steeply and evenly tapered. A leader of under 8 feet has a tendency to fault on the turn-over and turn the fly back upon it. The ideal taper is from a diameter, for lack of a better gauge, of about two-thirds of the diameter of the point of the reel line. That is, if the reel line has an "H" point of ·025 inch diameter the leader butt should be of ·016 inch (16 lb. test) to ·018 inch (19 lb. test) monofil. Use of so thick a leader head will doubtless horrify many, but the primary objective in presentation is to ensure a good turn-over of the point. Unless a leader is designed in this way, the turn-over becomes inconsistent at all times, particularly in wind. Moreover, if the leader is to be a long one of, say, 12 feet for chalk-stream work, the thicker the butt, the greater the latitude in stepping down to the point. I have read much advice about the graduation of monofil leaders, and have tried out a considerable number of these designs which

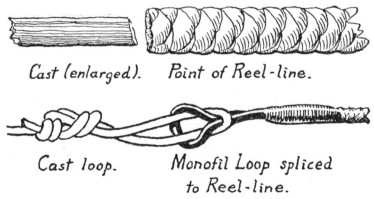

Cast (enlarged).   Point of Reel-line.

Cast loop.   Monofil Loop spliced
to Reel-line.

FIG. 47. *The cast should taper upwards so that the top section is two-thirds of the diameter of the point of the reel line. The most satisfactory connection is made by splicing a monofil loop to the point of the reel line, to which the cast is joined as shown.*

were supposed to perform miracles. There has been very little difference in performance so long as the tapering was not bordering on the eccentric! I suspect that Charles Cotton was right, three centuries ago, when he said that the rod and line of the angler should "taper from your very hand to your hook". Any even taper will perform well if the cast is good, and at the price of monofil, it is better that the angler should experiment for himself.

The leader for fishing with the dry fly is of the utmost importance. Its importance is maintained, to some extent, in wet-fly fishing; but in lake fishing, and fishing for grilse and sea-trout, although turn-over remains important, accuracy and delicacy of presentation are not so vital unless the experienced angler is fishing low water and employing every artifice he knows to bring fish to the fly. In such cases the angler will know enough about his game to make further comment unnecessary.

When we turn to the salmon leader, I can well remember my surprise at the casual approach of one very experienced angler who taught me a great deal about the game. "It matters little what you use," he said. "So long as it is strong enough, about 11 feet long, and the knots are properly tied." After some experiment I think he was about right, though I like a tapered leader, in three sections of about equal length. Also, I prefer the butt-end to keep the relationship of two-thirds diameter of the line point.

Conclusions. It may be considered that a great deal of space has been given to this commentary on tackle in a chapter which deals with casting, and too little to the methods of using tackle. I make no apology for this, because over a period of many years' wandering round the angling world, I have come to the conclusion that much of the poor casting that one sees is due to the fact that fly-fishermen are attempting to cast with tackle which makes it almost impossible for them to cast well. Their tackle "works somehow": that is all. It is frequently asserted that there are three parts to a cast: a man, a rod and a line. And that all three must be suited to each other. I incline to question this. An experienced caster with a good style will put up a good performance with any well-balanced rod and line. He may fancy one type of equipment more than another, and probably his performance will be fractionally better with the kit he fancies. What he will detect immediately is any lack of balance between rod and line.

THE OVERHEAD TROUT-FLY CAST

Before beginning any dissertation on casting methods, I should like to acknowledge my debt to Captain T. L. Edwards so far as anything I know is concerned. Apart from an outstanding record in the international tournament lists, he has both studied and taught casting for over thirty years, and has set many a noted angler on the way to better casting. Latterly, I have instructed a number of beginners, and indeed some anglers of experience, in casting. I have also watched others engaged in teaching casting. The conclusion I have reached is that the method of Captain Edwards, for all that it differs from that of several other teachers, is immeasurably more effective than any other method. The results are achieved more quickly, and the style, when it follows the teaching, is really sound.

Let us, then, move into action with these methods.

Grip. The caster holds a medium-action 8½ foot rod, with a No. 3 line, an 8 foot leader and a tuft of frayed yarn instead of a fly. He is on the edge of water, since grass practice is to be avoided if possible, as it tends to cause what we call a "lazy lift" when the angler comes to water. The caster strips three yards of line from the reel with a disengaged finger and begins to wave the rod backwards and forwards until the stripped line has been worked up the rings by this motion. His grip on the rod is firm, but in no circumstances tight, since strain of any sort is foreign to the good cast. The most relaxed grip is that in which the "V" formed by the thumb and the inside of the forefinger is on the top of the rod, parallel with the line of cast. The thumb or forefinger at the back of the rod is restrictive of action. The only purpose of having the thumb at the back of the rod is in the long cast, when it aids the power of rod torque being put in by the caster. The forefinger up the rod is supposed to aid accuracy, but if so, the majority of accuracy stars in the World Championships are missing an advantage, since they do not favour such a grip.

Action of casting. Outside the tip of the rod, the caster will have about 9 feet of dressed reel line and the 8 foot leader. Continuing to wave the rod, he strips more line until he can feel the weight of line flexing the rod nicely in both back cast and fore cast. The average novice masters this backward and forward movement quite well after very brief practice. It is when the moment comes for release that trouble comes. He pushes the rod hand forward, usually at hip level, with a convulsive twitch, and the line falls in an untidy bundle at his feet. The cast is a combined action of forearm and wrist, and can only be taught by some method which demonstrates this clearly to the novice. This method, the only effective one I know, is to make the caster, after his initial rod waving, sit on a chair or some object about the height of a chair. Let him then pillow his rod-hand elbow on his knee and begin his rod waving afresh. From this sitting position, provided he does not allow the elbow to leave the knee, his forearm and wrist movements cannot be other than correct. After a few dozen casts, or rather waves of the rod and line, from this position, he can get to his feet and try to repeat the action from that position. If he fails, let him return to the sitting position and start again. In a very short time, this drill is effective in giving him the rudiments of forearm-wrist action.

Timing. Once he has mastered this action, he can move to the next stage. He will get the line out after a manner of speaking, but his cast will not have the sting and precision of the expert. These features come with correct timing (the nature of which has been the subject of comment in the explanation of casting mechanics), and with correct timing alone. A simple example of timing is the action of hitting a nail into a piece of wood with a hammer. The whole action in this case is not an exact parallel with the cast because the hammer is raised slowly, without the need to flex the shaft, and then brought down with a blow which increases in speed to the instant of impact. A cast is, in fact, a double hammer blow; the first to drive the line behind the caster, and the second to drive it forward. Let the caster then return to his sitting position and imagine that he has a wall behind him with a nail in it. Let him imagine that the rod is his hammer, and that he must drive the nail in, behind him, over his rod-hand shoulder. He should watch the action of the rod with care. He will find that the tip curves forward to its maximum between 11 o'clock and 12 o'clock. By the time 12 o'clock has been reached, the tip will have reverted to the straight and inert position, and will then tend to curve the reverse way as the line unfolds backwards and begins to make its weight felt. If the rod is not moved, the line will fall to the ground and the rod will revert to the straight, but if the caster can pick the moment when the backward flex of the rod is at its greatest, and move the rod forward, he will find that the flex of the rod increases and the "feel" of the weight of the line is greatly accentuated. If the forward movement of the rod is continued, the line will be thrown forward as the flex of the rod straightens, but it will not be a good fore cast, in all probability. The reason will simply be that the forward movement of the rod will be no more than a hammer blow in which the hammer is allowed to fall on the nail, without force being applied. If the caster now imagines that he has a nail in wood before him, at about chest level, and tries to drive that nail in with the forecast, as he did with the back cast then the line will fly out with snap and velocity. Shortening this parallel, the force is applied in the back cast between 10 and 11 o'clock, and in the fore cast between 11 and 10 o'clock. Confusion is also caused by failure to appreciate *when*, in the back cast, the forearm action is supplemented by wrist action. The back cast begins with the rod held roughly parallel with the water. The first movement is a forearm lift, without any action in the wrist, from 9 o'clock to 10 o'clock. At 10 o'clock the wrist action comes in and drives up the power very fast, so that the full power *is expended* before the 12 o'clock position has been reached. It is better to expend the power too early, than too late, since early power application tends too throw the line upward behind the caster. This leaves some latitude for the downward pull of gravity as the line is extended, lacking velocity, behind the caster. Even if the line drops

o

slightly, it will still maintain a good position when the tip moves into the fore cast and fills it with fresh velocity. The bad cast is almost invariably caused, in my experience, by late application of power in the back cast and by a spread of power in the fore cast, instead of the late snap of the hammer blow which I have described.

The caster, once he has mastered forearm-wrist movement, and timing, has reached the last stage of the fly cast.

Use of off-rod hand. So far, he has been holding up just so much line as flexed the rod comfortably, with the reel end held beneath his finger to prevent involuntary draw off of line against the check of the reel. Let him now take the reel end of the line from beneath his finger, draw off another foot or two of line, and hold it in the off-rod hand. This hand should be held motionless, level with, and

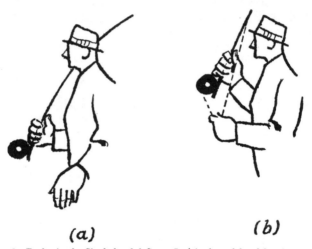

(a)   **(b)**

Fig. 48. *Faults in the Single-handed Cast: In (a) the rod hand has been kept at hip level and the rod has been allowed to flop back behind the caster by slackening the grip. In (b) the correct position is shown. The forearm has been raised to bring the hand to chin level, the wrist has flexed slightly and the rod is held in a firm but relaxed grip.*

a few inches in front of, its corresponding hip. If he starts casting again, he will detect a difference. There will be increased snap in the cast. This is due to a mechanical factor caused by his off-rod hold on the line, and it adds velocity to the movements of the line outside the rod-tip. Moreover, as he progresses with his casting, he will find a tendency to *use* the off-rod hand, instead of keeping it stationary. This tendency should not be resisted. The almost imperceptible draw away of line during the back cast, and slack off of the line in the fore cast, are the hall-marks of the finished caster. Moreover, the "shoot" of the loop of line held in the off-rod hand, towards the end of the fore cast, makes for an improved lay of the line.

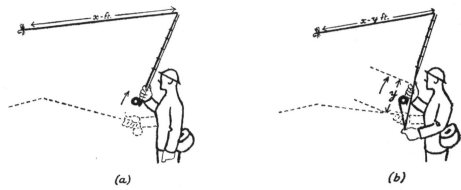

FIG. 49. *The action of the off-rod hand in the single-handed fly cast: The most important factor in line control is the velocity of the line outside the rod tip. In (a) the caster has merely lifted the length of x-feet of line. In (b) he has held the line below the butt ring. Although he started to lift the same x-feet of line, the length of line outside the tip at the backward position has been reduced by the length of the lift of the rod hand—the over-all velocity of the line being increased accordingly. It is on this principle that the exaggerated draw-off of the line in the distance cast on lakes is founded.*

This method of casting is common to all casts with the single-handed rod. The only variation is the exaggeration of the off-rod hand pull to give the full distance cast. Any introduction to this highly specialized cast, useful only in lake fishing, would call for some space. It is fully described in textbooks on casting, and beyond the observation that it makes casts of over 40 yards with suitable equipment comparatively easy, it must be left at that. It may be worth noting that, in recent British Casting Championships, an average of 48 yards was cast with a fast 9 foot bamboo rod and a standard forward-taper ·056 inch belly (No. 5) line. The longest of the scoring casts was 52 yards.

THE OVERHEAD DOUBLE-HANDED FLY CAST

Position of hands. This cast is, as I have observed earlier, no more than the single-handed cast with the lower hand supporting a rod which is too heavy to be manipulated by one hand. The initial cause of trouble with this cast, even among competent single-handed casters, is a tendency to allow the lower hand to stray about the front of the body during the cast. As a start, the caster can do worse than use Captain Edwards's gimmick of hooking the thumb of the lower hand in the coat or trouser buttons. The point of keeping the lower hand in something like a stationary position during the cast is simply that it acts in the nature of a fulcrum. Movement of it destroys the full power of rod flex, and, if moved laterally, causes the rod-tip to move in a curve and cause "cut". This feature of the cast is due to a circular movement by the rod-tip, so that the line, instead

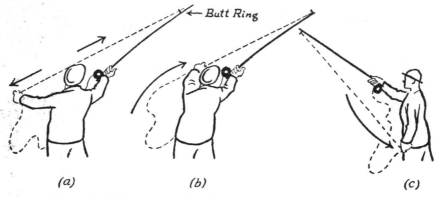

(a)   (b)   (c)

FIG. 50. *The action of the off-rod hand in the single-handed distance cast for lake fishing: The caster holds a certain amount of slack line between the reel and and his left hand. As he brings the rod back (a) he increases its flex by moving the left hand in the opposite direction. This action also increases the line velocity. As the line unfolds behind him he allows its weight to draw the left hand upwards towards the butt ring (b). As he comes into the fore cast, he pulls the left hand down hard (c). This increases the forward velocity of the line and increases rod flex. Immediately he feels the weight of the line going forward, he releases his hold and the extending line draws out the slack to increase the length of the cast. This is commonly called "shooting" line.*

of moving in a single plane back and fore, moves in a curved plane and loses velocity.

Timing. The principles of rod flex and timing are exactly the same in both the single-handed and double-handed casts. If the caster will concentrate on the upper hand when executing the double-

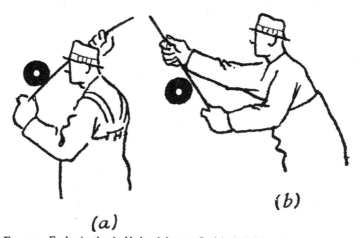

(a)

(b)

FIG. 51. *Faults in the double-handed cast: In (a) the left hand has been allowed to stray across the front of the body and the rod has flopped back behind the caster. In (b) the right shoulder has been pushed through, which causes "cut"; and the left hand has strayed forward instead of being brought back to a point roughly beneath the heart.*

handed cast, and imagine that the rod is still a single-handed instrument, he will experience no difficulty. After a little practice, possibly
starting with the coat button gimmick, he will find that he can safely
allow freedom of action to the lower hand. Although it may move
a few inches, it will never stray across an imaginary line drawn down
the centre of the body, and will always finish tucked well into the
body below the heart as the peak of power is reached in the fore cast.

THE ROLL CAST AND VARIATIONS

Fundamentally, there are only two casts in fishing: the "overhead"
cast that I have described, and the roll cast. The term "overhead"
is not a good one, because, no matter in what plane the rod is held
from the vertical to the horizontal, the cast is precisely the same. The
roll cast, with its variations the Spey and the Double-Spey, is a most
important one. The principles that govern it are different from those
governing the overhead cast.

The roll cast is a method of projecting the line from the angler
without raising it and throwing it backwards in order to straighten
it before the forward cast. The cast is clearly important to the
angler when he is fishing away from a wall of trees or rock, which
would interfere with his back cast if he used the straightforward
overhead cast. The roll cast is sometimes differentiated from the
"switch" cast on the ground that, in the former, the loop of line
ahead of the angler is never lifted wholly from the water, while in
the latter it is in fact lifted clear just before delivery. It is not easy
to see this distinction in two identical movements, and for practical
purposes, both the roll cast and the switch cast are the same.

Method of execution. The first requisite of the straightforward roll
cast is that the line should lie extended ahead of the angler. The rod
is raised slowly to a point slightly past the vertical, causing the line
to bag in an even curve from the tip of the rod to the water. The
success of the cast is entirely dependent on the evenness of this curve.
If the curve is even at the moment the rod-tip begins to travel forward, the cast always goes out under a minimum of power, but if
the slightest irregularity is thrown into the curve by a jerk, or by
pushing the whole rod forward as delivery starts, the cast will be
poor. It is for this reason that the raising of the rod must be slow
and smooth. It is also the reason why a rod with slow, or butt,
action (see Fig. 46(a)) is the best for the roll cast or its variations. From
the extreme of the back position, the rod is thrust forward hard. But
again, the thrust must be timed and not a mere violent push. The
forward motion begins slowly and accelerates to a peak of power at
10 o'clock. The line will then roll out and ultimately, if the cast has
been executed properly, straighten out ahead of the angler. In
executing this cast with the single-handed rod, the body enters little
into the cast, but with the double-handed rod it is most important

that the weight of the body should be transferred to the rear foot during the backward movement, and transferred again to the front foot during the forward movement. The forward foot will be that on the side of the lower hand. The vital factors in this cast are absolutely smooth, integrated movement throughout, and the start of the fore cast while the curve of the line still shows, or gives the feeling of, a degree of tension owing to the drag of the point of the line against the resistance of the water surface. A good caster, who has learned the action thoroughly, can lift a short line in such a way that, just before the moment of forward thrust, the point of the line is raised clear of the water. This, as I have said, has been called the "switch", but the action is precisely that of the roll and there is no merit, that I can see, in lifting the line in this way unless there happens to be some marginal obstruction in front of the angler, such as weed or rock, which would interfere with the even fall of the curve.

The principles of the roll cast are precisely the same for any rod and line, single-handed or double-handed. In the double-handed cast, the fulcrum effect of the lower hand is exactly the same as in the overhead cast, and the lower hand should, at the peak of power, tuck itself into the body beneath the heart.

Changing direction. In the roll cast, as I have described it, there has been no change of direction, but in practical fishing the angler rarely picks the line up and casts it back in the same direction. So that a means must be devised for picking up the line from one direction and changing to another, without fouling the body of the caster with the line during the process. This brings us to the Spey cast, and its modification, the Double-Spey cast.

The first principle to observe in any cast is that, if the line is not lying on the surface, it is more difficult (if not impossible) to lift it cleanly. In the overhead cast, when a change of direction is required, the first step is to bring the line to the surface, either by lifting the tip of the rod or, if the line is deep sunk, by roll-casting in the direction in which the line is lying, once or twice. The rod is then pointed in the direction in which the new cast is to travel, lifted in the ordinary way, and the cast made. Any attempt to change direction while the line is aerialized is fundamentally bad casting. When we come to the roll cast, particularly with a heavy salmon line extended to some length, it is not sufficient to point the rod to the new direction and attempt the lift and drive forward, since the essence of the roll cast is that the curved line shall lie roughly in line with the new direction. A movement must therefore be made which brings the line into a position from which it can be driven forward. This is the Spey movement.

The Spey cast. Let us suppose the cast has fished itself out directly downstream of the angler, who is fishing on the left bank of the river. He wishes to make a new cast at an angle of about 45 degrees, cross-stream. First, he raises the rod-tip to 10 o'clock; or, if the line is deeply sunk, rolls straight downstream to bring the line to the surface. Then, with the rod-tip held high at the 10 o'clock position, he starts his action. The rod-tip is swept in a downward curve across the front of his body, often called the "U" movement of this cast. The bottom of the "U" will be roughly in the line of new direction. When it reaches the bottom point, the rod-tip is then raised until eventually it is at a point slightly past the vertical, from which the angler would start a normal roll cast. But although I have referred to a sweep of the line by this movement, it is anything but a sweep in the true sense; that is, a gradual movement in which speed is even throughout. The vital factor of this so-called sweep is that it starts slowly and reaches a peak of power, very similar to that in any other cast, at a point slightly to the upstream side of the angler. This has the effect of *whisking* the line, still in a drooping curve, to a position in which the point lies roughly on the line of the new cast, and the rest of the line falls in a curve slightly to the upstream side of that line. The angler is then properly poised for an ordinary roll cast, with the line in a position from which it can be cast.

That is the Spey cast. The only point to be added is that it can only be cast with the right hand up the double-handed rod, from the left bank of the river, and with the left hand up the rod from the right bank of the river. In both cases the forward foot is that corresponding to the hand, and the importance of correct transfer of body weight between the feet is no less than in the case of the double-handed roll cast.

The Double-Spey cast. On occasions, the downstream wind is so strong that it is impossible to put sufficient power into the "U" movement to get the line into a position from which it can be rolled forward, and yet clear the body of the angler as it turns over. This calls for the Double-Spey action. Let us suppose the angler is on the left bank, with the line fished out directly below him. He first reverses his feet, so that the left foot is forward. He then reverses his hand positions so that the left hand is up the rod. The line is then drawn steadily upstream until the rod-tip is well upstream of the angler. The rod-tip is lifted, the "U" movement is put in from the upstream position, in a downstream direction, and the roll cast is then made over the left shoulder. The converse applies to this cast from the right bank of the river. This is the Double-Spey cast.

Changing hands. It may sound as though this calls for ambidextrous casting, which lies beyond the capacity of most anglers, but it will be found, after a very short practice, that there is a great deal of difference between casting with either hand with a single-handed rod and casting with either hand up the rod with the double-handed rod. The latter is comparatively easy. If any angler wishes to attain some measure of single-handed casting with the unaccustomed hand, there is a method of practice which, to me at any rate, did not prove unduly troublesome. For one season, every time I left the river to walk back to the car, I took the fly off and "cast" my way back, using the left hand. (I am right-handed.) The only real difficulty is to master the draw-off with the off-rod hand. But after a season's persistence, I found that I could change hands with some confidence. I have never been as comfortable with the left-hand cast, but this is partly due to the fact that I have found so little use for it. In the normal way, it is quicker to change to a back-hand cast, and only in a few places on any river does one find the bank-side vegetation, or other obstruction, such that the only way of covering a fish is with a left-hand cast as opposed to a back-handed cast with the right hand.

CASTING IN A WIND

Although I have touched on the problem of wind in dealing with lines, nothing has been said about the special action of the caster when he contends with wind. A line is a weight with a considerable surface upon which air resistance can make itself felt. The ratio of effect depends on the angle of incidence. Take the simple instance of a line suspended loosely in a vertical position and tethered at each end. The wind would cause a heavy "bag" as it hit the line surface roughly at right angles to the long dimension. If the line were held end-on, however, pointing into the wind, the effect would be relatively slight. There is a feature of the fly cast which has been called, somewhat mysteriously, "the bow". The bow of the cast can be either wide, or tight.

It is evident that the wide bow has far more susceptibility to air resistance than the tight bow. The feature of the tight bow is of vital importance in the tournament distance cast, and in the casts of Tarrantino, for instance, the line appears almost to rub along itself during the turn-over. The wide bow develops if the rod-tip describes a wide arc, while the tight bow can only be cast if the movement of the tip is kept as nearly as possible to a straight line. It need hardly be added that the line velocity of a tight-bow cast is immeasurably greater than that of a wide-bow cast, and that, for this reason, the tighter the bow, the less line surface is presented to the wind and the greater the force of the line in boring through the wind. If a good caster is watched in his work against the wind, it will be noted that he takes his rod back very shortly in the back cast, since the wind helps the line out and this short movement reduces the length, and therefore the curve, of the rod-tip. He then drives very hard into the fore cast and puts the power in later than in the normal cast. For all that he may not realize the fact, his action is designed to move the rod-tip in as nearly a straight line as possible and to present as little of the line surface to the retarding force of the wind as possible. In the double-handed salmon cast, the butt hand should be raised during the application of power, again very late in the fore cast. The rod-tip often enters the water at the end of this cast. This is no fault, but rather an indication that the power has been put in at the right place.

Only two other points need mention. The first is that the slower the action of the rod, the wider the bow must be. A really tight bow can only be cast with a very stiff rod, and therefore a line of sufficient weight to flex that rod. The failure of light lines in a wind is partly due to the nature of the rod with which they have to be matched, and therefore to the width of the bow which is inevitable. An interesting corollary, of course, is that if a rod can be found which will flex correctly to the weight of a light line, so that a tight bow can be cast, the combination will work well in a wind for all the inherent lightness of the line.

The second point is that the same principles apply whether the cast has to be made into a head-wind or in a cross-wind. The basis of the cast in a troublesome wind is the increase of line velocity.

CONCLUSION

My final comment on the subject of casts may seem paradoxical after so long a dissertation: it is that casting cannot be learned from a book! I will carry the paradox even further by saying that an hour or two with a *good* instructor (a rare breed, I fear) will improve the angler's casting far more quickly than any study of the written word. The instructor can see the faults, whereas the angler's actions, for all that he may think they follow precisely the recommendations of the book, may frequently depart widely from those recommendations. Again, the good instructor will know immediately, after a cast or two with the angler's equipment, whether it is at fault.

The main trouble, at the present day, is to find a good instructor. Much instruction is given by keepers and gillies. Though these gentlemen cast well enough for their own purposes, their knowledge of tackle and its refinements is usually superficial, and they have made no study of casting as a science. Their practical casting is a long way behind accomplished standards, so that what they see is the visible evidence of a fault, without being able to analyse the cause of what they see.

As an instance of what I mean, they note that the caster breaks his wrist in the back cast and allows the rod to flop behind him— with disastrous results. So they recommend the stiff wrist, which cures one fault by introducing another, of which the caster must rid himself before he begins to cast well. Again, they persist with the advice that the rod should be stopped at 12 o'clock; whereas if they knew the root cause of the backward slash of the rod, they would realize that it could not be cured, and turned into the correct action, by putting an inevitable jerk into the back cast as the rod is stopped deliberately.

A weak wrist action is nearly always due to failure to combine the forearm movement with the wrist action, and teaching (and practice) of the correct forearm-wrist action is the only cure. The backward slash of the rod past the vertical is always due to the fact that the power of the back cast has not been expended, as it must be, before the 12 o'clock position has been reached. The only cure is to experiment with this trick of compressing the power into the early move of the back cast. These points can be conveyed in a book, and reference can be made to them in case of trouble.

The intelligent caster will therefore combine the analysis of the book with the visual findings of his instructor. If the instruction is good, the whole will fit together. If the instruction is unsound, the eye of the instructor is at least reliable; and the instruction on the cure can be modified in the light of what the caster already knows of casting technique.

CHAPTER IX

FLY DRESSING
by
PETER DEANE

FLY dressing is a comparatively easy business. Any fly-fisherman can tie flies, regardless of whether they are for salmon, sea-trout or brown trout. It is rather like handwriting, which we take for granted; some, of course, do it far better than others. Many write naturally well and a few develop their writing to such a pitch it becomes an art in itself known as calligraphy, much in the same way as well-known fly dressers have developed their skill.

On occasions the perfectly-dressed fly fails as miserably as the crude one; so, apart from the personal satisfaction of tying well, the less impressive efforts of enthusiastic amateurs can and often do hold their own. The real gratification comes from taking a fish on something you have tied yourself and not to what extent your skill is admired by fellow fly-fishermen, though it would be smug to suggest that one is indifferent to such admiration.

My aim is to show the beginner how to dress a series of flies selected for their simplicity in construction, the availability of materials (an important point in these days), and attractiveness to fish, involving the basic techniques from which more complicated flies can eventually be tied. The order in which I have arranged the instructions is important. The first lesson is a hackled dry fly, which I consider the easiest for a beginner to try his hand at. This does not mean I consider dry-fly fishing more or less important than any other kind; it is just an ideal starting-point.

The object of each lesson is to give the simplest instruction *step by step*, so that the first finished fly can be used to catch fish, irrespective of what it may look like. Each lesson is complete in its own sphere and the basis for other patterns of that type. Stress is put on the instruction, the easiest way to use the materials, advice, the amount of material required, and how and from where to select it. Many refinements are omitted on purpose. If the reader wants to progress he will do so, regardless of this. Before starting on the lessons, however, it is necessary to say something of the tools and materials which will be required.

MATERIALS

There is such a vast number of difficult materials that one can spend any amount of building up a collection, so I offer the same advice as everyone else who has written on the subject: buy the minimum and add to it as required. Fly dressers take almost as much pride in their materials as they do in the flies they make with them. With economy in mind and the prior knowledge that the beginner will, through trial and error, be bound to waste a certain amount, I have adopted the following course. At the beginning of each instruction in tying a particular type of fly I am giving the dressing and materials required to make it. Some materials used in one pattern can be used in another and in such cases this will be referred to at the time. The sooner one becomes familiar with the types of hooks, silks, furs, feathers and equipment available, the better. The following firms specialize in supplying materials for the fly dresser: Messrs. S. & E. G. Messeena, Tom C. Saville, and E. Veniard, all of whom supply excellent catalogues on request.

I have no intention of discussing materials to any great extent, as the subject is too big to be included here. A perfunctory survey with each lesson accompanied by an added comment where essential will suffice for practical purposes. I must, however, say something about hackles.

Hackles. Every fly-fisherman knows the importance of a hackle on a fly, whether it be a floating or sunk pattern. A good cock hackle makes a dry fly float better, gives "kick" or life to some wet flies (others are tied with hen hackles), and acts as an "attractor" when dyed a bright colour and used on salmon flies. Their importance cannot be over-estimated. Unfortunately, cock necks from which all sizes of individual hackles can be selected are in very short supply. This is most unfortunate, as they are the basis of all fly-tying and there is little likelihood of the position regarding them improving at present.

Even so, the beginner can take heart, as the situation is not quite so bad as one would think for dry flies. Much has been written about cock hackles—stiff in the fibres, sparkling, well-graduated shape with small fibres at the tip and slightly longer ones at the base of the stalk. They look wonderful and flatter even a novice's work but, despite what the authorities say, they do not always make the best floaters. The cock hackle which makes a fly float best of all has a quality which the old-fashioned dressers call "spring". Any cock hackle has spring when its tips have a pronounced curve. By holding it by its tip and running the finger and thumb of the other hand down the stalk so the fibres stand out at right angles, you will notice that the tip of each fibre has what to all intents and purposes looks like a little foot on it. Such hackles, which may appear ugly in reality, make splendid floaters and the so-called feet make it cock well on the water and float far longer than any hackle with super-pointed fibres. Dark red cock hackles (Indian Game) have a pronounced tendency for being well sprung and are usually readily obtainable. It is only fair to add that they also have a tendency for lacking in graduation, i.e. sometimes the fibres at the tip are longer than those at the base. Irrespective of this, for making your fly float they have no equal.

The dealers will always send you the best hackles available, and whilst cock necks are limited the full neck is often obtainable loose in a packet. The snag here, of course, is that it is far easier to select a hackle for a particular size of hook from a skin (i.e. neck) than to hunt about in the contents of a packet spread over the table. If hackles do not come up to one's expectations, there is little one can do about it, but luckily this applies to cocks' hackles only, the majority of other feathers being as good as ever and in fair supply.

TOOLS AND ACCESSORIES

Fly-tying vice. There are various patterns on the market, and the beginner should choose one which will hold both small trout hooks and large salmon "irons", as they are called. Fig. 52 shows the two main types in use.

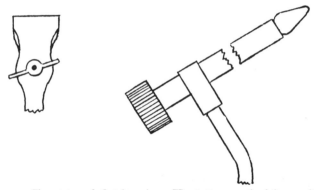

FIG. 52. *Two types of fly-tying vices. The pattern on the left resembles a miniature workshop vice on a long stem, the jaws being operated by a butterfly nut. That on the right, of which there are several variations, is of the collet type, operated by a milled head.*

Catch. Some vices have a small rubber button attached in which to hold the silk when you want both hands free. This, however, is necessarily situated at the foot of the vice itself, where it is virtually useless, so it is advisable to make your own catch, which can be done as follows. Slip a small metal washer over the point of a screw so that it slides down to the head, drive the screw into the centre of a piece of india rubber about the size of a halfpenny, and screw this into the edge of the table or work bench about five inches to the right of where the vice will be (Fig. 53). The silk can then be held firmly between the rubber and the bench at any time during the operations. Substitutes for this are a pair of hackle pliers suspended from the silk or a device known as a bobbin-holder.

Hackle pliers. The jaws of these pliers are opened by pressing each

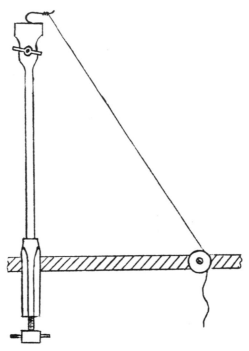

FIG. 53. *The "catch" in use. This consists of a rubber button screwed into the edge of the work bench, as shown.*

side of the shoulders between the finger and thumb and they close automatically when the pressure is released. Their main purpose is to hold a hackle while it is being wound round the hook shank. Two pairs will be required, preferably of different sizes.

Scissors. These should have curved blades and be the best quality you can afford.

Tweezers. A pair with sharp points is required for picking up hooks and materials.

Dubbing needle. This can be made from any large needle driven eye-first into a wooden or cork handle.

Pen-knife and razor blade. The former with a blunt blade, the latter sharp.

Nail. This should be about 1½ inches long and is driven into the edge of the work bench well out of the way but within reach of your right hand, so that you can hang your lengths of waxed silk on it to prevent them tangling.

Camel-hair brush. For applying varnish. The smallest size obtainable.

Apron. This will be found most useful, as apart from keeping pieces of feather, etc., off one's clothes, any tools or materials which fall from the table will be collected in one's lap, thereby saving endless time in searching on the floor. A white one is best, as small hooks show up plainly against a white background.

Bench or work table. It will make your work far easier if you can find one to keep permanently for fly-tying and nothing else. Apart from the improvised silk-holding button and nail, which must be driven into the edge, it is so much better to have a resting-place for the numerous boxes and packets, which mount up surprisingly quickly. You may even have to stop work in the middle of tying a fly, in which case the tying silk is just slipped into the catch and the fly can be completed on your return, whether it be a few minutes or a few days later, taking up the work where you left off.

Storage boxes. For storing feathers of any type old cigar boxes are as good as anything, the cedar wood from which they are made acting as a moth-repellent. Other types of container should be sprinkled with naphtha flakes, which may be obtained from the chemist.

Fly-tyer's wax. A piece of this will be required for waxing the tying silk at the outset of operations.

Varnishes. A bottle of colourless Cellire, a bottle of spirit varnish and a bottle of black varnish. These are for varnishing the heads of flies.

Methylated spirit for cleaning the fingers.

Cotton-wool. A packet of cheap cotton-wool for applying the methylated spirit.

Acetone. A small bottle for cleaning the brush.

Tying silk. Pearsall's "Gossamer" brand in various colours. This is sold on small reels for fly-tying purposes.

Hooks. These will be required in various sizes, both for salmon and trout. They are usually sold in packets of a dozen, fifty or a hundred. Generally, up-eyed hooks are used for dry flies and down-eyed for wet flies. The wide-gape hook is a popular type.

Before making an actual start on a trout fly there are two operations which must be learnt—those of starting and finishing a fly. It is much easier to learn them on a bare shank and it will save endless time in future if they are mastered at the outset. They consist of:

1. Winding waxed silk round the shank from the eye to the bend of the hook and back again.

2. The whip finish.

When you can carry out these two simple operations your first attempt at tying an actual fly should take under fifteen minutes.

FIRST LESSON. WINDING THE SILK

To simplify this and subsequent lessons I am numbering each successive stage. Proceed as follows:

1. Set up the vice on your table or bench by screwing the clamp firmly to the edge, making sure that it is about five inches to the left of the rubber catch.

2. Place these materials in easy reach: a piece of wax, a reel of yellow silk, methylated spirit, a small piece of cotton-wool, a pen-knife and a size 1 trout hook.

3. With your pen-knife cut or dig off a small piece of wax, about the size of a pea, and hold it between the lips (not in the mouth). This softens the wax quickly. If you have warm hands, just hold it in the fingers.

4. Still keeping the wax between the lips, cut off a length of tying silk about 18 inches long and hold it in the middle between the finger and thumb of the right hand. Take the wax from the lips with the finger and thumb of the left hand, mould it and then press it as flat as possible. When soft, pull first one end of the silk then the other through the wax, so that the complete length is covered. Hang your waxed silk over the nail put in table-edge for that purpose. Wax five more pieces of the same length and put a soft wax pellet on top of your reel of silk so that it sticks to it—then you won't lose it. Finally, clean your fingers with a piece of cotton-wool and spirit.

5. Take one hook and inspect the barb, point and eye. Always make a point of doing this—nothing is more annoying than tying a fly only to discard it as you have discovered the hook is faulty.

6. Unscrew the jaws of your vice slightly and place the hook between them. The point of the hook should be covered by the jaws, which is easier to accomplish in a wide-jawed vice operated by a winged nut screw than in the collet type, in which the jaws end in a point. Failure to cover the hook in this manner results in a tendency to break the silk against the point in winding it round the shank, which during your first attempt is all-too easily done. Then tighten up the jaws.

7. Test your hook for temper by flicking it up and down with the thumb-nail on the eye. If the temper is correct it will spring back to its original position; if too soft it will not do this; if too hard it may snap.

8. Take a piece of waxed silk and pull it through the fingers to clean off any surplus wax. Hold one end between the finger and thumb of the left hand and four inches higher up with the finger and thumb of the right hand, keeping the silk taut between the hands.

9. Place the taut silk against the hook shank, the right hand uppermost, about the length of a hyphen to the left of the eye.

10. Still keeping the silk taut between the hands, wind it with the right hand closely three or four times round the shank, working towards the bend of the hook. If the silk has been kept taut the turns made by the right hand will not only have gone round the

LOW WATER
PATTERNS:
Silver Blue
Spinning Jenny
Sweep (*Hairwing*)
Rhy Ness (*Norwe-
gian*)

HAIR-WING
PATTERNS:
Black Doctor
Silver Doctor
Thunder & Light-
ning

Hairy Mary
Old Charlie
Black Mary

CONVENTIONAL
PATTERNS:
Jock Scott
Mar Lodge

TUBE-FLIES:
Black & Yellow
Jungle, Black & Red
Basset Hound

PLATE I: SALMON FLIES
(From flies dressed by Peter Deane)

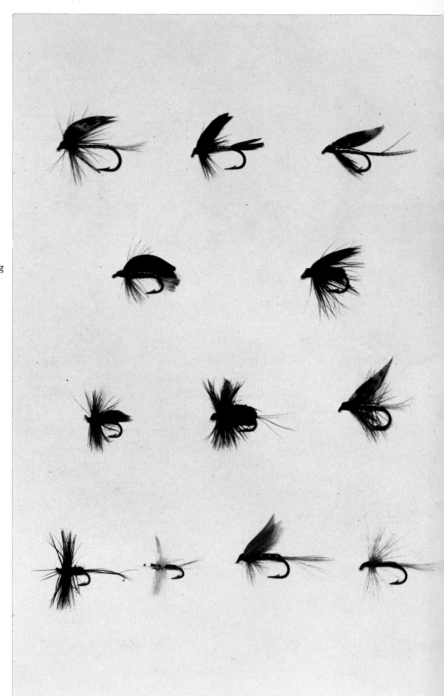

Left to right

Silver Invicta
Butcher
Silver March Brown

Greenwell Yellow Tag
Alder

Sedge
Hawthorn
Invicta

Hackled Black Net
Pale Watery Spinner
Red Spinner
Blue Upright

PLATE II: SEA-TROUT AND DRY-FLIES

shank, but also round the length of silk held by the end in the left hand. Continue to wind three more turns, still towards the bend.

11. Let the silk go with the left hand and place the long end, still kept taut, in the catch; if there is no catch, attach the hackle pliers to the end. (Fig 54).

12. If this has been done correctly the silk will hold firm on the shank. Cut off the waste silk.

Fig. 54. *Winding the Silk. The taut end of the tying silk on the right of this and subsequent diagrams is secured in the rubber catch (not shown).*

13. Take the silk out of the catch and hold it between the finger and thumb of the right hand about four inches below the hook shank. If you work with too long a piece of silk, manipulation, irrespective of what stage you are at, is just that much more difficult; in other words, work with a comparatively short length and as you require more silk just slide your hand down. Now wind slowly in close, even turns towards the bend of the hook, keeping the silk taut the whole time.

14. On reaching the bend (do not take silk beyond the straight part of the shank) wind back in slow even turns, each turn touching but not overlapping its neighbour. Stop about ⅛ inch short of the eye and place the silk in the catch. The work is now ready for the next lesson.

Comment. This may seem an extremely long-winded way to explain such a simple operation, but it is important and a good foundation always simplifies the rest of the work. After a few tries the beginner will manage it in a second or two and carry it out automatically.

SECOND LESSON. THE WHIP FINISH

This is another simple operation which may be learned at the first attempt or, in some cases, after a little practice. The fact still remains, until the beginner can do this with confidence he cannot finish any flies securely, no matter how expertly he has dressed them. For this purpose we must imagine the whole fly is completely tied and only needs a whip finish at the head of the hook to make secure.

1. Take the silk out of the catch and hold it with the forefinger and thumb of the right hand about 3 inches below the eye of the hook with the *forefinger on top of the silk, thumb underneath.* The elbow

P

should be pointing to the right and the arm approximately parallel with the edge of the table.

2. Without moving the arm, rotate the forefinger and thumb (turning away from your body) so that the thumb comes on top and the forefinger underneath. Do not release your grip and keep the silk taut between the hook and fingers. The loose end of the silk should fall automatically across the length held in the right hand, making an approximate letter "D" (Fig. 55).

3. Keeping the silk taut with the right hand, take hold of it with the forefinger and thumb of the left hand, the forefinger uppermost just above where it was gripped with the fingers of the right hand. Then take the right hand away (Fig. 56).

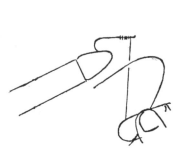
Fig. 55. *The Whip Finish* (1).

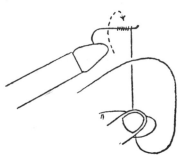
Fig. 56. *The Whip Finish* (2).

4. Still keeping the silk taut between the left hand and hook, with the right hand slide the loose end of the silk lying across the taut silk up to the eye of the hook. This is made easier if the left hand holding the silk is raised up towards the chin, still keeping the silk taut.

5. Bring the short end of the silk straight upwards and move the free right hand behind the vice, so that it is in the neighbourhood of the head of the fly; with it take the taut silk from the left hand and wind round the shank just short of the hook eye. During the whole of this operation it will be found considerably easier if the short length of the silk is kept taut. Take over with the left hand, then the right hand, until this has been done three or four times, working towards the eye. Practice will soon show the most convenient position to change hands. It will be seen that the short taut length of the silk has been wrapped round not only the end of the hook, but also the bight of silk formed when the position of the fingers was rotated at stage 2, i.e. in making the letter "D".

6. With the right hand insert the dubbing needle in the loop. Keep this loop taut with the needle and relax the left hand (Fig. 57).

7. Pull on the loose end of the silk with the left hand and the binding will tighten on the head of the fly.

8. Just before the final tightening, slip out the dubbing needle.

9. Pull the loose end tight and snip off the end of the silk with the scissors, leaving a fraction of silk showing. If cut off dead tight it could possibly work loose. Practice this until you have absolute confidence.

Comment. Once you can bind the silk on a hook and execute a whip finish on a dressed shank, two very important hurdles have been surmounted. Friends of mine who in the past have watched

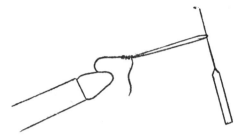

FIG. 57. *The Whip Finish* (3).

me tie flies have often asked me to let them try. In all cases the flies they tied were good, considering they were not familiar with handling the materials, but in every instance they came unstuck at the whip finish, hopelessly so. For that reason, as well as others, I stress the importance of learning it first.

THIRD LESSON. A HACKLED DRY FLY

Pattern Red Hackle.
Dressing:
Hook Size 1 (new scale), up-eyed, wide gape.
Silk Pearsall's yellow Gossamer, shade 5.
Whisks Three or four long red cock fibres.
Body Peacock herl
Hackle Red cock.

Having had some practice winding silk on a hook and the whip finish, the beginner should be able to manage this fly without too much difficulty.

Materials required:
One peacock eye feather.
A red cock's neck or packet of hackles.
A reel of yellow Gossamer tying silk.
A size 1 hook (new scale) up-eyed, wide gape.

1. Wax a few pieces of yellow silk about 18 inches long, and hang them over the nail.

2. Take a piece of waxed silk, pull it through the fingers, then wind on the hook shank, starting just short of the eye and working towards bend in close, even turns. Stop at the bend, having cut off

the waste end of the silk before getting there. Place the silk in the catch.

3. Pick up your cock neck and select a large, stiff hackle for the tail or whisks of the fly. This will generally be found on the sides of the neck. These hackles, apart from being extra stiff, usually have a pronounced curve, ideal for tail whisks.

4. Looking down on the best side of the hackle (the back of a hackle is duller than the front) tear off four or five fibres from the left-hand side of the hackle stalk. The left-hand fibres for some reason or other sit better on the hook, irrespective of which side of the neck the hackle was taken in the first place. Holding the fibres between the finger and thumb of the left hand, taking advantage of the natural curve of the fibres, place them on top of the hook shank where the silk binding has stopped at the bend. Take two close turns of silk round the base of the whisks and one turn underneath them. This will make the whisks cock up, and finally take one more turn round the base. Place the silk in the catch, keeping it taut. (Fig. 58).

FIG. 58. *Red Hackle. The whisks tied in.*

5. Pick up the peacock eye, best side towards you. Select one stand (known as a herl) from the bottom left-hand side of the eye. A single strand of herl has "a flue" on it, longer on one side than the other. It is the longer flue which makes the body. Hold the herl between the finger and thumb of the left hand and place the butt (the thick end) against the hook close up against the point where the whisks are tied in with about ¼ inch pointing towards the eye of the hook.

6. Wind the silk in close turns towards the eye, binding in the bases of the whisks and peacock herl. Stop about $\frac{1}{16}$ inch short of the eye of the hook. Any surplus ends of whisks or herl sticking out beyond this point are then trimmed off with the scissors.

7. Hold the peacock herl near the tip with the finger and thumb and wind the strand in close, even turns up the shank towards eye, stopping just a fraction beyond where the turns of silk ended. Attach the hackle pliers to the herl, but not too near the tip, as it breaks easily. The fly will now appear as in Fig. 59. Take the silk out of the catch and wind it three times round the shank under the hackle pliers, thus securing the herl. Make sure you take close, even turns, as it is essential to leave enough room to tie in your hackle.

Place the silk in the catch again. If you have wound the correct side of the herl, the body will have a pronounced taper; if the wrong side,

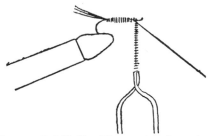

Fig. 59. *Red Hackle. The peacock herl wound on.*

the flue will not give a bushy effect and the quill to which the flue is attached will predominate.

8. Cut off the end of the herl. To do this insert the scissors *over* the silk and under the eye of the hook. This safeguards cutting the silk inadvertently, which is all-too easily done at first. The body is now completed and there should be a marked space between the end of the body, the turns of silk used to secure it, and the eye of the hook. Judgement of this, of course, comes with practice.

9. Take up the cock neck again and select a hackle for the size of the hook. Tear off the soft fibres at the base of stalk.

10. With the best side of the hackle towards you, tie it in by the base at the point where the body ends with three close turns of silk

Fig. 60. *Red Hackle. The hackle tied in by the butt.*

(Fig. 60). Put the silk in the catch and cut off base of the hackle just short of the eye and *not* beyond it.

11. Attach the hackle pliers to tip of hackle, taking a fair amount of tip in the pliers, and wind in a clockwise direction round the shank between the body and the eye of the hook. Keep the hackle fully extended whilst winding, as it makes it far easier (Fig. 61). The first two turns should be taken slightly towards the left, i.e. as close as possible to the body, then four or five turns towards the right, and remember to leave enough space for the whip finish. Leave the hackle pliers attached to the hackle-tip and let them

hang. Wind two tight turns of silk over the hackle-tip with the pliers attached. The taut silk is then placed in the catch.

12. Cut off the hackle-tip with the scissors, again taking great care not to cut the silk. The safest way to do this is to insert the scissors curve downwards to the right of the silk in the catch and un-

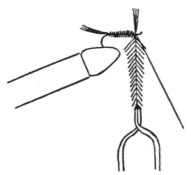

FIG. 61. *Red Hackle. Winding the hackle.*

der the eye of the hook. Extend the hackle pliers attached to the tip to the right of vice and snip off the hackle-point. This gives a clear view of what and where you are cutting.

13. Take the silk out of the catch and wind one tight turn in front of the hackle, making the turn slightly towards the left rather than encroaching over the actual eye.

14. If the last turn of the hackle is too near the eye of the hook (a common fault with the beginner), stroke the hackle fibres with the fingers so that they tend to lie towards the bend of the hook. It will then be found easier to see how much space you have left to form the whip finish, which can now be done.

15. Dip the paint-brush in acetone to clean it, wipe off the surplus on your apron, and apply a drop of thin, clear varnish to the head.

16. Clear the eye of varnish with the dubbing needle if necessary and stroke the hackle fibres upright if they are inclined to lie backwards.

Comments. You can ring numerous changes on this pattern, using,

FIG. 62. *Red Hackle. The finished fly.*

for example, any coloured hackle with whisks to match, or a different kind of body material. Sometimes it is necessary to use two hackles, e.g. for flies dressed on larger hooks or if the water is on the rough side and you need more hackle to support the hook. The method I adopt is to tie in one hackle first, wind it on and bind down with two turns of silk, cut off tip, then tie in the other hackle and proceed as before. Quite often a fly has hackles of different colours or types, for example a red cock and partridge hackle. In all cases tie in the hackle mentioned first in the dressing and follow with the other.

FOURTH LESSON. A HACKLED WET FLY

Pattern Hackle Blue Dun.
Dressing:
Hook Size 2 (new scale) down-eyed, wide gape.
Silk Yellow.
Whisks Three fibres from blue dun hen hackle tied in short.
Body Stripped quill from peacock eye.
Ribbing Gold wire.
Hackle Blue dun hen hackle.
Materials required:
> One small reel of gold wire, size 27.
> One hen neck dyed medium blue dun, or if not available a packet of hackles, and one peacock eye feather.
> A reel of yellow Gossamer tying silk.
> A size 2 hook (new scale) down-eyed, wide gape.

Stripping the quill. Take the peacock eye as used with the previous pattern and pull off some herls at their base from the right-hand side. It will be noted these individual herls have a pronounced curl. Place an old magazine, preferably one with glossy pages, on your bench and put one herl on the magazine, with the butt-end pointing towards you. Hold the butt down with the left thumb and the upper part with the index finger, so that there is a space between finger and thumb of about 3 inches. Take your pen-knife and, starting an inch below your index finger, gently scrape the flue on this side of the herl in short downward strokes; do not press too hard otherwise you will cut the quill. Continue to work down towards the butt.

Reverse the herl and carry out the same procedure, if need be turning the herl several times. It will then be noted the stripped quill has two colours running up and down its length, almost white and darkish brown. The better the contrast between these colours, the better the quill. Strip several herls and place them on one side; you will probably spoil a number before you find how much pressure you can use with your knife. The tip is, to use a blunt blade and work in short lengths.

Tying Instructions:
1. Wind your yellow waxed silk on the hook shank in even turns towards the bend; cut off the surplus silk and put the silk in the catch.
2. Now take one of the large blue hen hackles and pull off four fibres, tying them in at the bend. This time the fibres should only protrude beyond the bend of the hook for approximately ½ an inch.

Again take advantage of the natural curve of the fibres, but do not take a turn of silk under them as we did in the dry-fly pattern. Place the silk in the catch.

3. Take the reel of gold wire, cut off a length of about 6 inches and tie it in at the base with two turns of silk; do *not* cut off any surplus wire pointing towards the eye at this stage.

4. Still keeping tension on the silk with the tying hand, pick up the stripped quill and tie in with the darker colour *uppermost*. Place the silk in the catch. The fly should now appear something like this (Fig. 63).

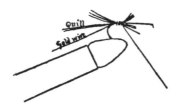

FIG. 63. *Hackle Blue Dun. The whisks, gold wire and quill tied in.*

5. At this stage you have tied in the tails, the gold wire and stripped quill, all of which should have their waste ends pointing towards the eye. Again do not cut them off but bind them all down along the shank in close even turns, stopping to allow room to tie in your hackle and make the whip finish. These waste ends can be put to good use as they help to make a foundation for the body. If any waste ends protrude from where you have stopped winding your silk, trim them off with the scissors.

6. Take the silk back half-way down the body and then forward again until you have given the body the proper shape, something like a carrot. Place the silk in the catch.

7. Wind the quill in even turns to the end of the body and secure it with two turns of silk, but do not cut off the end of the quill. If you have wound your quill correctly it should show equal parts of light and dark, which gives the impression of the segments on the body of a natural fly.

8. Place the silk in the catch and wind the gold wire round the quill body, keeping a firm tension on the wire with each turn (about four spirals in all).

9. Bind the wire down with two tight turns, cut off the ends of the

FIG. 64. *Hackle Blue Dun. The body completed.*

wire and quill, and put another turn round for good measure. The fly should now look as in Fig. 64.

10. Select a small blue hen hackle. The subsequent procedure is just the reverse of that employed for the dry fly. To assist what is known as "a good entry" for any sunk pattern, the hackle has to be "doubled", which is quite an easy process. The object of this is to make a fly sink as soon as it touches the water and offer as little resistance as possible. Figs. 65 and 66 show the process of doubling

FIG. 65. *Doubling a Hackle* (1). *The hackle in position for doubling, with hackle pliers attached to each end.*

a hackle. Actually, the one illustrated is a cock's hackle, but the procedure is exactly the same with a hen's. Apart from softer fibres, the reader will have noticed that hen hackles have rounded tips and cock hackles pointed ones.

11. Having doubled your hackle, tie it in by the tip where the

FIG. 66. *Doubling a Hackle* (2). *The basal fibres are stroked to the left with the thumb, after which the hackle is gradually slid over the forefinger and the operation repeated until it is doubled from end to end, except for the extreme tip. The second pair of hackle pliers is still attached to the tip of the hackle but is hidden by the fingers.*

doubling ends and the tip starts, with two tight turns of silk, cut off the hackle tip and place the silk in the catch.

12. Attach the hackle pliers to the base of the stalk, and keeping a firm tension on the pliers, wind the hackle round the shank, the first turn being hard up against the end of the body. Stroke the fibres back with the free hand, take the next turn in front of the first and finally one more turn, making three complete turns in all. See that the fibres lie well back and tie off.

FIG. 67. *Hackle Blue Dun. The finished fly.*

13. Cut off the hackle stalk and whip finish.

Comment. A wet fly is usually dressed with the minimum of hackle. This is our first use of tinsel. It is commonly either gold or silver, but coloured ones are now available. All tinsels are graded in size, i.e. very thin for small flies and heavier grades for bigger ones. They also vary in type and the ones in general use are wires, flat tinsel and oval tinsel. The secret of all tinselling is this. If you bind in any tinsel, irrespective of type or size to cover and/or rib the whole or part of the body, the waste ends should always correspond with the length of the body to be covered. The reason for this will be apparent in a later lesson.

FIFTH LESSON. A NYMPH

Pattern Olive Nymph
Dressing:
Hook Size 2 (new scale) down-eyed, wide gape.
Silk Yellow.
Whisks 3 short red cock fibres.
Body Yellow tying silk.
Ribbing Gold wire.
Wing Cases Rook or crow wing.
Thorax Chestnut seal's fur.
Materials required:
A rook's or crow's wing.
A reel of gold wire, size 27.
A reel of yellow Gossamer tying silk.
A small packet of chestnut seal's fur.
A size 2 hook, down-eyed, wide gape.
A red cock's hackle.
Tying instructions:
1. Wind the waxed tying silk in the usual way, down to the bend of the hook but not beyond it.

2. Tie in three rather soft red cock fibres very short, so that they protrude less than beyond the bend of the hook.

3. Tie in a length of gold wire as in the previous pattern.

4. Wind the silk in close even turns half-way up the shank, then put the silk in the catch; follow this with the gold wire ribbing about five or six turns. Bind it down and cut off the surplus wire. Place the silk in the catch again.

5. Take up a black wing and select one of the larger wing feathers (primaries) and pull it out. Half-way up this feather cut out at its base a section about ¼ inch in width (Fig. 68). Hold this section

FIG. 68. *Nymph. A section of primary wing feather prepared for cutting out to form the wing cases.*

by the base, and by gently pulling on the tips with the finger and thumb of the left hand, endeavour to get the fibres equal in length. This can be done surprisingly easily, but do not separate one fibre from another in the process. Now fold the section in half, good side outwards, so that the wing is exactly half as wide as it was before folding.

6. Tie in the tips of the wing section on top of the hook shank where the body and gold ribbing ends. Bind down the surplus ends of the wing and wind the silk back to the wing strip. Place the silk in the catch and trim off any surplus ends of wing near the eye.

7. The next thing is to make the thorax, which consists simply of a small knob of seal's fur representing the part of the body between the head and the abdomen. When any type of fur is spun on a hook, whether it be a whole or only part of it, the process is known as "dubbing". Take a small pinch of seal's fur and put it in the palm of the left hand, then with the fingers endeavour to tease out every individual fibre, separating them as much as possible. Then, with the finger-tips of the right hand, roll the fibres back and forth so that the fur is formed into a spindle thickening in the centre and tapering off at each end. For this particular pattern on a size 2 hook the seal's fur should be approximately ½ inch from end to end. It should be on the loose side, but not so loose that when you pick it up by one end it falls apart. This judgement of the right amount comes quite soon. Having tried several methods of spinning dubbing I have adopted the one below, as it is not only the easiest, but does not require the silk to be re-waxed.

8. Take a turn of silk hard up against the wing-case strip so that it lies towards the bend of the hook and well out of the way. Take up your spindle of seal's fur by one end with the finger and thumb of the left hand, lay the tip on the shank just beyond where the wing

cases were tied in. Take one complete turn of silk round this tip
and then bring the silk up so it is absolutely vertical and kept taut.
Gently ease the other tip of the spindle so that it is touching the
upright silk as far as possible along its whole length (Fig. 69).
Still keeping the silk taut and upright, twist the tip of the spindle
round the silk with the free hand and go on twisting both silk and
fur until the entire length of fur is round the silk. This should only
take four or five twists.

9. Take the end of the silk wrapped with the dubbing and, with
the silk still kept taut, take one turn inclined to the left, the next to
the right and the remainder in the middle, with one last turn of silk
near the eye. Do not worry if it is untidy. Put the silk in the catch.
Make sure the eye is clear of fur; if not snip it with the scissors
(Fig. 70).

10. Now bring the wing-case strip tight over the top of the seal's

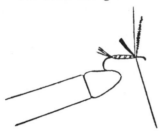

FIG. 69. *Nymph. The spindle of
seal's fur ready for spinning on the
tying silk.*

FIG. 70. *Nymph. The seal's fur spun
and wound to form the thorax, with the
strip of web to represent the wing cases
projecting behind it.*

fur, take two turns of silk over the end of the strip by the eye, lift
up the end of the strip and wind two turns in front of it (Fig. 71),
then whip finish. Lastly trim the waste end of the flap so you have a
little projection of about one-tenth of an inch.

Comment. I do not think it necessary to represent legs of an insect
in the nymphal stage, but if the tier should wish it, he can easily
tease out a few strands of seal's fur with the dubbing needle from
underneath the thorax to achieve this. G. E. M. Skues, however,
used short hen hackles for this purpose, and in his later patterns
omitted the wing cases.

FIG. 71. *Nymph. The strip of web tied
down over the thorax to form the wing cases.*

FIG. 72. *Nymph. The
finished fly.*

SIXTH LESSON. A HACKLE MAYFLY

Pattern French partridge Mayfly.
Dressing :
Hook Size 4 long-shanked Mayfly hook.
Silk Yellow, shade 5.
Whisks 4 Cock pheasant tail fibres.
Body Yellow raffia.
Ribbing Gold oval size 14 and orange silk, shade 19.
Hackles Red cock, partridge dyed medium olive, French
  partridge.

Material required :
  One cock pheasant centre tail feather.
  One strand of raffia.
  One red cock's neck.
  One packet of partridge hackles dyed medium olive.
  One packet of very small French partridge hackles.
  One reel of oval gold tinsel, size 14.
  One reel of yellow Gossamer tying silk, shade 5.
  One reel of orange Gossamer tying silk, shade 19.
  One long-shanked Mayfly hook, size 4.

Preparation. Cut a length of raffia about 6 inches long. This
material has a habit of becoming twisted along its length, so when
you untwist you will possibly find, instead of a piece about ¼ inch
in width it is a good deal wider. Place the unfolded length on your
bench and prick it with the dubbing needle about 1 inch from one
end; push in the needle and tear the raffia to the tip. Do this till
this end is divided up into lengths about 1/10 inch in width. Reverse
the raffia; put a finger on the torn ends and with the dubbing needle
continue to divide up the piece of raffia so there are now a number
of rather narrow strips. The narrower the strip, the easier it is to
make a body. If you use a bulky bit of raffia it is quite impossible.
  Tying Instructions.
  1. Wind on the waxed silk to the bend of the hook and tie in four
long pheasant-tail fibres, again taking advantage of the natural
curve. Remember, as in the previous dry-fly pattern, to put one
turn of silk under the pheasant-tail fibres to make them cock up;
place the silk in the catch.
  2. Cut off a piece of hot orange tying silk (do not wax) about 9
inches in length, double it so that you get equal lengths and tie in
at the tail.
  3. Cut off a piece of oval gold tinsel about 6 inches long and with
the thumb and finger-nails rip one end and you will find that the
gold cover comes off. Pull off a short length of this tinsel covering,
say about ¼ inch, and a cotton core will be exposed. Cut off the
unravelled gold covering and tie in at the tail where the gold ends

and the cotton core begins. The reason for this is you can "bed down" all oval tinsels better when tied in this way.

4. Carry the tying silk half-way up the shank in close even turns, tying down the pheasant-tail butts, the core of gold tinsel, and the doubled end of orange silk. Put the silk in the catch.

5. Pick up the length of prepared raffia and tie it in with the worse side towards you, where the body ends; the surplus should point towards the bend of the hook and come half-way down it (Fig. 73). This is known as tying in at the shoulder of a fly. All

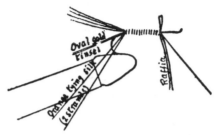

FIG. 73. *Hackle Mayfly. The whisks, tinsel, ribbing silk and raffia tied in.*

raffia floss and wool bodies should be made in this way. It makes a neater body and, equally important, is far easier to shape.

6. Start winding the raffia back to the bend of the hook, each turn slightly overlapping the next—care being taken that the best side of the raffia is showing. When you reach the bend, wind back again to the shoulder, then half-way down the body and back to the shoulder. By this time the body should have taken on the proper shape. If not, when you wind back to the shoulder for the last time, make each turn very close together. Tie off the raffia body with two turns of silk but do not cut off the waste end. Put silk in the catch.

7. Now go back to the tail of the fly and wind round the oval gold tinsel in rather wide turns, say about five. Bind down.

8. Twist the loose ends of the orange silk together and wind round the body in between each turn of gold. Bind down and cut off all waste ends. Put silk in the catch. The body is now complete and should look like this (Fig. 74).

FIG. 74. *Hackle Mayfly. The body completed.*

9. Select a rather long, large cock hackle from your red neck which, when the fibres are extended, is about the diameter of a half-penny. Clean off the weak fibres and tie in by its base tight up against the end of the raffia body, then wind on as many turns as the hackle will allow. Keep these turns close together. Bind down and cut off the tip. It is essential to get a good red hackle because it is this that gives the fly its main floating capacity.

10. Select a dyed partridge hackle, clean off the fluff on the stem, and tie in by its base as close to the red hackle as you can (Fig. 75). Wind as many turns as possible, cut off the tip and tie off.

11. Double a French partridge hackle as previously described,

FIG. 75. *Hackle Mayfly. The partridge hackle tied in immediately in front of the red cock's hackle, already wound.*

FIG. 76. *Hackle Mayfly. The finished fly.*

tie it in by the tip, cut this off and wind on as many turns as possible, keeping the first turn hard up against the previous hackle.

12. Cut off the stalk and whip finish. By manœuvring the French partridge hackle fibres with the fingers they will stand out at right-angles. In reality this hackle is so soft that it is only used for its colour value. The points to bear in mind are (i) Keep the body on the short side—half the hook shank is ample. (ii) Wind the first two hackles with tight turns, otherwise you will find you have little enough room to wind the last one, let alone make a whip finish.

SEVENTH LESSON. A WINGED LOCH OR SEA-TROUT FLY

Pattern Grouse and Silver.
Dressing:
Hook Size 5 (new scale), down-eyed, wide gape.
Silk Yellow.
Tail Golden pheasant topping.
Body Flat silver tinsel, size 4.
Ribs Oval silver tinsel, size 14.
Hackle Black hen.
Wings Grouse tail feather.

Materials required:
> One golden pheasant crest.
> One black hen's neck, or packet of hackles.
> One grouse tail feather.
> One reel of flat silver tinsel, size 4.
> One reel of oval silver tinsel, size 14.
> One reel of yellow Gossamer tying silk.
> One size 5 hook (new scale), down-eyed, wide gape.

This is the reader's first attempt at winging of any sort. The pattern is the simplest of its type I know, and involves a number of techniques which are used in all winged wet flies. It is easy to tie, easy to wing, and if the beginner has been able to progress with the previous patterns, he should find no difficulty in tying this one.

Tying Instructions:

1. Wind on your waxed silk to the bend of the hook. Place the silk in the catch.

2. Pick up your golden pheasant crest which, incidentally, is an excellent investment as it can be used for a great number of flies, and select one small topping from near the beak-end. Tie this topping in by the base on top of the hook, again taking advantage of its natural curve. Do not cut off any waste.

3. Take a length of oval silver tinsel, expose the core for about ½ inch and tie in as in the previous pattern of the tail end.

4. Cut off a piece of flat silver tinsel about 6 inches long; tie in at the base. The surplus end should correspond roughly to the length of the body.

5. Take the silk in very close even turns up the shank to the end of the body, bearing in mind that after the body is completed, a doubled hackle and a wing have to be allowed for. Place the silk in the catch.

6. Take hold of the end of your flat silver tinsel and wind it round the body in taut, even turns, each turn touching but not overlapping its neighbour. Bind off with two turns of silk but do not cut off the waste end. If the tinsel has become tarnished, it is a good tip at this stage to clean it. This can be done quite simply with a very narrow piece of chamois leather. It is for this reason that the waste end of the tinsel has not been cut off, otherwise when cleaning it is likely to unravel.

7. Rib the body with the oval tinsel for about four or five turns. If there are any small gaps in the flat tinsel try to hide them with the oval silver. Tie off with two turns of silk and place the silk in the catch. As an added insurance against the body coming undone (and tinsel bodies can easily be damaged by the teeth of the fish), when cutting off the oval silver, unravel a small length by pulling on the covering and cutting off, after having taken an extra turn of silk round the end.

8. Select a black hen hackle, double it, tie in by its tip and wind it

Left to right

WET FLIES:
Snipe & Purple
Blue Upright
Orange Partridge
Gold-Ribbed Hare's
  Ear
Poult Bloa

Grannom
March Brown
Dark Needle
Greenwell's Glory
Gravel Bed

THE REV. E. POWELL'S DRY FLIES:
Paragon
Buzz Olive
Doctor

GRAYLING FLIES:
Witch
Red Tag
Bradshaw's Fancy
Austrian Wasp
  (*King*)

LAKE FLIES:
Golden Olive
Red Palmer
Zulu
Peter Ross

Grouse & Claret
Invicta
Woodcock & Green

PLATE III: FLIES FOR RAIN-FED RIVERS, LAKES, AND GRAYLING
(From flies dressed by Peter Deane)

Left to right

Duns:
Iron Blue
Orange Quill
Dark Olive (*Walker*)

Pale Evening (*Kite*)
Mayfly
Pale Watery

Spinners:
Pheasant Tail
Mayfly
Lunn's Particular

Sedges & Diptera:
Red Sedge (*Kite*)
Caperer (*Lunn*)
Cinnamon Sedge
Hawthorn Fly
Black Gnat

Nymphs
Pheasant-tail
  Nymph (*Sawyer*)
Pale Watery Nymph
  (*Sawyer*)
Medium Olive
  Nymph (*Skues*)
Pale Watery Nymph
  Skues)

PLATE IV: CHALK-STREAM FLIES
(From flies dressed by Peter Deane)

round, making sure the fibres are inclined towards the hook. Bind down and place the silk in the catch.

9. The next step is completely unorthodox and will undoubtedly be frowned upon by many fly dressers of experience. It is simply this: instead of moulding the black hen fibres round the neck of the hook down below the shank, I cut off all fibres above the shank (Fig. 77). This facilitates the fly sinking quickly and enables one (especially a beginner) to tie in the wing with less difficulty.

FIG. 77. *Grouse and Silver. The body completed and the hackle wound, with the fibres trimmed off above the hook shank.*

10. Pick up the grouse tail feather and cut off a section at least 1 inch wide at its base. Double this, best side outwards, *exactly* in half and double again. Do not attempt to make the fibres equal as was done with the wing section for the nymph. On examining the wing just made, it is imperative that there should be no more fibres on one side than the other. If this is the case, when the wing is tied in it will meet with dismal failure. If there are more fibres on one side, these can be simply taken out by "combing through" with the dubbing needle along the bottom of the formed wing section.

11. Pick up the base of the folded wing section between the finger and thumb of the left hand and place it exactly on top of the hook shank. If you can get a portion of your finger and thumb down either side of the neck of the fly it will facilitate this process.

12. Picking up the tying silk about 4 inches (no more) below the eye of the hook, bring the silk up beneath the ball of the thumb loosely over the neck and down through the forefinger and thumb. Then, without relaxing the grip on the wing section, pull the silk tight in a downward direction. Repeat this once more and relax the grip with the left hand. With more luck than judgement, it is possible that the wing has now been tied on to the top of the hook shank and is fairly straight. If this is so, take two more turns of silk round the waste ends of the wing (Fig. 78).

13. Cut off any surplus wing beyond the eye and make a neat-shaped head before making a whip finish. It is possible that on examination one side of the wing is longer than the other. If this is the case, cut the whole wing straight across at the appropriate part and re-shape the tip with the scissors. This may sound a rather

Q

crude method but it does not seem to upset the fish and, with a little care, a neat wing can be made.

FIG. 78. *Grouse and Silver. The wing tied in.*

FIG. 79. *Grouse and Silver. The finished fly.*

EIGHTH LESSON. A HAIR-WINGED SALMON FLY

Pattern Hairy Mary.
Dressing :
Hook Size 4, salmon.
Tying Silk Yellow.
The Tag Flat gold tinsel size 3.
Tail Golden pheasant topping.
Body Black Mirabou floss.
Ribs Oval silver size 16.
Hackle Dyed blue cock, rather long in the fibre.
Wing Natural brown buck tail fibres with about six strands of calf's tail fibre dyed yellow over the buck tail.
Head Black.
Materials required :
    One golden pheasant crest.
    One packet of dyed blue cock hackles, for salmon flies.
    One natural buck tail with black-tipped fibres.
    One calf's tail dyed yellow.
    One reel of flat gold tinsel, size 3.
    One reel of oval silver tinsel, size 16.
    One reel of yellow Gossamer tying silk.
    One reel of black Mirabou floss silk.
    One size 4 salmon iron.

This is a very simple and popular pattern, making an ideal introduction for hair-wing salmon flies. It kills well in all sizes and on most rivers. The body is quite orthodox and similar to a number of others of elementary design.

Tying Instructions :

If you have difficulty in making a hook of this size hold secure in your vice, a simple remedy is to cut a small square of chamois leather or flannel, or thin sheet copper, a little under $\frac{1}{2}$ inch square. Fold this in half, slip into the jaws and place your hook between the two pieces of material. Tighten the jaws and the hook should hold.

1. Following the same procedure as for trout flies, binding on your waxed silk near the eye. The best starting-point with a salmon fly is just before the end of the "return", which is the place on an ordinary forged salmon iron where the eye of the hook is tapered off and runs parallel for a short distance with the shank proper. Sometimes the tapered end of the return is not quite flush with the shank but a few turns of silk will bring them together. It is important this should be done, as the made body of a salmon fly usually terminates round this point. Take the silk down a few more turns and place it in the catch.

2. Cut off a length of flat gold tinsel (say, 6 inches) and tie it in at this point.

3. Continue to take the silk down over the gold tinsel till you reach a place directly above the point of the hook or a fraction beyond it. Then wind back about six or seven close even turns and place the silk in the catch.

4. Take the end of your flat gold tinsel and wind in close even turns until you reach the silk in the catch; bind down with three tight turns of silk and cut off the end of the tinsel. You have now made the tag (Fig. 80).

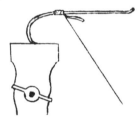

FIG. 80. *Hairy Mary. The tag formed.*

5. Select a well-curved golden pheasant topping for the tail and tie it in on top of the end of the gold tag with two firm turns of silk, making sure that there is no gap between the gold tag and the topping. If there is, do not worry overmuch at this stage as this can be remedied a little later on. Place the silk in the catch.

6. Cut off a length of the large oval silver, expose the core, and tie in close to the tail.

7. Take the silk up the shank in even turns to just beyond the return, tying down in the process the butt of the topping and the core of the oval silver. Place the silk in the catch.

8. Cut off a length of black Mirabou floss, at least 12 inches. On examination this floss is seen to consist of two threads (sometimes four) twisted together. Separate these threads, tie one in where the body ends with two turns of silk and place the silk in the catch. If the core of your oval silver did not correspond with the length of your salmon fly body, make the surplus piece of black floss meet the place where the core ends. If the core did in fact cover the

length of the body, keep the end of the black floss to about one-third of the length of the entire body. This will obviously help to give it shape when the floss is wrapped round.

9. Take up your length of black floss and wind it down towards the tail in rather close, even turns. If by chance there is a gap between the tail and the tinsel, you can take your floss down a fraction over the tail to cover this. Now wind back to where it was tied in with rather wider turns. In other words, as you wind the floss back the material should tend to splay itself and give a final covering. Go back again for three or four turns then back to the starting-point by which time your body should have taken on a definite shape. In a salmon fly of this type shaping is really quite unnecessary and only gives a neater over-all appearance.

10. Wind the oval silver tinsel in tight turns up the body, about five in all, bind down the end, expose the core, and add another turn or two of silk before cutting off the surplus.

11. Select a medium-size blue cock hackle, double it, and tie in by the tip. It happens in this particular pattern that the hackle fibres are rather longer than usual, but this is not imperative. If one selects a hackle long in the fibres, these, when tied in, should be able to touch the point of the hook. Normally they are considerably shorter. Wind on the hackle, place the scissors on top of the hook shank and cut off all hackle fibres above this point. If the reader prefers to be a little more professional, he may stroke the top fibres down so that they lie below the hook shank instead. A little pressure between the finger and thumb will induce them to stay in this position.

12. Now for the wing. There should be a definite space left between the hackle and the eye of the hook to allow room for this, and it is a good idea, especially with hair wings, if a silk foundation is made for the wing. All you do is to wind the silk in even, close turns to the eye and back again. With hair wings it is essential that they should be tied in securely, otherwise they tend to pull out and literally come to pieces in the water. To ensure security, the first thing you do is to coat the foundation you have just made with spirit varnish. Pick up your buck tail which, you will have noticed, is completely white on one side and natural brown on the other. Go about one-third of the way up from the base of the tail of the brown hair, sink your scissors right into the middle and cut out a bunch. First, hold these firmly by the tips with the forefinger and thumb of the left hand. With the right forefinger and thumb comb out any loose or soft under-fur from the bunch held by the tips—this is important. Should the bunch be tied in with the soft under-fur it will come adrift. Having combed out the unwanted hair, hold the bunch in the forefinger and thumb of the right hand and level it out; by this I mean get all the tips level. When this is done, hold it again in the middle of the bunch, be sure your spirit varnish on the

wing foundation has not dried out (if it has, re-varnish), place your compact bunch of buck tail on top of the hook shank so that the tip of the furs extend just beyond the bend of the hook and no farther, and tie down with several turns of silk. It will be found if the first few turns of silk round the bunch of hair are tied too tight that the hairs will tend to separate and fan out (Fig. 81). To avoid this make the first two or three turns on the loose side and then tighten.

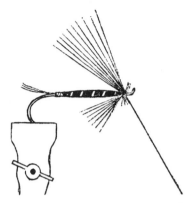

FIG. 81. *Hairy Mary. Showing how the hairs of the wing tend to splay out if the first few turns of tying silk securing them are pulled too tight to start with.* *

13. Take the silk down to the eye and back again. Put the silk in the catch (Fig. 82). Grasp the surplus ends of the buck tail wing with the forefinger and thumb of the left hand, lift up clear of the eye and snip off. Bind down again with two or three more turns, then put another coat of varnish on top of the head.

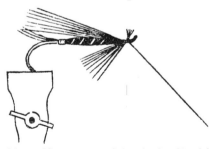

FIG. 82. *Hairy Mary. The proper set of the wing is achieved by making the first few turns of silk rather loose at the outset and subsequently drawing them taut.*

14. Select four or five fibres from your yellow calf's tail to correspond with the length of the buck tail wing and tie them in on top.

15. Cut off the surplus and now, if you have not already done so, shape your head so that it tapers towards the eye, and finally, whip finish. A well-shaped head improves the appearance of a salmon fly

* In figs. 81, 82 and 83, tails should spring from fore end of tag. —Ed.

a great deal and can be easily achieved. Unfortunately hair-wing salmon flies are apt to have bulkier heads than feather-wing ones, but this cannot be helped.

FIG. 83. *Hairy Mary. The finished fly.*

16. Allow the spirit varnish at least twenty-four hours to dry and then apply your black varnish, which completes the fly.

NINTH LESSON. A TUBE-FLY

Pattern Irish Blue.
Dressing:
Body 1-inch Polythene tube.
Wing Blue hackle fibres and grey squirrel tail fur.
Tying silk Black.
Materials required:
A length of Polythene tubing.
One packet of dyed blue cock's hackles.
One grey squirrel tail.
One reel of black Gossamer silk.

Comments. The tube-fly for salmon fishing is now the current rage. It is the simplest form of lure one can imagine, and consists of a Polythene tube of anything from a $\frac{1}{4}$ inch to 2 inches long, a hair or feather wing and, in some cases, a body, but many consider the latter superfluous. The main consideration to bear in mind is, that whatever the length of the tube, the wing, when made of hair, should be at least twice as long. The reason for this is that when the tube is threaded on to the point of your cast and a treble attached, this can be buried in the tips of the hair and tends to make the wing splay out, which assists movement when in the water.

Preparation before tying. All sorts of devices have been thought up to hold your tube so that you can tie the material upon it. The easiest I know is this. Take any low-water salmon hook, say a size 1, snip off the eye with a pair of pliers, place the hook in the vice and slip the Polythene tube over the shank. To stop the tube rolling round when one ties the silk on the head, push it sufficiently far down the shank so that a portion of it goes round the bend.

Tying Instructions:

1. Select whatever length of tubing you require—a 1-inch tube is recommended for a start—and push it on to your hook shank.

2. Take a length of waxed silk and wind it on to the top end of the tube. Carry this down for at least a quarter of an inch, back again to the start and then half-way down again. Cover this binding with spirit varnish and place silk in the catch.

3. Take your grey squirrel tail and cut from its base about 9–10 longish fibres. Hold them by the tips and, as with the buck tail, comb out any soft hair. Place the bunch of hair on top of the binding and take a half-dozen turns round it. Place silk in the catch, and cut off surplus hair flush with the end of the Polythene tube (Fig. 84).

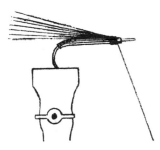

Fig. 84. *Irish Blue. The first section of wing tied in on top of the tube. (The hook, with the eye cut off, is only used as a mandrel during the tying process, and is subsequently withdrawn.)*

4. Twist the tube a fraction away from you and tie in at this point half a dozen fibres taken from a dyed blue hackle. These need only be as long as the tube or even shorter.

5. Twist the tube again away from you and tie in another equal amount of squirrel tail.

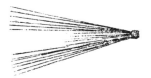

Fig. 85. *Irish Blue. The finished fly. (The blue hackle fibres are in the centre.)*

6. Twist again and add a few more fibres of dyed blue cock. Repeat this once more with the squirrel tail and dyed blue fibres.

7. Make an even head and whip finish.

8. Cover the head with spirit varnish, allow it to dry, and finally varnish with black.

CHAPTER X

THE ENTOMOLOGY OF LAKES AND RIVERS
by
C. F. WALKER

INTRODUCTION

WHETHER the fly-fisher is deliberately using representations of natural insects or merely general flies with fancy names, I believe that the majority of trout which take his artificial do so because they mistake it, if not for the species of fly on which they are feeding, at all events for the type of food they are accustomed to see at that particular time of year. This, moreover, is equally true of both wet and dry flies, and of lakes as well as rivers, despite the fact that, to the human eye, some of the patterns sold as loch flies bear little resemblance to any known form of animal life. If this premise is accepted, it follows that some knowledge of the insects on which trout feed is essential to the angler who would make the most of his opportunities. This does not imply that he need become an entomologist in the scientific sense, but merely that he should learn enough about the appearance, behaviour and habitats of these insects to enable him to fish his artificials intelligently and with that degree of confidence which begets success.

To deal fully with the subject of aquatic entomology a whole book would be required, and indeed a number of books have already been devoted to it. Of these, the most recent and comprehensive is *An Angler's Entomology*, by J. R. Harris, which I can strongly recommend to those who wish to pursue this fascinating study in greater detail. In the present chapter I can attempt no more than a brief description of the insects which are of importance to fish and fishermen, but this should be enough for the practical man who simply wants to better his chances of catching trout and, incidentally, to increase his enjoyment in catching them. I may add that nearly all the insects described have been found and studied by me in their native haunts (and not a few bred in my aquarium), for second-hand descriptions are all-too apt to result in old errors being perpetuated.

The food of trout. At the outset it should be stressed that trout, being extremely catholic in their tastes, will at times be prepared to eat almost any kind of insects which chance or a puff of wind may blow on to the water, not excluding such apparently unpalatable objects as wasps and bees. Those who have read Leonard West's book, *The Natural Trout Fly and its Imitation*, may recall that it includes descriptions and illustrations of no less than 102 insects, a great many of which are land-bred species which the average angler would be unlikely to see on the water once in a lifetime. Such comprehensive treatment, however, defeats its own object by making the subject of entomology unnecessarily complicated, and for present purposes, with a few important exceptions, I am confining myself to the true aquatic species.

It must also be realized that a substantial proportion of the trout's diet consists of creatures which, for one reason or another, it is virtually impossible to imitate in fur and feather. This includes such things as plankton crustacea (a very important source of food supply in lakes), snails, newts, tadpoles, larvae of many kinds, and caddis in their cases. With the exception of the last-named, which form an essential link in the life-history of the sedge-flies, these are omitted from my descriptions, together with small fish and the larger crustaceans, which, although they are probably represented by certain loch patterns, do not truly come under the heading of entomology.

Nomenclature. Before we proceed to the descriptions it will be as well, for the benefit of the beginner, to explain the principle on which insects—and indeed the whole of the animal and vegetable kingdoms—are arranged and named by the scientists. They are divided into a number of different groups, known as orders, families, sub-families, genera and species, the insects within each group bearing a stronger resemblance to one another as we proceed down the scale, until we come to species, in which they are all virtually identical. The naming system, which is based on that introduced by the Swedish naturalist, Linnaeus, two hundred years ago, only takes account of the genera and species. These generic and specific names, usually of a descriptive character, may be likened respectively to our own surnames and Christian names, but they appear in the reverse order. It may be objected that the angler has no need to trouble himself with scientific names, and I agree that one does not want to hear Latin and Greek bandied about by the waterside. It is, nevertheless, essential to include these names with the written descriptions of insects, for several reasons. First, the classical languages are international; second, some British insects have no vernacular names; third, some vernacular names are applied to different flies in different parts of the country, while, conversely, some flies are known by more than one such name. With the scientific names these ambiguities can never occur.

Habitats of insects. The habitats are included in the descriptions of each insect, and it should be noted that although many species are found in both flowing and static water, others occur in only one or the other kind. Unfortunately it is not as easy as might be thought to draw a hard-and-fast line between the two, since some rivers contain almost stagnant pools, which so far as the insects are concerned possess all the characteristics of a lake, while on the other hand there are stream-fed lakes with a strong current extending for some distance beyond the point of inflow, where the conditions resemble those of a river. Furthermore, there are certain species which, although primarily adapted for life in rivers, can sometimes be found on the stony margins of large lakes where the wave action creates a sufficient degree of aeration for them to exist in the absence of a current. It is, of course, on the requirements of the nymph or larva that the choice of habitat depends, and all land-bred insects, which only reach the water fortuitously and in the winged stage, may be found either on lakes or rivers.

DESCRIPTIVE LIST OF INSECTS
Order: EPHEMEROPTERA (*Day-flies*)

The day-flies are of the highest importance to the chalk-stream fisherman, of considerable importance to those who fish in rain-fed rivers, and by no means so unimportant on lakes as some writers on the subject would have us believe. The same species, however, do not in every case inhabit all three types of water.

This is the only order in which it is both necessary and practicable for the angler to learn to recognize the different species: necessary because hatches of each species frequently occur in sufficient numbers for the trout to feed on them exclusively, and practicable because they are few enough to be easily memorized. There are, in fact, only forty-seven British species all told, of which no more than half are sufficiently common and well-liked by the trout to merit the angler's attention. The remainder are omitted from my descriptive list.

In the descriptions of the flies, the colour of the back, or upper side, is given for recognition purposes, but in every case the under side is paler; a point to be borne in mind when selecting materials for dry flies. With the exception of Halford, who dealt only with the chalk-stream species, I do not know of any writer on entomology who gives the sizes of flies when describing them. Yet as the British day-flies vary in length from about three-sixteenths to three-quarters of an inch, it has always seemed to me that some acquaintance with their *relative* sizes would be of considerable help to the beginner who is learning to recognize them. I therefore mention the size of each species, employing relative terms for this purpose and taking as my standard the Medium Olive dun, which measures about 8 mm. from the front of the head to the extremity of the abdomen. Species of this length are described as medium-sized, those measuring from 9 to 10 mm. as large, from 6 to 7 mm. as small, and the few which lie outside these limits as very large or very small. It should be borne in mind, however, that certain species vary considerably in size, and where this is so the fact is stated. In most cases the female is slightly larger than her mate, and the length of the fore wing slightly greater than that of the body.

The life-cycle consists of four stages: egg, nymph, dun and spinner, and it is of interest to note that the day-flies are the only insects which go through two winged stages. After a short period, varying with the species and temperature of the water, the minute nymph, or larva, as it is more usually known at this early stage, emerges from the egg and at once starts to feed, mainly on algal growths. As it increases in size it undergoes a series of moults, until at the end of a year (or in the case of the Mayfly probably two years) it attains maturity. Then, when the time is ripe, it either swims to the surface or, in some species, climbs up a weed stem, the skin splits down the back, and the subimago, or dun, bursts forth. The newly-emerged fly, after drying its wings, then takes off and flies to the bank, where it hides itself amongst the foliage until the time arrives for the final metamorphosis, which may take place within a few minutes or not for a day or two, according to the species and atmospheric conditions.

Now the skin splits once more and the perfect insect, known as an imago or spinner, emerges, leaving its cast-off garment on the leaf or grass blade where the transformation took place. The wings of the insect are now clear and iridescent (those of the dun being semi-opaque and fringed with hairs), the body has changed colour, and the cerci, or tails, are considerably longer. If a female, it will now go into hiding once more: if a male, it will presently join others of its species and the whole assembly will begin the nuptial dance, rising and falling alternately above the banks, or sometimes in the shelter of bushes. This usually takes place in the evening, and has the effect of attracting the females, who in ones and twos approach the dancers, to be immediately seized by the nearest males and carried off for a brief aerial honeymoon.

As the last act in the little drama the now-fertilized females return to the water to deposit their eggs. For this purpose some species crawl down a weed stem, some dip repeatedly on to the surface, leaving a batch of eggs at each visit, while others drop the whole consignment from the air. But whichever method is adopted, the female, her duty done, ends by collapsing upon the water with outspread wings; the spent spinner of the fisherman. The males, on the other hand, have no need to revisit the water at all, and unless they are blown on to the surface accidentally they die inland.

From the foregoing account it will be evident that the trout have five separate opportunities of feeding on the day-flies: as immature nymphs on the bottom or amongst the weed-beds; as ripe nymphs either rising to the surface or in the act of hatching; as newly-hatched duns drying their wings before taking off; as female spinners in the act of depositing their eggs; and finally as spent spinners lying helpless on the surface of the water. The trout do not neglect these opportunities, though in the case of a few species, as we shall see in due course, the duns leave the water so quickly after emergence that the fish do not get a proper chance of taking them in this stage.

The day-fly nymphs fall into four categories: the burrowers, the crawlers, the swimmers (which may in turn be divided into fast and slow movers), and the flat nymphs which live under stones. It is not really necessary, and would in any case be difficult, for the angler to learn to recognize the individual species in their nymphal stage; so, as nymphs of the same genus are very much alike, a single description will suffice in each case. The duns require separate treatment according to species, though except in the case of the Blue-winged Olive, the sexes in this stage resemble each other closely enough to be dealt with together. (The males can be distinguished by the presence at the extremity of the abdomen of a pair of claspers for the purpose of holding the female during the mating process.) In the spinner stage, however, there is in nearly every case a very marked difference in body colour between the sexes, and although it is with

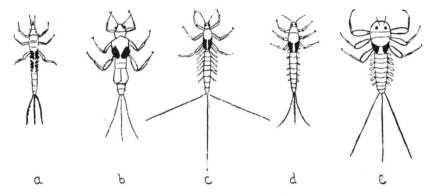

a   b   c   d   e

Fig. 86. *Types of day-fly nymphs. a, Burrowing. b, Crawling. c, Slow swimming. d, Fast swimming. e, Flat type living amongst stones. (For the sake of comparison of details all the nymphs have been drawn the same length. Actually, the Mayfly nymph (a) would be four or five times as long as the Broadwing nymph (b) the remainder being of intermediate lengths.)*

the females that fish and fishermen are primarily concerned, the males are described as well to enable the reader to identify them during the nuptial dance; a useful clue to the species of females which may be expected on the water later in the evening.

Although all day-fly nymphs carry three tails, in the winged stages of certain genera these are reduced to two. Some genera, moreover, have two wings and others four, so that the combination of wings and tails helps to reduce the possibilities when deciding the genus of a dun or spinner seen at close quarters. A note of these characteristics will be found beneath each genus.

Family: EPHEMERIDAE
Genus: *Ephemera*
Characteristics: Four wings and three tails.
The nymphs are of the burrowing type, living in the silt at the

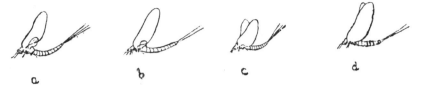

a   b   c   d

FIG. 87. *Day-flies: wing and tail combinations. a, 4 wings and 3 tails (May-flies, B.W.O., Sepia and Claret duns). b, 4 wings and 2 tails (Olives, Iron Blues, Pale Wateries, March Browns, August or Autumn dun and Yellow Upright). c, 2 wings and 3 tails (Broadwings). d, 2 wings and 2 tails (Pond and Lake Olives and Pale Evening dun). Only the commoner species are mentioned here, but all the British Ephemeroptera fall into one or another of these patterns.*

bottom of a lake or river. They are long and comparatively slender, brown in colour, and with plume-like gills which are folded over the back. Their tails are relatively short and fringed with short hairs. As they approach maturity wing-pads develop on the back; a feature common to all the day-fly nymphs which need not, therefore, be repeated in describing those of other genera. They spring from the middle thoracic segment and when fully grown extend over the first two segments of the abdomen.

GREEN MAYFLY, OR GREEN DRAKE
Ephemera danica

This is the common Mayfly of rivers and lakes, and has a preference for alkaline waters. It is a very large fly and hatches from the end of May to the beginning of June.

The dun[1] has broad, triangular fore wings and relatively large hind wings, their colour being greenish yellow with dark brown veins and dark markings on the fore wings. The thorax is dark olive-brown and the abdomen pale straw yellow with brown markings down the back which become more pronounced towards the tail end, those on the first five segments sometimes being either small or entirely absent. The legs are olive-brown and the tails almost black. The male is noticeably smaller than the female and of a darker shade throughout.

The male spinner, or Black Drake, has transparent wings strongly veined and marked with blackish brown. The thorax is black and the abdomen ivory-white, marked down the back in the same way as the dun. The legs and tails are black.

The female spinner is sometimes known as the Grey Drake, and after oviposition by the rather ridiculous name of Spent Gnat. The wings are transparent with a blue-grey sheen and brown veins, the thorax brown, and the abdomen similar to that of the male but with paler brown markings. The legs and tails are dark greyish-brown.

---

[1] The term dun is here used for the sake of uniformity, although, strictly speaking, it is not applicable to the larger Ephemeroptera, whose subimagines are not dun-coloured.

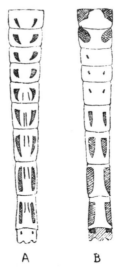

FIG. 88. *Mayfly body markings. A,* The Brown Mayfly (*Ephemera vulgata.*)
B, The Green Mayfly (*Ephemera danica*).

BROWN MAYFLY
Ephemera vulgata

Despite its name,[1] this species is much less common than the previous one, being chiefly confined to very sluggish rivers with a muddy bottom, such as those of the eastern counties. In view of this it is rather curious that this insect is seldom found in lakes, though I have seen it in some numbers on the Bourley lakes, near Aldershot. Its size and time of appearance are the same as for *E. danica.*

The dun has brownish wings, more mottled with brown than those of *E. danica,* while the colour of the abdomen is brownish-yellow, and the markings, which are roughly triangular in shape, are present on every segment. The legs and tails are dark brown.

The spinners, male and female, are virtually browner versions of the *danica* spinners, and can be distinguished from them by the markings on the back, described above.

A third British species, *E. lineata,* resembles the foregoing, but is too rare to merit a separate description.

Family: LEPTOPHLEBIIDAE

Genus: *Leptophlebia*

Characteristics: Four wings and three tails.

The nymphs are of the swimming type, but are not very agile in their movements. They are torpedo-shaped and very dark brown in

---

[1] This can doubtless be accounted for by the fact that *E. danica* was originally named *vulgata* by Pictet.

colour, which makes them hard to distinguish against a peaty bottom. From each side of the abdomen project seven pairs of gills resembling leaves with very long points. These gills are mobile, so that by moving them to and fro the nymphs can create a current along their bodies which enables them to live in still water. The tails are very long—at least as long as the body—and are held wide apart: a most distinctive feature of these nymphs, which is preserved in their winged stages.

SEPIA
Leptophlebia marginata

The vernacular name was suggested by me in a recent book, sepia being the predominating colour of the insect in all three stages. It hatches from mid-April to mid-May, and is found in lakes and slow streams. It is a large fly somewhat local in distribution, but abundant where it occurs.

The dun has light sepia wings with a darker area near the tips of the fore wings, the two main veins being yellow and the remainder dark sepia, forming a strongly-marked criss-cross pattern. The thorax and abdomen are dark sepia, the legs warm sepia and the tails almost black. Unlike most of the day-flies, the males are slightly large than the females.

The male spinner has transparent wings with a faint brownish tinge, veined and marked in the same way as the wings of the dun. The thorax is black and the abdomen dark sepia, becoming darker towards the tail. Legs and tails as in the dun.

The female spinner is similar to the male as to wings, thorax, legs and tails, but the sepia abdomen has an undertone of yellow, especially in the three terminal segments.

CLARET
Leptophlebia vespertina

Both the vernacular and scientific names of this species are misleading, as it is not claret-coloured and the duns normally emerge at midday. Its size is medium to small and its habitats the same as those of the Sepia, with a preference for a peaty bottom, but it has a wider distribution. The main hatches take place from mid-May to mid-June.

The dun has dark grey fore wings, not unlike those of the Iron Blue dun, for which it is probably often mistaken, but it can be readily distinguished from the latter by its pale buff hind wings, which show up very clearly some distance away. The thorax is black and the abdomen variable in colour, being either dark brown or dark grey in the female and dark brown or glossy black in the male. The legs are dark brown and the tails grey-brown with faintly marked rings.

The male spinner has transparent wings, which are completely colourless except for two yellow veins near the fore margin. The thorax is black and the abdomen reddish-grey with dark brown terminal segments. The legs are brown and the tails pale grey-brown with pronounced dark rings.

The female spinner is virtually a smaller edition of *L. marginata*, with the same yellow undertone showing through the abdominal segments.

Family: EPHEMERELLIDAE

Genus: *Ephemerella*

Characteristics: Four wings and three tails.

The nymphs are of the crawling type and live on the bottom amongst weeds and stones. They are relatively broader than any of the nymphs previously described and dark brown in colour. The plate-like gills are situated on the back, and do not project beyond the sides of the body. There are five pairs of these, of which the fifth pair is very small and hidden beneath the fourth. The tails are short and fringed with short scattered bristles.

BLUE-WINGED OLIVE

Ephemerella ignita

The B.W.O., as it is commonly known to fishermen, has a very wide distribution and is found in rivers of all types, though it does not occur in lakes. On the Hampshire chalk streams it seldom appears before mid-June, but on many other rivers it starts to hatch in April or May and continues throughout the season. It possesses several unusual characteristics, of which the following deserve mention. Firstly, it often appears to have considerable difficulty in withdrawing its body and tails from the nymphal skin, with the result that the hatching dun is an easy prey for the trout. Secondly, although it is commonly associated with the evening rise, when it is taken with avidity and a distinctive kidney-shaped boil on the surface, it sometimes emerges in broad daylight, and the trouts' reactions to it are then more uncertain. On the Driffield Beck, in Yorkshire, for example, I have seen it taken eagerly all day long, whereas on the Test it usually seems to be ignored before sunset. Thirdly, the female spinners deposit their eggs in a very distinctive manner. Instead of returning singly to the water, they usually congregate in large swarms, often numbering many thousands, and fly upstream in procession, each spinner carrying a greenish ball of eggs at the extremity of the abdomen, which is curled forwards underneath the body. On reaching a suitable place, sometimes where a bridge or mill forms an obstruction across the river, the eggs are dropped from the air, after which the spinners fall spent upon the water, and the trout frequently assemble at such places at dusk to await the large meal thus provided for them. The normal type of B.W.O. is a medium-sized fly, but has relatively long wings, which make it appear larger than the Medium Olive. Occasionally, however, a much smaller form is to be seen, which has led many anglers to suppose, mistakenly, that the vernacular name covers two distinct species.

The male dun has medium smoke-blue wings, an olive-brown thorax, and a brown abdomen with an orange undertone (which no doubt accounts for the success of the Orange Quill when these flies are on the water). The legs are olive-grey and the tails, which often become twisted and crumpled in the difficult process of emergence, are grey with dark rings.

The female dun differs from the male in the colour of the body, the thorax being olive and the abdomen a variable shade of olive or yellow-green.

The male spinner has transparent wings with brown veins, a dark brown thorax and dark red-brown abdomen. The legs are yellowish and the tails amber with dark rings near the base, becoming grey towards their tips.

The female spinner, commonly known as the Sherry spinner, undergoes a considerable colour-change during her short existence. On transposition her body is yellowish green, but after laying her eggs it turns to red, often a very brilliant shade. "Red as any lobster" is how J. W. Dunne described it, but at all events it is not the colour of any reputable brand of sherry, despite the popular name.

Family: CAENIDAE

Genus: *Caenis*

Characteristics: Two wings and three tails.

The nymphs are of the burrowing type, living in the surface of the silt, which adheres in small particles to their bodies and forms a very effective form of camouflage, as they are much the same colour as mud. They are short and relatively broad, with a pronounced "waist" between the wing-pads and the second pair of gills, which take the form of large flaps lying on the back of the nymph. These totally obscure the remaining gills, except the first pair, which are no more than minute filaments scarcely visible to the naked eye. The tails are about two-thirds of the length of the body and are fringed with short bristles.

DUSKY BROADWING

Caenis robusta

Although sometimes referred to collectively as the Angler's Curse—a name applied indiscriminately to many small aquatic insects—the Caenidae have not hitherto possessed any vernacular names of their own. I have therefore suggested elsewhere that they should be known as Broadwings, from their most striking characteristic, with appropriate prefixes to distinguish the species. The Dusky Broadwing, first found in the nymphal stage by Dr. T. T. Macan on the Norfolk Broads in 1951, has since been reported from

R

three further English stations: Two Lakes, near Romsey, Hampshire (where I found the duns and spinners in 1958), a pond near Reading, Berkshire, and a canal in Shropshire. But in view of the widely differing conditions in these four places, coupled with the fact that it has recently been reported from all over Europe, it is probably much more common in England than this meagre record suggests, and as it becomes better known will no doubt turn up in many other parts of the country. It will be noted that it has so far only been found in still water (at all events in England), but there seems no reason why it should not also exist in rivers, and this may prove to be the case when further reports come to hand. The angler has a unique opportunity of increasing our knowledge of this species by forwarding specimens answering to this description to the Entomological section of the Natural History Museum for identification. *C. robusta* is a small fly, though as its Latin name suggests, the largest of the Broadwings. It hatches in the late evening from the end of May to early August.

The dun has very broad opaque wings of a watery-grey colour, marked with prominent brown veins near their fore margins. The thorax is dark brown and the abdomen pale creamy grey with variable dusky markings all the way down the back. (This is the only one of the Broadwings in which such markings appear on every segment.) The legs and tails are off-white. The duns of this and all other species of the genus change to spinners within a very short time —sometimes only a matter of minutes—of emergence.

The spinners of both sexes resemble the duns, except that their tails become longer. This is especially noticeable in the male, whose tails are some three times as long as its short, stumpy body. The method of oviposition, which is I believe unique, merits a brief description. After alighting on the water, the gravid female spinner extrudes her eggs in a single stream, held together by a gelatinous membrane and spreading out in the shape of a fan, the whole mass eventually falling off and sinking to the bottom. When thus engaged, of course, she presents a sitting target to the trout.

YELLOW BROADWING
Caenis horaria

This is quite a common species, occurring both in lakes and rivers, especially where there is silt on the bottom. It is a very small fly, and the duns emerge in late evening from June to August.

The dun is virtually a smaller edition of the foregoing species, except that in this case the abdomen is pale yellow and the greyish markings appear only on the first five or six segments.

The spinners are similar, but with much longer tails than in the dun stage.

There are three other species of this genus, but as two of them hatch in the early mornings, before most anglers are astir, and the third is too small to imitate, they do not merit detailed description here.

Family: BAËTIDAE

Genus: *Baëtis*

Characteristics: Four wings, of which the hinder pair are very small, and two tails. Marginal intercalary veins double.

The nymphs are of the swimming type, with long torpedo-shaped bodies corresponding in colour to their respective duns. Seven leaf-shaped gills project from each side of the abdomen, and as these are not adapted for life in still water all species of this genus are found

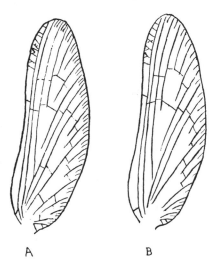

A   B

FIG. 89. *Fore wings of Baëtidae. In the genus* Baëtis *the small marginal intercalary veins are paired, as shown in A. In the rest of the family* (Centroptilum, Cloëon *and* Procloëon) *these veins are single, as in B.*

only in rivers. The centre tail is shorter than the outer pair, all three being fringed with hairs as an aid to swimming.

PALE WATERY

Baëtis bioculatus

The vernacular name, which was employed by Halford to cover four different insects, is now most commonly applied to this species. It is a small fly, common in rivers and streams, with a slight preference for alkaline water. It appears from May to September, but as the dun is very quick off the water it is less often taken in this stage than as a nymph or spinner.

The dun has pale watery-grey wings, a light brown-olive thorax, and pale green-olive abdomen, becoming yellower towards the tail. The legs are pale olive-grey and the tails pale grey.

The male spinner has transparent wings with colourless veins, a dark brown thorax, and pale yellowish-white abdomen, terminating in three dark brown segments. The legs and tails are greenish-white, and it can be distinguished from other small spinners of a similar type by the colour of the eyes, which are lemon yellow.

The female spinner differs from the male in the colour of the body, which is golden-brown throughout.

SMALL DARK OLIVE
Baëtis scambus

This is another of Halford's Pale Watery duns, though as will be seen from the description, it certainly does not merit this name. Skues called it the July dun, but although it may be seen in this month I have found it in the greatest numbers in April and September. I therefore prefer Harris's name of Small Dark Olive, which aptly describes its appearance. It is a small species, common in the faster rivers, both alkaline and acid.

The dun has dark grey wings, not quite so dark or so blue as those of the Iron Blue, for which, however, it could be mistaken at a little distance. The thorax is brown-olive and the abdomen medium green-olive, becoming more yellow towards the tail. The legs are pale yellowish and the tails pale grey.

The male spinner is a slightly darker version of *bioculatus*, from which it can be readily distinguished by its red-brown eyes.

The female spinner differs from her *bioculatus* counterpart in the colour of the body, which is dark brown and tinged with olive in the early stages.

MEDIUM OLIVE
Baëtis vernus
Baëtis tenax

These two species are so alike that some authorities now doubt whether they are, in fact, distinct. (A third species, *B. buceratus*, is too rare to be included.) The Medium Olive is very common in rivers and streams of all kinds and is widely distributed throughout this country. It is of medium size and hatches all through the fishing season.

The dun has medium-grey wings, often tinged with yellow, which was doubtless responsible for its old name, Yellow dun. The thorax is olive-brown and the abdomen yellowish-brown, in which the olive tint from which the modern name is derived is often hard to detect. The legs are olive shading to dark grey, and the tails pale grey.

The male spinner has transparent wings, the two main veins being brownish. The thorax is black, the first six segments of the abdomen olive-grey and the terminal segments brown. The legs are olive-grey and the tails off-white.

The female spinner has a yellowish-brown body, which changes to red-brown when spent.

LARGE DARK OLIVE
Baëtis rhodani

This is the Blue dun of our forebears, a very common species of rivers and streams. It hatches from October until the end of April, and as the trout fisherman only sees it when it is nearing the end of its season, it is sometimes known as the Dark Spring Olive. It is a large fly, and a very popular one with the trout. (*B. atrebatinus* is similar in appearance but relatively scarce.)

The dun has dark grey wings, much the same tone as those of the B.W.O. but of a less blue shade. The thorax is dark grey tinged with olive, and the abdomen dark olive. The legs are olive shading to grey, and the tails grey with faint rings near the base.

The male spinner has transparent wings with dark brown main veins, a black thorax, and olive-grey abdomen with brown terminal segments. The legs shade from olive to grey and the tails are pale grey with reddish rings.

The female spinner is a larger and darker version of that of the Medium Olive, becoming dark mahogany-brown when spent.

IRON BLUE
Baëtis pumilus
Baëtis niger

For practical purposes the two species may be treated as identical, the differences between them being too minute to be discerned with the naked eye. The Iron Blue is common and widespread in rivers and streams of all kinds, and despite its small size is often taken by the trout in preference to any other species which may be on the water at the same time. The main hatches occur in May, especially on cold, windy days, and there is a second brood in September.

The dun has very dark grey wings and thorax, the abdomen of the male being the same colour and that of the female a very dark olive-brown. The legs are dark olive to dark grey, and the tails dark grey.

The male spinner, known to our forbears as the Jenny spinner, is a beautiful little fly with transparent wings, black thorax, and dark brown terminal segments, the intermediate segments being white and translucent. The legs and tails are almost white, and the eyes dark red-brown.

The female spinner is sometimes known as the Claret spinner, but as this causes confusion with the spinner of the Claret dun, the name is best avoided. She has colourless wings, a black thorax, dark red-brown, abdomen, olive-brown legs and pale grey tails.

Family: BAËTIDAE

Genus: *Centroptilum*

Characteristics: Four wings, the hinder pair being much narrower than those of the preceding genus, and two tails. Marginal intercalary veins single.

The nymphs are of the swimming type and resemble those of the genus *Baëtis*, except that the gills are more pointed and the three tails of equal length.

LITTLE SKY BLUE

Centroptilum luteolum

This was the third fly classed by Halford as a Pale Watery dun, and it is still sometimes known by this name. Later, D. H. Turing called it the Lesser Spurwing, the generic name being derived from the Greek κεντρως (spur) and πτιλου (wing), but as the spurs on the hind wings are too small to be seen with the naked eye and are in any case not confined to this genus, I prefer Harris's name, Little Sky Blue. It is a small fly, common in rivers and streams, and may also be found in lakes under the conditions described on page 250. It hatches from May onwards.

The dun bears a superficial resemblance to *Baëtis bioculatus*, but the colour of the wings is slightly paler, the hind wings are narrower and end in a sharp point, and the body is more honey-coloured than olive.

The male spinner may be distinguished from *BB. bioculatus* and *scambus* by the shape of the hind wings and colour of the eyes, which are bright Indian red.

The female spinner, called by Harris the Little Amber spinner, has a yellowish-brown body which becomes amber when spent. It can be distinguished from the *B. bioculatus* spinner by the shape of the hind wings and the venation of the fore wings (Figs. 89 and 90).

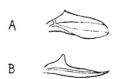

A

B

FIG. 90. *Hind wings. A,* Pale Watery dun (*Baëtis bioculatus*). *B,* Little Sky Blue, or Lesser Spurwing (*Centroptilum luteolum*).

The other member of this genus, *C. pennulatum*, is not of general importance, being very local in distribution and uncertain in its appearance even in its known habitats. It is a good deal larger than *luteolum* and has smoky-blue wings and a greyish body in the dun stage. This was the fourth of Halford's Pale Watery duns, but is now known either as the Blue-winged Pale Watery or the Greater Spurwing. It has not been recorded from lakes.

Family: BAËTIDAE

Genus: *Cloëon*

Characteristics: Two wings and two tails. Marginal intercalary veins single.

The nymphs are of the swimming type and of much the same shape as others of the family already described. Their colour is very variable, some being mottled in different shades of dull brown, others a warm chestnut-brown all over, and others again strongly marked with emerald green. They have seven pairs of gills, of which the first six are double and mobile, which enables them to live in still water, the last pair being single and fixed, probably acting as baffle-plates. The tails, which show a characteristic downward curve towards their tips, are of equal length and fringed with hairs. They are remarkably agile swimmers.

POND OLIVE

Cloëon dipterum

The vernacular name was suggested by Harris on account of its more frequent appearance in ponds than in large lakes, though it is a high summer temperature, rather than the actual area of water, which governs its choice of habitat. It is also found occasionally in the sluggish pools of rivers. The first hatches appear in May, after which it continues throughout the fishing season, the flies of successive broods gradually diminishing in size from large or medium to small as the summer advances. Both species of *Cloëon* become airborne almost instantaneously on emergence, and are consequently not very often taken as duns.

The dun varies in colour as well as size. The wings, which are broad at the base to compensate for the absence of hind wings, are medium grey, slightly darker in the male than in the female. The thorax is brown-olive, the abdomen of the male grey with brown terminal segments and of the female brown-olive with yellow terminal segments and red streaks. I have, however, found female specimens in which the yellow colour was much more pronounced throughout, and even a few with bodies the same colour as in the spinner (q.v.) The legs are pale yellow-olive and grey, and the tails pale grey or buff with reddish rings.

The male spinner has transparent wings with colourless veins, dark brown thorax, and reddish-grey abdomen becoming red-brown towards the tail. The legs are pale watery grey and the tails pale grey with dark red rings.

The female spinner is a most beautiful fly, with yellow veins and a broad yellow band along the fore margin of the wings, yellow ochre thorax, and abdomen the colour of a ripe apricot, streaked with red. The legs are pale yellow and the tails pale buff ringed with red.

LAKE OLIVE

Cloëon simile

This species can stand lower temperatures than the Pond Olive, and therefore tends to prefer the larger lakes, though the two are often found together in the same water. Like the other, it begins to hatch in May, but then seems to peter out until September, when a second brood appears. In size it is medium to large, but although Harris states that flies of the autumn brood are smaller than those of spring, I have not observed this myself.

The dun has medium grey wings suffused with brown or olive, a brown-olive thorax, and grey-brown or olive-brown abdomen. The legs are pale olive shading to grey, and the tails dark grey without rings. The general effect is of a dingier-looking fly than the Pond Olive, but in cases of doubt it can be distinguished from the other by the number of small cross-veins in what is known as the pterostigmatic area, on the fore margins of the wings towards their tips. The Lake Olive has from nine to eleven of these small veins, and the Pond Olive only from three to five (Fig. 91).

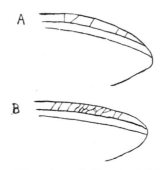

FIG. 91. *Outer sections of fore wings. A,* The Pond Olive (*Cloëon dipterum*) *has from 3 to 5 pterostigmatic veins. B,* The Lake Olive (*Cloëon simile*) *has from 9 to 11 of these veins.*

The male spinner has transparent wings faintly stained with yellow-brown and brownish veins. The thorax is dark brown, almost black, the abdomen warm brown becoming red towards the tail end, grey legs, and grey-brown tails with dark rings near the base.

The female spinner is similar but with a dark red-brown abdomen and brown legs.

Family: BAËTIDAE

Genus: *Procloëon*

Characteristics: Two wings and two tails. Marginal intercalary veins single.

The nymph is a swimmer and of the same general appearance as the *Cloëon* nymphs, except that all the gills are single and the tails are more heavily fringed with hairs and held closer together.

PALE EVENING

Procloëon pseudorufulum

This is the only member of the genus, which stands very close to *Cloëon*, in which this species was formerly placed. Although I have found the spinners on a lake it is very doubtful whether they were bred there, and its true habitat seems to be the slow-flowing type of river. It is a small fly and may occur throughout the summer months, the main hatches being from June to August. The duns emerge in the late evenings, often so late that they are probably either overlooked by the angler or mistaken in the semi-darkness for one of the small Pale Watery duns.

The dun has pale greyish-white wings, often tinged with green near the base, a pale honey-coloured thorax and abdomen with reddish markings, pale yellow legs, and watery grey tails.

The male spinner has transparent wings with colourless veins, a brown thorax, and translucent white abdomen with red-brown terminal segments. The legs are pale olive and grey, and the tails white. The eyes are lemon-yellow like those of *Baëtis bioculatus*, but it can be distinguished from that species by its two wings.

The female spinner has a pale yellow ochre thorax and abdomen becoming amber towards the tail, with amber markings down the back and fine dark lines on each side of the middle segments. The legs and tails are pale watery grey.

Family: ECDYONURIDAE
Genus: *Rhithrogena*
Characteristics: Four wings and two tails.

The nymphs are of the flat type, living amongst stones on the bottom, over which they can move at high speed. Their bodies, particularly the head and thorax, together with the upper joints of the legs, are flattened and very broad in proportion to their length. Their colour is dark brown mottled with yellowish brown. The gills are prominent features and consist of plates and bunches of filaments, the first pair being very large and meeting beneath the body. These help to keep the nymph attached to the surface of the stones in a fast current. The tails are relatively long, devoid of hair, and held wide apart.

YELLOW UPRIGHT
Rhithrogena semicolorata

The vernacular name is not very descriptive of this species, which is neither yellow nor more upright than any others of its kind. Nevertheless, it seems preferable to retain the name by which it has for long been widely known, rather than introduce a new one, such as Olive Upright, which was proposed by Harris. It is common in fast stony rivers and streams and is of great importance on the Usk and Welsh Dee, but although I have taken a single specimen on the Itchen and have heard of others, it cannot be classed as a chalk-stream fly. It is a large species whose main hatches occur from late May to July.

The dun has medium grey fore wings and paler hind wings, a grey-green thorax, and olive abdomen. The legs are pale olive and the tails grey. At a little distance it might be mistaken for a large Olive dun, but a certain means of identification is the presence of a dark streak on the femoral, or upper, joint of each leg in both the dun and spinner stages.

The male spinner has transparent wings with brown veins and a yellow-brown stain near the base. (Courtney Williams states that it is this yellowish stain, coupled with the spinner's habit of ascending in a vertical position during the nuptial flight, which gives the species its vernacular name.) The thorax and abdomen are dark olive-brown, and the legs and tails brown.

The female spinner has a medium reddish brown body and pale amber legs and tails.

MARCH BROWN

Rhithrogena haarupi

For many years the March Brown was identified as *Ecdyurus* (now known as *Ecdyonurus*) *venosus*, but in 1931 it was discovered that there were, in fact, two species very similar in appearance but hatching at different times of the year and belonging to different genera. *R. haarupi* was henceforth recognized as the true March Brown, emerging from late March to early May, while *E. venosus* does not appear until the other's season has ended. It is a very large fly and a common one on rapid, stony rivers, but is unknown on the chalk streams. A distinctive feature is its sudden appearance in large numbers at intervals throughout a spring day, but the trout feed more often on the ascending nymphs than on the duns.

The dun has light yellowish-brown wings and prominent brown veins, the cross-veins, which have dark borders, being absent from two areas in the centre of the fore wings, producing the effect of two pale blotches. The thorax and abdomen are dark brown, darker in the male than the female, the legs olive-brown and the tails grey-brown.

The male and female spinners resemble the duns, except that the wings are transparent and only tinged with brown towards the base.

Family: ECDYONURIDAE

Genus: *Ecdyonurus*

Characteristics: Four wings and two tails.

The nymphs are of the flat type and similar to the preceding ones in general shape, but the first pair of gills are small and do not meet beneath the body. The most distinctive feature of this genus, however, is the front segment of the thorax, known as the pronotum, which ends on each side in a point projecting backwards over the second segment.

LATE OR FALSE MARCH BROWN

Ecdyonurus venosus

This is the species referred to as being formerly identified as the

March Brown, and is common in the same types of rivers as those in which *R. haarupi* is found, though it does not hatch in such profusion. It is a very large fly, appearing from May onwards.

The dun resembles *R. haarupi* except that there are no pale areas in the centre of the fore wings.

The male and female spinners, known as Great Red spinners, can be distinguished from those of *R. haarupi* by the colour of their bodies, in this case a bright red-brown.

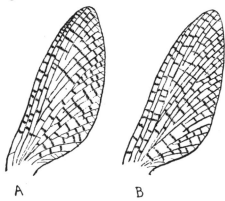

A   B

FIG. 92. *Fore wings. A,* March Brown *(Rhithrogena haarupi). B,* False March Brown *(Ecdyonurus venosus). Note the pale areas in A due to the absence of cross veins near the centre of the wings.*

AUGUST OR AUTUMN DUN

Ecdyonurus dispar

The habitats of this species are the same as for the foregoing, but it is also sometimes found on the shores of large lakes under the conditions described on page 250. This is another very large fly, though slightly smaller than *venosus*. It may be found from June to October, the main hatches being in July and August.

The dun is very similar to *E. venosus*, but the cross veins lack the dark borders, and consequently do not appear so prominent.

The male and female spinners are scarcely distinguishable from those of *E. venosus* except in the matter of size.

This disposes of all the commoner species except two: the Turkey Brown (*Paraleptophlebia submarginata*), which is very similar in appearance to the Sepia, and the Yellow May (*Heptagenia sulphurea*), a large pale yellow fly except for the male spinner, which is dark brown. Both these species have long been known to anglers, but the fact is that they are seldom taken by trout—possibly because they do not hatch in such large numbers as other day-flies.

The following less common flies have now been given names by Harris:

YELLOW EVENING (DUN) (*Ephemerella notata*), a close relative of the B.W.O. but resembling the Yellow May dun in appearance.

PURPLE (DUN) (*Paraleptophlebia cincta*), somewhat resembling large Iron Blues, but with three tails.

SUMMER MAYFLIES (3 species of *Siphlonurus*), very large flies known to me as Large Summer duns and found chiefly in lakes.

BROWN MAY (DUN) (*Heptagenia fuscogrisea*), a very large fly bearing a general resemblance to the March Brown.

DARK (DUN) (*Heptagenia lateralis*), a dark dun-coloured relative of the foregoing.

LARGE GREEN (DUN) (*Ecdyonurus insignis*), a greenish-grey relative of the Late March Brown and August dun.

Order: TRICHOPTERA (*Sedge-or Caddis-flies*).

Although they are of considerable importance, both on rivers and lakes, the sedge-flies, with a few exceptions, do not hatch simultaneously in such large numbers as the day-flies, wherefore the angler has no need to learn to recognize the individual species or to carry more than one or two general patterns to represent them. This, perhaps, is just as well, since 189 species of British Trichoptera have been recorded.

The life-cycle consists of four stages: egg, larva, pupa and imago, or adult. The egg-laying habits vary with the species, some depositing their eggs on weeds or stones, others in the open water. On emerging from the eggs the majority of caddis larvae then proceed to build cases for themselves, in which the whole of their under-water existence is passed. These cases are made from many different kinds of material, such as sand, gravel, small stones, weed or bits of stick, each species having its own special method of construction. There are, however, a few kinds of caddis larvae which do not make cases, but live instead in silken tunnels attached to weeds or stones, from which they sometimes emerge in search of food. It is, incidentally, incorrect to refer to caddis larvae as nymphs, as some anglers do. Strictly speaking, the term nymph should only be applied to those larvae which bear a recognisable resemblance to their respective adults, such as those of the day-flies, dragon-flies, stone-flies and water-boatmen. All others should be called larvae, and should not be confused with pupae.

On reaching maturity the caddis larva pupates in a similar manner to a butterfly or moth, the case-making species spinning cocoons inside their cases and the others in shelters specially constructed for the purpose. When fully developed the pupa bites its way out of its home and either swims or climbs up a weed stem to the surface, whereupon the winged fly emerges and struggles across the water to the bank, where mating takes place. The trout feed on the larvae (case and all), pupae, newly-emerged adults and egg-laying females. Those which escape the attentions of the fish and other predators live a good deal longer than the day-flies, probably for more than a week, while specimens bred in captivity and artificially fed have been known to exist for a matter of months.

As the sedge-flies vary greatly in size and appearance, according to their species, they can only be described in general terms, which will suffice to enable the reader to recognize them as members of the order Trichoptera. References to a few specific flies will be found at the end of the general description.

The larvae of the non-case-making species somewhat resemble caterpillars, but with longer legs and, in some cases, abdominal gills. The case-making species are generally fatter and more grub-like in appearance, but this is of no more than academic interest to the angler, who cannot well imitate a hard caddis case in fur and feather. Both types have short caudal appendages ending in hooks, by means of which they can maintain a grip on the shelters in which they live.

The pupae have fat, juicy-looking bodies and a rather hump-backed appearance. The antennae, springing from the head, and the legs, from the thorax, lie beneath the body, while the four wing-pads slope downwards from the thorax towards the under side of the abdomen. The centre pair of legs are longer than the others and fringed with hairs to assist the pupa in swimming to the surface.

The adults are not unlike moths in appearance, except that their wings are covered with hairs instead of scales. The fore-wings are slightly longer than the hind wings and hide them when the insect is at rest with both pairs folded back over the body in the form of a ridge tent. The antennae and legs are long in proportion to the body, and there are no tails. The wings of most species are some shade of brown or grey, either plain or patterned, and the bodies brown, grey or green. The size varies according to species from a quarter of an inch or less up to an inch in length.

GRANNOM

Brachycentrus subnubilus

This is the only sedge-fly which the angler need learn to identify, as it is the only species favoured by the trout to hatch in any quantity.

It is confined to running water and I have seen heavy hatches on the Don and lower Test, but it seems to be less common, especially on the chalk streams, than it used to be. Where it does occur, however, it provides a sight worth seeing, and an opportunity which no angler can afford to miss. So sudden are the hatches that at one moment the river will appear lifeless, and in the next the whole surface will be covered with these littles flies and boiling with the rises of trout, who go almost mad in their eagerness to make the most of what they probably know is but a fleeting chance of a good meal. Their usual procedure is to chase the ascending pupae towards the surface and to take them either just before or in the act of hatching.

The Grannom is one of the smaller sedge-flies,[1] with a greyish body less than half an inch long and grey wings with buff patches.

[1] The measurements used to denote the sizes of day-flies do not apply to the Trichoptera or other orders here described, where the sizes mentioned are purely arbitrary and relative.

The mature female carries a ball of blue-green eggs at the extremity of her abdomen and most artificials are dressed with a green tag to suggest this, though in fact the Grannom is usually taken before it reaches this stage. The hatches take place in April and May.

The only other sedge-flies likely to be seen in large numbers are the Silverhorns, a name covering several very small species belonging to the genera *Mystacides* and *Leptocerus*. These are well-known to every angler on account of their habit of gyrating above the water in large swarms, but although an occasional immature fish will be seen jumping after them in the air, the fact is that they seldom figure on the trouts' menu. One or other species will usually be found, both in still and running water, throughout the summer months, but they are not worth the angler's serious consideration.

The majority of sedge-flies emerge in the late evening, the Grannom and the Caperer (*Sericostoma personatum*) being the most notable exceptions. The latter is a medium-sized sedge-fly with mahogany-brown wings, which is of some importance on the chalk streams in May and June. It is, incidentally, a good example of the confusion which may arise through the use of vernacular names. Halford called it the Welshman's Button, a name properly belonging to a beetle, but it is now more often known as the Caperer, which to add to the muddle is also applied by some to *Halesus radiatus*, a quite different species emerging in the evening in late summer.

The following English names are also in use:

CINNAMON SEDGE (*Limnephilus lunatus*, Halford).
GREAT RED SEDGE (*Phryganea grandis* and *striata*. Trad).
GREY FLAG (*Hydropsyche* species, Irish).
GREY SEDGE (*Odontocerum albicorne*, Mosely).
MEDIUM SEDGE (*Goëra pilosa* female, Halford).
SMALL DARK SEDGE (*Goëra pilosa* male, Halford).
SILVER SEDGE (*Lepidostoma hirtum*, Harris).

Some of these names are more often used to denote the artificial flies than their natural prototypes, and there are besides these several similarly-named artificials, which do not seem to have been copied from any specific insects. This probably applies to the Little Red Sedge, one of Skues's favourite patterns, and to the Orange and Kimbridge Sedges formerly in vogue on the chalk streams.

There is no need for the angler to learn to identify the species mentioned in the above list.

Order: PLECOPTERA (*Stone-flies*).

It seems to be the custom to place the stone-flies immediately after the sedge-flies in angling entomologies, though in fact they are of less importance to the fly-fisherman than some of the insects we shall meet later in this chapter. True, the stone-flies are taken by the trout in certain stages of their existence, but so far as the angler

is concerned their chief function is to provide bait, in the shape of
the nymphs of the larger species, for the "creeper" fisherman of the
North, and I agree with Courtney Williams that artificial stone-flies
seldom justify their existence.

Nevertheless, the Plecoptera are true aquatic insects, and as fly-
fishermen have imitated, or attempted to imitate, them for several
centuries, they deserve some mention here. The angler should at all
events be able to recognize a stone-fly as such when he sees one,
though he need not trouble himself overmuch with the individual
species. Of these thirty-four have been recorded in Britain, mostly
from stony streams and rivers. Only nine species occur in lakes.

The life-cycle consists of only three stages: egg, nymph and adult.
There is no pupal stage. The eggs are laid on the surface of the
water in much the same way as those of the day-flies, the precise
method varying in the different genera. On emergence the nymphs
live amongst the stones on the bottom, or in a few cases in water
moss. As they attain their full growth—usually after one year as
nymphs but in some genera up to three years—they crawl ashore,
often at night, and take shelter amongst the stones and vegetation
on the bank, where the adults emerge. Mating then takes place on
the ground. Trout take the nymphs while they are crawling about
on the bottom, but as it would be difficult to make an artificial
behave in the same way, they are of little account to the fly-fisherman
at this stage. Owing to their habit of emerging on the bank, the
newly-hatched adults are not seen by the fish, whose only opportunity of taking the winged flies, therefore, is when the females
return to the water to deposit their eggs.

The nymphs are not unlike day-fly nymphs in their general shape,
but they have much longer antennae, stouter legs, often fringed with
hairs, and only two tails, while the gills are either absent or spring
from the thorax or the points of junction of the legs or tails with the
body, instead of from the abdomen. As they approach maturity
two pairs of wing-pads develop on the back, springing from the
second and third thoracic segments respectively. The general
colouration of the nymphs varies with the species. They are poor
swimmers, and usually progress by crawling, in which they are
assisted by the presence of a stout claw at the extremity of each leg.

The adults have four wings of nearly equal length, which are
folded flat along the back when at rest. In the males of some species,
however, the wings are so attenuated that the insects are unable to
fly. The antennae are long, though not so long as those of the sedge-
flies, and the tails variable in length, in some cases being no more
than short stumps. The colour of the stone-flies is usually some
shade of brown or yellow, and their size varies from about three-
sixteenths up to more than an inch in length, the females being
larger than the males.

The following English names are employed by anglers:

EARLY BROWNS (*Nemouridae* species, esp. *Protonemura meyeri*).
FEBRUARY RED (*Taeniopteryx nebulosa* female).
NEEDLE BROWNS, or NEEDLE FLIES (*Leuctra* species).
LARGE STONEFLIES or MAYFLIES[1] (*Perlidae* species and the larger species of *Perlodidae*).
WILLOW FLY (*Leuctra geniculata*).
YELLOW SALLY (*Isoperla grammatica*).

Order: DIPTERA (*Two-winged flies*).

There are something like 3,000 species of this order, which includes the common house-flies, the crane-flies, gnats, midges and mosquitoes. Most of them only figure on the trouts' menu in the shape of accidental windfalls, but there are some truly aquatic families and others which, although land-bred, fall on to the water in sufficient numbers to bring about a general rise. It is with these two classes that we are concerned here.

Family: CHIRONOMIDAE (*Midges or Buzzers*).

There are some 400 British species of this aquatic family, some of which are to be found throughout the season in every area of static water from the smallest pond to the largest lake, and as they form one of the principle articles of insect diet of the trout of such waters they are of great importance to the lake angler. They also occur in the sluggish pools and reaches of some rivers, but generally speaking are not of much account to the river fisherman. The majority of Chironomids are too small to imitate, but the genus *Chironomus* includes. a number of relatively large species which are well worth the angler's attention.

The life-cycle consists of four stages: egg, larva, pupa and adult. The eggs are laid on the surface of the water, and the larvae live either amongst the water weeds or in small tubes composed of mud, but they can and do swim about. When fully grown they pupate, and in due course the pupae swim up to the surface, where the adult flies emerge. The trout take the larvae, pupae, newly-hatched flies and finally the egg-laying females, but they are most often taken in the pupal stage, when they hang suspended vertically just beneath the surface for a short time before hatching, thereby presenting the fish with an easy prey. The larvae, as will be realized from the accompanying description, are virtually impossible to imitate successfully, but the lake angler who carries one or two good patterns representing the pupa and adult—more especially the former— is assured of some good sport.

The larvae resemble very small worms, a resemblance which is heightened in many species whose blood contains haemoglobin, which gives them a red colour and incidentally enables them to live in deep water. The remainder are usually coloured pale olive.

[1] Thereby causing confusion with the day-flies of the genus *Ephemera*.

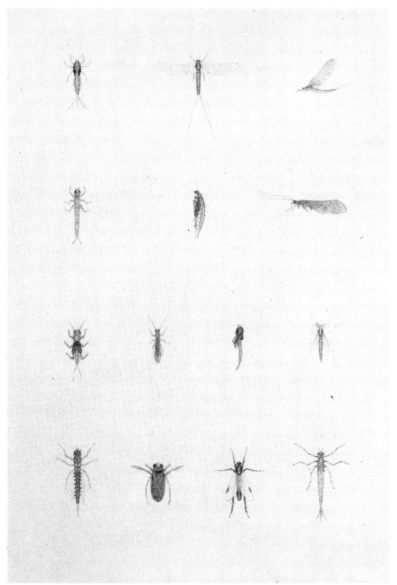

Drawn by C. F. Walker

34. Typical forms of the insect food of trout. (Life size.)

EPHEMEROPTERA   Day-fly nymph.   Spent spinner.   Dun.

TRICHOPTERA.   Free caddis larva.   Caddis pupa.   Adult sedge-fly.

PLECOPTERA   Stone-fly nymph.   Adult stone fly.   Chironomid pupa.   Adult midge and DIPTERA.

MISCELLANEOUS.   Alder larva.   Corixid.   A land-bred Dipteran.   Damsel fly nymph.

Blue Winged Olives:
dun and spinner.

Olive nymph.

Yellow Upright:
Spent female spinner.

Hawthorn fly.

Green Mayfly (male).

Adult Stone-fly:
Early Brown.

Sedge-fly: Speckled Peter.

Stone-fly nymph:
Early Brown

E. Horsfall Turner

35. **Some specific** insects on which trout feed.

The pupae begin to resemble their respective adults in colour and shape, except that the legs and embryo wings are tucked away beneath the body. The abdomen is slender and tapering, and the thorax, which occupies about a third of the length of the body, is very bulky in proportion. From the head arises a tuft of filaments which act as breathing tubes.

The adults have semi-transparent wings, which are held horizontally in the form of a V when the insects are at rest. The legs are very long and widely spread, and the male carries a prominent pair of antennae resembling small feathers. The swarms of Chironomids which are often to be seen amongst the bushes on the shores of lakes are the males awaiting the arrival of their mates.

The larger Chironomids are from a quarter to half an inch in length and they are of many different colours, the most common being golden-olive, bright green, brown, and black. The following English names have been identified with specific insects, but colour alone is not a sufficient guide to species because there are several of each colour, while individual species may vary considerably in this respect:

GOLDEN DUN MIDGE *(Chironomus plumosus).*

GREEN MIDGE *(Chironomus viridis).*

OLIVE MIDGE or BLAGDON BUZZER *(Chironomus tentans).*

Family: CULICIDAE
Sub-family: CHAOBORINAE *(Phantom midges).*

The Phantom midges belong to the mosquito family, but bear a strong resemblance to the Chironomids and have the same life cycle. There are only four British species.

The larvae, from which the family takes its English name, are completely transparent, although this does not save them from the keen-eyed trout, who frequently take them in large numbers.

The pupae are similar in general appearance to those of the Chironomids, but are relatively shorter and fatter, and the breathing filaments are replaced by a pair of ear-like appendages.

The adults could easily be mistaken for Chironomids without a lens, which reveals the presence of a fringe of fine hairs round the wings. The only one of the four species I have found myself is *Chaoborus crystallinus,* a rather spectacular insect nearly half an inch long with a pale blue-green body striped with black on the thorax.

Family: BIBIONIDAE
Genus: *Bibio*

There are two species of this genus which, although terrestrial, are of some importance to both the lake and river fisherman on account of their predilection for tumbling into the water during or after mating. In general appearance they bear a superficial resemblance to house-flies.

S

Life-cycle : Egg, larva, pupa and adult. The larvae live and pupate in the earth or in the roots of plants, often in the vicinity of water, which seems to have a strange and frequently fatal attraction for the adults, once they are on the wing. The trout, of course, can only take them in the winged stage, when chance or some mysterious compulsion causes them to end their short existence on the surface of a lake or stream.

BLACK GNAT
Bibio johannis

Although the Black Gnat has for many years been identified with *Bibio johannis*, it has recently been pointed out that there are several other insects of different genera to which the English name could be equally well applied. They are a familiar sight to every angler as they gyrate over the water, often in huge swarms, in a similar manner to the Silverhorns. Sometimes these swarms disperse inland and not a single fly is seen on the water: at other times every single one seems to come down until the whole surface is strewn with them for several hours at a stretch. On such occasions sport is apt to be magnificent, for not only do these flies attract the biggest trout, but the fish seem to know they have plenty of time and instead of rushing madly about as they do after Grannom, they remain in their chosen places taking a fly here and there with a deliberate and purposeful rise. In view of the competition which confronts the artificial fly, however, accurate casting, a good pattern, and considerable patience are required if the angler is to make the most of his opportunity. The name *johannis* refers to the fact that this species is most prevalent around Midsummer (St. John's) day, though the heaviest hatches I have seen—which may well have included other species—have been in Mayfly-time and again in August.

It is, of course, unnecessary to describe the larva and pupa, which the fish never see, and to avoid multiplying scientific names I am taking *B. johannis* as the type.

The adult has iridescent wings which are carried flat over the back when at rest but are often outspread when the fly lies spent upon the water. The body of the male is slender and cylindrical, that of the female fatter and egg-shaped. It is an old quip that the Black Gnat is neither black nor a gnat, but while it is true that the body is really dark olive, it looks black enough at a little distance to justify the first part of the name. The length of the female is about a quarter of an inch, the male being slightly longer.

HAWTHORN FLY
Bibio marci

This species takes its Latin name from the alleged date of its first appearance, namely St. Mark's day (April 5th), but in this case the English name is more accurate, as it usually arrives with the hawthorn blossom. For the same reason it is yet another claimant to the name of Mayfly in some parts of the country. As in the case of the Black Gnat, it seems probable that anglers have confused two or more similar species, which might account for the apparent discrepancy in dates, but for practical purposes we will consider them as one.

I am inclined to think that the Hawthorn is a more local insect than the Black Gnat, and it certainly does not appear in anything like the same profusion, nor does it seem quite so fond of taking a bath. Consequently, although each individual fly represents a larger mouthful, and may tempt the trout on this account, it is seldom the cause of a general rise of fish. Indeed, the only really big hatch of Hawthorns I have ever witnessed was completely ignored by the trout, but from the experience of others it is evident that at certain times and places it is of some importance as an angling fly.

The adult resembles a Black Gnat but on a larger scale and with a blacker body. A distinctive feature, faithfully copied by most fly-dressers, is a pair of long, hairy hind legs, which it trails astern when in flight. It is nearly half an inch in length.

This completes the tale of the more important Dipterans, but there are a few others which merit brief mention.

REED SMUTS, which belong to the family Simulidae, are true aquatic insects and sometimes hatch in such large numbers as to occupy the trouts' exclusive attention. They are, however, really too small to imitate satisfactorily, and although a minute hackle pattern may score an occasional success, the angler is likely to experience an unhappy, not to say exasperating, time when the fish are engaged in "smutting". They occur in rivers throughout the summer months, and resemble miniature Black Gnats in appearance, but with relatively thicker bodies and shorter wings.

CRANE-FLIES of the Tipulidae family, popularly known as Daddy- or Harry-long-legs, often fall on to the water in late summer, when they receive a warm reception from the trout. Several ingenious patterns have been devised with legs represented by knotted strands of herl, but the majority of trout which succumb to the "Daddy", especially on the Irish loughs, are victims of the natural fly used as a dap. There are many different species, varying in size, but they are too well-known to require description.

The GRAVEL BED (*Anisomera burmeisteri*) has long been known to fishermen and although of rather local distribution can be productive of fine sport where it occurs. I once witnessed a splendid rise to this fly on the Don, but mistakenly diagnosed Grannom, which had been hatching freely on the previous day. On discovering my mistake (thanks to a friendly angler on the opposite bank who was busily filling his basket) I rushed back to my hotel and dressed a couple of patterns, but by the time I returned it was all over. Those who fish the rivers of the north and west, therefore, would do well to be prepared for hatches of the Gravel bed during the month of

May. As its name suggests, it hatches out in the gravel beds by the riverside, and it is not unlike a Chironomid in appearance, with greyish wings, a dark lead-coloured body 3/16th of an inch in length, and long, almost black legs.

Sub-order: MEGALOPTERA

Family: SIALIDAE

Genus: *Sialis*.

ALDER

Sialis lutaria. Sialis fuliginosa.

These two species, of which *lutaria* is the commoner, are sufficiently alike to be treated as one. The Alder, or Orl-fly, as it was formerly known, is such a familiar sight by the waterside in May and June that it has been known to and imitated by anglers for centuries. Yet the fact is that it is not a wholly aquatic insect and in its winged state does not come on to the water except by accident, when it is very seldom taken by the trout. The undoubted success of the artificial Alder, therefore, is presumably due to its resemblance to some other insect—possibly a caddis pupa ascending to hatch, since most fishermen are agreed that it does best as a sunk fly. The larva, on the other hand, though unknown to the majority of fishermen, forms quite an important article of the trouts' diet at certain times of the year, but to understand the true position of the Alder in the angling scene it is necessary to know something of the fly's rather unusual life-history.

The life-cycle consists of egg, larva, pupa and adult, of which only the second stage is passed in the water. The eggs are laid on vegetation close to the waterside, and as soon as the small larvae emerge they make their way at once to the lake or river, as the case may be, there to live in the mud or silt for the best part of a year, feeding on other small larvae and nymphs. In the following March or April they crawl or swim ashore and proceed to pupate in holes in the bank. There the adults finally emerge, and as both mating and oviposition take place on shore, it will be appreciated that the trout only see the Alder in its larval stage, unless the winged fly is unlucky enough to fall into the water, when in my experience it is invariably ignored. The larvae, however, are eaten in some numbers during their shoreward migration in the spring, and sometimes again towards the end of the season, when the new generation have attained a worth-while size.

The larva is an uncouth-looking beast, mottled in shades of brown and dull yellow and shaped rather like a carrot. It carries a pair of claw-like mandibles, and the abdomen is fringed with seven pairs of pointed tracheal gills. It is quite a fair swimmer and has a curious habit of rearing up the front half of its body when closely approached, doubtless for the purpose of intimidating potential enemies.

The pupa sheds the gills and tapering tail of the larva, and develops two pairs of wing-pads and a pair of antennae, which together with the legs are stowed away, beneath the abdomen as in the sedge pupa. But as the trout never see the Alder in the pupal stage, this is of no more than academic interest to the angler.

The adult might be mistaken for a sedge-fly by the uninitiated, but the wings are rather more rounded in outline and are devoid of hairs. The body and legs are almost black, and the wings sepia brown with prominent dark veins. The length of the body is about half an inch, the wings being slightly longer.

Order: HEMIPTERA-HETEROPTERA (*Water bugs*)

This order includes a wide variety of aquatic insects differing considerably in appearance and habits, such as the water cricket, water measurer, water scorpions, pond skaters and water-boatmen. Considering the boundless opportunities they provide, it is a surprising fact that the great majority of them are very seldom eaten by trout, virtually the only exceptions to this being the Lesser water-boatmen of the family Corixidae. The remainder can therefore be safely ignored.

Family: CORIXIDAE (*Lesser Water-boatmen*)

This family contains 26 British species and one variety of the genus *Corixa*, together with three species of allied genera. Except to the scientist, who is concerned with minute anatomical details, they are all very much alike except in the matter of size, which ranges from about one-eighth to half an inch, measured lengthways. Although they occur in some rivers, they are of more importance to the lake fisherman, the trout of different lakes seeming to vary in their partiality for them, regardless of the numbers available. Blagdon is the most notable example of a lake in which the Corixids form a significant proportion of the trouts' food throughout the summer, while records from many other waters show that they are taken chiefly in April, May, June and September. They can be distinguished from the rather similar water-boatmen of the Notonectidae family (which the fish seldom take) by the fact that the Notonectids always swim on their backs.

The life-cycle consists of egg, nymph and adult, the nymphs in this case being no more than immature specimens of their respective adults. They normally live on the bed of the lake, but have to swim to the surface at intervals to renew their air supplies, and it is when thus engaged, no doubt, that they attract the trouts' attention. Although they live under water they are able to fly, and sometimes shift their quarters by this means from one lake to another during the summer months.

The adults bear a superficial resemblance to beetles, to which, however, they are unrelated. Seen from above they are boat-shaped, with large yellowish heads and a pattern of alternate light and dark brown stripes running across the body and wing cases, or hemielytra, which are folded across the back. Their under sides are flat and a dirty cream colour. The front legs are short and stout, the second pair long and thin, and the hindmost pair, which are used as paddles, are fringed with hairs and held nearly at right angles to the body when the insect is at rest. The air is stored between the wing-cases and abdomen, giving the appearance of a silver halo as the Corixid turns downwards from the surface after renewing its supplies.

Order: ODONATA

Sub-orders: (ANISOPTERA (Dragon-flies).
(ZYGOPTERA (Damsel-flies).

These beautiful creatures are to be found in almost every lake and pond, as well as in some rivers, during the summer months, but although the trout sometimes eat them in surprising numbers they are too large to imitate satisfactorily except as immature nymphs, of which a good pattern often proves quite successful. There are 27 British species of Anisoptera and 17 of Zygoptera.

The Life-cycle consists of egg, nymph and adult. The eggs are laid either on the surface of the water or an emergent weed, the different species, as always, differing in their methods. The nymphs, or naiads as they are sometimes called, live at the bottom or amongst weeds and are mostly carnivorous. On reaching maturity the nymph crawls up the stem of a water plant to a position well clear of the surface, where the adult emerges; a process which may take over an hour to complete. The trout take both nymphs and winged flies—the latter probably in the shape of females in the act of laying their eggs, though immature fish may sometimes be seen making abortive attempts to seize them in the air as they hover over the water.

The nymphs of the true dragon-flies are squat, ungainly-looking creatures, varying in size and shape according to their species. They are fitted with a primitive form of jet-propulsion, which enables them to move at considerable speed over short distances. Damsel-fly nymphs are quite different in appearance and easier to imitate, being more like the nymphs of day-flies but with longer legs and three tracheal gills at the tail end. They usually proceed at a slow crawl, but can swim after a fashion with an undulating movement of the body. Both types possess a curious piece of apparatus known as a mask, which is a kind of retractable grab used for the purpose of seizing their prey.

The adults need no description, being a familiar sight to every child who has dabbled in a pond. It may be noted, however, that the damsel-flies can be distinguished not only by their more slender build, but also by their habit of folding their wings over their backs when at rest, whereas the dragon-flies hold them spread apart in the flying position.

Order: COLEOPTERA (*Beetles*)

There are no less than 3,700 British beetles, of which several hundred species are either aquatic or amphibious in their habits. It might be thought from this—and has indeed been stated by not a few writers—that beetles form an important source of trout food, but generally speaking this is not the case. At certain times and places, it is true, some of the terrestrial species are taken in large numbers, but for some strange reason trout do not appear to relish the water beetles, which are seldom found in autopsies. It may be that the fish only become interested in the Coleoptera when they are present in some quantities, and that this condition is only fulfilled when some of the land-bred species are hatching in the vicinity of rivers or lakes. This seems to happen more frequently in Wales than elsewhere, especially in the cases of the Coch-y-bonddu beetle, which Courtney Williams has identified as *Phyllopertha horticola,* and the Cockchafer or Maybug (*Melolontha melolontha.*) The former hatches in June and July and the latter in May and June, and both sometimes fall on to the water in very large numbers. I have never witnessed this myself, but I remember seeing the streets of Brecon so covered with Cockchafers that it was impossible to walk without treading on them, and I was told that anglers on the nearby Taly-bont reservoir enjoy excellent sport on such occasions. When visiting waters where beetles are to be expected, therefore, the fisherman would do well to provide himself with an appropriate pattern, though as a general "fly" I feel that the value of the artificial beetle has been somewhat overrated.

The life-cycle consists of egg, larva, pupa and adult, but the trout do not, of course, have an opportunity of taking the larvae and pupae of the terrestrial species. Even the aquatic beetles usually pupate out of their reach, either in the bank or on emergent vegetation, while their larvae are very rarely found in autopsies, possibly because they are equipped with prehensile claws which enable them to cling so tightly to the weeds that they are difficult to dislodge. It is therefore unnecessary to describe the Coleoptera in these stages.

The adults vary greatly in shape and size, the aforementioned Coch-y-bonddu being an oval-shaped beetle about half an inch long and coloured reddish brown and black, with black legs. The Cockchafer is too well-known to need description. Most of the water beetles are more or less boat-shaped, and may be distinguished from the land-bred species by their flatter legs, fringed with hairs, which enable them to swim. They have to surface for air at intervals like the Corixids, which makes it all the more surprising that they are so seldom eaten by trout.

Order: HYMENOPTERA

The only insects of this order with which the angler need concern himself are the ants, of which there are several species coloured red, brown or black. They are, of course, land-bred, but when a swarm flies across a lake or river during the late summer months many of them fall into the water, and the trout seem to be inordinately fond of them. It has been said that an artificial ant is very seldom required but that when it *is* wanted it is wanted very badly, which no doubt is true, though in thirty years of fly-fishing I never had occasion to use one myself. The ants, of course, require no description from me, and their life-history is too complex to be included here. Those who may be interested, however, will find a detailed description of the ants' remarkable story in Courtney Williams's excellent work, *A Dictionary of Trout Flies*.

CHAPTER XI

RIVER MANAGEMENT
by
F. T. K. PENTELOW

THE three governing factors in looking after a fishery are what you want, what the fish want and what your neighbours, by land and water, are prepared to put up with. The owner or lessee wants to catch a large number of good-sized fish: the sport must not be too easy or it becomes monotonous and loses its attraction, and it must not be too difficult or the angler and his guests become discouraged and frustrated. The fish want, primarily, homes and food; homes so that they will stay in the water and food so that they will grow quickly. It may be desirable that there should be good spawning ground as well, but that, though natural and economical, is not essential, and indeed absence of natural spawning makes management of the stock a great deal easier. One's neighbours' rights must be respected: his land must not be flooded nor matters so arranged that his water is drained away or obstructed: in general his rights are protected by the law, either common or statutory, and though heaven forbid that every fisherman should have to be a lawyer, it is well to know the rudiments of his legal rights and duties and in most cases the local river board is a handy source of information and advice.

THE FISHERMAN'S REQUIREMENTS

It is easy to say that if you look after the fish the fisherman's needs will be met but this is only a half truth. True, if you don't look after the fish the fisherman cannot be satisfied, but we have to remember that in a perfect world for fish anglers would have no place. They are as much predators and pests as otters, herons, mergansers or pike in a chalk stream, and their needs and interests do not coincide with those of their prey.

Banks. The first requirement of the angler is access to the water, and management of the banks makes as much difference to his comfort and success as any other management practice. Banks should first of all be firm and that is so whether the water is fished from them or by wading. A marshy bank is a misery to fish from and a horror to traverse: how many of us have left a gumboot in a bog and taken an unexpected stockinged step into black liquid ooze! Therefore see that land drains are clear and if the banks are low use any convenient material to raise them a few inches. So long as the drains are clear it doesn't matter if the banks are a foot or two higher than the adjoining field. Material to strengthen them often becomes available from the river itself; mud and shoals removed to improve the flow, cut weeds, tree branches and of course any solid material than can be begged. It may be necessary to protect the bank from the river by sheet piling, and indeed where the fishery has been neglected it often pays to narrow the channel by driving in sheet piling (either wood or steel will do but the latter is more permanent) and filling in behind it.

Bridges and Stiles. The ditches and tributaries entering the river should be bridged; a stout wooden plank is generally quite adequate

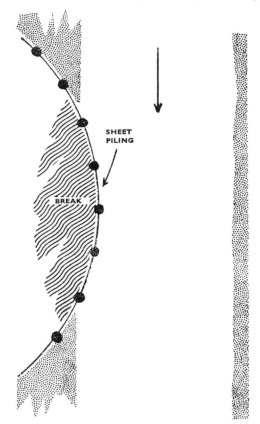

SHEET PILING

BREAK

FIG. 93. *Repairs to a broken bank*

provided the ditch is narrow enough and it is a very good idea to nail rabbit wire over the plank; it is common practice in the chalk-stream rivers and it gives a safe and certain foothold: damp wood can be as slippery as ice. Bigger streams will need a proper bridge and the building of that must be adapted to local circumstances: the two essentials are that it should be well supported (remember that wooden supports will eventually rot, so keep an eye on them) and that the approaches should be adequate. A stream of this sort is often a "wet fence" and divides one field from another; in that case the bridge will have to be fitted with a gate or stile. A stile should be used if possible for gates get left open, but when building the stile remember you will probably be climbing it in waders and they have a hampering effect. Hedges and fences require crossing places and stiles near the bank are a great advantage; they save a lot of unprofitable walking and avoid those nasty tears from barbed wire; they may even make it possible to follow a big fish if it should be your good fortune to hook one.

Trees and bushes. Anglers frequently have a bivalent attitude towards botany; they love the flowers and the fresh green of the spring and summer countryside but they abominate trees and bushes (and figwort) which play havoc with the back cast, and many a salmon fisherman has a jaundiced view of the leaf fall in the autumn. The proper "gardening" of the river bank therefore requires careful consideration and involves a lot of trouble if the best of both worlds is to be achieved. A tidy, mown river bank, innocent of trees and bushes within thirty yards of the water's edge would be anathema to most of us, even though it made a cast a certain and joyous exercise. Not only would it look and feel highly artificial, it would make it unnecessarily difficult to catch fish; they would too often see the angler before he saw them and took the appropriate action. Unless you are desirous of going in for ornamentation, there is no need to plant anything on the bank. Plenty of everything will grow there and the proper course is selective removal and trimming, leaving enough to give shade and cover to the fish (and provide them with caterpillars, beetles and other casual tit-bits) but giving the angler a fair chance to fish in comfort. It is often a good idea to leave a screen of herbaceous vegetation, reeds, rushes and willow-herb, but not thistles and nettles, along the edge of the water, so that the fisherman can fish from behind them. He can be pretty well hidden from the fish and it saves a lot of kneeling and crawling. Low branches of trees over the water or trailing in it should be ruthlessly pruned. There will almost certainly be a trout under the tree and it ought to be possible, if not easy, to bring one's fly over him.

Lastly, if the water is fished by wading, see that there are a few places where access is easy, either by keeping a clear path through a streamside thicket or seeing that the bank is of such a slope that one can walk down it.

Weed cutting. Attention to the river itself and the river-bed is largely in the interest of the fish and not of the fisherman, but weed cutting is of benefit to both and may be dealt with here. It must be admitted that to the fisherman all weed is a nuisance. It makes the fish invisible and too often produces surface growths, either leaves or flower heads. The best fish when hooked dive for it and the cast gets fouled and breaks; it collects mud, and lastly but not least, it never knows when to stop growing and is liable to fill the river completely and make fishing impossible. Nevertheless, in some streams, though not in all, weed is essential for the fish. It gives them cover and the fauna in the weeds provides a sizeable proportion of their food. So it is impossible to say "out with it, I will have none of it"; it must be treated properly and used to the best advantage.

First of all, it is probably quite unnecessary for the fishery manager to worry about the kind of weed growing in the water. There is precious little evidence that any kind of weed is better than any other, and if the water is kept in suitable condition for trout the appropriate kinds of weed will grow, and those that are undesirable like ribbon weeds and rushes will not. In particular, do not despise the Canadian water-weed; it has a bad name, but that seems quite unjustified. You must therefore take weeds as they come and control them so that they do not spread unduly. Undoubtedly the best way of doing this is by trimming with a scythe, either by wading or from a punt, and keeping each weed-bed to the desired shape and area. Unfortunately in these days of scarce hand labour this is very difficult to do and more heroic measures have to be taken. Many have looked to chemical control to solve the problem, but so far there is no hope of weed-control in free flowing water in this direction. With the currents prevailing in trout streams the amount of weed killer required to maintain the necessary concentration for the requisite time is beyond all reason; moreover, nearly all of them are toxic to fish as well as to weeds. There are, however, hopes that it may be possible to make up weed killers in the form of pellets which can be placed in the mud among the roots of the plants and that by this method selected areas of weed can be exterminated without any poison getting into the water. Experiments on these lines are being actively pursued, but so far complete success has not been achieved. It is worth keeping an eye on what the chemical manufacturers are doing, for this kind of thing could be a very great help in river management.

However, for the present we must use mechanical methods, and if the labour for river "gardening" cannot be obtained we must look to more wholesale, but admittedly less satisfactory and selective methods.

The chain scythe, made of scythe blades fastened together with a flexible joint and worked to and fro downstream from either bank or between two punts, is old and well tried; it clears an area reasonably well and in favourable circumstances can be used with discrimination so that occasional weed-beds are left and the river-bed is not shaved bare. Then there are weedcutting boats which are fitted with knives below the water. They trim off the weeds at the depth they are set to, but they are expensive and can only be used in fairly deep water. Finally, there is the drag-line excavator which grabs out the weeds in great lumps and deposits them on the banks. Again, this is an expensive business and only worth while where the growth is very abundant over long stretches, as it is in the Hampshire Avon. In theory the machine could be used selectively, but in practice the operator is unlikely to be a fisherman, or indeed to be able to see very clearly what he is removing, and the method will inevitably turn out to be pretty wholesale destruction.

If the weed growth is not kept in check by the fisherman it may become so prolific as to hold up the water and cause flooding of riparian land. In those circumstances if the river is designated "main river" on the map of the River Board area, the River Board will be bound to remove it in the interest of land drainage. They will do it in the cheapest and most efficient way, but the clearance is likely to be drastic and the fisherman is frequently not at all pleased with the result. Generally the engineer will be sympathetic to fishery interests and his operations will be so conducted as to cause as little harm as possible, but remember that his job is to get the water away, he may have a long length of river to deal with in a very short time, he has to do it because the others concerned, owners or lessees, are incapable of keeping the weeds down, and the service is free. A weed-filled river is not fishable and though the bed may be clean, bare and lacking in shelter for a time, the weeds will grow again and the water will again be fishable.

Disposal of weeds. The removal of weeds really belongs to the section of this chapter dealing with one's duty towards one's neighbour, but for convenience it may be included here. If you do nothing the current will take all the cut weeds out of your water, but to leave it at that is a pretty raw deal for your fellows below. Their water will be unfishable and their own weed problem will be made a great deal worse. Therefore it is good manners to remove on to your own banks as much as you possibly can. Weed racks (preferably temporary) will concentrate the cut weed at points where it can be conveniently dragged out on to the banks, or the wealthy may obtain small petrol-driven mechanical elevators which will save the labour of doing it by hand. Nevertheless, with the best will in the world, weedcutting will make the water turbid and fragments of floating weed are bound to go downstream and, generally speaking, the water below will be unfishable for a time. Therefore it is very good practice for the fishery owners to concert their weedcutting programmes so they all know what is afoot, and though they will have, unwillingly perhaps, to accept that their water may be unfishable on a certain day, they can at least avoid asking an important guest to fish on that day!

WHAT THE FISH WANT

Harbourage for fish. We have none of us been a fish, so what they really want we can never truly know; we have to judge their needs from their growth and behaviour and our observations and deductions from them may both be faulty. Nevertheless, we can make a pretty fair assessment of what they have to have; what is less certain is whether we get the priorities right. Many of us have tended to put food to eat and oxygen to breathe at the top of the list, but it may well be that in the fish's scheme of things a good home counts for more than anything else and this therefore will be discussed first.

Recent work by Mr. E. D. Le Cren at Windermere has shown that trout of all ages show just the same sort of "territorial" behaviour as do the robins and blackbirds in our gardens. Each trout has a little portion of the stream that is his and intruders entering it are attacked and, if possible, driven off; the occupant does not, however, normally interfere with fish outside his territory. What determines the boundaries of the territory is not yet known, but the fish's sight seems to have something to do with it. "Out of sight, out of mind" may be the philosophy of fish territory in solitary species like trout. Consequently irregularities in the river-bed, weed-beds, holes under banks, rocks, submerged logs and generally any diversification of the stream bed is a help to the housing problem. In a bare stream with a smooth bed the fish may have to be out of sight-range of their neighbours if they are to be happy and settled.

In rivers which are, or can be made, what the engineer calls "self-cleansing" there is not much need to bother about the housing question. The current will, by eroding soft material and leaving hard, produce irregularities in the river-bed and patches of weed will do the rest. Of course a smooth rock channel is rather barren, but if the current is so fast as to keep it clear of boulders and stones it is too great to permit the artificial introduction of them, for they will go in the next flood and possibly fill up a good pool below. In places where the current is a good deal slower and the bed is composed of small pebbles it has been said that the introduction of large boulders or concrete blocks improves the fish-holding capacity, and it may do so if the gravel is weedless and loose enough to be moved by smallish floods. However, such places are not so very common; mostly the bed will be fairly stable except in major floods and will grow weeds. "Let well alone" is good advice when applied to trout streams as to many other things.

Mud and shallows. A "self-cleansing" stream is one where the current conditions are such that on the average material erodes from the river-bed: a "non-self-cleansing" stream is one where over a period material is deposited on the river-bed faster than it is eroded away, so that in time the river channel fills up. It is these which give rise to most of the problems of managing a trout fishery. The effect shows itself in a muddy bed or a wide and shallow shoal of gravel and sand. Mud is the trout fisherman's worst and most dangerous natural enemy. It is uniform and featureless, it has an oxygen-absorbing capacity which may deoxygenate the overlying water on warm nights, and though the idea that area for area it produces less food than gravel is almost certainly wrong, trout do not like it. A shallow is a good deal less offensive in appearance, the water ripples cheerfully over it, the bed looks clean and bright and if the sun shines it makes a most attractive picture. But if it is shallow enough it will be as barren as a muddy river, for fish are not happy with their backs out of water.

Whether a river erodes its bed or fills it up depends solely on the current and these evils arise from too little of it. Current is essentially due to gravity and therefore the primary factor is the fall of the land: steep land, a torrent, flat land, stagnation. The fall of a river from the source to the sea is for practical purposes fixed by geography and there is very little we can do about it; we can sometimes speed up the current by shortening the channel and slow it above or hasten it below by building weirs, but we cannot alter the total fall and the lower reaches of the fenland rivers, for instance, will always be muddy and slow. However, the current is also dependent on the quantity of water and the size of the channel it passes through. The flow of the river is conveniently measured in cubic feet per second (cusecs) and if, for example, the channel is 5 feet wide and 2 feet deep and water flows through it at 1 foot per second, the discharge is 10 cusecs. If the channel is reduced to 2½ feet by 2 feet, then the rate of flow must be 2 feet per second to produce the same total discharge.

Now, in our trout streams mud and shallows often occur because the river is too big for the amount of water it carries: this may arise because the quantity of water has been reduced by abstraction (like many of the chalk streams of Hertfordshire), or because the banks have eroded and fallen in, or because the channel has been enlarged for navigation purposes and the locks, sluices and controls have now become derelict, or even because the channel has been widened and deepened to accommodate flood flow and so save riparian land from inundation. In all these cases it is often possible to provide more fishable water by narrowing the channel; the increased flow will wash away mud and leave clean gravel, or cut a deeper channel in pebbly sand and give more harbourage for trout.

The places where a permanent restriction of the channel is either necessary or desirable are quite few, and very careful consideration should be given to any such project before embarking upon it. Remember that the channel has to accommodate the flow in flood as well as in drought and that a river which is depositing mud when the water is low may well be eroding its bed when it is high. So before embarking on such a scheme make very certain that you are not going to involve yourself in problems of flooding and bank and bed erosion, which may be far worse than the existing conditions.

If the channel is really too big for the river in all its stages then the best thing to do is to line out the new channel with sheet piling and fill in behind it. You will naturally use as much material from the river-bed as you can for it will be cheap and handy, but you will have to import a surprising amount of stuff and the harder it is the better. At the end of the stretch under treatment do not forget to key the piling carefully and well into the old bank: otherwise water will cut through behind it and everything will be wasted.

However, most channel restrictions will be temporary, to create a run and to remove mud at times when the river is low, and this fortunately is very much less of an undertaking. The best thing for this purpose is the old-fashioned stuffed hurdle or wattle fencing staked to the river-bed, as has been used on the Test and Itchen for generations. The hurdles are put in so as to direct the current in the right direction, to make a run or to wash away some mud or even to erode away a weed-bed. Experiment and experience have to be used to find the best places but unless the river is very wide it is necessary to have the hurdles in pairs, opposite each other, or the current deflected by one may wash away the opposite bank. The hurdles can be taken out before the winter and are better out at any time if a flood is expected. Finally some people use sheets of corrugated iron instead of hurdles; it is cheap and *very* nasty.

Weirs. Another way of improving the fish-holding capacity of a shallow stream is to build low weirs across it. They, of course, give a greater depth and therefore more cover above them, their effect on slowing down the current may encourage weed growth and the water cascading over the weir will erode a hole below it which, with the falling turbulent water, gives more cover. It is often maintained that the oxygenating effect of the weir is good, too, but unless the water is polluted this is doubtful for it may be quite offset by the stagnation and silting above the weir.

Such weirs should be low, not raising the water level by more than a foot. Higher dams restrict fish movement and that is certainly a bad thing where salmon and sea trout are concerned and probably also for brown trout too. In salmon rivers it is sometimes a good idea to build croys out from the bank, to concentrate the current which often erodes a hole in which a fish will lie below the croy, to protect the bank from erosion and to make a stance from which to fish.

Finally, if you contemplate engineering works of this kind, consult your river board engineer. He is an expert on the subject and will know whether what you propose will produce the desired results or have effects which are unforeseen and unwanted. Moreover, if the river is designated as "main river" on the river board map you will have to obtain the formal consent of the Board anyway, and the engineer is a good man to consult at the earliest stage.

36, 37. A chalk stream before and after being cleared of weed and bankside
vegetation. (Note the protective screen left along the margin.)

38. Clearing a trout stream of coarse fish with the electric machine.

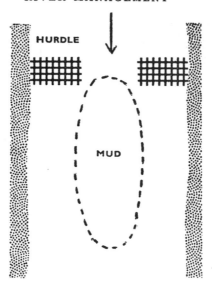

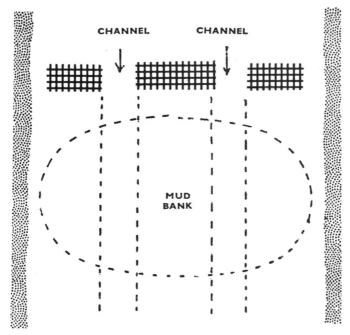

FIG. 94. *Clearing a stream of mud. This is effected by hurdles placed in position temporarily as shown.*

T

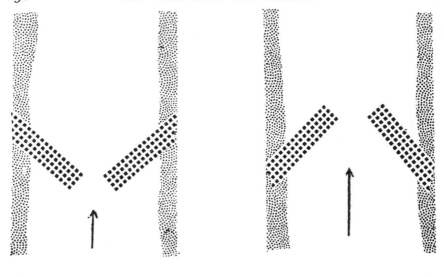

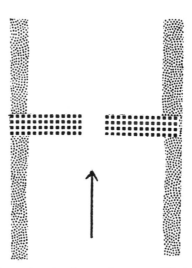

FIG. 95. *Restricting a channel to increase the current. This is accomplished by the construction of croys, which can also be used as fishing platforms. Skilled advice should be sought as to the most suitable angles of emplacement for different sets of conditions.*

FOOD SUPPLY

Fish like all other animals need food in order to live and grow. Those we are concerned with, salmon and trout, are in nature carnivorous, but adult salmon, unlike parr and smolts, appear to take no food in fresh water.

Trout and salmon in their feeding stages can, of course, be fed on artificial foods in rivers as they can in ponds, but that is scarcely ever done in this country and, indeed, since we like to catch "wild" fish (even if they have spent all their earlier life in a stew), to feed them in a river would seem akin to shooting barnyard hens or hunting a bagged fox.

So we leave our fish to find their own living in the river or stream in which they find themselves. Any healthy unpolluted and permanent stream appears to produce adequate food for the natural population of fish in it and human interference can seldom do much good or harm. What a river produces depends essentially on the amount of light it receives and the nutrient salts it carries: the former depends on the climate and the second on the geology of the river basin and neither of these is easily altered. A stream heavily overgrown with trees and bushes will produce less food than one in full daylight and overshadowing is therefore to be avoided for other reasons than preventing fishing, but some shade is desirable for other reasons, so do not be too drastic. Moreover, it has recently been discovered that a large proportion of trout food is in the form of "drift", i.e. insects and other creatures which fall into the water from overhanging vegetation, and trees help to replenish this larder.

Manuring. Incidentally, if anyone thinks that by artificial manuring the nutrient status of a stream can be improved he had better do some arithmetic; ten million gallons a day is quite a low flow for a trout stream and a gallon of water weighs about 10 lb., so to increase the amount of phosphate or nitrate or lime by one part per million one would have to add 100 lb. a day, or about 18 tons a year! In fact the only practicable method of fertilization is by sewage effluents: in a nutritively poor water they can, if of good quality and not too great in quantity, do a lot of good!

Introduction of food. Many people have experimented optimistically with the introduction of food organisms, freshwater shrimps, crayfish, Mayflies, fly boards, snails and even fodder fish but it is very doubtful whether anyone has had any success. The truth is that in a wild and uncontrolled environment like a river the organisms present are adapted to their environment and there are, we think, sufficient numbers and kinds to make full use of the resources available; unfortunately we do not know what are the controlling factors and until we do, any interference with existing conditions is as likely to do harm as to do good and perhaps most likely to have no effect at all.

Although it may at present be impracticable to increase the food supply, there may be some possibility of it preventing it being reduced. The greatest destroyer of food is a flood of sufficient intensity to move the river-bed and rivers with lakes and reservoirs on their course are much less likely to suffer this disaster than those which run directly off steep mountains, but generally speaking the sort of engineering works necessary for flood control are beyond the scope of the fishery owners, though they can benefit them when they are undertaken for other purposes. The other way in which food can be saved is by removing competitive species such as dace, roach and chub, together with grayling, if you are prepared to forego sport with the fly-rod during the autumn months. With nylon nets and electric fishing machines there is no great difficulty about such operations.

OXYGEN

Fish, like us, need oxygen to breathe and they get it from the water as we do from the air. The water is supplied by solution from the air and by the photosynthetic activity of green plants in daylight. It is used up by fish in respiration and by decaying organic matter and in a healthy stream the oxygen is replenished at a faster rate than it is used, so that there is always plenty for the fish. If there is too much decaying organic matter, or even living plants respiring at night, the oxygen may be used up faster than it is supplied and fish may suffer. The commonest cause of this trouble is pollution and if there is good reason to suspect that, the river board should be asked to investigate. Apart from that the usual practices of good fishery management, preventing the accumulation of mud and keeping weed growth to reasonable amounts, will be all that is necessary to keep the oxygen conditions right for the fish.

CONTROL OF PREDATORS

Coarse fish. It is a good thing to keep down the numbers of pike, perch, chub and eels in a stream where "salmon or trout are specially preserved", to use the words of the Salmon and Freshwater Fisheries Act, 1923. This must be done by netting or electric fishing and you may need the permission of the river board. In this country it is still a statutory offence, punishable by heavy penalties, to use poison to take fish, and this applies to all fish even if they are reckoned undesirable. In America the poisoning out of unwanted species is common fishery practice, but there are conflicting views about it in this country and our laws still remain as they were. If you are getting rid of coarse fish remember that some of your fellow anglers may be very glad of them and that the Salmon and Trout Association and the National Federation have a scheme whereby those who have fish to dispose of can be put in touch with those who want them.

Birds. Dealing with predatory birds is now a somewhat difficult matter; they can, of course, still be shot with as much ease or otherwise as ever, but since the Protection of Birds Act of 1954 was passed the general law is that almost all birds are protected and may only be killed if taken in the act of doing damage. For our purpose the exceptions are cormorants, greater and lesser black-backed gulls, herring gulls and in Scotland only, goosanders and red-breasted mergansers. They may be shot by "authorized persons" at any time, but it will be noticed that the list does not include herons or kingfishers. It is essential that anyone contemplating action against any bird should make himself acquainted with the provisions of the Act.

Otters. The only British mammal known to prey on fish is the otter and it is doubtful if they are ever numerous enough to cause the fisherman serious concern. Moreover, they are known to eat eels and it is generally thought that in this way they compensate for the harm they may do by eating salmon and trout.

STOCKING

No fishery can be maintained unless there are young fish coming along to replace the natural mortality (which at all ages and in all species with which we are concerned is almost certainly greater than that due to fishing) and those taken by fishermen. So obvious is this that for about a century it has over-coloured all thinking about fishery management, and "stocking policy" has almost become synonymous with that expression.

The plain fact is that where there exists a natural population of salmon, sea-trout or brown trout the fish are much better at maintaining it than anyone else; they will lay sufficient eggs and all stages will be subject to the various population checks, so that the stream produces a natural quantity of takeable fish.

Salmon and sea-trout. In the case of salmon and sea-trout, man has so far found no way of improving on nature. It seems pretty certain that introducing eggs, fry or parr will have no effect on the number of smolts going to sea, for they will merely compete with their naturally-produced contemporaries and the weakest (which may well be the stocked fish) will go to the wall. Swedish experience suggests that the stock might be increased by adding smolts, but that has not been tested where they compete with a natural stock and is, in any event, a very expensive process, so for the present it cannot be recommended. Of course, if there are in the fishery streams with suitable spawning grounds which contain no salmon or sea-trout, because they are denied access by natural or artificial obstructions, then the stock can be increased by seeding the spawning ground with eggs, preferably in the eyed stage, in Kashmir or Vibert boxes, or by stocking with fry which have been reared in a hatchery until they are ready to feed. The losses will be very heavy, certainly over 99 per cent, but there seems to be no advantage in stocking with older fish, which is much more expensive and difficult.

Brown trout. Where brown trout only are concerned, they are under much better control and there is more chance that interference will produce the desired result. Nevertheless if the natural stock of fish is satisfactory in numbers and size, let well alone. Both Plunket-Greene and Laming have vividly described the ill results from un-wise stocking of the Bourne and Itchen respectively. There are, however, waters where the natural stock is not all that could be desired : it may consist of many fish of too small a size or of very big ones which are far too few to give sport; again there are lakes and rivers where there is no spawning ground and they can only be maintained as trout fisheries by artificial stocking. In the first case little can be done, though perhaps a drastic reduction of stock, if persisted in, may improve the growth-rate of the survivors. It would be possible to stock with fish of the desired size, but this would have only a temporary effect and the object would be to have sport with them before they moved out of the fishery. A very few large fish is likely to be the situation where the river is big and deep and naturally more suited to chub, dace and roach than to trout. Here, if the other species are harried with nets and electric machines, a good head of sizeable trout can be maintained by stocking. My own view is that the most economical fish to buy are the biggest you can afford. They should grow to takeable size as soon after stocking as possible, for the longer they are in the river the greater will the loss in numbers be. Certainly conditions are unsuitable for anything less than well-grown yearlings, and American work on the loss from one year to another suggests that the fish have a better chance in a hatchery than in a river. Where a river or lake has no natural stock then there is much more choice in size of fish. The famous lakes of the Bristol Waterworks Company are stocked with fry, many are stocked with yearlings, and there is no information as to which is the better : it may well be a question of economics, but that has not been worked out, or if it has, the results have not been published.

Rainbow trout. Finally, if you want rainbow trout you will have to stock annually, for the rivers where they will breed are numbered on the fingers of one hand.

CARE OF THE SPAWNING-BEDS

Fish know much better than we do what makes a suitable spawn-ing-bed and it is not certain that we can help them very much. It used to be the practice to rake or harrow spawning-beds to loosen the gravel and disperse silt. Whether this did any good is not known : it is true that silt is bad for eggs, but the hen would have got rid of a lot of it herself whilst cutting the redd, and loose gravel is

more easily washed away in a flood. If you believe in the practice
then make sure you do it before the fish spawn and not afterwards;
sea-trout will sometimes spawn quite early in October.

FISHERY MANAGEMENT AND YOUR NEIGHBOUR

Remember you are not alone in your interest in a river: other
people have rights and they may not share your views. Primarily it
is a matter of consideration and good manners. Do not dam a
stream to such a height that land is flooded, particularly if it does
not belong to you: do not interfere with the free movement of fish
up and down stream for it is illegal: do not divert the water to the
disadvantage of your downstream neighbour.

Lastly, consult your river board's fishery officer. You may not
always see eye to eye with him or he with you, but he does have an
overall picture and a good deal of expert knowledge and may well
make helpful suggestions if he is in your confidence.

CLASSIFIED INDEX

Books mentioned in the text
Angler's Entomology, An, 248
Creel of Willow, A, 188
Dictionary of Trout Flies, A, 280
Fly Fishing for Salmon, 39
Keeper of the Stream, 116
Mental Evolution in Animals, 84
Minor Tactics of the Chalk Stream, 116
Natural Trout Fly and its Imitation,
  The, 248
Nymph Fishing for Chalk Stream Trout,
  116
Nymphs and the Trout, 111, 116
Sunshine and the Dry Fly, 86
Where the Bright Waters Meet, 123

Casting a Fly, 193 et seq
  Casting in a wind, 216
  Conclusion, 217
  Mechanics of the cast, The, 194–8
  — Aerial manipulation, 195
  — Basic principles, 194
  — Rod action, 196
  Overhead double-handed fly cast,
    The, 211–13
  — Position of hands, 211
  — Timing, 212
  Overhead trout-fly cast, The, 207–
    11
  — Action of casting, 208
  — Grip, 208
  — Timing, 209
  — Use of off-rod hand, 210
  Roll cast and variations, The, 213–
    16
  — Changing direction, 214
  — Changing hands, 215
  — Double-Spey cast, The, 215
  — Method of execution, 213
  — Spey cast, The, 214
  Tackle, 198–207
  — Conclusions, 207
  — General application, 202
  — Leaders or casts, 205
  — Lines, 200
  — Reels, 205
  — Rods, 198

Chalk streams, brown trout in, 113 et
  seq
Artificial flies
  — Black Gnat, 120, 128, 137, 145
  — Caenis spinner, 126
  — Fairey's Irresistible, 124
  — Ginger Quill, 120
  — Hawthorn-fly, 127, 145
  — Iron Blue, 145
  — Kite's sedge, 127, 145
  — Lunn's Caperer, 127
  — Lunn's Particular, 120
  — Mayfly, 145
  — Mayfly spinner, 121, 125, 126, 145
  — Olive dun, 123, 145
  — Orange Quill, 126, 145
  — Pale Evening dun, 119, 125, 145
  — Pale Watery dun, 124, 145
  — Pheasant-tail nymph, 120, 139,
    145
  — Pheasant-tail Red spinner, 120,
    126, 145
  — Red Quill, 120
  — Red spinner, 119, 136
  — Sedge fly, 145
  — Slow-water Olive spinner, 126
  See also table on p. 145
Basic methods, 114–17
  — Dry-fly fishing, 114
  — Nymph fishing, 115
Chalk-stream season, The, 117–19
  — Duration, 117
  — First phase, The, 118
  — Main phases, 117
  — Second phase, The, 118
  — Third phase, The, 119
Clothes and tackle, 128–30
  — Amadou, 130
  — Bag, 130
  — Cast, 129
  — Dressing the part, 128
  — Fly-box, 130
  — Grease, 130
  — Lines, 129
  — Oil, 130
  — Reel, 129
  — Rod, 129
  — Ruler, 130
  — Spring balance, 130

Clothes and tackle (contd.)
— Waders, 129
— Working tools, 129
Contents of the fly-box, The, 119–28
— All-round dry-fly patterns, 120
— Happy mean, The, 121
— Introduction, 119
— Nymph in relation to the dry
    fly, The, 119
— Winged and hackled flies, 128
(For names of flies see "Artificial
flies" in this section and "Natural
insects").

Dry fly in theory and practice, 131–8
— Basic theory, 131
— Choice of bank, 132
— Handling a hooked trout, 137
— Locating a trout, 132
— Main problem, The, 132
— Making a start, 131
— Nymphing fish, 137
— Opening fire, 135
— Preliminaries, 131
— Reconnaissance, 135
— Some advice, 136
— Smutting fish, 137
Introduction, 113–14
— Chalk-stream characteristics, 113
— Chalk country, The, 114
— End and the means, The, 114
— Importance of fly production, 113
— Limitations on fishing methods,
    113
— Maintenance of trout stocks, 113
Nymph-fishing technique, 138–44
— Artificial nymphs, 138
— Basic technique, 141
— Evening nymph fishing, 141
— Natural nymphs, 138
— Nymphs in fast water, 141
— Nymphs in slow water, 141
— Nymph pitching, 143
— Patterns necessary, 139
— Practice, 144
— Tackle, 139
— Tailing trout, 140
— Test of suitability, A, 139
— Timing the strike, 143
— When to fish the nymph, 140
— Windy days, 140

Entomology of lakes and rivers, The,
    248 et seq
Artificial flies.
— Kimbridge sedge, 270
— Little Red sedge, 270

— Orange Quill, 257
— Orange sedge, 270
Descriptive list of insects, 250–80
— Families
— — Baëtidae, 259
— — Bibionidae, 273
— — Caenidae, 257
— — Chironomidae, 272
— — Corixidae, 277
— — Culicidae, 273
— — Ecdyonuridae, 265
— — Ephemerellidae, 256
— — Ephemeridae, 252
— — Leptophlebiidae, 254
— — Nemouridae, 272
— — Notonectidae, 277
— — Perlidae, 272
— — Perlodidae, 272
— — Sialidae, 276
— — Simulidae, 275
— — Tipulidae, 275
— Genera.
— — Anisomera, 275
— — Baëtis, 259
— — Bibio, 273
— — Brachycentrus, 269
— — Caenis, 257
— — Centroptilum, 261
— — Chaoborus, 273
— — Chironomus, 272
— — Cloëon, 262
— — Corixa, 277
— — Ecdyonurus, 268
— — Ephemera, 252
— — Ephemerella, 256, 267
— — Goëra, 270
— — Halesus, 270
— — Heptagenia, 267, 268
— — Hydropsyche, 270
— — Isoperla, 272
— — Lepidostoma, 270
— — Leptocerus, 270
— — Leptophlebia, 254
— — Leuctra, 272
— — Limnephilus, 270
— — Melolontha, 279
— — Mystacides, 270
— — Odontocerum, 270
— — Paraleptophlebia, 268
— — Phryganea, 270
— — Phyllopertha, 279
— — Procloëon, 264
— — Protonemura, 272
— — Rhithrogena, 265
— — Sericostoma, 270
— — Sialis, 276
— — Siphlonurus, 268

Descriptive list of insects (contd.)
— — *Taniopteryx*, 272
— Natural orders.
— — Coleoptera, 279
— — Diptera, 272–76
— — Ephemeroptera, 250–67
— — Hemiptera-Heteroptera, 277–78
— — Hymenoptera, 280–81
— — Odonata, 278
— — Plecoptera, 270–72
— — Trichoptera, 268–70
— Sub-family
— — Chaoborinae, 273
— Sub-orders
— — Anisoptera, 278
— — Megaloptera, 276–77
— — Zygoptera, 278
(For vernacular names of individual species see under "Natural insects'.)
Introduction, 248–50
— Food of trout, The, 248
— Habitats of insects, 249
— Nomenclature, 249

Fishermen and authors mentioned in the text.
Balfour-Kinnear, G.P.R., 43
Blakey, Robert, 84
Blyth, Ben, 104, 105
Canaway, W. H., 188
Carey, Brig. General H. E., 119
Clegg, Thomas, 70, 79, 99, 100
Cholmondeley-Pennell, H. 96, 201
Connett, Eugene, 109
Cotton, Charles, 188, 207
Courtney Williams, A., 97, 266, 271, 279, 280
Crosfield, Ernest, 33
Daubry, 193
Dieckman, 193
Dunne, J. W., 86
Edwards, Capt. T. L., 207, 208, 211
Fairey, Sir Richard, 124
Francis Francis, 114
Halford, F. M., 90, 96, 114, 115, 119, 120, 172, 250, 259, 262, 270
Hall, H. S., 114
Harris, Prof, J. R., 97, 106, 248, 264, 265
Hewitt, E. R., 98, 202
Hills, J. W., 119, 121
Hollings, 104
Hutton, J. A., 22
Kingsmill-Moore, T. C., 77
Kolseth, 193

La Branche, G. M. L., 105, 108, 109
Laming, Percy, 47, 294
Le Cren, E. D., 286
Leney, 170, 175
Lewis, Dai, 98, 193
Lunn, William, 135
Lupton, Phillip, 109
Macan, Dr. T. T., 257
Marryat, G. S., 114
Marsden, J. C., 140
McCaskie, Dr. N., 128
Mitchell, Sir Robert, 175
Morgan, Prof. Lloyd, 84
Mottley, C. M., 171 n.
Oglesby, A. V., 109
Owen, Jack, 104, 105
Pashley, Robert, 193
Plunket Greene, H., 123 294
Powell, Rev. E., 108
Pryce, 103, 104
Rennie, Prof, John, 96
Romanes, G. R. J., 84, 85, 89
Saundby, Sir Robert, 171 n.
Sawyer, Frank, 98, 111, 116, 138, 139
Schöpp, 193
Skues, G. E. M., 91, 93, 96, 111, 114, 115, 117, 127, 138, 139, 172, 176
Stephens, Wilson, 111
Stoddart, T. T., 84
Tarrantino, 193, 216
Thomson, Prof, A. J., 84
Turing, H. D., 262
Waddington, Richard, 27, 33, 39, 43
Walker, Comdr. C. F., 173, 177
Ward, Dr. Francis, 84
West, Leonard, 248
Wood, A. H. E., 26, 30, 31, 33, 38, 39, 40, 43, 87
Wood, Ian, 50
Wulff, Lee, 27

Fly Dressing, 219 *et seq*
Lessons
— Hackle Mayfly, 237
— Hackled dry fly, 227
— Hackled wet fly, 231
— Hair-winged salmon fly, 242
— Nymph, 234
— Tube-fly, 246
— Whip finish, 225
— Winding the silk, 223
— Winged loch or sea trout fly, 239
Materials, 219–21
— Hackles, 220
(*See also each lesson*)

Patterns described
— French Partridge Mayfly, 237
— Grouse and Silver, 239
— Hackle Blue Dun, 231
— Hairy Mary, 242
— Irish Blue, 246
— Olive nymph, 234
— Red Hackle, 237
Tools and accessories, 221-3
— Acetone, 223
— Apron, 222
— Bench or work table, 223
— Bobbin-holder, 221
— Camel-hair brush, 222
— Catch, 221
— Cotton wool, 223
— Dubbing needle, 222
— Fly-tying vice, 221
— Hackle pliers, 221
— Hooks, 223
— Methylated spirit, 223
— Nail, 222
— Pen-knife, 222
— Razor blade, 222
— Scissors, 222
— Storage boxes, 223
— Tying Silk, 223
— Varnishes 223
— Wax, fly-tyer's, 223

Grayling, 180 et seq
Anatomy of, 181
Artificial flies
— Bradshaw's Fancy, 190
— Bumbles, 190
— Greenwell's Glory, 190, 191
— King's Austrian Wasp, 190
— Poult Bloa, 190
— Red Tag, 190, 191
— Sherry spinner, 190
— Tup's Indispensable, 190
— Variants, 190
— Water-hen Bloa, 190
— Wickham's Fancy, 190, 191
— Witch, 190
Artificial fly and the use of cover,
The, 188
— Flies, 188
— Taking cover, 188
Coloration, 182
Conclusion, 191
Dry-fly fishing, 188-90
— Fly patterns, 190
— Tackle, 190
— Tactics, 189
Habitats, 183-4

— Alkaline content and tempera-
ture, 183
— Food supply, 183
— River conditions, 183
— Stocking experiments, 184
Origins of grayling, 180
Shoaling habits, 186
— Lies, 186
Spawning, 184-5
— weights, 185
Surface food, 187-8
— Method of rising, 187
Wet-fly fishing, 190-1
— Nymphs, 191
— Striking, 191
— Tackle and flies, 190
— Upstream or down? 191

Lakes, brown trout in, 146 et seq
Artificial flies
— Alexandra, 156
— Black Pennell, 156
— Black Spider, 156, 162
— Blae and Black, 155
— Butcher, 156, 158
— Claret and Mallard, 157
— Coch-y-bonddu, 156
— Golden Olive, 155
— Greenwell's Glory, 155, 157
— Grouse and Green, 155
— Hardy's Favourite, 156
— Invicta, 155, 157
— March Brown, 154, 157
— March Brown Spider, 156
— Peter Ross, 157, 158
— Red Palmer, 156
— Teal and Black, 156
— Teal and Green, 155
— Teal and Red, 157, 158
— Teal and Silver, 156
— Woodcock and Hare's Ear, 155
— Woodcock and Yellow, 156
— Worm-fly, 157
— Zulu, 156
Boat fishing, 166-9
— Boats, 166
— Fishing the drift, 166
— Hooking a trout, 167
— Tactics, 167
(See also under "Shore v. boat
fishing").
Dry-fly fishing, 160-2
— Drag, 161
— Fly patterns, 162
— Hooking a trout, 161
— Practical application, 161
— When to fish dry, 160

Finding the fish, 147–50
— Artificial reservoirs, 149
— Bed of the lake, The, 148
— Effect of wind, The, 148
— Other features, 149
Introduction, 146
Lake fishing season, The, 152–3
— Effects of temperature, The, 152
— End of the season, The, 153
— Summer fishing, 153
More about the trout, 150–2
— Food supply, 150
— Movement of trout, 151
Shore fishing, 163–6
— Choice of beat, 163
— Method of fishing, 164
— Wading, 163
Shore v. Boat fishing, 162–3
Tackle for lake fishing, 146–7
— Casts, 147
— Landing nets, 147
— Lines, 147
— Reels, 146
— Rods, 146
Wet-fly fishing, 153–9
— Artificial fly, The, 153
— Change of method, 157
— Effect of light, The, 157
— Fishing the artificial, 155
— Fly patterns, 155
— Fly sizes, 158
— Hooking a trout, 159
— Nymphs & Chironomid pupae, 154
— Practical application, 159
— Small fish, 156
— Surface insects, 156
— Water boatmen, 156
Lakes mentioned in the text
Blagdon reservoir, 146
Bristol Waterworks' lakes, 294
L. Labe, 172, 173
L. Leven, 158
L. Lomond, 49, 50
L. Mask, 77
L. Ness, 49
L. Shasta, 170
L. Shore, 171 n.
L. Taupo, 175, 178
L. Te Anu, 175
L. Watten, 146
Talybont reservoir, 279
Two Lakes, near Romsey, 258

Natural insects
Alder, 128, 173, 276
Ants, 128, 177, 280

August or Autumn dun, 267
Baëtis nymphs, 259
Beetles, 110, 154, 183, 279, 283
Black Gnat, 118-20, 122, 127, 128, 145, 274
Blue-winged Olive, 60, 107, 119, 120, 122, 125, 126, 145, 256
Blue-winged Pale Watery or Greater Spurwing, 124, 262
Broadwings (general), 122, 126, 177. (See also under Dusky and Yellow Broadwings).
Brown May (dun), 268
Brown Mayfly, 254
Caenis nymphs, 257
Caperer, 270
Centroptilum nymphs, 262
Claret, 177, 255
Chironomidae or midges, 154, 155, 172, 177, 272
Cinnamon sedge, 270
Cloëon nymphs, 263
Coch-y-bonddu beetle, 279
Cockchafer or Maybug, 279
Crane-fly or Daddy-longlegs, 77, 177, 275
Damsel and Dragon-flies, 172, 177, 278
Dark (dun) 268
Duns (general) 101, 108, 111, 113, 118, 131, 132, 135, 140, 156, 172, 174, 177, 250, 251
Dusky Broadwing, 257
Early Brown, 272
Ecdyonurus nymphs, 266
Ephemera nymphs, 252, 253
Ephemerella nymphs, 256
False or Late March Brown, 267
February Red, 272
Grannom, 269, 275
Gravel Bed, 275
Great Red sedge, 270
Green Mayfly or Green Drake, 253
Grey Flag, 270
Grey sedge, 270
Hawthorn fly, 88, 111, 118, 122, 127, 128, 145, 274
Iron Blue, 122, 123, 127, 138, 145, 261
Lake Olive, 77, 118 n., 177, 263
Large Green (dun), 268
Large (Dark) Olive, 122, 123, 261
Large or Greater Spurwing (see under B-W Pale Watery)
Large Stone-flies, 272
Leptophlebia nymphs, 254

Natural insects (*contd.*)

Little Claret (I. B.) spinner, 127, 261
Little Sky Blue or Lesser Spurwing, 118, 122, 124, 126, 138, 141, 262
March Brown, 266
Mayfly, 77, 118, 120, 122, 125, 126, 129, 145, 157, 172, 177, 251, 253, 291
Medium Olive, 122, 123, 172, 250, 260
Medium sedge, 270
Needle Browns, 272
Nymphs (general), 69, 96, 98, 101, 105, 113, 115, 116, 119, 138-41, 145, 151, 154, 155, 191, 250, 251, 252
Olives (general), 118, 120, 122, 123, 127, 137, 138, 141, 145, 179
Pale Evening, 118, 120, 122, 125, 145, 264
Pale Watery, 59, 107, 118, 122-4, 138, 139, 141, 145, 176, 259
Phantom midges, 273
Pond Olive, 118 n., 141, 177, 263
Pond skaters, 277
Procloëon nymphs, 264
Purple (dun), 268
Red (Olive) spinner, 127, 145
Reed Smuts, 106, 107, 137, 177, 275
Rhithrogena nymphs, 265
Sedge or caddis flies (general), 59, 67-71, 76, 113, 118, 119, 122, 127, 131, 140, 145, 150, 156, 172, 174, 179, 249, 268-70
Sepia, 177, 255
Sherry (B.W.O.) spinner, 119, 127, 145, 256
Silver sedge, 270
Slow-water Olives, 122, 124, 126, 138, 139, 141, (see also under Lake & Pond Olives)
Small (Dark) Olive, 122, 123, 141, 145, 260
Small Dark sedge, 270
Small Spurwing (see under Little Sky Blue)
Spinners (general), 101, 108, 111, 113, 118, 126, 127, 131, 132, 156, 172, 177, 250, 251
Stone-flies, 270-2
Summer Mayflies or Large Summer duns, 268
Turkey Brown, 122, 267
Water-Boatmen, 156, 172, 277
Water cricket, 277
Water measurer, 277

Water scorpions, 277
Willow fly, 119, 128, 272
Yellow Broadwing, 258
Yellow Evening (dun) 267
Yellow May (dun) 122, 267
Yellow Sally, 272
Yellow Upright, 265
(See also table on p. 145)

Rainbow trout, 170 *et seq*
Artificial flies
— Black & Peacock Spider, 173
— Black Palmer, 173, 174
— Blue demoiselle, 177
— Broadwing spinner, 177
— Brown Ant, 177
— Coachman, 174, 176, 178
— Craig's Night Time, 173
— Crane-fly, 177
— Gold-ribbed Hare's Ear, 172
— Mayfly nymph, 177
— Midge pupa, 178
— Missionary, 173
— Olive, 178
— Pale Watery, 176
— Pale Watery nymph, 176
— Peacock and Black, 173
— Peter Ross, 173, 174, 178
— Pheasant-tail, 177
— Reckless William, 174
— Reed Smut, 177
— Silver-bodied March Brown, 173
— Teal and Red, 173
— Water-louse, 173
— Wickham's Fancy, 172-4, 178
Large reservoirs, 171-4
— Flies, 172
— Food of rainbows, The, 171
— Tactics, 172
Natural history, 170-1
— Koakanee 170
— Rainbow waters, 171
— *Salmo kamloops*, 170
— S. *shasta*, 170
— S. *stonei*, 170
— Steelheads, 170 & n., 178
Rivers, 178-9
— Flies, 178
Small reservoirs & gravel pits, 174-8
— Flies, 177
— Manner of feeding, 175
— Playing a rainbow, 175
— Stocking, 175
Rain-fed rivers, brown trout in, 82 *et seq*
Artificial flies
— Beetle, 88, 107, 108, 110

Rain-fed rivers (*contd.*)
— Black and Silver, 100
— Black Pennell, 110
— Blue dun, 104
— Butcher, 100
— Coch-y-bonddu, 104, 110
— Greenwell's Glory, 104
— Hare's Ear, 100, 107
— Hawthorn-fly, 88
— John Storey, 107
— March Brown, 104
— Orange Quill, 107
— Pale Watery, 107
— Pheasant-tail, 100
— Pheasant-tail nymph, 98
— Red spinner, 107
— Variant, 110
Artificial flies, 96–100
— Trout vision and the artificial
    fly, 97
Characteristics of trout, 84–96
— Emotions of trout, 84
— Short-rising, 85
— Vision of trout, 90
Conclusion, 111
Dibbing, 110
Dry-fly fishing, 106–9
— Downstream method, 108
— Floating v. sunk cast, 109
— Upstream methods, 108
Lies of trout, The, 100–2
Methods of fly-fishing, 102–3
More about the wet fly, 109–10
Types of rivers, 82–3
— Nature of river beds, 83
Wet-fly fishing, 103–5
— Downstream method, 103
— Upstream v. downstream, 104
River Management, 281 *et seq*
Care of the spawning beds, 294
Control of predators, 292–93
— Birds, 293
— Coarse fish, 292
— Otters, 293
Fisherman's requirements, The,
    281–285
— Banks, 281
— Bridges and stiles, 282
— Disposal of weeds, 285
— Trees and bushes, 283
— Weed cutting, 283
Fishery Management and your
    neighbours, 295
Food supply, 291–2
— Introduction of food, 291
— Manuring, 291
Oxygen, 292

Stocking, 293–4
— Brown trout, 294
— Rainbow trout, 294
— Salmon & sea-trout, 293
What the fish want, 285–8
— Harbourage for fish, 285
— Mud and shallows, 286
— Weirs, 288
Rivers mentioned in the text
Anton, 120
Avon (Hampshire), 114, 116, 118–
    121, 123, 126, 127, 131, 136, 180,
    182, 186
Bourne, 114, 120, 121, 123, 294
Chess, 171, 172, 178
Clwyedog, 103
Colne, 171, 178
Dee, Welsh, 265
Derwent (Derbyshire), 171, 178
Derwent (Yorkshire), 88, 186
Don, 269, 275
Driffield Beck, 256
Ebble, 114, 126
Eden, 89
Humber, 180
Itchen, 114, 117, 120, 121, 123–6,
    139, 180, 265, 288, 294
Kennet, 114, 125–7, 180, 182
Lambourn, 182, 184
Macloud, 170
Marteg, 103
Medway, 184
Melgum, 185
Nadder, 120, 125–7
Severn, 103, 105, 186
Shal Bourne, 120
Spey, 18
Stour (Kent), 184
Swale, 186
Teifi, 105
Test, 114, 117, 120, 121, 123–5, 128,
    129, 131, 140, 141, 180, 186, 256,
    269, 288
Usk, 105, 265
Wye (Derbyshire), 170–2, 175, 176,
    178
Wye (Herefordshire), 22, 103, 105
Wylye, 113, 117, 120, 121, 123, 126,
    129, 186

Salmon, 17 *et seq*
Fishing the sunk fly, 27–36
— Cast and lines, 28
— Casting, 35
— Choice of fly, 27
— Hooking a fish, 33
— Landing a fish, 34

Salmon (*contd.*)
— Playing a fish, 33
— Tactics, 28
— Temperature, 35
Fly-fishing: general, 27
Fly patterns
— Green Highlander, 39
— Hairy Mary, 26, 38, 39, 50
— Jock Scott, 26, 28
— Logie, 38, 39
— Mar Lodge, 26
— Silver Blue, 38, 53
— Silver Doctor, 28
— Stoat's Tail, 26, 38, 39, 40
— Thunder-and-Lightning, 26, 28, 53
— Tube-flies, 26, 33, 38, 40, 41, 48
Greased-line fishing, 36–49
— Changing tactics, 47
— Controlled-drag method, 46
— Effect of spates, 46
— Effect of sun, 48
— Equipment for, 37
— Flies, 38
— General remarks, 39
— Hooking a fish, 41
— Patience, on, 48
— Playing a fish, 44
— Popular and Wood methods, 39
— Practice, 48
— Where salmon lie, 44
Introduction, 17
Loch-fishing, 49–53
— Boats, 50
— Conclusion, 53
— Flies, 50
— Further tactics, 51
— Hooking a fish, 51
— Landing a fish, 51
— Lies of salmon, The, 50
— Link with the sea, The, 49
— Playing a fish, 51
— Tackle, 50
— Tactics, 50
— Wind-knots, 53
Natural history of the salmon, 18–22
— Characteristics of rivers, 22
— Egg to smolt, from, 19
— Return to the river, The, 20
— Salmon's requirements, The, 18
— Scale reading, 22
— Spawning, 18
Tackle, 23–6

— Accessories, 26
— Casts, 25
— Flies, 25
— Lines, 25
— Reels, 25
— Rods, 23
Sea-trout, 54 *et seq*
Artificial flies
— Black Doctor, 60
— Blae-and-Silver, 70
— Buzzard-and-Silver, 70
— Coch-y-bonddu, 60
— Gold Butcher, 80
— Gold Mallard, 60, 70, 80
— Half-stone, 60
— Hare's Ear and Gold, 60
— Haslam, 60
— Invicta, 60
— Lures, 60, 79, 80
— Magpie Scad, 60
— Olive dun, 60
— Palmer, 69
— Peter Ross, 60
— Red spinner, 60
— Tube-flies, 60
Dry-fly fishing, 68–69
Fly-fishing: general, 60–1
Lake fishing, 73–8
— Dapping, 77
— Lies of sea-trout, 73
— Tackle for, 75
— Tactics, 75
Natural history, 54–6
Night fishing, 69–72
— Tactics, 70
Playing and netting, 72–3
Rivers and weather, 61–2
Tackle, 56–60
— Casts, 58
— Flies, 59
— Lines, 57
— Reels, 57
— Rods, 56
Tidal-water fishing, 79–81
— Brackish-water fishing, 80
— Estuary fishing, 79
— Voe fishing, 79
Wet-fly fishing, 62-68
— Camouflage, 63
— Casting, 64
— Effect of currents, 64
— Preservation and working of fly, 65
— Time of day, 62